The Harvard Classics

Registered Edition

Julius Caesar

W. T. Mar

THE HARVARD CLASSICS
EDITED BY CHARLES W. ELIOT, LL.D.

With Introductions and Notes

Plutarch's Lives

of Themistocles ■ Pericles ■ Aristides
Alcibiades and Coriolanus
Demosthenes and Cicero
Caesar and Antony

IN THE TRANSLATION CALLED DRYDEN'S
CORRECTED AND REVISED BY
ARTHUR HUGH CLOUGH

Grolier Enterprises Corp.
DANBURY, CONNECTICUT

Contents

Introductory Note

Plutarch, the great biographer of antiquity, had not the fortune himself to find a biographer. For the facts of his life we are dependent wholly upon the fragmentary information that he scattered casually throughout his writings. From these we learn that he was born in the small Boeotian town of Chaeroneia in Greece, between 46 and 51 A.D., of a family of good standing and long residence there; that he married a certain Timoxena, to whom he wrote a tender letter of consolation on the death of their daughter; and that he had four sons, to two of whom he dedicated one of his philosophical treatises. He began the study of philosophy at Athens, travelled to Alexandria and in various parts of Italy, and sojourned for a considerable period in Rome; but he seems to have continued to regard Chaeroneia as his home, and here he did a large part of his writing and took his share in public service. As a lecturer and teacher of philosophy he achieved considerable repute, and the nature of his doctrine may be gathered from the treatises in which the substance of many of the lectures has been preserved. His death is placed between 120 and 130 A.D.

The ruling passion of Plutarch's life was ethical. His miscellaneous writings are known collectively as his "Morals," and though they deal with a great variety of themes, the prevailing interest is so strongly centred on conduct that the title is not unsuitable. Many of the subjects of his biographies, even, are treated as models of virtue or warnings against vice, and as a rule he was more concerned about portraying character than about intricacies of political history.

The "Parallel Lives of Famous Greeks and Romans" have their name from the author's plan of setting side by side a Greek statesman, soldier, or orator, and a Roman of eminence in the same field, in order to gain illumination from the comparison; and in this way he covered almost the whole history of Greece and Rome from legendary times to his own day. He collected his facts with care and at the expense of great labor, and for many periods he is the chief, sometimes the only, source of information now accessible. In general, the Greek lives are more learned than the Roman, partly, no doubt, because of the greater difficulty of getting information as to Roman affairs when he was writing in Greece, partly because, as he tells us, his mastery of Latin was incomplete.

The biographical as distinct from the historical purpose was entirely deliberate. "It must be borne in mind," he says in his life of Alexander the Great, "that my design is not to write histories but lives. And the most glorious exploits do not always furnish us with the clearest discoveries of virtue or vice in men; sometimes a matter of less moment, an expression or a jest, informs us better of their characters and inclinations, than the most famous sieges, the greatest armaments, or the bloodiest battles whatsoever. Therefore, as portrait-painters are more exact in the lines and features of the face, in which the character is seen, than in the other parts of the body, so I must be allowed to give my more particular attention to the marks and indications of the souls of men, and while I endeavor by these to portray their lives, may be free to leave more weighty matters and great battles to be treated of by others." Most of the critical comment passed upon the "Lives" is but an elaboration of these statements of their author. The proportions and the significance of political events were often hidden from him, but in his portraiture of men he has laid the world under a perpetual debt.

The influence of these Lives it is almost impossible to exaggerate. All classes of people have taken delight in them, from kings to shepherds, and it is safe to say that the influence has always been wholesome. Not only do they supply a mass of information, vividly and picturesquely presented, regarding the leading personalities of some of the greatest periods of the world's history, but they offer in concrete and inspiring form the ideals of human character in the antique world incarnated in a series of great heroic figures. Of few books can it be said with such assurance that they will remain a permanent possession of the race.

The present translation is that made originally by a group of scholars in the end of the seventeenth century and published with a life of Plutarch by Dryden. This, usually called the Dryden translation, was revised in 1859 by Arthur Hugh Clough, who corrected it by the standards of modern scholarship, so that it took the place which it still occupies as the best version in English for the purposes of the general reader.

■

THEMISTOCLES

THE birth of Themistocles was somewhat too obscure to do him honor. His father, Neocles, was not of the distinguished people of Athens, but of the township of Phrearrhi, and of the tribe Leontis; and by his mother's side, as it is reported, he was base-born.

> I am not of the noble Grecian race,
> I'm poor Abrotonon, and born in Thrace;
> Let the Greek women scorn me, if they please,
> I was the mother of Themistocles.

Yet Phanias writes that the mother of Themistocles was not of Thrace, but of Caria, and that her name was not Abrotonon, but Euterpe; and Neanthes adds farther that she was of Halicarnassus in Caria. And, as illegitimate children, including those that were of the half-blood or had but one parent an Athenian, had to attend at the Cynosarges (a wrestling-place outside the gates, dedicated to Hercules, who was also of half-blood amongst the gods, having had a mortal woman for his mother), Themistocles persuaded several of the young men of high birth to accompany him to anoint and exercise themselves together at Cynosarges; an ingenious device for destroying the distinction between the noble and the base-born, and between those of the whole and those of the half-blood of Athens. However, it is certain that he was related to the house of the Lycomedæ; for Simonides records, that he rebuilt the chapel of Phlya, belonging to that family, and beautified it with pictures and other ornaments, after it had been burnt by the Persians.

It is confessed by all that from his youth he was of a vehement and impetuous nature, of a quick apprehension, and a strong and aspiring bent for action and great affairs. The holidays and intervals in his studies he did not spend in play or idleness, as other children, but would be always inventing or arranging some oration or declamation to himself, the subject of which was generally the excusing or accusing his companions, so that his master would often say to him, "You, my boy, will be nothing small, but great one way or other, for good or else for bad." He received reluctantly and carelessly instructions given him to improve his manners and behavior, or to teach him any pleasing or graceful accomplishment, but whatever was said to improve him in sagacity, or in management of affairs, he would give attention to, beyond one of his years, from confidence in his natural capacities for such things. And thus afterwards, when in company where people engaged themselves in what are commonly thought the liberal and elegant amusements, he was obliged to defend himself against the observations of those who considered themselves highly accomplished, by the somewhat arrogant retort, that he certainly could not make use of any stringed instrument, could only, were a small and obscure city put into his hands, make it great and glorious. Notwithstanding this, Stesimbrotus says that Themistocles was a hearer of Anaxagoras, and that he studied natural philosophy under Melissus, contrary to chronology; for Melissus commanded the Samians in their siege by Pericles, who was much Themistocles's junior; and with Pericles, also, Anaxagoras was intimate. They, therefore, might rather be credited, who report, that Themistocles was an admirer of Mnesiphilus the Phrearrhian, who was neither rhetorician nor natural philosopher, but a professor of that which was then called wisdom, consisting in a sort of political shrewdness and practical sagacity, which had begun and continued, almost like a sect of philosophy, from Solon; but those who came afterwards, and mixed it with pleadings and legal artifices, and transformed the practical part of it into a mere art of speaking and an exercise of words, were generally called sophists. Themistocles resorted to Mnesiphilus when he had already embarked in politics.

In the first essays of his youth he was not regular nor happily balanced; he allowed himself to follow mere natural character, which, without the control of reason and instruction, is apt to hurry, upon either side, into sudden and violent courses, and very often to break away and determine upon the worst; as he afterwards owned himself, saying, that the wildest colts make the best horses, if they only get properly trained and broken in. But those who upon this fasten stories of their own invention, as of his being disowned by his father, and that his mother died for grief of her son's ill fame, certainly calumniate him; and there are others who relate, on the contrary, how that to deter him from public business, and to let him see how the vulgar behave themselves towards their leaders when they have at last no farther use of them, his father showed him the old galleys as they lay forsaken and cast about upon the sea-shore.

Yet it is evident that his mind was early imbued with the keenest interest in public affairs, and the most passionate ambition for distinction. Eager from the first to obtain the highest place, he unhesitatingly accepted the hatred of the most powerful and influential leaders in the city, but more especially of Aristides, the son of Lysimachus, who always opposed him. And yet all this great enmity between them arose, it appears, from a very boyish occasion, both being attached to the beautiful Stesilaus of Ceos, as Ariston the philosopher tells us; ever after which, they took opposite sides, and were rivals in politics. Not but that the incompatibility of their lives and manners may seem to have increased the difference, for Aristides was of a mild nature, and of a nobler sort of character, and, in public matters, acting always with a view, not to glory or popularity, but to the best interests of the state consistently with safety and honesty, he was often forced to oppose Themistocles, and interfere against the increase of his influence, seeing him stirring up the people to all kinds of enterprises, and introducing various innovations. For it is said that Themistocles was so transported with the thoughts of glory, and so inflamed with the passion for great actions, that, though he was still young when the battle of Marathon was fought against the Persians, upon the skilful conduct of the general, Miltiades, being everywhere talked about, he was observed to be thoughtful, and reserved, alone by himself; he passed the nights without sleep, and avoided all his usual places of recreation, and to those who wondered at the change, and inquired the reason of it, he gave the answer, that "the trophy of Miltiades would not let him sleep." And when others were of opinion that the battle of Marathon would be an end to the war, Themistocles thought that it was but the beginning of far greater conflicts, and for these, to the benefit of all Greece, he kept himself in continual readiness, and his city also in proper training, foreseeing from far before what would happen.

And, first of all, the Athenians being accustomed to divide amongst themselves the revenue proceeding from the silver mines at Laurium, he was the only man that durst propose to the people that this distribution should cease, and that with the money ships should be built to make war against the Æginetans, who were the most flourishing people in all Greece, and by the number of their ships held the sovereignty of the sea; and Themistocles thus was more easily able to persuade them, avoiding all mention of danger from Darius or the Persians who were at a great distance, and their coming very uncertain, and at that time not much to be feared; but, by a seasonable employment of the emulation and anger felt by the Athenians against the Æginetans, he induced them to preparation. So that with this money an hundred ships were built, with which they afterwards fought against Xerxes. And, henceforward, little by little, turning and drawing the city down towards the sea, in the belief, that, whereas by land they were not a fit match for their next neighbors, with their ships they might be able to repel the Persians and command Greece, thus, as Plato says, from steady soldiers he turned them into mariners and seamen tossed about the sea, and gave occasion for the reproach against him, that he took away from the Athenians the spear and the shield, and bound them to the bench and the oar. These measures he carried in the assembly, against the opposition, as Stesimbrotus relates, of Miltiades; and whether or no he hereby injured the purity and true balance of government, may be a question for philosophers, but that the deliverance of Greece came at that time from the sea, and that these galleys restored Athens again after it was destroyed, were others wanting, Xerxes himself would be sufficient evidence, who, though his land-forces were still entire, after his defeat at sea, fled away, and thought himself no longer able to encounter the Greeks; and, as it seems to me, left Mardonius behind him, not out of any hopes he could have to bring them into subjection, but to hinder them from pursuing him.

Themistocles is said to have been eager in the acquisition of riches, according to some, that he might be the more liberal; for loving to sacrifice often, and to be splendid in his entertainment of strangers, he required a plentiful revenue; yet he is accused by others of having been parsimonious and sordid to that degree that he would sell provisions which were sent to him as a present. He desired Diphilides, who was a breeder of horses, to give him a colt, and when he refused it, threatened that in a short time he would turn his house into a wooden[1] horse, intimating that he would stir up dispute and litigation between him and some of his relations.

He went beyond all men in the passion for distinction. When he was still young and unknown in the world, he entreated Epicles of Hermione, who had a good hand at the lute and was much sought after by the Athenians, to come and practise at home with him, being ambitious of having people inquire after his house and frequent his company. When he came to the Olympic games, and was so splendid in his equipage and entertainments, in his rich tents and furniture, that he strove to outdo Cimon, he displeased the Greeks, who thought that such magnificence might be allowed in one who was a young man and of a great family but was a great piece of insolence in one as yet undistinguished, and without title or means for making any such display. In a dramatic contest, the play he paid for won the prize, which was then a matter that excited much emulation; he put up a tablet in record of it, with the inscription, "Themistocles of Phrearrhi was at the charge of it; Phrynichus made it; Adimantus was archon." He was well liked by the common people, would salute every particular citizen by his own name, and always show himself a just judge in questions of business between private men; he said to Simonides, the poet of Ceos, who desired something of him, when he was commander of the army, that was not reasonable, "Simonides, you would be no good poet if you wrote false measure, nor should I be a good magistrate if for favor I made false law." And at another time, laughing at Simonides, he said, that he was a man of little judgment to speak against the Corinthians, who were inhabitants of a great city, and to have his own picture drawn so often, having so ill-looking a face.

[1] Full of people ready for fighting. like the Trojan horse.

Gradually growing to be great, and winning the favor of the people, he at last gained the day with his faction over that of Aristides, and procured his banishment by ostracism. When the king of Persia was now advancing against Greece, and the Athenians were in consultation who should be general, and many withdrew themselves of their own accord, being terrified with the greatness of the danger, there was one Epicydes, a popular speaker, son to Euphemides, a man of an eloquent tongue, but of a faint heart, and a slave to riches, who was desirous of the command, and was looked upon to be in a fair way to carry it by the number of votes; but Themistocles, fearing that, if the command should fall into such hands, all would be lost, bought off Epicydes and his pretensions, it is said, for a sum of money.

When the king of Persia sent messengers into Greece, with an interpreter, to demand earth and water, as an acknowledgment of subjection, Themistocles, by the consent of the people, seized upon the interpreter, and put him to death, for presuming to publish the barbarian orders and decrees in the Greek language; this is one of the actions he is commended for, as also for what he did to Arthmius of Zelea, who brought gold from the king of Persia to corrupt the Greeks, and was, by an order from Themistocles, degraded and disfranchised, he and his children and his posterity; but that which most of all redounded to his credit was, that he put an end to all the civil wars of Greece, composed their differences, and persuaded them to lay aside all enmity during the war with the Persians; and in this great work, Chileus the Arcadian was, it is said, of great assistance to him.

Having taken upon himself the command of the Athenian forces, he immediately endeavored to persuade the citizens to leave the city, and to embark upon their galleys, and meet with the Persians at a great distance from Greece; but many being against this, he led a large force, together with the Lacedæmonians, into Tempe, that in this pass they might maintain the safety of Thessaly, which had not as yet declared for the king; but when they returned without performing any thing, and it was known that not only the Thessalians, but all as far as Bœotia, were going over to Xerxes, then the Athenians more willingly hearkened to the advice of Themistocles to fight by sea, and sent him with a fleet to guard the straits of Artemisium.

When the contingents met here, the Greeks would have the Lacedæmonians to command, and Eurybiades to be their admiral; but the Athenians, who surpassed all the rest together in number of vessels, would not submit to come after any other, till Themistocles, perceiving the danger of this contest, yielded his own command to Eurybiades, and got the Athenians to submit, extenuating the loss by persuading them, that if in this war they behaved themselves like men, he would answer for it after that, that the Greeks, of their own will, would submit to their command. And by this moderation of his, it is evident that he was the chief means of the deliverance of Greece, and gained the Athenians the glory of alike surpassing their enemies in valor, and their confederates in wisdom.

As soon as the Persian armada arrived at Aphetæ, Eurybiades was astonished to see such a vast number of vessels before him, and, being informed that two hundred more were sailing round behind the island of Sciathus, he immediately determined to retire farther into Greece, and to sail back into some part of Peloponnesus, where their land army and their fleet might join, for he looked upon the Persian forces to be altogether unassailable by sea. But the Eubœans, fearing that the Greeks would forsake them, and leave them to the mercy of the enemy, sent Pelagon to confer privately with Themistocles, taking with him a good sum of money, which, as Herodotus reports, he accepted and gave to Eurybiades. In this affair none of his own countrymen opposed him so much as Architeles, captain of the sacred galley, who, having no money to supply his seamen, was eager to go home; but Themistocles so incensed the Athenians against him, that they set upon him and left him not so much as his supper, at which Architeles was much surprised, and took it very ill; but Themistocles immediately sent him in a chest a service of provisions, and at the bottom of it a talent of silver, desiring him to sup to-night, and to-morrow provide for his seamen; if not, he would report it amongst the Athenians that he had received money from the enemy. So Phanias the Lesbian tells the story.

Though the fights between the Greeks and Persians in the straits of Eubœa were not so important as to make any final decision of the war, yet the experience which the Greeks obtained in them was of great advantage; for thus, by actual trial and in real danger, they found out, that neither number of ships, nor riches and ornaments, nor boasting shouts, nor barbarous songs of victory, were any way terrible to men that knew how to fight, and were resolved to come hand to hand with their enemies; these things they were to despise, and to come up close and grapple with their foes. This, Pindar appears to have seen, and says justly enough of the fight at Artemisium, that

> "There the sons of Athens set
> The stone that freedom stands on yet."

For the first step towards victory undoubtedly is to gain courage. Artemisium is in Eubœa, beyond the city of Histiæa, a sea-beach open to the north; most nearly opposite to it stands Olizon, in the country which formerly was under Philoctetes; there is a small temple there, dedicated to Diana, surnamed of the Dawn, and trees about it, around which again stand pillars of white marble; and if you rub them with your hand, they send forth both the smell and color of saffron. On one of the pillars these verses are engraved,—

> "With numerous tribes from Asia's regions brought
> The sons of Athens on these waters fought;
> Erecting, after they had quelled the Mede,
> To Artemis this record of the deed."

There is a place still to be seen upon this shore, where, in the middle of a great heap of sand, they take out from the bottom a dark powder like ashes, or something that has passed the fire; and here, it is supposed, the shipwrecks and bodies of the dead were burnt.

But when news came from Thermopylæ to Artemisium, informing them that king Leonidas was slain, and that Xerxes had made himself master of all the passages by land, they returned back to the interior of Greece, the Athenians having the command of the rear, the place of honor and danger, and much elated by what had been done.

As Themistocles sailed along the coast, he took notice of the harbors and fit places for the enemies' ships to come to land at, and engraved large letters in such stones as he found there by chance, as also in others which he set up on purpose near to the landing-places, or where they were to water; in which inscriptions he called upon the Ionians to forsake the Medes, if it were possible, and come over to the Greeks, who were their proper founders and fathers, and were now hazarding all for their liberties; but, if this could not be done, at any rate to impede and disturb the Persians in all engagements. He hoped that these writings would prevail with the Ionians to revolt, or raise some trouble by making their fidelity doubtful to the Persians.

Now, though Xerxes had already passed through Doris and invaded the country of Phocis, and was burning and destroying the cities of the Phocians, yet the Greeks sent them no relief; and, though the Athenians earnestly desired them to meet the Persians in Bœotia, before they could come into Attica, as they themselves had come forward by sea at Artemisium, they gave no ear to their request, being wholly intent upon Peloponnesus, and resolved to gather all their forces together within the Isthmus, and to build a wall from sea to sea in that narrow neck of land; so that the Athenians were enraged to see themselves betrayed, and at the same time afflicted and dejected at their own destitution. For to fight alone against such a numerous army was to no purpose, and the only expedient now left them was to leave their city and cling to their ships; which the people were very unwilling to submit to, imagining that it would signify little now to gain a victory, and not understanding how there could be deliverance any longer after they had once forsaken the temples of their gods and exposed the tombs and monuments of their ancestors to the fury of their enemies.

Themistocles, being at a loss, and not able to draw the people over to his opinion by any human reason, set his machines to work, as in a theatre, and employed prodigies and oracles. The serpent of Minerva, kept in the inner part of her temple, disappeared; the priests gave it out to the people that the offerings which were set for it were found untouched, and declared, by the suggestion of Themistocles, that the goddess had left the city, and taken her flight before them towards the sea. And he often urged them with the oracle[2] which bade them trust to walls of wood, showing them that

[2] "While all things else are taken," said the oracle, "within the boundary of Cecrops and the covert of divine Cithæron, Zeus grants to Athena that the wall of wood alone shall remain uncaptured; that shall help thee and thy children. Stay not for horsemen and an host of men on foot, coming from the mainland; retire turning thy back; one day yet thou shalt show thy face. O divine Salamis, but thou shalt slay children of women, either at the scattering of Demeter or at the gathering."

walls of wood could signify nothing else but ships; and that the island of Salamis was termed in it, not miserable or unhappy, but had the epithet of divine, for that it should one day be associated with a great good fortune of the Greeks. At length his opinion prevailed, and he obtained a decree that the city should be committed to the protection of Minerva, "queen of Athens;" that they who were of age to bear arms should embark, and that each should see to sending away his children, women, and slaves where he could. This decree being confirmed, most of the Athenians removed their parents, wives, and children to Trœzen, where they were received with eager good-will by the Trœzenians, who passed a vote that they should be maintained at the public charge, by a daily payment of two obols to every one, and leave be given to the children to gather fruit where they pleased, and schoolmasters paid to instruct them. This vote was proposed by Nicagoras.

There was no public treasure at that time in Athens; but the council of Areopagus, as Aristotle says, distributed to every one that served, eight drachmas, which was a great help to the manning of the fleet; but Clidemus ascribes this also to the art of Themistocles. When the Athenians were on their way down to the haven of Piræus, the shield with the head of Medusa was missing; and he, under the pretext of searching for it, ransacked all places, and found among their goods considerable sums of money concealed, which he applied to the public use; and with this the soldiers and seamen were well provided for their voyage.

When the whole city of Athens were going on board, it afforded a spectacle worthy of pity alike and admiration, to see them thus send away their fathers and children before them, and, unmoved with their cries and tears, pass over into the island. But that which stirred compassion most of all was, that many old men, by reason of their great age, were left behind; and even the tame domestic animals could not be seen without some pity, running about the town and howling, as desirous to be carried along with their masters that had kept them; among which it is reported that Xanthippus, the father of Pericles, had a dog that would not endure to stay behind, but leaped into the sea, and swam along by the galley's side till he came to the island of Salamis, where he fainted away and died, and that spot in the island, which is still called the Dog's Grave, is said to be his.

Among the great actions of Themistocles at this crisis, the recall of Aristides was not the least, for, before the war, he had been ostracized by the party which Themistocles headed, and was in banishment; but now, perceiving that the people regretted his absence, and were fearful that he might go over to the Persians to revenge himself, and thereby ruin the affairs of Greece, Themistocles proposed a decree that those who were banished for a time might return again, to give assistance by word and deed to the cause of Greece with the rest of their fellow-citizens.

Eurybiades, by reason of the greatness of Sparta, was admiral of the Greek fleet, but yet was faint-hearted in time of danger, and willing to weigh anchor and set sail for the isthmus of Corinth, near which the land army lay encamped; which Themistocles resisted; and this was the occasion of the well-known words, when Eurybiades, to check his impatience, told him that at the Olympic games they that start up before the rest are lashed; "And they," replied Themistocles, "that are left behind are not crowned." Again, Eurybiades lifting up his staff as if he were going to strike, Themistocles said, "Strike if you will, but hear"; Eurybiades, wondering much at his moderation, desired him to speak, and Themistocles now brought him to a better understanding. And when one who stood by him told him that it did not become those who had neither city nor house to lose, to persuade others to relinquish their habitations and forsake their countries, Themistocles gave this reply: "We have indeed left our houses and our walls, base fellow, not thinking it fit to become slaves for the sake of things that have no life nor soul; and yet our city is the greatest of all Greece, consisting of two hundred galleys, which are here to defend you, if you please; but if you run away and betray us, as you did once before, the Greeks shall soon hear news of the Athenians possessing as fair a country, and as large and free a city, as that they have lost." These expressions of Themistocles made Eurybiades suspect that if he retreated the Athenians would fall off from him. When one of Eretria began to oppose him, he said, "Have you any thing to say of war, that are like an ink-fish? you have a sword, but no heart."[3] Some say that while Themistocles was thus speaking things upon the deck, an owl was seen flying to the right hand of the fleet, which came and sate upon the top of the mast; and this happy omen so far disposed the Greeks to follow his advice, that they presently prepared to fight. Yet, when the enemy's fleet was arrived at the haven of Phalerum, upon the coast of Attica, and with the number of their ships concealed all the shore, and when they saw the king himself in person come down with his land army to the sea-side, with all his forces united, then the good counsel of Themistocles was soon forgotten, and the Peloponnesians cast their eyes again towards the Isthmus, and took it very ill if any one spoke against their returning home; and, resolving to depart that night, the pilots had order what course to steer.

Themistocles, in great distress that the Greeks should retire, and lose the advantage of the narrow seas and strait passage, and slip home every one to his own city, considered with himself, and contrived that stratagem that was carried out by Sicinnus. This Sicinnus was a Persian captive, but a great lover of Themistocles, and the attendant of his children. Upon this occasion, he sent him privately to Xerxes, commanding him to tell the king, that Themistocles, the admiral of the Athenians, having espoused his interest, wished to be the first to inform him that the Greeks were ready to make their escape, and that he counselled him to hinder their flight, to set upon them while they were in this confusion and at a distance from their land army, and hereby destroy all their forces by sea. Xerxes was very joyful at this message, and received it as from one who wished him all that was good, and immediately issued instructions to the commanders of his ships, that they should instantly set out with two hundred galleys to encompass all the islands, and enclose all the straits and passages, that none of the Greeks might escape, and that they should afterwards follow with the rest of their fleet at leisure. This being done, Aristides, the son of Lysimachus, was the first man that perceived it, and went to the tent of Themistocles, not

[3] The *Teuthis,* loligo, or cuttlefish, is said to have a bone or cartilage shaped like a sword, and was conceived to have no heart.

out of any friendship, for he had been formerly banished by his means, as has been related, but to inform him how they were encompassed by their enemies. Themistocles, knowing the generosity of Aristides, and much struck by his visit at that time, imparted to him all that he had transacted by Sicinnus, and entreated him, that, as he would be more readily believed among the Greeks, he would make use of his credit to help to induce them to stay and fight their enemies in the narrow seas. Aristides applauded Themistocles, and went to the other commanders and captains of the galleys, and encouraged them to engage; yet they did not perfectly assent to him, till a galley of Tenos, which deserted from the Persians, of which Panætius was commander, came in, while they were still doubting, and confirmed the news that all the straits and passages were beset; and then their rage and fury, as well as their necessity, provoked them all to fight.

As soon as it was day, Xerxes placed himself high up, to view his fleet, and how it was set in order. Phanodemus says, he sat upon a promontory above the temple of Hercules, where the coast of Attica is separated from the island by a narrow channel; but Acestodorus writes, that it was in the confines of Megara, upon those hills which are called the Horns, where he sat in a chair of gold, with many secretaries about him to write down all that was done.

When Themistocles was about to sacrifice, close to the admiral's galley, there were three prisoners brought to him, fine looking men, and richly dressed in ornamented clothing and gold, said to be the children of Artayctes and Sandauce, sister to Xerxes. As soon as the prophet Euphrantides saw them, and observed that at the same time the fire blazed out from the offerings with a more than ordinary flame, and that a man sneezed on the right, which was an intimation of a fortunate event, he took Themistocles by the hand, and bade him consecrate the three young men for sacrifice, and offer them up with prayers for victory to Bacchus the Devourer: so should the Greeks not only save themselves, but also obtain victory. Themistocles was much disturbed at this strange and terrible prophecy, but the common people, who, in any difficult crisis and great exigency, ever look for relief rather to strange and extravagant than to reasonable means, calling upon Bacchus with one voice, led the captives to the altar, and compelled the execution of the sacrifice as the prophet had commanded. This is reported by Phanias the Lesbian, a philosopher well read in history.

The number of the enemy's ships the poet Æschylus gives in his tragedy called the Persians, as on his certain knowledge, in the following words—

> "Xerxes, I know, did into battle lead
> One thousand ships; of more than usual speed
> Seven and two hundred. So is it agreed."

The Athenians had a hundred and eighty; in every ship eighteen men fought upon the deck, four of whom were archers and the rest men-at-arms.

As Themistocles had fixed upon the most advantageous place, so, with no less sagacity, he chose the best time of fighting; for he would not run the prows of his galleys against the Persians, nor begin the fight till the time of day was come, when there regularly blows in a fresh breeze from the open sea, and brings in with it a strong swell into the channel; which was no inconvenience to the Greek ships, which were low-built, and little above the water, but did much hurt to the Persians, which had high sterns and lofty decks, and were heavy and cumbrous in their movements, as it presented them broadside to the quick charges of the Greeks, who kept their eyes upon the motions of Themistocles, as their best example, and more particularly because, opposed to his ship, Ariamenes, admiral to Xerxes, a brave man, and by far the best and worthiest of the king's brothers, was seen throwing darts and shooting arrows from his huge galley, as from the walls of a castle. Aminias the Decelean and Sosicles the Pedian, who sailed in the same vessel, upon the ships meeting stem to stem, and transfixing each the other with their brazen prows, so that they were fastened together, when Ariamenes attempted to board theirs, ran at him with their pikes, and thrust him into the sea; his body, as it floated amongst other shipwrecks, was known to Artemisia, and carried to Xerxes.

It is reported, that, in the middle of the fight, a great flame rose into the air above the city of Eleusis, and that sounds and voices were heard through all the Thriasian plain, as far as the sea, sounding like a number of men accompanying and escorting the mystic Iacchus, and that a mist seemed to form and rise from the place from whence the sounds came, and, passing forward, fell upon the galleys. Others believed that they saw apparitions, in the shape of armed men, reaching out their hands from the island of Ægina before the Grecian galleys; and supposed they were the Æacidæ, whom they had invoked to their aid before the battle. The first man that took a ship was Lycomedes the Athenian, captain of a galley, who cut down its ensign, and dedicated it to Apollo, the Laurel-crowned. And as the Persians fought in a narrow arm of the sea, and could bring but part of their fleet to fight, and fell foul of one another, the Greeks thus equalled them in strength, and fought with them till the evening, forced them back, and obtained, as says Simonides, that noble and famous victory, than which neither amongst the Greeks nor barbarians was ever known more glorious exploit on the seas; by the joint valor, indeed, and zeal of all who fought, but by the wisdom and sagacity of Themistocles.

After this sea-fight, Xerxes, enraged at his ill-fortune, attempted, by casting great heaps of earth and stones into the sea, to stop up the channel and to make a dam, upon which he might lead his land-forces over into the island of Salamis.

Themistocles, being desirous to try the opinion of Aristides, told him that he proposed to set sail for the Hellespont, to break the bridge of ships, so as to shut up, he said, Asia a prisoner within Europe; but Aristides, disliking the design, said, "We have hitherto fought with an enemy who has regarded little else but his pleasure and luxury; but if we shut him up within Greece, and drive him to necessity, he that is master of such great forces will no longer sit quietly with an umbrella of gold over his head, looking upon the fight for his pleasure; but in such a strait will attempt all things; he will be resolute, and appear himself in person upon all occasions, he will soon correct his errors, and supply what he has formerly omitted through remissness, and will be better advised in all things. Therefore, it is noways our interest, Themistocles," he said, "to take away the bridge that is already made, but rather to build another, if it were possible, that he might make his retreat with the more expedition." To which Themistocles answered, "If this be requisite, we must immediately use all diligence, art, and industry, to rid ourselves of him as soon as may be;" and to this purpose he found out among the captives one of the king of Persia's eunuchs, named Arnaces, whom he sent to the king, to inform him that the Greeks, being now victorious by sea, had decreed to sail to the Hellespont, where the boats were fastened together, and destroy the bridge; but that Themistocles, being concerned for the king, revealed this to him, that he might hasten towards the Asiatic seas, and pass over into his own dominions; and in the mean time would cause delays, and hinder the confederates from pursuing him. Xerxes no sooner heard this, but, being very much terrified, he proceeded to retreat out of Greece with all speed. The prudence of Themistocles and Aristides in this was afterwards more fully understood at the battle of Platæa, where Mardonius, with a very small fraction of the forces of Xerxes, put the Greeks in danger of losing all.

Herodotus writes, that, of all the cities of Greece, Ægina was held to have performed the best service in the war; while all single men yielded to Themistocles, though, out of envy, unwillingly; and when they returned to the entrance of Peloponnesus, where the several commanders delivered their suffrages at the altar, to determine who was most worthy, every one gave the first vote for himself and the second for Themistocles. The Lacedæmonians carried him with them to Sparta, where, giving the rewards of valor to Eurybiades, and of wisdom and conduct to Themistocles, they crowned him with olive, presented him with the best chariot in the city, and sent three hundred young men to accompany him to the confines of their country. And at the next Olympic games, when Themistocles entered the course, the spectators took no farther notice of those who were contesting the prizes, but spent the whole day in looking upon him, showing him to the strangers, admiring him, and applauding him by clapping their hands, and other expressions of joy, so that he himself, much gratified, confessed to his friends that he then reaped the fruit of all his labors for the Greeks.

He was, indeed, by nature, a great lover of honor, as is evident from the anecdotes recorded of him. When chosen admiral by the Athenians, he would not quite conclude any single matter of business, either public or private, but deferred all till the day they were to set sail, that, by despatching a great quantity of business all at once, and having to meet a great variety of people, he might make an appearance of greatness and power. Viewing the dead bodies cast up by the sea, he perceived bracelets and necklaces of gold about them, yet passed on, only showing them to a friend that followed him, saying, "Take you these things, for you are not Themistocles." He said to Antiphates, a handsome young man, who had formerly avoided, but now in his glory courted him, "Time, young man, has taught us both a lesson." He said that the Athenians did not honor him or admire him, but made, as it were, a sort of plane-tree of him; sheltered themselves under him in bad weather, and, as soon as it was fine, plucked his leaves and cut his branches. When the Seriphian told him that he had not obtained this honor by himself, but by the greatness of his city, he replied, "You speak truth; I should never have been famous if I had been of Seriphus; nor you, had you been of Athens." When another of the generals, who thought he had performed considerable service for the Athenians, boastingly compared his actions with those of Themistocles, he told him that once upon a time the Day after the Festival found fault with the Festival: "On you there is nothing but hurry and trouble and preparation, but, when I come, everybody sits down quietly and enjoys himself;" which the Festival admitted was true, but "if I had not come first, you would not have come at all." "Even so," he said, "if Themistocles had not come before, where had you been now?" Laughing at his own son, who got his mother, and, by his mother's means, his father also, to indulge him, he told him that he had the most power of any one in Greece: "For the Athenians command the rest of Greece, I command the Athenians, your mother commands me, and you command your mother." Loving to be singular in all things, when he had land to sell, he ordered the crier to give notice that there were good neighbors near it. Of two who made love to his daughter, he preferred the man of worth to the one who was rich, saying he desired a man without riches, rather than riches without a man. Such was the character of his sayings.

After these things, he began to rebuild and fortify the city of Athens, bribing, as Theopompus reports, the Lacedæmonian ephors not to be against it, but, as most relate it, overreaching and deceiving them. For, under pretext of an embassy, he went to Sparta, where, upon the Lacedæmonians charging him with rebuilding the walls, and Poliarchus coming on purpose from Ægina to denounce it, he denied the fact, bidding them to send people to Athens to see whether it was so or no; by which delay he got time for the building of the wall, and also placed these ambassadors in the hands of his countrymen as hostages for him; and so, when the Lacedæmonians knew the truth, they did him no hurt, but, suppressing all display of their anger for the present, sent him away.

Next he proceeded to establish the harbor of Piræus, observing the great natural advantages of the locality and desirous to unite the whole city with the sea, and to reverse, in a manner, the policy of ancient Athenian kings, who, endeavoring to withdraw their subjects from the sea, and to accustom them to live, not by sailing about, but by planting and tilling the earth, spread the story of the dispute between Minerva and Neptune for the sovereignty of Athens, in which Minerva, by producing to the judges an olive tree, was declared to have won; whereas Themistocles did not only knead up, as Aristophanes says, the port and the city into one, but made the city absolutely the dependant and the adjunct of the port, and the land of the sea, which increased the power and confidence of the people against nobility; the authority coming into the hands of sailors and boatswains and pilots. Thus it was one of the orders of the thirty tyrants, that the hustings in the assembly, which had faced towards the sea, should be turned round towards the land; implying their opinion that the empire by sea had been the origin of the democracy, and that the farming population were not so much opposed to oligarchy.

Themistocles, however, formed yet higher designs with a view to naval supremacy. For, after the departure of Xerxes, when the Grecian fleet was arrived at Pagasæ, where they wintered, Themistocles, in a public oration to the people of Athens, told them that he had a design to perform something that would tend greatly to their interests and safety, but was of such a nature, that it could not be made generally public. The Athenians ordered him to impart it to Aristides only; and, if he approved of it, to put it in practice. And when Themistocles had discovered to him that his design was to burn the Grecian fleet in the haven of Pagasæ, Aristides, coming out to the people, gave this report of the stratagem contrived by Themistocles, that no proposal could be more politic, or more dishonorable; on which the Athenians commanded Themistocles to think no farther of it.

When the Lacedæmonians proposed, at the general council of the Amphictyonians, that the representatives of those cities which were not in the league, nor had fought against the Persians, should be excluded, Themistocles, fearing that the Thessalians, with those of Thebes, Argos, and others, being thrown out of the council, the Lacedæmonians would become wholly masters of the votes, and do what they pleased, supported the deputies of the cities, and prevailed with the members then sitting to alter their opinion in this point, showing them that there were but one and thirty cities which had partaken in the war, and that most of these, also, were very small; how intolerable would it be, if the rest of Greece should be excluded, and the general council should come to be ruled by two or three great cities. By this, chiefly, he incurred the displeasure of the Lacedæmonians, whose honors and favors were now shown to Cimon, with a view to making him the opponent of the state policy of Themistocles.

He was also burdensome to the confederates, sailing about the islands and collecting money from them. Herodotus says, that, requiring money of those of the island of Andros, he told them that he had brought with him two goddesses, Persuasion and Force; and they answered him that they had also two great goddesses, which prohibited them from giving him any money, Poverty and Impossibility. Timocreon, the Rhodian poet, reprehends him somewhat bitterly for being wrought upon by money to let some who were banished return, while abandoning himself, who was his guest and friend. The verses are these:—

"Pausanias you may praise, and Xanthippus he be for,
For Leutychidas, a third; Aristides, I proclaim,
From the sacred Athens came,
The one true man of all; for Themistocles Latona doth abhor,

"The liar, traitor, cheat, who, to gain his filthy pay,
Timocreon, his friend, neglected to restore
To his native Rhodian shore;
Three silver talents took, and departed (curses with him) on his way,

"Restoring people here, expelling there, and killing here,
Filling evermore his purse: and at the Isthmus gave a treat,
To be laughed at, of cold meat,
Which they ate, and prayed the gods some one else might give the feast another year."

But after the sentence and banishment of Themistocles, Timocreon reviles him yet more immoderately and wildly in a poem which begins thus:—

"Unto all the Greeks repair
O Muse, and tell these verses there,
As is fitting and is fair."

The story is, that it was put to the question whether Timocreon should be banished for siding with the Persians, and Themistocles gave his vote against him. So when Themistocles was accused of intriguing with the Medes, Timocreon made these lines upon him:—

"So now Timocreon, indeed, is not the sole friend of the Mede,
There are some knaves besides; nor is it only mine that fails,
But other foxes have lost tails.—"

When the citizens of Athens began to listen willingly to those who traduced and reproached him, he was forced, with somewhat obnoxious frequency, to put them in mind of the great services he had performed, and ask those who were offended with him whether they were weary with receiving benefits often from the same person, so rendering himself more odious. And he yet more provoked the people by building a temple to Diana with the epithet of Aristobule, or Diana of Best Counsel; intimating thereby, that he had given the best counsel, not only to the Athenians, but to all Greece. He built this temple near his own house, in the district called Melite, where now the public officers carry out the bodies of such as are executed, and throw the halters and clothes of those that are strangled or otherwise put to death. There is to this day a small figure of Themistocles in the temple of Diana of Best Counsel, which represents him to be a person, not only of a noble mind, but also of a most heroic aspect. At length the Athenians banished him, making use of the ostracism to humble his eminence and authority, as they ordinarily did with all whom they thought too powerful, or, by their greatness, disproportionable to the equality thought requisite in a popular government. For the ostracism was instituted, not so much to punish the offender, as to mitigate and pacify the violence of the envious, who delighted to humble eminent men, and who, by fixing this disgrace upon them, might vent some part of their rancor.

Themistocles being banished from Athens, while he stayed at Argos the detection of Pausanias happened, which gave such advantage to his enemies, that Leobotes of Agraule, son of Alcmæon, indicted him of treason, the Spartans supporting him in the accusation.

When Pausanias went about this treasonable design, he concealed it at first from Themistocles, though he were his intimate friend; but when he saw him expelled out of the commonwealth, and how impatiently he took his banishment, he ventured to communicate it to him, and desired his assistance, showing him the king of Persia's letters, and exasperating him against the Greeks, as a villainous, ungrateful people. However, Themistocles immediately rejected the proposals of Pausanias, and wholly refused to be a party in the enterprise, though he never revealed his communications, nor disclosed the conspiracy to any man, either hoping that Pausanias would desist from his intentions, or expecting that so inconsiderate an attempt after such chimerical objects would be discovered by other means.

After that Pausanias was put to death, letters and writings being found concerning this matter, which rendered Themistocles suspected, the Lacedæmonians were clamorous against him, and his enemies among the Athenians accused him; when, being absent from Athens, he made his defence by letters, especially against the points that had been previously alleged against him. In answer to the malicious detractions of his enemies, he merely wrote to the citizens, urging that he who was always ambitious to govern, and not of a character or a disposition to serve, would never sell himself and his country into slavery to a barbarous and hostile nation.

Notwithstanding this, the people, being persuaded by his accusers, sent officers to take him and bring him away to be tried before a council of the Greeks, but, having timely notice of it, he passed over into the island of Corcyra, where the state was under obligations to him; for, being chosen as arbitrator in a difference between them and the Corinthians, he decided the controversy by ordering the Corinthians to pay down twenty talents, and declaring the town and island of Leucas a joint colony from both cities. From thence he fled into Epirus, and, the Athenians and Lacedæmonians still pursuing him, he threw himself upon chances of safety that seemed all but desperate. For he fled for refuge to Admetus, king of the Molossians, who had formerly made some request to the Athenians, when Themistocles was in the height of his authority, and had been disdainfully used and insulted by him, and had let it appear plain enough, that, could he lay hold of him, he would take his revenge. Yet in this misfortune, Themistocles, fearing the recent hatred of his neighbors and fellow-citizens more than the old displeasure of the king, put himself at his mercy, and became an humble suppliant to Admetus, after a peculiar manner, different from the custom of other countries. For taking the king's son, who was then a child, in his arms, he laid himself down at his hearth, this being the most sacred and only manner of supplication, among the Molossians, which was not to be refused. And some say that his wife, Phthia, intimated to Themistocles this way of petitioning, and placed her young son with him before the hearth; others, that king Admetus, that he might be under a religious obligation not to deliver him up to his pursuers, prepared and enacted with him a sort of stage-play to this effect. At this time, Epicrates of Acharnæ privately conveyed his wife and children out of Athens, and sent them hither, for which afterwards Cimon condemned him and put him to death as Stesimbrotus reports, and yet somehow, either forgetting this himself, or making Themistocles to be little mindful of it, says presently that he sailed into Sicily, and desired in marriage the daughter of Hiero, tyrant of Syracuse, promising to bring the

Greeks under his power; and, on Hiero refusing him, departed thence into Asia; but this is not probable.

For Theophrastus writes, in his work on Monarchy, that when Hiero sent race-horses to the Olympian games, and erected a pavilion sumptuously furnished, Themistocles made an oration to the Greeks, inciting them to pull down the tyrant's tent, and not to suffer his horses to run. Thucydides says, that, passing over land to the Ægæan Sea, he took ship at Pydna in the bay of Therme, not being known to any one in the ship, till, being terrified to see the vessel driven by the winds near to Naxos, which was then besieged by the Athenians, he made himself known to the master and pilot, and, partly entreating them, partly threatening that if they went on shore he would accuse them, and make the Athenians to believe that they did not take him in out of ignorance, but that he had corrupted them with money from the beginning, he compelled them to bear off and stand out to sea, and sail forward towards the coast of Asia.

A great part of his estate was privately conveyed away by his friends, and sent after him by sea into Asia; besides which, there was discovered and confiscated to the value of fourscore talents, as Theophrastus writes; Theopompus says an hundred; though Themistocles was never worth three talents before he was concerned in public affairs.

When he arrived at Cyme, and understood that all along the coast there were many laid wait for him, and particularly Ergoteles and Pythodorus (for the game was worth the hunting for such as were thankful to make money by any means, the king of Persia having offered by public proclamation two hundred talents to him that should take him), he fled to Ægæ, a small city of the Æolians, where no one knew him but only his host Nicogenes, who was the richest man in Æolia, and well known to the great men of Inner Asia. While Themistocles lay hid for some days in his house, one night, after a sacrifice and supper ensuing, Olbius, the attendant upon Nicogenes's children, fell into a sort of frenzy and fit of inspiration, and cried out in verse,—

> "Night shall speak, and night instruct thee,
> By the voice of night conduct thee."

After this, Themistocles, going to bed, dreamed that he saw a snake coil itself up upon his belly, and so creep to his neck; then, as soon as it touched his face, it turned into an eagle, which spread its wings over him, and took him up and flew away with him a great distance; then there appeared a herald's golden wand, and upon this at last it set him down securely, after infinite terror and disturbance.

His departure was effected by Nicogenes by the following artifice; the barbarous nations, and amongst them the Persians especially, are extremely jealous, severe, and suspicious about their women, not only their wives, but also their bought slaves and concubines, whom they keep so strictly that no one ever sees them abroad; they spend their lives shut up within doors, and, when they take a journey, are carried in close tents, curtained in on all sides, and set upon a wagon. Such a travelling carriage being prepared for Themistocles, they hid him in it, and carried him on his journey, and told those whom they met or spoke with upon the road that they were conveying a young Greek woman out of Ionia to a nobleman at court.

Thucydides and Charon of Lampsacus say that Xerxes was dead, and that Themistocles had an interview with his son; but Ephorus, Dinon, Clitarchus, Heraclides, and many others, write that he came to Xerxes. The chronological tables better agree with the account of Thucydides, and yet neither can their statements be said to be quite set at rest.

When Themistocles was come to the critical point, he applied himself first to Artabanus, commander of a thousand men, telling him that he was a Greek, and desired to speak with the king about important affairs concerning which the king was extremely solicitous. Artabanus answered him, "O stranger, the laws of men are different, and one thing is honorable to one man, and to others another; but it is honorable for all to honor and observe their own laws. It is the habit of the Greeks, we are told, to honor, above all things, liberty and equality; but amongst our many excellent laws, we account this the most excellent, to honor the king, and to worship him, as the image of the great preserver of the universe; if, then, you shall consent to our laws, and fall down before the king and worship him, you may both see him and speak to him; but if your mind be otherwise, you must make use of others to intercede for you, for it is not the national custom here for the king to give audience to any one that doth not fall down before him." Themistocles, hearing this, replied, "Artabanus, I that come hither to increase the power and glory of the king, will not only submit myself to his laws, since so it hath pleased the god who exalteth the Persian empire to this greatness, but will also cause many more to be worshippers and adorers of the king. Let not this, therefore, be an impediment why I should not communicate to the king what I have to impart." Artabanus asking him, "Who must we tell him that you are? for your words signify you to be no ordinary person," Themistocles answered, "No man, O Artabanus, must be informed of this before the king himself." Thus Phanias relates; to which Eratosthenes, in his treatise on Riches, adds, that it was by the means of a woman of Eretria, who was kept by Artabanus, that he obtained this audience and interview with him.

When he was introduced to the king, and had paid his reverence to him, he stood silent, till the king commanding the interpreter to ask him who he was, he replied, "O king, I am Themistocles the Athenian, driven into banishment by the Greeks. The evils that I have done to the Persians are numerous; but my benefits to them yet greater, in withholding the Greeks from pursuit, so soon as the deliverance of my own country allowed me to show kindness also to you. I come with a mind suited to my present calamities; prepared alike for favors and for anger; to welcome your gracious reconciliation, and to deprecate your wrath. Take my own countrymen for witnesses of the services I have done for Persia, and make use of this occasion to show the world your virtue, rather than to satisfy your indignation. If you save me, you will save your suppliant; if otherwise, will destroy an enemy of the Greeks." He talked also of divine admonition, such as the vision which he saw at Nicogenes's house, and the direction given him by the oracle of Dodona, where Jupiter commanded him to go to him that had a name like his, by which he understood that he was sent from Jupiter to him, seeing that they both were great, and had the name of kings.

The king heard him attentively, and, though he admired his temper and courage, gave him no answer at that time; but, when he was with his intimate friends, rejoiced in his great good fortune, and esteemed himself very happy in this, and prayed to his god Arimanius, that all his enemies might be ever of the same mind with the Greeks, to abuse and expel the bravest men amongst them. Then he sacrificed to the gods, and presently fell to drinking, and was so well pleased, that in the night, in the middle of his sleep, he cried out for joy three times, "I have Themistocles the Athenian."

In the morning, calling together the chief of his court, he had Themistocles brought before him, who expected no good of it, when he saw, for example, the guards fiercely set against him as soon as they learnt his name, and giving him ill language. As he came forward towards the king, who was seated, the rest keeping silence, passing by Roxanes, a commander of a thousand men, he heard him, with a slight groan, say, without stirring out of his place, "You subtle Greek serpent, the king's good genius hath brought thee hither." Yet, when he came into the presence, and again fell down, the king saluted him, and spake to him kindly, telling him he was now indebted to him two hundred talents; for it was just and reasonable that he should receive the reward which was proposed to whosoever should bring Themistocles; and promising much more, and encouraging him, he commanded him to speak freely what he would concerning the affairs of Greece. Themistocles replied, that a man's discourse was like to a rich Persian carpet, the beautiful figures and patterns of which can only be shown by spreading and extending it out; when it is contracted and folded up, they are obscured and lost; and, therefore, he desired time. The king being pleased with the comparison, and bidding him take what time he would, he desired a year; in which time, having learnt the Persian language sufficiently, he spoke with the king by himself without the help of an interpreter, it being supposed that he discoursed only about the affairs of Greece; but there happening, at the same time, great alterations at court, and removals of the king's favorites, he drew upon himself the envy of the great people, who imagined that he had taken the boldness to speak concerning them. For the favors shown to other strangers were nothing in comparison with the honors conferred on him; the king invited him to partake of his own pastimes and recreations both at home and abroad, carrying him with him a-hunting, and made him his intimate so far that he permitted him to see the queen-mother, and converse frequently with her. By the king's command, he also was made acquainted with the Magian learning.

When Demaratus the Lacedæmonian, being ordered by the king to ask whatsoever he pleased, and it should immediately be granted him, desired that he might make his public entrance, and be carried in state through the city of Sardis, with the tiara set in the royal manner upon his head, Mithropaustes, cousin to the king, touched him on the head, and told him that he had no brains for the royal tiara to cover, and if Jupiter should give him his lightning and thunder, he would not any the more be Jupiter for that; the king also repulsed him with anger, resolving never to be reconciled to him, but to be inexorable to all supplications on his behalf. Yet Themistocles pacified him, and prevailed with him to forgive him. And it is reported, that the succeeding kings, in whose reigns there was a greater communication between the Greeks and Persians, when they invited any considerable Greek into their service, to encourage him, would write, and promise him that he should be as great with them as Themistocles had been. They relate, also, how Themistocles, when he was in great prosperity, and courted by many, seeing himself splendidly served at his table, turned to his children and said, "Children, we had been undone if we had not been undone." Most writers say that he had three cities given him, Magnesia, Myus, and Lampsacus, to maintain him in bread, meat, and wine. Neanthes of Cyzicus, and Phanias, add two more, the city of Palæscepsis, to provide him with clothes, and Percote, with bedding and furniture for his house.

As he was going down towards the sea-coast to take measures against Greece, a Persian whose name was Epixyes, governor of the upper Phrygia, laid wait to kill him, having for that purpose provided a long time before a number of Pisidians, who were to set upon him when he should stop to rest at a city that is called Lion's-head. But Themistocles, sleeping in the middle of the day, saw the Mother of the gods appear to him in a dream and say unto him, "Themistocles, keep back from the Lion's-head, for fear you fall into the lion's jaws; for this advice I expect that your daughter Mnesiptolema should be my servant." Themistocles was much astonished, and, when he had made his vows to the goddess, left the broad road, and, making a circuit, went another way, changing his intended station to avoid that place, and at night took up his rest in the fields. But one of the sumpter-horses, which carried the furniture for his tent, having fallen that day into the river, his servants spread out the tapestry, which was wet, and hung it up to dry; in the meantime the Pisidians made towards them with their swords drawn, and, not discerning exactly by the moon what it was that was stretched out, thought it to be the tent of Themistocles, and that they should find him resting himself within it but when they came near, and lifted up the hangings, those who watched there fell upon them and took them. Themistocles, having escaped this great danger, in admiration of the goodness of the goddess that appeared to him, built, in memory of it, a temple in the city of Magnesia, which he dedicated to Dindymene, Mother of the gods, in which he consecrated and devoted his daughter Mnesiptolema to her service.

When he came to Sardis, he visited the temples of the gods, and observing, at his leisure, their buildings, ornaments, and the number of their offerings, he saw in the temple of the Mother of the gods the statue of a virgin in brass, two cubits high, called the water-bringer. Themistocles had caused this to be made and set up when he was surveyor of waters at Athens, out of the fines of those whom he detected in drawing off and diverting the public water by pipes for their private use; and whether he had some regret to see this image in captivity, or was desirous to let the Athenians see in what great credit and authority he was with the king, he entered into a treaty with the governor of Lydia to persuade him to send this statue back to Athens, which so enraged the Persian officer, that he told him he would write the king word of it. Themistocles, being affrighted hereat, got access to his wives and concubines, by presents of money to whom, he appeased the fury of the governor; and afterwards behaved with more reserve and circumspection, fearing the envy of the Persians, and did not, as Theopompus writes, continue to travel about Asia, but lived quietly in his own house in Magnesia, where for a long time he passed his days in great security, being courted by all, and enjoying rich presents, and honored equally with the greatest persons in the Persian empire; the king, at that time, not minding his concerns with Greece, being taken up with the affairs of Inner Asia.

But when Egypt revolted, being assisted by the Athenians, and the Greek galleys roved about as far as Cyprus and Cilicia, and Cimon had made himself master of the seas, the king turned his thoughts thither, and, bending his mind chiefly to resist the Greeks, and to check the growth of their power against him, began to raise forces, and send out commanders, and to despatch messengers to Themistocles at Magnesia, to put him in mind of his promise, and to summon him to act against the Greeks. Yet this did not increase his hatred nor exasperate him against the Athenians, neither was he any way elevated with the thoughts of the honor and powerful command he was to have in this war; but judging, perhaps, that the object would not be attained, the Greeks having at that time, beside other great commanders, Cimon, in particular, who was gaining wonderful military successes; but chiefly, being ashamed to sully the glory of his former great actions, and of his many victories and trophies, he determined to put a conclusion to his life, agreeable to its previous course. He sacrificed to the gods, and invited his friends; and, having entertained them and shaken hands with them, drank bull's blood, as is the usual story; as others state, a poison producing instant death; and ended his days in the city of Magnesia, having lived sixty-five years, most of which he had spent in politics and in the wars, in government and command. The king, being informed of the cause and manner of his death, admired him more than ever, and continued to show kindness to his friends and relations.

Themistocles left three sons by Archippe, daughter to Lysander of Alopece,—Archeptolis, Polyeuctus, and Cleophantus. Plato the philosopher mentions the last as a most excellent horseman, but otherwise insignificant person; of two sons yet older than these, Neocles and Diocles, Neocles died when he was young by the bite of a horse, and Diocles was adopted by his grandfather, Lysander. He had many daughters, of whom Mnesiptolema, whom he had by a second marriage, was wife to Archeptolis, her brother by another mother; Italia was married to Panthoides, of the island of Chios; Sybaris to Nicomedes the Athenian. After the death of Themistocles, his nephew, Phrasicles, went to Magnesia, and married, with her brothers' consent, another daughter, Nicomache, and took charge of her sister Asia, the youngest of all the children.

The Magnesians possess a splendid sepulchre of Themistocles, placed in the middle of their market-place. It is not worth while taking notice of what Andocides states in his Address to his Friends concerning his remains, how the Athenians robbed his tomb, and threw his ashes into the air; for he feigns this, to exasperate the oligarchical faction against the people; and there is no man living but knows that Phylarchus simply invents in his history; where he all but uses an actual stage machine, and brings in Neocles and Demopolis as the sons of Themistocles, to incite or move compassion, as if he were writing a tragedy. Diodorus the cosmographer says, in his work on Tombs, but by conjecture rather than of certain knowledge, that near to the heaven of Piræus, where the land runs out like an elbow from the promontory of Alcimus, when you have doubled the cape and passed inward where the sea is always calm, there is a large piece of masonry, and upon this the tomb of Themistocles, in the shape of an altar; and Plato the comedian confirms this, he believes, in these verses,—

> "Thy tomb is fairly placed upon the strand,
> Where merchants still shall greet it with the land;
> Still in and out 't will see them come and go,
> And watch the galleys as they race below."

Various honors also and privileges were granted to the kindred of Themistocles at Magnesia, which were observed down to our times, and were enjoyed by another Themistocles of Athens, with whom I had an intimate acquaintance and friendship in the house of Ammonius the philosopher.

PERICLES

CÆSAR[1] once, seeing some wealthy strangers at Rome, carrying up and down with them in their arms and bosoms young puppy-dogs and monkeys, embracing and making much of them, took occasion not unnaturally to ask whether the women in their country were not used to bear children; by that prince-like reprimand gravely reflecting upon persons who spend and lavish upon brute beasts that affection and kindness which nature has implanted in us to be bestowed on those of our own kind. With like reason may we blame those who misuse that love of inquiry and observation which nature has implanted in our souls, by expending it on objects unworthy of the attention either of their eyes or their ears, while they disregard such as are excellent in themselves, and would do them good.

The mere outward sense, being passive in responding to the impression of the objects that come in its way and strike upon it, perhaps cannot help entertaining and taking notice of every thing that addresses it, be it what it will, useful or unuseful; but, in the exercise of his mental perception, every man, if he chooses, has a natural power to turn himself upon all occasions, and to change and shift with the greatest ease to what he shall himself judge desirable. So that it becomes a man's duty to pursue and make after the best and choicest of everything, that he may not only employ his contemplation, but may also be improved by it. For as that color is most suitable to the eye whose freshness and pleasantness stimulates and strengthens the sight, so a man ought to apply his intellectual perception to such objects as, with the sense of delight, are apt to call it forth, and allure it to its own proper good and advantage.

Such objects we find in the acts of virtue, which also produce in the minds of mere readers about them, an emulation and eager-

[1] Probably Augustus.

ness that may lead them on to imitation. In other things there does not immediately follow upon the admiration and liking of the thing done, any strong desire of doing the like. Nay, many times, on the very contrary, when we are pleased with the work, we slight and set little by the workman or artist himself, as, for instance, in perfumes and purple dyes, we are taken with the things themselves well enough, but do not think dyers and perfumers otherwise than low and sordid people. It was not said amiss by Antisthenes, when people told him that one Ismenias was an excellent piper, "It may be so," said he, "but he is but a wretched human being, otherwise he would not have been an excellent piper." And king Philip, to the same purpose, told his son Alexander, who once at a merry-meeting played a piece of music charmingly and skilfully, "Are you not ashamed, son, to play so well?" For it is enough for a king or prince to find leisure sometimes to hear others sing, and he does the muses quite honor enough when he pleases to be but present, while others engage in such exercises and trials of skill.

He who busies himself in mean occupations produces, in the very pains he takes about things of little or no use, an evidence against himself of his negligence and indisposition to what is really good. Nor did any generous and ingenuous young man, at the sight of the statue of Jupiter at Pisa, ever desire to be a Phidias, or, on seeing that of Juno at Argos, long to be a Polycletus, or feel induced by his pleasure in their poems to wish to be an Anacreon or Philetas or Archilochus. For it does not necessarily follow, that, if a piece of work please for its gracefulness, therefore he that wrought it deserves our admiration. Whence it is that neither do such things really profit or advantage the beholders, upon the sight of which no zeal arises for the imitation of them, nor any impulse or inclination, which may prompt any desire or endeavor of doing the like. But virtue, by the bare statement of its actions, can so affect men's minds as to create at once both admiration of the things done and desire to imitate the doers of them. The goods of fortune we would possess and would enjoy; those of virtue we long to practise and exercise; we are content to receive the former from others, the latter we wish others to experience from us. Moral good is a practical tise; and influences the mind and character not by a mere imitation which we look at, but, by the statement of the fact, creates a moral purpose which we form.

And so we have thought fit to spend our time and pains in writing of the lives of famous persons; and have composed this tenth book upon that subject, containing the life of Pericles, and that of Fabius Maximus, who carried on the war against Hannibal, men alike, as in their other virtues and good parts, so especially in their mild and upright temper and demeanor, and in that capacity to bear the cross-grained humors of their fellow-citizens and colleagues in office which made them both most useful and serviceable to the interests of their countries. Whether we take a right aim at our intended purpose, it is left to the reader to judge by what he shall here find.

Pericles was of the tribe Acamantis, and the township Cholargus, of the noblest birth both on his father's and mother's side. Xanthippus, his father, who defeated the king of Persia's generals in the battle at Mycale, took to wife Agariste, the grandchild of Clisthenes, who drove out the sons of Pisistratus, and nobly put an end to their tyrannical usurpation, and moreover made a body of laws, and settled a model of government admirably tempered and suited for the harmony and safety of the people.

His mother, being near her time, fancied in a dream that she was brought to bed of a lion, and a few days after was delivered of Pericles, in other respects perfectly formed, only his head was somewhat longish and out of proportion. For which reason almost all the images and statues that were made of him have the head covered with a helmet, the workmen apparently being willing not to expose him. The poets of Athens called him *Schinocephalos,* or squill-head, from *schinos,* a squill, or sea-onion. One of the comic poets, Cratinus, in the Chirons, tells us that—

> "Old Chronos once took queen Sedition to wife;
> Which two brought to life
> That tyrant far-famed,
> Whom the gods the supreme skull-compeller[2] have named."

[2] Kephalegeretes, a play on Nephelegeretes, the cloud-compeller.

And, in the Nemesis, addresses him—

> "Come, Jove, thou *head* of gods."

And a second, Teleclides, says, that now, in embarrassment with political difficulties, he sits in the city,—

> "Fainting underneath the load
> Of his own head; and now abroad,
> From his huge galley of a pate,
> Sends forth trouble to the state."

And a third, Eupolis, in the comedy called the Demi, in a series of questions about each of the demagogues, whom he makes in the play to come up from hell, upon Pericles being named last, exclaims,—

> "And here by way of summary, now we've done,
> Behold, in brief, the heads of all in one."

The master that taught him music, most authors are agreed, was Damon (whose name, they say, ought to be pronounced with the first syllable short). Though Aristotle tells us that he was thoroughly practised in all accomplishments of this kind by Pythoclides. Damon, it is not unlikely, being a sophist, out of policy, sheltered himself under the profession of music to conceal from people in general his skill in other things, and under this pretence attended Pericles, the young athlete of politics, so to say, as his training-master in these exercises. Damon's lyre, however, did not prove altogether a successful blind; he was banished the country by ostracism for ten years, as a dangerous inter-meddler and a favorer of arbitrary power, and, by this means, gave the stage occasion to play upon him. As, for instance, Plato, the comic poet, introduces a character, who questions him—

> "Tell me, if you please,
> Since you're the Chiron who taught Pericles."

Pericles, also, was a hearer of Zeno, the Eleatic, who treated of natural philosophy in the same manner as Parmenides did, but had also perfected himself in an art of his own for refuting and silencing opponents in argument; as Timon of Phlius describes it,—

> "Also the two-edged tongue of mighty Zeno, who,
> Say what one would, could argue it untrue."

But he that saw most of Pericles, and furnished him most especially with a weight and grandeur of sense, superior to all arts of popularity, and in general gave him his elevation and sublimity of purpose and of character, was Anaxagoras of Clazomenæ; whom the men of those times called by the name of Nous, that is, mind, or intelligence, whether in admiration of the great and extraordinary gift he displayed for the science of nature, or because that he was the first of the philosophers who did not refer the first ordering of the world to fortune or chance, nor to necessity or compulsion, but to a pure, unadulterated intelligence, which in all other existing mixed and compound things acts as a principle of discrimination, and of combination of like with like.

For this man, Pericles entertained an extraordinary esteem and admiration, and, filling himself with this lofty, and, as they call it, up-in-the-air sort of thought, derived hence not merely, as was natural, elevation of purpose and dignity of language, raised far above the base and dishonest buffooneries of mob-eloquence, but, besides this, a composure of countenance, and a serenity and calmness in all his movements, which no occurrence whilst he was speaking could disturb, a sustained and even tone of voice, and various other advantages of a similar kind, which produced the greatest effect on his hearers. Once, after being reviled and ill-spoken of all day long in his own hearing by some vile and abandoned fellow in the open market-place, where he was engaged in the despatch of some urgent affair, he continued his business in perfect silence, and in the evening returned home composedly, the man still dogging him at the heels, and pelting him all the way with abuse and foul language; and stepping into his house, it being this time dark, he ordered one of his servants to take a light, and to go along with the man and see him safe home. Ion, it is true, the dramatic poet, says that Pericles's manner in company was somewhat over-assuming and pompous; and that into his high bearing there entered a good deal of slightingness and scorn of others; he reserves his commendation for Cimon's ease and pliancy and natural grace in society. Ion, however, who must needs make virtue, like a show of tragedies, include some comic scenes,[3] we shall not altogether rely upon; Zeno used to bid those who called Pericles's gravity the affectation of a charlatan, to go and affect the like themselves; inasmuch as this mere counterfeiting might in time insensibly instil into them a real love and knowledge of those noble qualities.

Nor were these the only advantages which Pericles derived from Anaxagoras's acquaintance; he seems also to have become, by his instructions, superior to that superstition with which an ignorant wonder at appearances, for example, in the heavens possesses the minds of people unacquainted with their causes, eager for the supernatural, and excitable through an inexperience which the knowledge of natural causes removes, replacing wild and timid superstition by the good hope and assurance of an intelligent piety.

There is a story, that once Pericles had brought to him from a country farm of his, a ram's head with one horn, and that Lampon, the diviner, upon seeing the horn grow strong and solid out of the midst of the forehead, gave it as his judgment, that, there being at that time two potent factions, parties, or interests in the city, the one of Thucydides and the other of Pericles, the government would come about to that one of them in whose ground or estate this token or indication of fate had shown itself. But that Anaxagoras, cleaving the skull in sunder, showed to the bystanders that the brain had not filled up its natural place, but being oblong, like an egg, had collected from all parts of the vessel which contained it, in a point to that place from whence the root of the horn took its rise. And that, for that time, Anaxagoras was much admired for his explanation by those that were present; and Lampon no less a little while after, when Thucydides was overpowered, and the whole affairs of the state and government came into the hands of Pericles.

And yet, in my opinion, it is no absurdity to say that they were both in the right, both natural philosopher and diviner, one justly detecting the cause of this event, by which it was produced, the other the end for which it was designed. For it was the business of the one to find out and give an account of what it was made, and in what manner and by what means it grew as it did; and of the other

[3] Three tragedies represented in succession were followed by a burlesque, the so-called *satyric* drama, which has no connection, it must be remembered, with the moral satire of the Romans, but takes its name from the grotesque satyrs of the Greek woods.

to foretell to what end and purpose it was so made, and what it might mean or portend. Those who say that to find out the cause of a prodigy is in effect to destroy its supposed signification as such, do not take notice that, at the same time, together with divine prodigies, they also do away with signs and signals of human art and concert, as, for instance, the clashings of quoits, fire-beacons, and the shadows on sun-dials, every one of which things has its cause, and by that cause and contrivance is a sign of something else. But these are subjects, perhaps, that would better befit another place.

Pericles, while yet but a young man, stood in considerable apprehension of the people, as he was thought in face and figure to be very like the tyrant Pisistratus, and those of great age remarked upon the sweetness of his voice, and his volubility and rapidity in speaking, and were struck with amazement at the resemblance. Reflecting, too, that he had a considerable estate, and was descended of a noble family, and had friends of great influence, he was fearful all this might bring him to be banished as a dangerous person; and for this reason meddled not at all with state affairs, but in military service showed himself of a brave and intrepid nature. But when Aristides was now dead, and Themistocles driven out, and Cimon was for the most part kept abroad by the expeditions he made in parts out of Greece, Pericles, seeing things in this posture, now advanced and took his side, not with the rich and few, but with the many and poor, contrary to his natural bent, which was far from democratical; but, most likely, fearing he might fall under suspicion of aiming at arbitrary power, and seeing Cimon on the side of the aristocracy, and much beloved by the better and more distinguished people, he joined the party of the people, with a view at once both to secure himself and procure means against Cimon.

He immediately entered, also, on quite a new course of life and management of his time. For he was never seen to walk in any street but that which led to the market-place and the council-hall, and he avoided invitations of friends to supper, and all friendly visiting and intercourse whatever; in all the time he had to do with the public, which was not a little, he was never known to have gone to any of his friends to a supper, except that once when his near kinsman Euryptolemus married, he remained present till the ceremony of the drink-offering,[4] and then immediately rose from table and went his way. For these friendly meetings are very quick to defeat any assumed superiority, and in intimate familiarity an exterior of gravity is hard to maintain. Real excellence, indeed, is most recognized when most openly looked into; and in really good men, nothing which meets the eyes of external observers so truly deserves their admiration, as their daily common life does that of their nearer friends. Pericles, however, to avoid any feeling of commonness, or any satiety on the part of the people, presented himself at intervals only, not speaking to every business, nor at all times coming into the assembly, but, as Critolaus says, reserving himself, like the Salaminian galley,[5] for great occasions, while matters of lesser importance were despatched by friends or other speakers under his direction. And of this number we are told Ephialtes made one, who broke the power of the council of Areopagus, giving the people, according to Plato's expression, so copious and so strong a draught of liberty, that, growing wild and unruly, like an unmanageable horse, it, as the comic poets say,—

"——got beyond all keeping in,
Champing at Eubœa, and among the islands leaping in."

The style of speaking most consonant to his form of life and the dignity of his views he found, so to say, in the tones of that instrument with which Anaxagoras had furnished him; of his teaching he continually availed himself, and deepened the colors of rhetoric with the dye of natural science. For having, in addition to his great natural genius, attained, by the study of nature, to use the words of the divine Plato, this height of intelligence, and this universal consummating power, and drawing hence whatever might be of advantage to him in the art of speaking, he showed himself far superior to all others. Upon which account, they say, he had his nickname given him, though some are of opinion he was named the Olympian from the public buildings with which he adorned the city; and others again, from his great power in public affairs,

[4] The *spondai*, or libations, which, like the modern grace, concluded the meal, and were followed by the dessert.

[5] The Salaminia and the Paralus were the two sacred state-galleys of Athens, used only on special missions.

whether of war or peace. Nor is it unlikely that the confluence of many attributes may have conferred it on him. However, the comedies represented at the time, which, both in good earnest and in merriment, let fly many hard words at him, plainly show that he got that appellation especially from his speaking; they speak of his "thundering and lightning" when he harangued the people, and of his wielding a dreadful thunderbolt in his tongue.

A saying also of Thucydides, the son of Melesias, stands on record, spoken by him by way of pleasantry upon Pericles's dexterity. Thucydides was one of the noble and distinguished citizens, and had been his greatest opponent; and, when Archidamus, the king of the Lacedæmonians, asked him whether he or Pericles were the better wrestler, he made this answer: "When I," said he, "have thrown him and given him a fair fall, by persisting that he had no fall, he gets the better of me, and makes the bystanders, in spite of their own eyes, believe him." The truth, however, is, that Pericles himself was very careful what and how he was to speak, insomuch that, whenever he went up to the hustings, he prayed the gods that no one word might unawares slip from him unsuitable to the matter and the occasion.

He has left nothing in writing behind him, except some decrees; and there are but very few of his sayings recorded; one, for example, is, that he said Ægina must, like a gathering in a man's eye, be removed from Piræus; and another, that he said he saw already war moving on its way towards them out of Peloponnesus. Again, when on a time Sophocles, who was his fellow-commissioner in the generalship, was going on board with him, and praised the beauty of a youth they met with in the way to the ship, "Sophocles," said he, "a general ought not only to have clean hands, but also clean eyes." And Stesimbrotus tells us, that, in his encomium on those who fell in battle at Samos, he said they were become immortal, as the gods were. "For," said he, "we do not see them themselves, but only by the honors we pay them, and by the benefits they do us, attribute to them immortality; and the like attributes belong also to those that die in the service of their country."

Since Thucydides describes the rule of Pericles as an aristocratical government, that went by the name of a democracy, but was, indeed, the supremacy of a single great man, while many others say, on the contrary, that by him the common people were first encouraged and led on to such evils as appropriations of subject territory; allowances for attending theatres, payments for performing public duties, and by these bad habits were, under the influence of his public measures, changed from a sober, thrifty people, that maintained themselves by their own labors, to lovers of expense, intemperance, and license, let us examine the cause of this change by the actual matters of fact.

At the first, as has been said, when he set himself against Cimon's great authority, he did caress the people. Finding himself come short of his competitor in wealth and money, by which advantages the other was enabled to take care of the poor, inviting every day some one or other of the citizens that was in want to supper, and bestowing clothes on the aged people, and breaking down the hedges and enclosures of his grounds, that all that would might freely gather what fruit they pleased, Pericles, thus outdone in popular arts, by the advice of one Damonides of Œa, as Aristotle states, turned to the distribution of the public moneys; and in a short time having bought the people over, what with moneys allowed for shows and for service on juries, and what with other forms of pay and largess, he made use of them against the council of Areopagus, of which he himself was no member, as having never been appointed by lot either chief archon, or lawgiver, or king, or captain.[6] For from of old these offices were conferred on persons by lot, and they who had acquitted themselves duly in the discharge of them were advanced to the court of Areopagus. And so Pericles, having secured his power and interest with the populace, directed the exertions of his party against this council with such success, that most of those causes and matters which had been used to be tried there, were, by the agency of Ephialtes, removed from its cognizance. Cimon, also, was banished by ostracism as a favorer of the Lacedæmonians and a hater of the people, though in wealth and noble

[6] Eponymus, Thesmothetes, Basileus, Polemarchus; titles of the different archons, the chief civic dignitaries, who, after the period of the Persian wars, were appointed, not by election, but simply by lot, from the whole body of citizens. Hence, at this time, the importance of the board of the ten *strategi*, or generals who were elected, and were always persons of real or supposed capacity.

birth he was among the first, and had won several most glorious victories over the barbarians, and had filled the city with money and spoils of war; as is recorded in the history of his life. So vast an authority had Pericles obtained among the people.

The ostracism was limited by law to ten years; but the Lacedæmonians, in the mean time, entering with a great army into the territory of Tanagra, and the Athenians going out against them, Cimon, coming from his banishment before his time was out, put himself in arms and array with those of his fellow-citizens that were of his own tribe, and desired by his deeds to wipe off the suspicion of his favoring the Lacedæmonians, by venturing his own person along with his countrymen. But Pericles's friends, gathering in a body, forced him to retire as a banished man. For which cause also Pericles seems to have exerted himself more in that than in any battle, and to have been conspicuous above all for his exposure of himself to danger. All Cimon's friends, also, to a man, fell together side by side, whom Pericles had accused with him of taking part with the Lacedæmonians. Defeated in this battle on their own frontiers, and expecting a new and perilous attack with return of spring, the Athenians now felt regret and sorrow for the loss of Cimon, and repentance for their expulsion of him. Pericles, being sensible of their feelings, did not hesitate or delay to gratify it, and himself made the motion for recalling him home. He, upon his return, concluded a peace betwixt the two cities; for the Lacedæmonians entertained as kindly feelings towards him as they did the reverse towards Pericles and the other popular leaders.

Yet some there are who say that Pericles did not propose the order for Cimon's return till some private articles of agreement had been made between them, and this by means of Elpinice, Cimon's sister; that Cimon, namely, should go out to sea with a fleet of two hundred ships, and be commander-in-chief abroad, with a design to reduce the king of Persia's territories, and that Pericles should have the power at home.

This Elpinice, it was thought, had before this time procured some favor for her brother Cimon at Pericles's hands, and induced him to be more remiss and gentle in urging the charge when Cimon was tried for his life; for Pericles was one of the committee appointed by the commons to plead against him. And when Elpinice came and besought him in her brother's behalf, he answered, with a smile, "O Elpinice, you are too old a woman to undertake such business as this." But, when he appeared to impeach him, he stood up but once to speak, merely to acquit himself of his commission, and went out of court, having done Cimon the least prejudice of any of his accusers.

How, then, can one believe Idomeneus, who charges Pericles as if he had by treachery procured the murder of Ephialtes, the popular statesman, one who was his friend, and of his own party in all his political course, out of jealousy, forsooth, and envy of his great reputation? This historian, it seems, having raked up these stories, I know not whence, has befouled with them a man who, perchance, was not altogether free from fault or blame, but yet had a noble spirit, and a soul that was bent on honor; and where such qualities are, there can no such cruel and brutal passion find harbor or gain admittance. As to Ephialtes, the truth of the story, as Aristotle has told it, is this: that having made himself formidable to the oligarchical party, by being an uncompromising asserter of the people's rights in calling to account and prosecuting those who any way wronged them, his enemies, lying in wait for him, by the means of Aristodicus the Tanagræan, privately despatched him.

Cimon, while he was admiral, ended his days in the Isle of Cyprus. And the aristocratical party, seeing that Pericles was already before this grown to be the greatest and foremost man of all the city, but nevertheless wishing there should be somebody set up against him, to blunt and turn the edge of his power, that it might not altogether prove a monarchy, put forward Thucydides of Alopece, a discreet person, and a near kinsman of Cimon's, to conduct the opposition against him; who, indeed, though less skilled in warlike affairs than Cimon was, yet was better versed in speaking and political business, and keeping close guard in the city, and engaging with Pericles on the hustings, in a short time brought the government to an equality of parties. For he would not suffer those who were called the honest and good (persons of worth and distinction) to be scattered up and down and mix themselves and be lost among the populace, as formerly, diminishing and obscuring their superiority amongst the masses; but taking them apart by themselves and uniting them in one body, by their combined weight he was able, as it were upon the balance, to make a counterpoise to the other party.

For, indeed, there was from the beginning a sort of concealed split, or seam, as it might be in a piece of iron, marking the different popular and aristocratical tendencies; but the open rivalry and contention of these two opponents made the gash deep, and severed the city into the two parties of the people and the few. And so Pericles, at that time more than at any other, let loose the reins to the people, and made his policy subservient to their pleasure, contriving continually to have some great public show or solemnity, some banquet, or some procession or other in the town to please them, coaxing his countrymen like children, with such delights and pleasures as were not, however, unedifying. Besides that every year he sent out three-score galleys, on board of which there went numbers of the citizens, who were in pay eight months, learning at the same time and practising the art of seamanship.

He sent, moreover, a thousand of them into the Chersonese as planters, to share the land among them by lot, and five hundred more into the isle of Naxos, and half that number to Andros, a thousand into Thrace to dwell among the Bisaltæ, and others into Italy, when the city Sybaris, which now was called Thurii, was to be repeopled. And this he did to ease and discharge the city of an idle, and, by reason of their idleness, a busy, meddling crowd of people; and at the same time to meet the necessities and restore the fortunes of the poor townsmen, and to intimidate, also, and check their allies from attempting any change, by posting such garrisons, as it were, in the midst of them.

That which gave most pleasure and ornament to the city of Athens, and the greatest admiration and even astonishment to all strangers, and that which now is Greece's only evidence that the power she boasts of and her ancient wealth are no romance or idle story, was his construction of the public and sacred buildings. Yet this was that of all his actions in the government which his enemies most looked askance upon and cavilled at in the popular assemblies, crying out how that the commonwealth of Athens had lost its reputation and was ill-spoken of abroad for removing the common treasure of the Greeks from the isle of Delos into their own custody; and how that their fairest excuse for so doing, namely, that they took it away for fear the barbarians should seize it, and on purpose to secure it in a safe place, this Pericles had made unavailable, and how that "Greece cannot but resent it as an insufferable affront, and consider herself to be tyrannized over openly, when she sees the treasure, which was contributed by her upon a necessity for the war, wantonly lavished out by us upon our city, to gild her all over, and to adorn and set her forth, as it were some vain woman, hung round with precious stones and figures and temples, which cost a world of money."

Pericles, on the other hand, informed the people, that they were in no way obliged to give any account of those moneys to their allies, so long as they maintained their defence, and kept off the barbarians from attacking them; while in the meantime they did not so much as supply one horse or man or ship, but only found money for the service; "which money," said he, "is not theirs that give it, but theirs that receive it, if so be they perform the conditions upon which they receive it." And that it was good reason, that, now the city was sufficiently provided and stored with all things necessary for the war, they should convert the overplus of its wealth to such undertakings, as would hereafter, when completed, give them eternal honor, and, for the present, while in process, freely supply all the inhabitants with plenty. With their variety of workmanship and of occasions for service, which summon all arts and trades and require all hands to be employed about them, they do actually put the whole city, in a manner, into state-pay; while at the same time she is both beautified and maintained by herself. For as those who are of age and strength for war are provided for and maintained in the armaments abroad by their pay out of the public stock, so, it being his desire and design that the undisciplined mechanic multitude that stayed at home should not go without their share of public salaries, and yet should not have them given them for sitting still and doing nothing, to that end he thought fit to bring in among them, with the approbation of the people, these vast projects of buildings and designs of works, that would be of some continuance before they were finished, and would give employment to numerous arts, so that the part of the people that stayed at home might, no less than those that were at sea or in garrisons or on expeditions, have a fair and just occasion of receiving the benefit and having their share of the public moneys.

The materials were stone, brass, ivory, gold, ebony, cypress-wood; and the arts or trades that wrought and fashioned them were smiths and carpenters, moulders, founders and braziers, stone-cutters, dyers, goldsmiths, ivory-workers, painters, embroiderers, turners; those again that conveyed them to the town for use, merchants and mariners and shipmasters by sea, and by land, cartwrights, cattle-breeders, waggoners, rope-makers, flax-workers, shoe-makers and leather-dressers, road-makers, miners. And every trade in the same nature, as a captain in an army has his particular company of soldiers under him, had its own hired company of journeymen and laborers belonging to it banded together as in array, to be as it were the instrument and body for the performance of the service. Thus, to say all in a word, the occasions and services of these public works distributed plenty through every age and condition.

As then grew the works up, no less stately in size than exquisite in form, the workmen striving to outvie the material and the design with the beauty of their workmanship, yet the most wonderful thing of all was the rapidity of their execution. Undertakings, any one of which singly might have required, they thought, for their completion, several successions and ages of men, were every one of them accomplished in the height and prime of one man's political service. Although they say, too, that Zeuxis once, having heard Agatharchus the painter boast of despatching his work with speed and ease, replied, "I take a long time." For ease and speed in doing a thing do not give the work lasting solidity or exactness of beauty; the expenditure of time allowed to a man's pains beforehand for the production of a thing is repaid by way of interest with a vital force for its preservation when once produced. For which reason Pericles's works are especially admired, as having been made quickly, to last long. For every particular piece of his work was immediately, even at that time, for its beauty and elegance, antique; and yet in its vigor and freshness looks to this day as if it were just executed. There is a sort of bloom of newness upon those works of his, preserving them from the touch of time, as if they had some perennial spirit and undying vitality mingled in the composition of them.

Phidias had the oversight of all the works, and was surveyor-general, though upon the various portions other great masters and workmen were employed. For Callicrates and Ictinus built the Parthenon; the chapel at Eleusis, where the mysteries were celebrated, was begun by Corœbus, who erected the pillars that stand upon the floor or pavement, and joined them to the architraves; and after his death Metagenes of Xypete added the frieze and the upper line of columns; Xenocles of Cholargus roofed or arched the lantern on the top of the temple of Castor and Pollux; and the long wall, which Socrates says he himself heard Pericles propose to the people, was undertaken by Callicrates. This work Cratinus ridicules, as long in finishing,—

> " 'Tis long since Pericles, if words would do it,
> Talk'd up the wall; yet adds not one mite to it."

The Odeum, or music-room, which in its interior was full of seats and ranges of pillars, and outside had its roof made to slope and descend from one single point at the top, was constructed, we are told, in imitation of the king of Persia's Pavilion; this likewise by Pericles's order; which Cratinus again, in his comedy called The Thracian Women, made an occasion of raillery,—

> "So, we see here,
> Jupiter Long-pate Pericles appear,
> Since ostracism time, he's laid aside his head,
> And wears the new Odeum in its stead."

Pericles, also, eager for distinction, then first obtained the decree for a contest in musical skill to be held yearly at the Panathenæa, and he himself, being chosen judge, arranged the order and method in which the competitors should sing and play on the flute and on the harp. And both at that time, and at other times also, they sat in this music-room to see and hear all such trials of skill.

The propylæa, or entrances to the Acropolis, were finished in five years' time, Mnesicles being the principal architect. A strange accident happened in the course of building, which showed that the goddess was not averse to the work, but was aiding and coöperating to bring it to perfection. One of the artificers, the quickest and the handiest workman among them all, with a slip of his foot fell down from a great height, and lay in a miserable condition, the physicians having no hopes of his recovery. When Pericles was in distress about this, Minerva appeared to him at night in a dream, and ordered a course of treatment, which he applied, and in a short time and with great ease cured the man. And upon this occasion it was that he set up a brass statue of Minerva, surnamed Health, in the citadel near the altar, which they say was there before. But it was Phidias who wrought the goddess's image in gold, and he has his name inscribed on the pedestal as the workman of it; and indeed the whole work in a manner was under his charge, and he had, as we have said already, the oversight over all the artists and workmen, through Pericles's friendship for him; and this, indeed, made him much envied, and his patron shamefully slandered with stories, as if Phidias were in the habit of receiving, for Pericles's use, free-born women that came to see the works. The comic writers of the town, when they had got hold of this story, made much of it, and bespattered him with all the ribaldry they could invent, charging him falsely with the wife of Menippus, one who was his friend and served as lieutenant under him in the wars; and with the birds kept by Pyrilampes, an acquaintance of Pericles, who, they pretended, used to give presents of peacocks to Pericles's female friends. And how can one wonder at any number of strange assertions from men whose whole lives were devoted to mockery, and who were ready at any time to sacrifice the reputation of their superiors to vulgar envy and spite, as to some evil genius, when even Stesimbrotus the Thasian has dared to lay to the charge of Pericles a monstrous and fabulous piece of criminality with his son's wife? So very difficult a matter is it to trace and find out the truth of any thing by history, when, on the one hand, those who afterwards write it find long periods of time intercepting their view, and, on the other hand, the contemporary records of any actions and lives, partly through envy and ill-will, partly through favor and flattery, pervert and distort truth.

When the orators, who sided with Thucydides and his party, were at one time crying out, as their custom was, against Pericles, as one who squandered away the public money, and made havoc of the state revenues, he rose in the open assembly and put the question to the people, whether they thought that he had laid out much; and they saying, "Too much, a great deal," "Then," said he, "since it is so, let the cost not go to your account, but to mine; and let the inscription upon the buildings stand in my name." When they heard him say thus, whether it were out of a surprise to see the greatness of his spirit, or out of emulation of the glory of the works, they cried aloud, bidding him to spend on, and lay out what he thought fit from the public purse, and to spare no cost, till all were finished.

At length, coming to a final contest with Thucydides, which of the two should ostracize the other out of the country, and having gone through this peril, he drew his antagonist out, and broke up the confederacy that had been organized against him. So that now all schism and division being at an end, and the city brought to evenness and unity, he got all Athens and all affairs that pertained to the Athenians into his own hands, their tributes, their armies, and their galleys, the islands, the sea, and their wide-extended power, partly over other Greeks and partly over barbarians, and all that empire, which they possessed, founded and fortified upon subject nations and royal friendships and alliances.

After this he was no longer the same man he had been before, nor as tame and gentle and familiar as formerly with the populace, so as readily to yield to their pleasures and to comply with the desires of the multitude, as a steersman shifts with the winds. Quitting that loose, remiss, and, in some cases, licentious court of the popular will, he turned those soft and flowery modulations to the austerity of aristocratical and regal rule; and employing this uprightly and undeviatingly for the country's best interests, he was able generally to lead the people along, with their own wills and consents, by persuading and showing them what was to be done; and sometimes, too, urging and pressing them forward extremely against their will, he made them, whether they would or no, yield submission to what was for their advantage. In which, to say the truth, he did but like a skilful physician, who, in a complicated and chronic disease, as he sees occasion, at one while allows his patient the moderate use of such things as please him, at another while gives him keen pains and drugs to work the cure. For there arising and growing up, as was natural, all manner of distempered feelings among a people which had so vast a command and dominion, he alone, as a great master, knowing how to handle and deal fitly with each one of them, and, in an especial manner, making that use of hopes and fears, as his two chief rudders, with the one to check the career of their confidence at any time, with the other to raise them up and cheer them when under any discouragement, plainly showed by this, that rhetoric, or the art of speaking, is, in Plato's language, the government of the souls of men, and that her chief business is to address the affections and passions, which are as it were the strings and keys to the soul, and require a skilful and careful touch to be played on as they should be. The source of this predominance was not barely his power of language, but, as Thucydides assures us, the reputation of his life, and the confidence felt in his character; his manifest freedom from every kind of corruption, and superiority to all considerations of money. Notwithstanding he had made the city of Athens, which was great of itself, as great and rich as can be imagined, and though he were himself in power and interest more than equal to many kings and absolute rulers, who some of them also bequeathed by will their power to their children, he, for his part, did not make the patrimony his father left him greater than it was by one drachma.

Thucydides, indeed, gives a plain statement of the greatness of his power; and the comic poets, in their spiteful manner, more than hint at it, styling his companions and friends the new Pisistratidæ, and calling on him to abjure any intention of usurpation, as one whose eminence was too great to be any longer proportionable to and compatible with a democracy or popular government. And Teleclides says the Athenians had surrendered up to him—

"The tribute of the cities, and with them, the cities too, to do with them as he pleases, and undo;
To build up, if he likes, stone walls around a town; and again, if so he likes, to pull them down;
Their treaties and alliances, power, empire, peace, and war, their wealth and their success forevermore."

Nor was all this the luck of some happy occasion; nor was it the mere bloom and grace of a policy that flourished for a season; but having for forty years together maintained the first place among statesmen such as Ephialtes and Leocrates and Myronides and Cimon and Tolmides and Thucydides were, after the defeat and banishment of Thucydides, for no less than fifteen years longer, in the exercise of one continuous unintermitted command in the office, to which he was annually reëlected, of General, he preserved his integrity unspotted; though otherwise he was not altogether idle or careless in looking after his pecuniary advantage; his paternal estate, which of right belonged to him, he so ordered that it might neither through negligence be wasted or lessened, nor yet, being so full of business as he was, cost him any great trouble or time with taking care of it; and put it into such a way of management as he thought to be the most easy for himself, and the most exact. All his yearly products and profits he sold together in a lump, and supplied his household needs afterward by buying every thing that he or his family wanted out of the market. Upon which account, his children, when they grew to age, were not well pleased with his management, and the women that lived with him were treated with little cost, and complained of his way of housekeeping, where every thing was ordered and set down from day to day, and reduced to the greatest exactness; since there was not there, as is usual in a great family and a plentiful estate, any thing to spare, or over and above; but all that went out or came in, all disbursements and all receipts, proceeded as it were by number and measure. His manager in all this was a single servant, Evangelus by name, a man either naturally gifted or instructed by Pericles so as to excel every one in this art of domestic economy.

All this, in truth, was very little in harmony with Anaxagoras's wisdom; if, indeed, it be true that he, by a kind of divine impulse and greatness of spirit, voluntarily quitted his house, and left his land to lie fallow and to be grazed by sheep like a common. But the life of a contemplative philosopher and that of an active statesman are, I presume, not the same thing; for the one merely employs, upon great and good objects of thought, an intelligence that requires no aid of instruments nor supply of any external materials; whereas the other, who tempers and applies his virtue to human uses, may have occasion for affluence, not as a matter of mere necessity, but as a noble thing; which was Pericles's case, who relieved numerous poor citizens.

However, there is a story, that Anaxagoras himself, while Pericles was taken up with public affairs, lay neglected, and that, now being grown old, he wrapped himself up with a resolution to die for want of food; which being by chance brought to Pericles's ear, he was horror-struck, and instantly ran thither, and used all the arguments and entreaties he could to him, lamenting not so much Anaxagoras's condition as his own, should he lose such a counsellor as he had found him to be; and that, upon this, Anaxagoras unfolded his robe, and showing himself, made answer: "Pericles," said he, "even those who have occasion for a lamp supply it with oil."

The Lacedæmonians beginning to show themselves troubled at the growth of the Athenian power, Pericles, on the other hand, to elevate the people's spirit yet more, and to raise them to the thought of great actions, proposed a decree, to summon all the Greeks in what part soever, whether of Europe or Asia, every city, little as well as great, to send their deputies to Athens to a general assembly, or convention, there to consult and advise concerning the Greek temples which the barbarians had burnt down, and the sacrifices which were due from them upon vows they had made to their gods for the safety of Greece when they fought against the barbarians; and also concerning the navigation of the sea, that they might henceforward all of them pass to and fro and trade securely, and be at peace among themselves.

Upon this errand, there were twenty men, of such as were above fifty years of age, sent by commission; five to summon the Ionians and Dorians in Asia, and the islanders as far as Lesbos and Rhodes; five to visit all the places in the Hellespont and Thrace, up to Byzantium; and other five besides these to go to Bœotia and Phocis and Peloponnesus, and from hence to pass through the Locrians over to the neighboring continent, as far as Acarnania and Ambracia; and the rest to take their course through Eubœa to the Œtæans and the Malian Gulf, and ro the Achæans of Phthiotis and the Thessalians; all of them to treat with the people as they passed, and to persuade them to come and take their part in the debates for settling the peace and jointly regulating the affairs of Greece.

Nothing was effected, nor did the cities meet by their deputies, as was desired; the Lacedæmonians, as it is said, crossing the design underhand, and the attempt being disappointed and baffled first in Peloponnesus. I thought fit, however, to introduce the mention of it, to show the spirit of the man and the greatness of his thoughts.

In his military conduct, he gained a great reputation for wariness; he would not by his good-will engage in any fight which had much uncertainty or hazard; he did not envy the glory of generals whose rash adventures fortune favored with brilliant success, however they were admired by others; nor did he think them worthy his imitation, but always used to say to his citizens that, so far as lay in his power, they should continue immortal, and live forever. Seeing Tolmides, the son of Tolmæus, upon the confidence of his former successes, and flushed with the honor his military actions had procured him, making preparation to attack the Bœotians in their own country, when there was no likely opportunity, and that he had prevailed with the bravest and most enterprising of the youth to enlist themselves as volunteers in the service, who besides his other force made up a thousand, he endeavored to withhold him and to advise him from it in the public assembly, telling him in a memorable saying of his, which still goes about, that, if he would not take Pericles's advice, yet he would not do amiss to wait and be ruled by time, the wisest counsellor of all. This saying, at that time, was but slightly commended; but within a few days after, when news was brought that Tolmides himself had been defeated and slain in battle near Coronea, and that many brave citizens had fallen with him, it gained him great repute as well as good-will among the people, for wisdom and for love of his countrymen.

But of all his expeditions, that to the Chersonese gave most satisfaction and pleasure, having proved the safety of the Greeks who inhabited there. For not only by carrying along with him a thousand fresh citizens of Athens he gave new strength and vigor to the cities, but also by belting the neck of land, which joins the peninsula to the continent, with bulwarks and forts from sea to sea, he put a stop to the inroads of the Thracians, who lay all about the Chersonese, and closed the door against a continual and grievous war, with which that country had been long harassed, lying exposed to the encroachments and influx of barbarous neighbors, and groaning under the evils of a predatory population both upon and within its borders.

Nor was he less admired and talked of abroad for his sailing round the Peloponnesus, having set out from Pegæ, or The Fountains, the port of Megara, with a hundred galleys. For he not only laid waste the sea-coast, as Tolmides had done before, but also, advancing far up into main land with the soldiers he had on board, by the terror of his appearance drove many within their walls; and at Nemea, with main force, routed and raised a trophy over the Sicyonians, who stood their ground and joined battle with him. And having taken on board a supply of soldiers into the galleys, out of Achaia, then in league with Athens, he crossed with the fleet to the opposite continent, and, sailing along by the mouth of the river Achelous, overran Acarnania, and shut up the Œniadæ within their city walls, and having ravaged and wasted their country, weighed anchor for home with the double advantage of having shown himself formidable to his enemies, and at the same time safe and energetic to his fellow-citizens; for there was not so much as any chance-miscarriage that happened, the whole voyage through, to those who were under his charge.

Entering also the Euxine Sea with a large and finely equipped fleet, he obtained for the Greek cities any new arrangements they wanted, and entered into friendly relations with them; and to the barbarous nations, and kings and chiefs round about them, displayed the greatness of the power of the Athenians, their perfect ability and confidence to sail wherever they had a mind, and to bring the whole sea under their control. He left the Sinopians thirteen ships of war, with soldiers under the command of Lamachus, to assist them against Timesileus the tyrant; and when he and his accomplices had been thrown out, obtained a decree that six hundred of the Athenians that were willing should sail to Sinope and plant themselves there with the Sinopians, sharing among them the houses and land which the tyrant and his party had previously held.

But in other things he did not comply with the giddy impulses of the citizens, nor quit his own resolutions to follow their fancies, when, carried away with the thought of their strength and great success, they were eager to interfere again in Egypt, and to disturb the king of Persia's maritime dominions. Nay, there were a good many who were, even then, possessed with that unblest and inauspicious passion for Sicily, which afterward the orators of Alcibiades's party blew up into a flame. There were some also who dreamt of Tuscany and of Carthage, and not without plausible reason in their present large dominion and the prosperous course of their affairs.

But Pericles curbed this passion for foreign conquest, and unsparingly pruned and cut down their ever busy fancies for a multitude of undertakings; and directed their power for the most part to securing and consolidating what they had already got, supposing it would be quite enough for them to do, if they could keep the Lacedæmonians in check; to whom he entertained all along a sense of opposition; which, as upon many other occasions, so he particularly showed by what he did in the time of the holy war. The Lacedæmonians, having gone with an army to Delphi, restored Apollo's temple, which the Phocians had got into their possession, to the Delphians; immediately after their departure, Pericles, with another army, came and restored the Phocians. And the Lacedæmonians having engraven the record of their privilege of consulting the oracle before others, which the Delphians gave them, upon the forehead of the brazen wolf which stands there, he, also, having received from the Phocians the like privilege for the Athenians, had it cut upon the same wolf of brass on his right side.

That he did well and wisely in thus restraining the exertions of the Athenians within the compass of Greece, the events themselves that happened afterward bore sufficient witness. For, in the first place, the Eubœans revolted, against whom he passed over with forces; and then, immediately after, news came that the Megarians were turned their enemies, and a hostile army was upon the borders of Attica, under the conduct of Plistoanax, king of the Lacedæmonians. Wherefore Pericles came with his army back again in all haste out of Eubœa, to meet the war which threatened at home; and did not venture to engage a numerous and brave army eager for battle; but perceiving that Plistoanax was a very young man, and governed himself mostly by the counsel and advice of Cleandrides, whom the ephors had sent with him, by reason of his youth, to be a kind of guardian and assistant to him, he privately made trial of this man's integrity, and, in a short time, having corrupted him with money, prevailed with him to withdraw the Peloponnesians out of Attica. When the army had retired and dispersed into their several states, the Lacedæmonians in anger fined their king in so large a sum of money, that, unable to pay it, he quitted Lacedæmon; while Cleandrides fled, and had sentence of death passed upon him in his absence. This was the father of Gylippus, who overpowered the Athenians in Sicily. And it seems that this covetousness was an hereditary disease transmitted from father to son; for Gylippus also afterwards was caught in foul practices, and expelled from Sparta for it. But this we have told at large in the account of Lysander.

When Pericles, in giving up his accounts of this expedition, stated a disbursement of ten talents, as laid out upon fit occasion, the people, without any question, nor troubling themselves to investigate the mystery, freely allowed of it. And some historians, in which number is Theophrastus the philosopher, have given it as a truth that Pericles every year used to send privately the sum of ten talents to Sparta, with which he complimented those in office, to keep off the war; not to purchase peace neither, but time, that he might prepare at leisure, and be the better able to carry on war hereafter.

Immediately after this, turning his forces against the revolters, and passing over into the island of Eubœa with fifty sail of ships and five thousand men in arms, he reduced their cities, and drove out the citizens of the Chalcidians, called Hippobotæ, horse-feeders, the chief persons for wealth and reputation among them; and removing all the Histiæans out of the country, brought in a plantation of Athenians in their room; making them his one example of severity, because they had captured an Attic ship and killed all on board.

After this, having made a truce between the Athenians and Lacedæmonians for thirty years, he ordered, by public decree, the expedition against the Isle of Samos, on the ground, that, when they were bid to leave off their war with the Milesians, they had not complied. And as these measures against the Samians are thought to have been taken to please Aspasia, this may be a fit point for inquiry about the woman, what art or charming faculty she had that enabled her to captivate, as she did, the greatest statesmen, and to give the philosophers occasion to speak so much about her, and that, too, not to her disparagement. That she was a Milesian by birth, the daughter of Axiochus, is a thing acknowledged. And they say it was in emulation of Thargelia, a courtesan of the old Ionian times, that she made her addresses to men of great power. Thargelia was a great beauty, extremely charming, and at the same time sagacious; she had numerous suitors among the Greeks, and brought all who had to do with her over to the Persian interest, and by their means, being men of the greatest power and station, sowed the seeds of the Median faction up and down in several cities.[7] Aspasia, some say, was courted and caressed by Pericles upon account of her knowledge and skill in politics. Socrates himself would sometimes go to visit her, and some of his acquaintance with him; and those who frequented her company would carry their wives with them to listen to her. Her occupation was any thing but creditable, her house being a home for young courtesans. Æschines tells us also, that Lysicles, a sheep-dealer, a man of low birth and character, by keeping Aspasia company after Pericles's death, came to be a chief man in Athens. And in Plato's Menexenus, though we do not take the introduction as quite serious, still thus much seems to be historical, that she had the repute of being resorted to by many of the Athenians for instruction in the art of speaking. Pericles's inclination for her seems, however, to have rather proceeded from the passion of love. He had a wife that was near of kin to him, who had been married first to Hipponicus, by whom she had Callias, surnamed the Rich; and also she brought Pericles, while she lived with him, two sons, Xanthippus and Paralus. Afterwards, when they did not

[7] She was married, says Athenæus, to fourteen husbands; a woman of great beauty and intellect.

well agree nor like to live together, he parted with her, with her own consent, to another man, and himself took Aspasia, and loved her with wonderful affection; every day, both as he went out and as he came in from the market-place, he saluted and kissed her.

In the comedies she goes by the nicknames of the new Omphale and Deianira, and again is styled Juno. Cratinus, in downright terms, calls her a harlot.

> "To find him a Juno the goddess of lust
> Bore that harlot past shame,
> Aspasia by name."

It should seem, also, that he had a son by her; Eupolis, in his Demi, introduced Pericles asking after his safety, and Myronides replying,

> "My son?" "He lives; a man he had been long,
> But that the harlot-mother did him wrong."

Aspasia, they say, became so celebrated and renowned, that Cyrus also, who made war against Artaxerxes for the Persian monarchy, gave her whom he loved the best of all his concubines the name of Aspasia, who before that was called Milto. She was a Phocæan by birth, the daughter of one Hermotimus, and, when Cyrus fell in battle, was carried to the king, and had great influence at court. These things coming into my memory as I am writing this story, it would be unnatural for me to omit them.

Pericles, however, was particularly charged with having proposed to the assembly the war against the Samians, from favor to the Milesians, upon the entreaty of Aspasia. For the two states were at war for the possession of Priene; and the Samians, getting the better, refused to lay down their arms and to have the controversy betwixt them decided by arbitration before the Athenians. Pericles, therefore, fitting out a fleet, went and broke up the oligarchical government at Samos, and, taking fifty of the principal men of the town as hostages, and as many of their children, sent them to the isle of Lemnos, there to be kept, though he had offers, as some relate, of a talent a piece for himself from each one of the hostages, and of many other presents from those who were anxious not to have a democracy. Moreover, Pissuthnes the Persian, one of the king's lieutenants, bearing some good-will to the Samians, sent him ten thousand pieces of gold to excuse the city. Pericles, however, would receive none of all this; but after he had taken that course with the Samians which he thought fit, and set up a democracy among them, sailed back to Athens.

But they, however, immediately revolted, Pissuthnes having privily got away their hostages for them, and provided them with means for the war. Whereupon Pericles came out with a fleet a second time against them, and found them not idle nor slinking away, but manfully resolved to try for the dominion of the sea. The issue was, that, after a sharp sea-fight about the island called Tragia, Pericles obtained a decisive victory, having with forty-four ships routed seventy of the enemy's, twenty of which were carrying soldiers.

Together with his victory and pursuit, having made himself master of the port, he laid siege to the Samians, and blocked them up, who yet, one way or other, still ventured to make sallies, and fight under the city walls. But after that another greater fleet from Athens was arrived, and that the Samians were now shut up with a close leaguer on every side, Pericles, taking with him sixty galleys, sailed out into the main sea, with the intention, as most authors give the account, to meet a squadron of Phœnician ships that were coming for the Samians' relief, and to fight them at as great distance as could be from the island; but, as Stesimbrotus says, with a design of putting over to Cyprus; which does not seem to be probable. But whichever of the two was his intent, it seems to have been a miscalculation. For on his departure, Melissus, the son of Ithagenes, a philosopher, being at that time general in Samos, despising either the small number of the ships that were left or the inexperience of the commanders, prevailed with the citizens to attack the Athenians. And the Samians having won the battle, and taken several of the men prisoners, and disabled several of the ships, were masters of the sea, and brought into port all necessaries they wanted for the war, which they had not before. Aristotle says, too, that Pericles himself had been once before this worsted by this Melissus in a sea-fight.

The Samians, that they might requite an affront which had before been put upon them, branded the Athenians, whom they took prisoners, in their foreheads, with the figure of an owl. For so the Athenians had marked them before with a Samæna, which is a sort of ship, low and flat in the prow, so as to look snub-nosed, but wide and large and well-spread in the hold, by which it both carries a large cargo and sails well. And it was so called, because the first of that kind was seen at Samos, having been built by order of Polycrates the tyrant. These brands upon the Samians' foreheads, they say, are the allusion in the passage of Aristophanes, where he says,—

"For, oh, the Samians are a lettered people."

Pericles, as soon as news was brought him of the disaster that had befallen his army, made all the haste he could to come in to their relief, and having defeated Melissus, who bore up against him, and put the enemy to flight, he immediately proceeded to hem them in with a wall, resolving to master them and take the town, rather with some cost and time, than with the wounds and hazards of his citizens. But as it was a hard matter to keep back the Athenians, who were vexed at the delay, and were eagerly bent to fight, he divided the whole multitude into eight parts, and arranged by lot that that part which had the white bean should have leave to feast and take their ease, while the other seven were fighting. And this is the reason, they say, that people, when at any time they have been merry, and enjoyed themselves, call it white day, in allusion to this white bean.

Ephorus the historian tells us besides, that Pericles made use of engines of battery in this siege, being much taken with the curiousness of the invention, with the aid and presence of Artemon himself, the engineer, who, being lame, used to be carried about in a litter, where the works required his attendance, and for that reason was called Periphoretus. But Heraclides Ponticus disproves this out of Anacreon's poems, where mention is made of this Artemon Periphoretus several ages before the Samian war, or any of these occurrences. And he says that Artemon, being a man who loved his ease, and had a great apprehension of danger, for the most part kept close within doors, having two of his servants to hold a brazen shield over his head, that nothing might fall upon him from above;

and if he were at any time forced upon necessity to go abroad, that he was carried about in a little hanging bed, close to the very ground, and that for this reason he was called Periphoretus.

In the ninth month, the Samians surrendering themselves and delivering up the town, Pericles pulled down their walls, and seized their shipping, and set a fine of a large sum of money upon them, part of which they paid down at once, and they agreed to bring in the rest by a certain time, and gave hostages for security. Duris the Samian makes a tragical drama out of these events, charging the Athenians and Pericles with a great deal of cruelty, which neither Thucydides, nor Ephorus, nor Aristotle have given any relation of, and probably with little regard to truth; how, for example, he brought the captains and soldiers of the galleys into the market-place at Miletus, and there having bound them fast to boards for ten days, then, when they were already all but half dead, gave order to have them killed by beating out their brains with clubs, and their dead bodies to be flung out into the open streets and fields, unburied. Duris, however, who even where he has no private feeling concerned, is not wont to keep his narrative within the limits of truth, is the more likely upon this occasion to have exaggerated the calamities which befell his country, to create odium against the Athenians. Pericles, however, after the reduction of Samos, returning back to Athens, took care that those who died in the war should be honorably buried, and made a funeral harangue, as the custom is, in their commendation at their graves, for which he gained great admiration. As he came down from the stage on which he spoke, the rest of the women came and complimented him, taking him by the hand, and crowning him with garlands and ribbons, like a victorious athlete in the games; but Elpinice, coming near to him, said, "These are brave deeds, Pericles, that you have done, and such as deserve our chaplets; who have lost us many a worthy citizen, not in a war with Phœnicians or Medes, like my brother Cimon, but for the overthrow of an allied and kindred city." As Elpinice spoke these words, he, smiling quietly, as it is said, returned her answer with this verse,—

"Old women should not seek to be perfumed."

Ion says of him, that, upon this exploit of his, conquering the Samians, he indulged very high and proud thoughts of himself: whereas Agamemnon was ten years a-taking a barbarous city, he had in nine months' time vanquished and taken the greatest and most powerful of the Ionians. And indeed it was not without reason that he assumed this glory to himself, for, in real truth, there was much uncertainty and great hazard in this war, if so be, as Thucydides tells us, the Samian state were within a very little of wresting the whole power and dominion of the sea out of the Athenians' hands.

After this was over, the Peloponnesian war beginning to break out in full tide, he advised the people to send help to the Corcyræans, who were attacked by the Corinthians, and to secure to themselves an island possessed of great naval resources, since the Peloponnesians were already all but in actual hostilities against them. The people readily consenting to the motion, and voting an aid and succor for them, he despatched Lacedæmonius, Cimon's son, having only ten ships with him, as it were out of a design to affront him; for there was a great kindness and friendship betwixt Cimon's family and the Lacedæmonians; so, in order that Lacedæmonius might lie the more open to a charge, or suspicion at least, of favoring the Lacedæmonians and playing false, if he performed no considerable exploit in this service, he allowed him a small number of ships, and sent him out against his will; and indeed he made it somewhat his business to hinder Cimon's sons from rising in the state, professing that by their very names they were not to be looked upon as native and true Athenians, but foreigners and strangers, one being called Lacedæmonius, another Thessalus, and the third Eleus; and they were all three of them, it was thought, born of an Arcadian woman. Being, however, ill spoken of on account of these ten galleys, as having afforded but a small supply to the people that were in need, and yet given a great advantage to those who might complain of the act of intervention, Pericles sent out a larger force afterward to Corcyra, which arrived after the fight was over. And when now the Corinthians, angry and indignant with the Athenians, accused them publicly at Lacedæmon, the Megarians joined with them, complaining that they were, contrary to common right and the articles of peace sworn to among the Greeks, kept out and driven away from every market and from all ports under the control of the Athenians. The Æginetans, also, professing to be ill-used and treated with violence, made supplications in private to the Lacedæmonians for redress, though not daring openly to call the Athenians in question. In the mean time, also, the city of Potidæa, under the dominion of the Athenians, but a colony formerly of the Corinthians, had revolted, and was beset with a formal siege, and was a further occasion of precipitating the war.

Yet notwithstanding all this, there being embassies sent to Athens, and Archidamus, the king of the Lacedæmonians, endeavoring to bring the greater part of the complaints and matters in dispute to a fair determination, and to pacify and allay the heats of the allies, it is very likely that the war would not upon any other grounds of quarrel have fallen upon the Athenians, could they have been prevailed with to repeal the ordinance against the Megarians, and to be reconciled to them. Upon which account, since Pericles was the man who mainly opposed it, and stirred up the people's passions to persist in their contention with the Megarians, he was regarded as the sole cause of the war.

They say, moreover, that ambassadors went, by order from Lacedæmon to Athens about this very business, and that when Pericles was urging a certain law which made it illegal to take down or withdraw the tablet of the decree, one of the ambassadors, Polyalces by name, said, "Well, do not take it down then, but *turn* it; there is no law, I suppose, which forbids that";[8] which, though prettily said, did not move Pericles from his resolution. There may have been, in all likelihood, something of a secret grudge and private animosity which he had against the Megarians. Yet, upon a public and open charge against them, that they had appropriated part of the sacred land on the frontier, he proposed a decree that a herald should be sent to them, and the same also to the Lacedæmonians, with an accusation of the Megarians; an order which certainly shows equitable and friendly proceeding enough. And after that the herald

[8] The word for *taking down,* in the literal sense, is also the technical term for revoking, or repealing; hence the Spartans play upon the two senses. "If you may not take it down, turn it, with its face to the wall."

who was sent, by name Anthemocritus, died, and it was believed that the Megarians had contrived his death, then Charinus proposed a decree against them, that there should be an irreconcilable and implacable enmity thenceforward betwixt the two commonwealths; and that if any one of the Megarians should but set his foot in Attica, he should be put to death; and that the commanders, when they take the usual oath, should, over and above that, swear that they will twice every year make an inroad into the Megarian country; and that Anthemocritus should be buried near the Thriasian Gates, which are now called the Dipylon, or Double Gate.

On the other hand, the Megarians, utterly denying and disowning the murder of Anthemocritus, throw the whole matter upon Aspasia and Pericles, availing themselves of the famous verses in the Acharnians,

> "To Megara some of our madcaps ran,
> And stole Simætha thence, their courtesan.
> Which exploit the Megarians to outdo,
> Came to Aspasia's house, and took off two."

The true occasion of the quarrel is not so easy to find out. But of inducing the refusal to annul the decree, all alike charge Pericles. Some say he met the request with a positive refusal, out of high spirit and a view of the state's best interests, accounting that the demand made in those embassies was designed for a trial of their compliance, and that a concession would be taken for a confession of weakness, as if they durst not do otherwise; while other some there are who say that it was rather out of arrogance and a wilful spirit of contention, to show his own strength, that he took occasion to slight the Lacedæmonians. The worst motive of all, which is confirmed by most witnesses, is to the following effect. Phidias the Moulder had, as has before been said, undertaken to make the statue of Minerva. Now he, being admitted to friendship with Pericles, and a great favorite of his, had many enemies upon this account, who envied and maligned him; who also, to make trial in a case of his, what kind of judges the commons would prove, should there be occasion to bring Pericles himself before them, having tampered with Menon, one who had been a workman with Phidias, stationed him in the market-place, with a petition desiring public security upon his discovery and impeachment of Phidias. The people admitting the man to tell his story, and the prosecution proceeding in the assembly, there was nothing of theft or cheat proved against him; for Phidias, from the very first beginning, by the advice of Pericles, had so wrought and wrapt the gold that was used in the work about the statue, that they might take it all off and make out the just weight of it, which Pericles at that time bade the accusers do. But the reputation of his works was what brought envy upon Phidias, especially that where he represents the fight of the Amazons upon the goddesses' shield, he had introduced a likeness of himself as a bald old man holding up a great stone with both hands, and had put in a very fine representation of Pericles fighting with an Amazon. And the position of the hand, which holds out the spear in front of the face, was ingeniously contrived to conceal in some degree the likeness, which, meantime, showed itself on either side.

Phidias then was carried away to prison, and there died of a disease; but, as some say, of poison, administered by the enemies of Pericles, to raise a slander, or a suspicion, at least, as though he had procured it. The informer Menon, upon Glycon's proposal, the people made free from payment of taxes and customs, and ordered the generals to take care that nobody should do him any hurt. About the same time, Aspasia was indicted of impiety, upon the complaint of Hermippus the comedian, who also laid further to her charge that she received into her house freeborn women for the uses of Pericles. And Diopithes proposed a decree, that public accusation should be laid against persons who neglected religion, or taught new doctrines about things above,[9] directing suspicion, by means of Anaxagoras, against Pericles himself. The people receiving and admitting these accusations and complaints, at length, by this means, they came to enact a decree, at the motion of Dracontides, that Pericles should bring in the accounts of the moneys he had expended, and lodge them with the Prytanes; and that the judges, carrying their suffrage from the altar in the Acropolis, should examine and determine the

[9] "Supera ac cœlestia," as Cicero translates the words *meteora* and *metarsia,* whence we have formed our *meteorology*. The whole Greek religion was based on certain conceptions of such phenomena, any tampering with which was, therefore, quickly resented.

business in the city. This last clause Hagnon took out of the decree, and moved that the causes should be tried before fifteen hundred jurors, whether they should be styled prosecutions for robbery, or bribery, or any kind of malversation. Aspasia, Pericles begged off, shedding, as Æschines says, many tears at the trial, and personally entreating the jurors. But fearing how it might go with Anaxagoras, he sent him out of the city. And finding that in Phidias's case he had miscarried with the people, being afraid of impeachment, he kindled the war, which hitherto had lingered and smothered, and blew it up into a flame; hoping, by that means, to disperse and scatter these complaints and charges, and to allay their jealousy; the city usually throwing herself upon him alone, and trusting to his sole conduct, upon the urgency of great affairs and public dangers, by reason of his authority and the sway he bore.

These are given out to have been the reasons which induced Pericles not to suffer the people of Athens to yield to the proposals of the Lacedæmonians; but their truth is uncertain.

The Lacedæmonians, for their part, feeling sure that if they could once remove him, they might be at what terms they pleased with the Athenians, sent them word that they should expel the "Pollution" with which Pericles on the mother's side was tainted, as Thucydides tells us. But the issue proved quite contrary to what those who sent the message expected; instead of bringing Pericles under suspicion and reproach, they raised him into yet greater credit and esteem with the citizens, as a man whom their enemies most hated and feared. In the same way, also, before Archidamus, who was at the head of the Peloponnesians, made his invasion into Attica, he told the Athenians beforehand, that if Archidamus, while he laid waste the rest of the country, should forbear and spare his estate, either on the ground of friendship or right of hospitality that was betwixt them, or on purpose to give his enemies an occasion of traducing him, that then he did freely bestow upon the state all that his land and the buildings upon it for the public use. The Lacedæmonians, therefore, and their allies, with a great army, invaded the Athenian territories, under the conduct of king Archidamus, and laying waste the country, marched on as far as Acharnæ, and there pitched their camp, presuming that the Athenians would never endure that, but would come out and fight them for their country's and their honor's sake. But Pericles looked upon it as dangerous to engage in battle, to the risk of the city itself, against sixty thousand men-at-arms of Peloponnesians and Bœotians; for so many they were in number that made the inroad at first; and he endeavored to appease those who were desirous to fight, and were grieved and discontented to see how things went, and gave them good words, saying, that "trees, when they are lopped and cut, grow up again in a short time, but men, being once lost, cannot easily be recovered." He did not convene the people into an assembly, for fear lest they should force him to act against his judgment; but, like a skilful steersman or pilot of a ship, who, when a sudden squall comes on, out at sea, makes all his arrangements, sees that all is tight and fast, and then follows the dictates of his skill, and minds the business of the ship, taking no notice of the tears and entreaties of the sea-sick and fearful passengers, so he, having shut up the city gates, and placed guards at all posts for security, followed his own reason and judgment, little regarding those that cried out against him and were angry at his management, although there were a great many of his friends that urged him with requests, and many of his enemies threatened and accused him for doing as he did, and many made songs and lampoons upon him, which were sung about the town to his disgrace, reproaching him with the cowardly exercise of his office of general, and the tame abandonment of everything to the enemy's hands.

Cleon, also, already was among his assailants, making use of the feeling against him as a step to the leadership of the people, as appears in the anapæstic verses of Hermippus.

"Satyr-king, instead of swords,
Will you always handle words?
Very brave indeed we find them,
But a Teles[10] lurks behind them.

"Yet to gnash your teeth you're seen,
When the little dagger keen,
Whetted every day anew,
Of sharp Cleon touches you."

[10] Apparently some notorious coward.

Pericles, however, was not at all moved by any attacks, but took all patiently, and submitted in silence to the disgrace they threw upon him and the ill-will they bore him; and, sending out a fleet of a hundred galleys to Peloponnesus, he did not go along with it in person, but stayed behind, that he might watch at home and keep the city under his own control, till the Peloponnesians broke up their camp and were gone. Yet to soothe the common people, jaded and distressed with the war, he relieved them with distributions of public moneys, and ordained new divisions of subject land. For having turned out all the people of Ægina, he parted the island among the Athenians, according to lot. Some comfort, also, and ease in their miseries, they might receive from what their enemies endured. For the fleet, sailing round the Peloponnese, ravaged a great deal of the country, and pillaged and plundered the towns and smaller cities; and by land he himself entered with an army the Megarian country, and made havoc of it all. Whence it is clear that the Peloponnesians, though they did the Athenians much mischief by land, yet suffering as much themselves from them by sea, would not have protracted the war to such a length, but would quickly have given it over, as Pericles at first foretold they would, had not some divine power crossed human purposes.

In the first place, the pestilential disease, or plague, seized upon the city, and ate up all the flower and prime of their youth and strength. Upon occasion of which, the people, distempered and afflicted in their souls, as well as in their bodies, were utterly enraged like madmen against Pericles, and, like patients grown delirious, sought to lay violent hands on their physician, or, as it were, their father. They had been possessed, by his enemies, with the belief that the occasion of the plague was the crowding of the country people together into the town, forced as they were now, in the heat of the summer-weather, to dwell many of them together even as they could, in small tenements and stifling hovels, and to be tied to a lazy course of life within doors, whereas before they lived in a pure, open and free air. The cause and author of all this, said they, is he who on account of the war has poured a multitude of people from the country in upon us within the walls, and uses all these many men that he has here upon no employ or service, but keeps them pent up like cattle, to be overrun with infection from one another, affording them neither shift of quarters nor any refreshments.

With the design to remedy these evils, and do the enemy some inconvenience, Pericles got a hundred and fifty galleys ready, and having embarked many tried soldiers, both foot and horse, was about to sail out, giving great hope to his citizens, and no less alarm to his enemies, upon the sight of so great a force. And now the vessels having their complement of men, and Pericles being gone aboard his own galley, it happened that the sun was eclipsed, and it grew dark on a sudden, to the affright of all, for this was looked upon as extremely ominous. Pericles, therefore, perceiving the steersman seized with fear and at a loss what to do, took his cloak and held it up before the man's face, and, screening him with it so that he could not see, asked him whether he imagined there was any great hurt, or the sign of any great hurt in this, and he answering No, "Why," said he, "and what does that differ from this, only that what has caused that darkness there, is something greater than a cloak?" This is a story which philosophers tell their scholars. Pericles, however, after putting out to sea, seems not to have done any other exploit befitting such preparations, and when he had laid siege to the holy city Epidaurus, which gave him some hope of surrender, miscarried in his design by reason of the sickness. For it not only seized upon the Athenians, but upon all others, too, that held any sort of communication with the army. Finding after this the Athenians ill affected and highly displeased with him, he tried and endeavored what he could to appease and re-encourage them. But he could not pacify or allay their anger, nor persuade or prevail with them any way, till they freely passed their votes upon him, resumed their power, took away his command from him, and fined him in a sum of money; which, by their account that say least, was fifteen talents, while they who reckon most, name fifty. The name prefixed to the accusation was Cleon, as Idomeneus tells us; Simmias, according to Theophrastus; and Heraclides Ponticus gives it as Lacratidas.

After this, public troubles were soon to leave him unmolested; the people, so to say, discharged their passion in their stroke, and lost their stings in the wound. But his domestic concerns were in an unhappy condition, many of his friends and acquaintance having died in the plague time, and those of his family having long since been in disorder and in a kind of mutiny against him. For the eldest of his lawfully begotten sons, Xanthippus by name, being naturally prodigal, and marrying a young and expensive wife, the daughter of Tisander, son of Epilycus, was highly offended at his father's economy in making him but a scanty allowance, by little and little at a time. He sent, therefore, to a friend one day, and borrowed some money of him in his father Pericles's name, pretending it was by his order. The man coming afterward to demand the debt, Pericles was so far from yielding to pay it, that he entered an action against him. Upon which the young man, Xanthippus, thought himself so ill used and disobliged, that he openly reviled his father; telling first, by way of ridicule, stories about his conversations at home, and the discourses he had with the sophists and scholars that came to his house. As for instance, how one who was a practiser of the five games of skill,[11] having with a dart or javelin unawares against his will struck and killed Epitimus the Pharsalian, his father spent a whole day with Protagoras in a serious dispute, whether the javelin, or the man that threw it, or the masters of the games who appointed these sports, were, according to the strictest and best reason, to be accounted the cause of this mischance. Beside this, Stesimbrotus tells us that it was Xanthippus who spread abroad among the people the infamous story concerning his own wife; and in general that this difference of the young man's with his father, and the breach betwixt them, continued never to be healed or made up till his death. For Xanthippus died in the plague time of the sickness. At which time Pericles also lost his sister, and the greatest part of his relations and friends, and those who had been most useful and serviceable to him in managing the affairs of state. However, he did not shrink or give in upon these occasions, nor betray or lower his high spirit and the greatness of his mind under all his misfortunes; he was not even so much as seen to weep or to mourn, or even attend

[11] These are recorded in a pentameter verse by Simonides.

Halma, podokeiēn, discon, aconta, palēn.
Leaping, and swiftness of foot, wrestling, the discus, the dart.

the burial of any of his friends or relations, till at last he lost his only remaining legitimate son. Subdued by this blow, and yet striving still, as far as he could, to maintain his principle, and to preserve and keep up the greatness of his soul, when he came, however, to perform the ceremony of putting a garland of flowers upon the head of the corpse, he was vanquished by his passion at the sight, so that he burst into exclamations, and shed copious tears, having never done any such thing in all his life before.

The city having made trial of other generals for the conduct of war, and orators for business of state, when they found there was no one who was of weight enough for such a charge, or of authority sufficient to be trusted with so great a command, regretted the loss of him, and invited him again to address and advise them, and to reassume the office of general. He, however, lay at home in dejection and mourning; but was persuaded by Alcibiades and others of his friends to come abroad and show himself to the people; who having, upon his appearance, made their acknowledgments, and apologized for their untowardly treatment of him, he undertook the public affairs once more; and, being chosen general, requested that the statute concerning base-born children, which he himself had formerly caused to be made, might be suspended; that so the name and race of his family might not, for absolute want of a lawful heir to succeed, be wholly lost and extinguished. The case of the statute was thus: Pericles, when long ago at the height of his power in the state, having then, as has been said, children lawfully begotten, proposed a law that those only should be reputed true citizens of Athens who were born of such parents as were both Athenians. After this, the king of Egypt having sent to the people, by way of present, forty thousand bushels of wheat, which were to be shared out among the citizens, a great many actions and suits about legitimacy occurred, by virtue of that edict; cases which, till that time, had not been known nor taken notice of; and several persons suffered by false accusations. There were little less than five thousand who were convicted and sold for slaves; those who, enduring the test, remained in the government and passed muster for true Athenians were found upon the poll to be fourteen thousand and forty persons in number.

It looked strange, that a law, which had been carried so far against so many people, should be cancelled again by the same man that made it; yet the present calamity and distress which Pericles labored under in his family broke through all objections, and prevailed with the Athenians to pity him, as one whose losses and misfortunes had sufficiently punished his former arrogance and haughtiness. His sufferings deserved, they thought, their pity, and even indignation, and his request was such as became a man to ask and men to grant; they gave him permission to enroll his son in the register of his fraternity, giving him his own name. This son afterward, after having defeated the Peloponnesians at Arginusæ, was with his fellow-generals, put to death by the people.

About the time when his son was enrolled, it should seem, the plague seized Pericles, not with sharp and violent fits, as it did others that had it, but with a dull and lingering distemper, attended with various changes and alterations, leisurely, by little and little, wasting the strength of his body, and undermining the noble faculties of his soul. So that Theophrastus, in his Morals, when discussing whether men's characters change with their circumstances, and their moral habits, disturbed by the ailings of their bodies, start aside from the rules of virtue, has left it upon record, that Pericles, when he was sick, showed one of his friends that came to visit him, an amulet or charm that the women had hung about his neck; as much as to say, that he was very sick indeed when he would admit of such a foolery as that was.

When he was now near his end, the best of the citizens and those of his friends who were left alive, sitting about him, were speaking of the greatness of his merit, and his power, and reckoning up his famous actions and the number of his victories; for there were no less than nine trophies, which, as their chief commander and conqueror of their enemies, he had set up, for the honor of the city. They talked thus together among themselves, as though he were unable to understand or mind what they said, but had now lost his consciousness. He had listened, however, all the while, and attended to all, and speaking out among them, said, that he wondered they should commend and take notice of things which were as much owing to fortune as to any thing else, and had happened to many other commanders, and, at the same time, should not speak or make mention of that which was the most excellent and greatest thing of all. "For," said he, "no Athenian, through my means, ever wore mourning."

He was indeed a character deserving our high admiration, not only for his equitable and mild temper, which all along in the many affairs of his life, and the great animosities which he incurred, he constantly maintained; but also for the high spirit and feeling which made him regard it the noblest of all his honors that, in the exercise of such immense power, he never had gratified his envy or his passion, nor ever had treated any enemy as irreconcilably opposed to him. And to me it appears that this one thing gives that otherwise childish and arrogant title a fitting and becoming significance; so dispassionate a temper, a life so pure and unblemished, in the height of power and place, might well be called Olympian, in accordance with our conceptions of the divine beings, to whom, as the natural authors of all good and of nothing evil, we ascribe the rule and government of the world. Not as the poets represent, who, while confounding us with their ignorant fancies, are themselves confuted by their own poems and fictions, and call the place, indeed, where they say the gods make their abode, a secure and quiet seat, free from all hazards and commotions, untroubled with winds or with clouds, and equally through all time illumined with soft serenity and a pure light, as though such were a home most agreeable for a blessed and immortal nature; and yet, in the meanwhile, affirm that the gods themselves are full of trouble and enmity and anger and other passions, which no way become or belong to even men that have any understanding. But this will, perhaps, seem a subject fitter for some other consideration, and that ought to be treated of in some other place.

The course of public affairs after his death produced a quick and speedy sense of the loss of Pericles. Those who, while he lived, resented his great authority, as that which eclipsed themselves, presently after his quitting the stage, making trial of other orators and demagogues, readily acknowledged that there never had been in nature such a disposition as his was, more moderate and reasonable in the height of that state he took upon him, or more grave and impressive in the mildness which he used. And that invidious, arbitrary power, to which formerly they gave the name of monarchy and tyranny, did then appear to have been the chief bulwark of public safety; so great a corruption and such a flood of mischief and vice followed, which he, by keeping weak and low, had withheld from notice, and had prevented from attaining incurable height through a licentious impunity.

ARISTIDES

ARISTIDES, the son of Lysimachus, was of the tribe Antiochis, and township of Alopece. As to his wealth, statements differ; some say he passed his life in extreme poverty, and left behind him two daughters whose indigence long kept them unmarried: but Demetrius, the Phalerian, in opposition to this general report, professes in his Socrates, to know a farm at Phalerum going by Aristides's name, where he was interred; and, as marks of his opulence, adduces first, the office of archon eponymus, which he obtained by the lot of the bean; which was confined to the highest assessed families, called the Pentacosiomedimni; second, the ostracism, which was not usually inflicted on the poorer citizens, but on those of great houses, whose station exposed them to envy; third and last, that he left certain tripods in the temple of Bacchus, offerings for his victory in conducting the representation of dramatic performances, which were even in our age still to be seen, retaining this inscription upon them, "The tribe Antiochis obtained the victory: Aristides defrayed the charges: Archestratus's play was acted." But this argument, though in appearance the strongest, is of the least moment of any. For Epaminondas, who all the world knows was educated, and lived his whole life, in much poverty, and also Plato, the philosopher, exhibited magnificent shows, the one an entertainment of flute-players, the other of dithyrambic singers; Dion, the Syracusan, supplying the expenses of the latter, and Pelopidas those of Epaminondas. For good men do not allow themselves in any inveterate and irreconcilable hostility to receiving presents from their friends, but while looking upon those that are accepted to be hoarded up and with avaricious intentions, as sordid and mean, they do not refuse such as, apart from all profit, gratify the pure love of honor and magnificence. Panætius, again, shows that Demetrius was deceived concerning the tripod by an identity of name. For, from the Persian war to the end of the Peloponnesian, there are upon record only two of the name of Aristides, who defrayed the expense of representing plays and gained the prize, neither of which was the same with the son of Lysimachus; but the father of the one was Xenophilus, and the other lived at a much later time, as the way of writing, which is that in use since the time of Euclides, and the addition of the name of Archestratus prove, a name which, in the time of the Persian war, no writer mentions, but which several, during the Peloponnesian war, record as that of a dramatic poet. The argument of Panætius requires to be more closely considered. But as for the ostracism, every one was liable to it, whom his reputation, birth, or eloquence raised above the common level; insomuch that even Damon, preceptor to Pericles, was thus banished, because he seemed a man of more than ordinary sense. And, moreover, Idomeneus says, that Aristides was not made archon by the lot of the bean, but the free election of the people. And if he held the office after the battle of Platæa, as Demetrius himself has written, it is very probable that his great reputation and success in the war, made him be preferred for his virtue to an office which others received in consideration of their wealth. But Demetrius manifestly is eager not only to exempt Aristides, but Socrates likewise, from poverty, as from a great evil; telling us that the latter had not only a house of his own, but also seventy minæ put out at interest with Crito.

Aristides being the friend and supporter of that Clisthenes, who settled the government after the expulsion of the tyrants, and emulating and admiring Lycurgus the Lacedæmonian above all politicians, adhered to the aristocratical principles of government; and had Themistocles, son of Neocles, his adversary on the side of the populace. Some say that, being boys and bred up together from their infancy, they were always at variance with each other in all their words and actions as well serious as playful, and that in this their early contention they soon made proof of their natural inclinations; the one being ready, adventurous, and subtle, engaging readily and eagerly in every thing; the other of a staid and settled temper, intent on the exercise of justice, not admitting any degree of falsity, indecorum, or trickery, no, not so much as at his play. Ariston of

Chios[1] says the first origin of the enmity which rose to so great a height, was a love affair; they were rivals for the affection of the beautiful Stesilaus of Ceos, and were passionate beyond all moderation, and did not lay aside their animosity when the beauty that had excited it passed away; but, as if it had only exercised them in it, immediately carried their heats and differences into public business.

Themistocles, therefore, joining an association of partisans, fortified himself with considerable strength; insomuch that when some one told him that were he impartial, he would make a good magistrate; "I wish," replied he, "I may never sit on that tribunal where my friends shall not plead a greater privilege than strangers." But Aristides walked, so to say, alone on his own path in politics, being unwilling, in the first place, to go along with his associates in ill doing, or to cause them vexation by not gratifying their wishes; and, secondly, observing that many were encouraged by the support they had in their friends to act injuriously, he was cautious; being of opinion that the integrity of his words and actions was the only right security for a good citizen.

However, Themistocles making many dangerous alterations, and withstanding and interrupting him in the whole series of his actions, Aristides also was necessitated to set himself against all Themistocles did, partly in self-defence, and partly to impede his power from still increasing by the favor of the multitude; esteeming it better to let slip some public conveniences, rather than that he by prevailing should become powerful in all things. In fine, when he once had opposed Themistocles in some measures that were expedient, and had got the better of him, he could not refrain from saying, when he left the assembly, that unless they sent Themistocles and himself to the barathrum,[2] there could be no safety for Athens. Another time, when urging some proposal upon the people, though there were much opposition and stirring against it, he yet was gaining

[1] More correctly, perhaps, both here and elsewhere, Ariston of Ceos. There were two philosophical writers of the name, Ariston of Chios, a stoic, and Ariston of Ceos, a Peripatetic.

[2] A pit into which the dead bodies of malefactors, or perhaps living malefactors themselves, were thrown. "The gallows" perhaps is the English term most nearly corresponding to the barathrum, as commonly spoken of in the Athenian popular language.

the day; but just as the president of the assembly was about to put it to the vote, perceiving by what had been said in debate the inexpediency of his advice, he let it fall. Also he often brought in his bills by other persons, lest Themistocles, through party spirit against him, should be any hindrance to the good of the public.

In all the vicissitudes of public affairs, the constancy he showed was admirable, not being elated with honors, and demeaning himself tranquilly and sedately in adversity; holding the opinion that he ought to offer himself to the service of his country without mercenary views and irrespectively of any reward, not only of riches, but even of glory itself. Hence it came, probably, that at the recital of these verses of Æschylus in the theatre, relating to Amphiaraus.

"For not at seeming just, but being so
He aims; and from his depth of soil below,
Harvests of wise and prudent counsels grow,"

the eyes of all the spectators turned on Aristides, as if this virtue, in an especial manner, belonged to him.

He was a most determined champion for justice, not only against feelings of friendship and favor, but wrath and malice. Thus it is reported of him that when prosecuting the law against one who was his enemy, on the judges after accusation refusing to hear the criminal, and proceeding immediately to pass sentence upon him, he rose in haste from his seat and joined in petition with him for a hearing, and that he might enjoy the privilege of the law. Another time, when judging between two private persons, on the one declaring his adversary had very much injured Aristides; "Tell me rather, good friend," he said, "what wrong he has done you; for it is your cause, not my own, which I now sit judge of." Being chosen to the charge of the public revenue, he made it appear, that not only those of his time, but the preceding officers, had alienated much treasure, and especially Themistocles:—

"Well known he was an able man to be,
But with his fingers apt to be too free."

Therefore, Themistocles associating several persons against Aristides, and impeaching him when he gave in his accounts, caused him to be condemned of robbing the public; so Idomeneus states; but the best and chiefest men of the city much resenting it, he was not only exempted from the fine imposed upon him, but likewise again called to the same employment. Pretending now to repent him of his former practice, and carrying himself with more remissness, he became acceptable to such as pillaged the treasury, by not detecting or calling them to an exact account. So that those who had their fill of the public money began highly to applaud Aristides, and sued to the people, making interest to have him once more chosen treasurer. But when they were upon the point of election, he reproved the Athenians. "When I discharged my office well and faithfully," said he, "I was insulted and abused; but now that I have allowed the public thieves in a variety of malpractices, I am considered an admirable patriot. I am more ashamed, therefore, of this present honor than of the former sentence; and I commiserate your condition, with whom it is more praiseworthy to oblige ill men than to conserve the revenue of the public." Saying thus, and proceeding to expose the thefts that had been committed, he stopped the mouths of those who cried him up and vouched for him, but gained real and true commendation from the best men.

When Datis, being sent by Darius under pretence of punishing the Athenians for their burning of Sardis, but in reality to reduce the Greeks under his dominion, landed at Marathon and laid waste the country, among the ten commanders appointed by the Athenians for the war, Miltiades was of the greatest name; but the second place, both for reputation and power, was possessed by Aristides: and when his opinion to join battle was added to that of Miltiades, it did much to incline the balance. Every leader by his day having the command in chief, when it came to Aristides's turn, he delivered it into the hands of Miltiades, showing his fellow officers, that it is not dishonorable to obey and follow wise and able men, but, on the contrary, noble and prudent. So appeasing their rivalry, and bringing them to acquiesce in one and the best advice, he confirmed Miltiades in the strength of an undivided and unmolested authority. For now every one, yielding his day of command, looked for orders only to him. During the fight the main body of the Athenians being the hardest put to it, the barbarians, for a long time, making opposition there against the tribes Leontis and Antiochis, Themistocles and Aristides being ranged together, fought valiantly; the one being of the tribe Leontis, the other of the Antiochis. But after they had beaten the barbarians back to their ships, and perceived that they sailed not for the isles, but were driven in by the force of sea and wind towards the country of Attica; fearing lest they should take the city, unprovided of defence, they hurried away thither with nine tribes, and reached it the same day. Aristides, being left with his tribe at Marathon to guard the plunder and prisoners, did not disappoint the opinion they had of him. Amidst the profusion of gold and silver, all sorts of apparel, and other property, more than can be mentioned, that were in the tents and the vessels which they had taken, he neither felt the desire to meddle with any thing himself, nor suffered others to do it; unless it might be some who took away any thing unknown to him; as Callias, the torch-bearer,[3] did. One of the barbarians, it seems, prostrated himself before this man, supposing him to be a king by his hair and fillet; and, when he had so done, taking him by the hand, showed him a great quantity of gold hid in a ditch. But Callias, most cruel and impious of men, took away the treasure, but slew the man, lest he should tell of him. Hence, they say, the comic poets gave his family the name of *Laccopluti,* or enriched by the ditch, alluding to the place where Callias found the gold. Aristides, immediately after this, was archon; although Demetrius, the Phalerian, says he held the office a little before he died, after the battle of Platæa. But in the records of the successors of Xanthippides, in whose year Mardonius was overthrown at Platæa, amongst very many there mentioned, there is not so much as one of the same name as Aristides: while immediately after Phænippus, during whose term of office they obtained the victory of Marathon, Aristides is registered.

Of all his virtues, the common people were most affected with his justice, because of its continual and common use; and thus, although of mean fortune and ordinary birth, he possessed himself of the most kingly and divine appellation of Just; which kings, however, and tyrants have never sought after; but have taken delight to be surnamed besiegers of cities, thunderers, conquerors, or eagles again,

[3] In the festivals of Eleusinian Ceres; an office hereditary in the family of Callias.

and hawks;[4] affecting, it seems, the reputation which proceeds from power and violence, rather than that of virtue. Although the divinity, to whom they desire to compare and assimilate themselves, excels, it is supposed, in three things, immortality, power, and virtue; of which three, the noblest and divinest is virtue. For the elements and vacuum have an everlasting existence; earthquakes, thunders, storms, and torrents have great power; but in justice and equity nothing participates except by means of reason and the knowledge of that which is divine. And thus, taking the three varieties of feeling commonly entertained towards the deity, the sense of his happiness, fear, and honor of him, people would seem to think him blest and happy for his exemption from death and corruption, to fear and dread him for his power and dominion, but to love, honor, and adore him for his justice. Yet though thus disposed, they covet that immortality which our nature is not capable of, and that power the greatest part of which is at the disposal of fortune; but give virtue, the only divine good really in our reach, the last place, most unwisely; since justice makes the life of such as are in prosperity, power, and authority the life of a god, and injustice turns it to that of a beast.

Aristides, therefore, had at first the fortune to be beloved for this surname, but at length envied. Especially when Themistocles spread a rumor amongst the people, that, by determining and judging all matters privately, he had destroyed the courts of judicature, and was secretly making way for a monarchy in his own person, without the assistance of guards. Moreover, the spirit of the people, now grown high, and confident with their late victory, naturally entertained feelings of dislike to all of more than common fame and reputation. Coming together, therefore, from all parts into the city, they banished Aristides by the ostracism, giving their jealousy of his reputation the name of fear of tyranny. For ostracism was not the punishment of any criminal act, but was speciously said to be the mere depression and humiliation of excessive greatness and power; and was in fact a gentle relief and mitigation of envious feeling, which was thus allowed to vent itself in inflicting no intolerable injury,

[4] Demetrius Poliorcetes, or the besieger, Ptolemy Ceraunus, or Thunder, and Demetrius Nicator, the conqueror, are the probable examples alluded to; with Pyrrhus who had the name of Aetus, the eagle, and Antiochus surnamed Hierax, the hawk.

only a ten years' banishment. But after it came to be exercised upon base and villainous fellows, they desisted from it; Hyperbolus, being the last whom they banished by the ostracism.

The cause of Hyperbolus's banishment is said to have been this. Alcibiades and Nicias, men that bore the greatest sway in the city, were of different factions. As the people, therefore, were about to vote the ostracism, and obviously to decree it against one of them, consulting together and uniting their parties, they contrived the banishment of Hyperbolus. Upon which the people, being offended, as if some contempt or affront was put upon the thing, left off and quite abolished it. It was performed, to be short, in this manner. Every one taking an *ostracon,* a sherd, that is, or piece of earthenware, wrote upon it the citizen's name he would have banished, and carried it to a certain part of the market-place surrounded with wooden rails. First, the magistrates numbered all the sherds in gross (for if there were less than six thousand, the ostracism was imperfect); then, laying every name by itself, they pronounced him whose name was written by the larger number, banished for ten years, with the enjoyment of his estate. As, therefore, they were writing the names on the sherds, it is reported that an illiterate clownish fellow, giving Aristides his sherd, supposing him a common citizen, begged him to write *Aristides* upon it; and he being surprised and asking if Aristides had ever done him any injury, "None at all," said he, "neither know I the man; but I am tired of hearing him everywhere called the Just." Aristides, hearing this, is said to have made no reply, but returned the sherd with his own name inscribed. At his departure from the city, lifting up his hands to heaven, he made a prayer, (the reverse, it would seem, of that of Achilles), that the Athenians might never have any occasion which should constrain them to remember Aristides.

Nevertheless, three years after, when Xerxes marched through Thessaly and Bœotia into the country of Attica, repealing the law, they decreed the return of the banished; chiefly fearing Aristides, lest, joining himself to the enemy, he should corrupt and bring over many of his fellow-citizens to the party of the barbarians; much mistaking the man, who, already before the decree, was exerting himself to excite and encourage the Greeks to the defence of their liberty. And afterwards, when Themistocles was general with absolute power, he assisted him in all ways both in action and counsel; rendering, in consideration of the common security, the greatest enemy he had the most glorious of men. For when Eurybiades was deliberating to desert the isle of Salamis, and the galleys of the barbarians putting out by night to sea surrounded and beset the narrow passage and islands, and nobody was aware how they were environed, Aristides, with great hazard, sailed from Ægina through the enemy's fleet; and coming by night to Themistocles's tent, and calling him out by himself; "If we have any discretion," said he, "Themistocles, laying aside at this time our vain and childish contention, let us enter upon a safe and honorable dispute, vying with each other for the preservation of Greece; you in the ruling and commanding, I in the subservient and advising part; even, indeed, as I now understand you to be alone adhering to the best advice, in counselling without any delay to engage in the straits. And in this, though our own party oppose, the enemy seems to assist you. For the sea behind, and all around us, is covered with their fleet; so that we are under a necessity of approving ourselves men of courage, and fighting, whether we will or no; for there is no room left us for flight." To which Themistocles answered, "I would not willingly, Aristides, be overcome by you on this occasion; and shall endeavor, in emulation of this good beginning, to outdo it in my actions." Also relating to him the stratagem he had framed against the barbarians, he entreated him to persuade Eurybiades and show him, how it was impossible they should save themselves without an engagement; as he was the more likely to be believed. Whence, in the council of war, Cleocritus, the Corinthian, telling Themistocles that Aristides did not like his advice, as he was present and said nothing, Aristides answered, That he should not have held his peace, if Themistocles had not been giving the best advice; and that he was now silent not out of any good-will to the person, but in approbation of his counsel.

Thus the Greek captains were employed. But Aristides perceiving Psyttalea, a small island that lies within the straits over against Salamis, to be filled by a body of the enemy, put aboard his small boats the most forward and courageous of his countrymen, and went ashore upon it; and, joining battle with the barbarians, slew them all, except such more remarkable persons as were taken alive. Amongst these were three children of Sandauce, the king's sister, whom he immediately sent away to Themistocles, and it is stated that in accordance with a certain oracle, they were, by the command of Euphrantides, the seer, sacrificed to Bacchus, called Omestes, or the devourer. But Aristides, placing armed men all around the island, lay in wait for such as were cast upon it, to the intent that none of his friends should perish, nor any of his enemies escape. For the closest engagement of the ships, and the main fury of the whole battle, seems to have been about this place; for which reason a trophy was erected in Psyttalea.

After the fight, Themistocles, to sound Aristides, told him they had performed a good piece of service, but there was a better yet to be done, the keeping Asia in Europe, by sailing forthwith to the Hellespont, and cutting in sunder the bridge. But Aristides, with an exclamation, bid him think no more of it, but deliberate and find out means for removing the Mede, as quickly as possible, out of Greece; lest being enclosed, through want of means to escape, necessity should compel him to force his way with so great an army. So Themistocles once more despatched Arnaces, the eunuch, his prisoner, giving him in command privately to advertise the king that he had diverted the Greeks from their intention of setting sail for the bridges, out of the desire he felt to preserve him.

Xerxes, being much terrified with this, immediately hasted to the Hellespont. But Mardonius was left with the most serviceable part of the army, about three hundred thousand men, and was a formidable enemy, confident in his infantry, and writing messages of defiance to the Greeks: "You have overcome by sea men accustomed to fight on land, and unskilled at the oar; but there lies now the open country of Thessaly; and the plains of Bœotia offer a broad and worthy field for brave men, either horse or foot, to contend in." But he sent privately to the Athenians, both by letter and word of mouth from the king, promising to rebuild their city, to give them a vast sum of money, and constitute them lords of all Greece on condition they were not engaged in the war. The Lacedæmonians, receiving news of this, and fearing, despatched an embassy to the Athenians, entreating that they would send their wives and children to Sparta, and receive support from them for their superannuated. For, being despoiled both of their city and country, the people were suffering extreme distress. Having given audience to the ambassadors, they returned an answer, upon the motion of Aristides, worthy of the highest admiration; declaring, that they forgave their enemies if they thought all things purchasable by wealth, than which they knew nothing of greater value; but that they felt offended at the Lacedæmonians, for looking only to their present poverty and exigence, without any remembrance of their valor and magnanimity, offering them their victuals, to fight in the cause of Greece. Aristides, making this proposal and bringing back the ambassadors into the assembly, charged them to tell the Lacedæmonians, that all the treasure on the earth or under it, was of less value with the people of Athens, than the liberty of Greece. And, showing the sun to those who came from Mardonius, "as long as that retains the same course, so long," said he, "shall the citizens of Athens wage war with the Persians for the country which has been wasted, and the temples that have been profaned and burnt by them." Moreover, he proposed a decree, that the priests should anathematize him who sent any herald to the Medes, or deserted the alliance of Greece.

When Mardonius made a second incursion into the country of Attica, the people passed over again into the isle of Salamis. Aristides, being sent to Lacedæmon, reproved them for their delay and neglect in abandoning Athens once more to the barbarians; and demanded their assistance for that part of Greece which was not yet lost. The Ephori, hearing this, made show of sporting all day, and of carelessly keeping holy day, (for they were then celebrating the Hyacinthian festival), but in the night, selecting five thousand Spartans, each of whom was attended by seven Helots, they sent them forth unknown to those from Athens. And when Aristides again reprehended them, they told him in derision that he either doted or dreamed, for the army was already at Oresteum, in their march towards the *strangers;* as they called the Persians. Aristides answered, that they jested unseasonably, deluding their friends, instead of their enemies. Thus says Idomeneus. But in the decree of

Aristides, not himself, but Cimon, Xanthippus, and Myronides are appointed ambassadors.

Being chosen general for the war, he repaired to Platæa, with eight thousand Athenians, where Pausanias, generalissimo of all Greece, joined him with the Spartans; and the forces of the other Greeks came in to them. The whole encampment of the barbarians extended all along the bank of the river Asopus, their numbers being so great, there was no enclosing them all, but their baggage and most valuable things were surrounded with a square bulwark, each side of which was the length of ten furlongs.

Tisamenus, the Elean, had prophesied to Pausanias and all the Greeks, and foretold them victory if they made no attempt upon the enemy, but stood on their defence. But Aristides sending to Delphi, the god answered, that the Athenians should overcome their enemies, in case they made supplication to Jupiter and Juno of Cithæron, Pan, and the nymphs Sphragitides, and sacrificed to the heroes Androcrates, Leucon, Pisander, Damocrates, Hypsion, Actæon, and Polyidus; and if they fought within their own territories in the plain of Ceres Eleusinia and Proserpine. Aristides was perplexed upon the tidings of this oracle: since the heroes to whom it commanded him to sacrifice had been chieftains of the Platæans, and the cave of the nymphs Sphragitides was on the top of Mount Cithæron, on the side facing the setting sun of summer time; in which place, as the story goes, there was formerly an oracle, and many that lived in the district were inspired with it, whom they called *Nympholepti*, possessed with the nymphs. But the plain of Ceres Eleusinia, and the offer of victory to the Athenians, if they fought in their own territories, recalled them again, and transferred the war into the country of Attica. In this juncture, Arimnestus, who commanded the Platæans, dreamed that Jupiter, the Saviour, asked him what the Greeks had resolved upon; and that he answered, "To-morrow, my Lord, we march our army to Eleusis, and there give the barbarians battle according to the directions of the oracle of Apollo." And that the god replied, they were utterly mistaken, for that the places spoken of by the oracle were within the bounds of Platæa, and if they sought there they should find them. This manifest vision having appeared to Arimnestus, when he awoke he sent for the most aged and experienced of his countrymen, with whom communicating and examining the matter, he found that near Hysiæ, at the foot of Mount Cithæron, there was a very ancient temple called the temple of Ceres Eleusinia and Proserpine. He therefore forthwith took Aristides to the place, which was very convenient for drawing up an army of foot, because the slopes at the bottom of the mountain Cithæron rendered the plain, where it comes up to the temple, unfit for the movements of cavalry. Also, in the same place, there was the fane of Androcrates, environed with a thick shady grove. And that the oracle might be accomplished in all particulars for the hope of victory, Arimnestus proposed, and the Platæans decreed, that the frontiers of their country towards Attica should be removed, and the land given to the Athenians, that they might fight in defence of Greece in their own proper territory. This zeal and liberality of the Platæans became so famous, that Alexander, many years after, when he had obtained the dominion of all Asia, upon erecting the walls of Platæa, caused proclamation to be made by the herald at the Olympic games, that the king did the Platæans this favor in consideration of their nobleness and magnanimity, because, in the war with the Medes, they freely gave up their land and zealously fought with the Greeks.

The Tegeatans, contesting the post of honor with the Athenians, demanded, that, according to custom, the Lacedæmonians being ranged on the right wing of the battle, they might have the left, alleging several matters in commendation of their ancestors. The Athenians being indignant at the claim, Aristides came forward; "To contend with the Tegeatans," said he, "for noble descent and valor, the present time permits not: but this we say to you, O you Spartans, and you the rest of the Greeks, that place neither takes away nor contributes courage: we shall endeavor by crediting and maintaining the post you assign us, to reflect no dishonor on our former performances. For we are come, not to differ with our friends, but to fight our enemies; not to extol our ancestors, but ourselves to behave as valiant men. This battle will manifest how much each city, captain, and private soldier is worth to Greece." The council of war, upon this address, decided for the Athenians, and gave them the other wing of the battle.

All Greece being in suspense, and especially the affairs of the Athenians unsettled, certain persons of great families and possessions having been impoverished by the war, and seeing all their authority and reputation in the city vanished with their wealth, and others in possession of their honors and places, convened privately at a house in Platæa, and conspired for the dissolution of the democratic government; and, if the plot should not succeed, to ruin the cause and betray all to the barbarians. These matters being in agitation in the camp, and many persons already corrupted, Aristides, perceiving the design, and dreading the present juncture of time, determined neither to let the business pass unanimadverted upon, nor yet altogether to expose it; not knowing how many the accusation might reach, and willing to set bounds to his justice with a view to the public convenience. Therefore, of many that were concerned, he apprehended eight only, two of whom, who were first proceeded against and most guilty, Æschines of Lampra, and Agesias of Acharnæ, made their escape out of the camp. The rest he dismissed; giving opportunity to such as thought themselves concealed, to take courage and repent; intimating that they had in the war a great tribunal, where they might clear their guilt by manifesting their sincere and good intentions towards their country.

After this, Mardonius made trial of the Grecian courage, by sending his whole number of horse, in which he thought himself much the stronger, against them, while they were all pitched at the foot of Mount Cithæron, in strong and rocky places, except the Megarians. They, being three thousand in number, were encamped on the plain, where they were damaged by the horse charging and making inroads upon them on all hands. They sent, therefore, in haste to Pausanias, demanding relief, as not being able alone to sustain the great numbers of the barbarians. Pausanias, hearing this, and perceiving the tents of the Megarians already hid by the multitude of darts and arrows, and themselves driven together into a narrow space, was at a loss himself how to aid them with his battalion of heavy-armed Lacedæmonians. He proposed it, therefore, as a point of emulation in valor and love of distinction, to the commanders and captains who were around him, if any would voluntarily take upon them the defence and succor of the Megarians. The rest being backward, Aristides undertook the enterprise for the Athenians, and sent Olympiodorus, the most valiant of his inferior officers, with three hundred chosen men and some archers under his command. These being soon in readiness, and running upon the enemy, as soon as Masistius, who commanded the barbarians' horse, a man of wonderful courage and of extraordinary bulk and comeliness of person, perceived it, turning his steed he made towards them. And they sustaining the shock and joining battle with him, there was a sharp conflict, as though by this encounter they were to try the success of the whole war. But after Masistius's horse received a wound, and flung him, and he falling could hardly raise himself through the weight of his armor, the Athenians, pressing upon him with blows, could not easily get at his person, armed as he was, his breast, his head, and his limbs all over, with gold and brass and iron; but one of them at last, running him in at the visor of his helmet, slew him; and the rest of the Persians, leaving the body, fled. The greatness of the Greek success was known, not by the multitude of the slain, (for an inconsiderable number were killed), but by the sorrow the barbarians expressed. For they shaved themselves, their horses, and mules for the death of Masistius, and filled the plain with howling and lamentation; having lost a person, who, next to Mardonius himself, was by many degrees the chief among them, both for valor and authority.

After this skirmish of the horse, they kept from fighting a long time; for the soothsayers, by the sacrifices, foretold the victory both to Greeks and Persians, if they stood upon the defensive part only, but if they became aggressors, the contrary. At length Mardonius, when he had but a few days' provision, and the Greek forces increased continually by some or other that came in to them, impatient of delay, determined to lie still no longer, but, passing Asopus by daybreak, to fall unexpectedly upon the Greeks; and signified the same over night to the captains of his host. But about midnight, a certain horseman stole into the Greek camp, and coming to the watch, desired them to call Aristides, the Athenian, to him. He coming speedily; "I am," said the stranger, "Alexander, king of the Macedonians, and am arrived here through the greatest danger in the world for the good-will I bear you, lest a sudden onset should dismay you, so as to behave in the fight worse than usual. For to-morrow Mardonius will give you battle, urged, not by any hope of success or courage, but by want of victuals since, indeed, the prophets prohibit him the battle, the sacrifices and oracles being unfavorable; and the army is in despondency and consternation; but necessity forces him to try his fortune, or sit still and endure the last extremity of want." Alexander, thus saying, entreated Aristides to take notice and remember him, but not to tell any other. But he told him, it was not convenient to conceal the matter from Pausanias (because he was general); as for any other, he would keep it secret from them till the battle was fought; but if the Greeks obtained the victory, that then no one should be ignorant of Alexander's good-will and kindness towards them. After this, the king of the Macedonians rode back again, and Aristides went to Pausanias's tent and told him; and they sent for the rest of the captains and gave orders that the army should be in battle array.

Here, according to Herodotus, Pausanias spoke to Aristides, desiring him to transfer the Athenians to the right wing of the army opposite to the Persians, (as they would do better service against them, having been experienced in their way of combat, and emboldened with former victories), and to give him the left, where the Medizing Greeks were to make their assault. The rest of the Athenian captains regarded this as an arrogant and interfering act on the part of Pausanias; because, while permitting the rest of the army to keep their stations, he removed them only from place to place, like so many Helots, opposing them to the greatest strength of the enemy. But Aristides said, they were altogether in the wrong. If so short a time ago they contested the left wing with the Tegeatans, and gloried in being preferred before them, now, when the Lacedæmonians give them place in the right, and yield them in a manner the leading of the army, how is it they are discontented with the honor that is done them, and do not look upon it as an advantage to have to fight, not against their countrymen and kindred, but barbarians, and such as were by nature their enemies? After this, the Athenians very readily changed places with the Lacedæmonians, and there went words amongst them as they were encouraging each other, that the enemy approached with no better arms or stouter hearts than those who fought the battle of Marathon; but had the same bows and arrows, and the same embroidered coats and gold, and the same delicate bodies and effeminate minds within; "while we have the same weapons and bodies, and our courage augmented by our victories; and fight not like others in defence of our country only, but for the trophies of Salamis and Marathon; that they may not be looked upon as due to Miltiades or fortune, but to the people of Athens." Thus, therefore, were they making haste to change the order of their battle. But the Thebans, understanding it by some deserters, forthwith acquainted Mardonius; and he, either for fear of the Athenians, or a desire to engage the Lacedæmonians, marched over his Persians to the other wing, and commanded the Greeks of his party to be posted opposite to the Athenians. But this change was observed on the other side, and Pausanias, wheeling about again, ranged himself on the right, and Mardonius, also at first, took the left wing over against the Lacedæmonians. So the day passed without action.

After this, the Greeks determined in council to remove their camp some distance, to possess themselves of a place convenient for watering; because the springs near them were polluted and destroyed by the barbarian cavalry. But night being come, and the captains setting out towards the place designed for their encamping, the soldiers were not very ready to follow, and keep in a body, but, as soon as they had quitted their first entrenchments, made towards the city of Platæa; and there was much tumult and disorder as they dispersed to various quarters and proceeded to pitch their tents. The Lacedæmonians, against their will, had the fortune to be left by the rest. For Amompharetus, a brave and daring man, who had long been burning with desire of the fight, and resented their many lingerings and delays, calling the removal of the camp a mere running away and flight, protested he would not desert his post, but would there remain with his company, and sustain the charge of Mardonius. And when Pausanias came to him and told him he did these things by the common vote and determination of the Greeks, Amompharetus taking up a great stone and flinging it at Pausanias's feet, and "by this token," said he, "do I give my suffrage for the battle, nor have I any concern with the cowardly consultations and decrees of other men." Pausanias, not knowing what to do in the present juncture, sent to the Athenians, who were drawing off, to stay to accompany him; and so he himself set off with the rest of the army for Platæa, hoping thus to make Amompharetus move.

Meantime, day came upon them; and Mardonius (for he was not ignorant of their deserting their camp) having his army in array, fell upon the Lacedæmonians with great shouting and noise of barbarous people, as if they were not about to join battle, but crush the Greeks in their flight. Which within a very little came to pass. For Pausanias, perceiving what was done, made a halt, and commanded every one to put themselves in order for the battle; but either through his anger with Amompharetus, or the disturbance he was in by reason of the sudden approach of the enemy, he forgot to give the signal to the Greeks in general. Whence it was, that they did not come in immediately, or in a body, to their assistance, but by small companies and straggling, when the fight was already begun. Pausanias, offering sacrifice, could not procure favorable omens, and so commanded the Lacedæmonians, setting down their shields at their feet to abide quietly and attend his directions, making no resistance to any of their enemies. And, he sacrificing again a second time, the horse charged, and some of the Lacedæmonians were wounded. At this time, also, Callicrates, who, we are told, was the most comely man in the army, being shot with an arrow and upon the point of expiring, said, that he lamented not his death (for he came from home to lay down his life in the defence of Greece) but that he died without action. The case was indeed hard, and the forbearance of the men wonderful; for they let the enemy charge without repelling them; and, expecting their proper opportunity from the gods and their general, suffered themselves to be wounded and slain in their ranks. And some say, that while Pausanias was at sacrifice and prayers, some space out of the battle-array, certain Lydians, falling suddenly upon him, plundered and scattered the sacrifice; and that Pausanias and his company, having no arms, beat them with staves and whips; and that in imitation of this attack, the whipping the boys about the altar, and after it the Lydian procession, are to this day practised in Sparta.

Pausanias, therefore, being troubled at these things, while the priest went on offering one sacrifice after another, turns himself towards the temple with tears in his eyes, and, lifting up his hands to heaven, besought Juno of Cithæron, and the other tutelar gods of the Platæans, if it were not in the fates for the Greeks to obtain the victory, that they might not perish, without performing some remarkable thing, and by their actions demonstrating to their enemies, that they waged war with men of courage, and soldiers. While Pausanias was thus in the act of supplication, the sacrifices appeared propitious, and the soothsayers foretold victory. The word being given, the Lacedæmonian battalion of foot seemed, on the sudden, like some one fierce animal, setting up his bristles, and betaking himself to the combat; and the barbarians perceived that they encountered with men who would fight it to the death. Therefore, holding their wicker-shields before them, they shot their arrows amongst the Lacedæmonians. But they, keeping together in the order of a phalanx, and falling upon the enemies, forced their shields out of their hands, and, striking with their pikes at the breasts and faces of the Persians, overthrew many of them; who, however, fell not either unrevenged or without courage. For taking hold of the spears with their bare hands, they broke many of them, and betook themselves not without effect to the sword; and making use of their falchions and scimitars, and wresting the Lacedæmonians' shields from them, and grappling with them, it was a long time that they made resistance.

Meanwhile, for some time, the Athenians stood still, waiting for the Lacedæmonians to come up. But when they heard much noise as of men engaged in fight, and a messenger, they say, came from Pausanias, to advertise them of what was going on, they soon hasted to their assistance. And as they passed through the plain to the place where the noise was, the Greeks, who took part with the enemy, came upon them. Aristides, as soon as he saw them, going a considerable space before the rest, cried out to them, conjuring them by the guardian gods of Greece to forbear the fight, and be no impediment or stop to those, who were going to succor the defenders of Greece. But when he perceived they gave no attention to him, and had prepared themselves for the battle, then turning from the present relief of the Lacedæmonians, he engaged them, being five thousand in number. But the greatest part soon gave way and retreated, as the barbarians also were put to flight. The sharpest conflict is said to have been against the Thebans, the chiefest and most powerful persons among them at that time siding zealously with the Medes, and leading the multitude not according to their own inclinations, but as being subjects of an oligarchy.

The battle being thus divided, the Lacedæmonians first beat off the Persians; and a Spartan, named Arimnestus, slew Mardonius by a blow on the head with a stone, as the oracle in the temple of Amphiaraus had foretold to him. For Mardonius sent a Lydian thither, and another person, a Carian, to the cave of Trophonius. This latter, the priest of the oracle answered in his own language. But the Lydian sleeping in the temple of Amphiaraus, it seemed to him that a minister of the divinity stood before him and commanded him to be gone; and on his refusing to do it, flung a great stone at his head, so that he thought himself slain with the blow. Such is the story.—They drove the fliers within their walls of wood; and, a little time after, the Athenians put the Thebans to flight, killing three hundred of the chiefest and of greatest note among them in the actual fight itself. For when they began to fly, news came that the army of the barbarians was besieged within their palisade: and so giving the Greeks opportunity to save themselves, they marched to assist at the fortifications; and coming in to the Lacedæmonians, who were altogether unhandy and unexperienced in storming, they took the camp with great slaughter of the enemy. For of three hundred thousand, forty thousand only are said to have escaped with Artabazus; while on the Greeks' side there perished in all thirteen hundred and sixty: of which fifty-two were Athenians, all of the tribe Æantis, that fought, says Clidemus, with the greatest courage of any; and for this reason the men of this tribe used to offer sacrifice for the victory, as enjoined by the oracle, to the nymphs Sphragitides at the expense of the public: ninety-one were Lacedæmonians, and sixteen Tegeatans. It is strange, therefore, upon what grounds Herodotus can say, that they only, and none other, encountered the enemy; for the number of the slain and their monuments testify that the victory was obtained by all in general; and if the rest had been standing still, while the inhabitants of three cities only had been engaged in the fight, they would not have set on the altar the inscription:—

> "The Greeks, when by their courage and their might,
> They had repelled the Persian in the fight,
> The common altar of freed Greece to be,
> Reared this to Jupiter who guards the free."

They fought this battle on the fourth day of the month Boëdromion, according to the Athenians, but according to the Bœotians, on the twenty-seventh of Panemus;—on which day there is still a convention of the Greeks at Platæa, and the Platæans still offer sacrifice for the victory to Jupiter of freedom. As for the difference of days, it is not to be wondered at, since even at the present time, when there is a far more accurate knowledge of astronomy, some begin the month at one time, and some at another.

After this, the Athenians not yielding the honor of the day to the Lacedæmonians, nor consenting they should erect a trophy, things were not far from being ruined by dissension amongst the armed Greeks; had not Aristides, by much soothing and counselling the commanders, especially Leocrates and Myronides, pacified and persuaded them to leave the thing to the decision of the Greeks. And on their proceeding to discuss the matter, Theogiton, the Megarian, declared the honor of the victory was to be given some other city, if they would prevent a civil war; after him Cleocritus of Corinth rising up, made people think he would ask the palm for the Corinthians, (for next to Sparta and Athens, Corinth was in greatest estimation); but he delivered his opinion, to the general admiration, in favor of the Platæans; and counselled to take away all contention by giving them the reward and glory of the victory, whose being honored could be distasteful to neither party. This being said, first Aristides gave consent in the name of the Athenians, and Pausanias, then, for the Lacedæmonians. So, being reconciled, they set apart eighty talents for the Platæans, with which they built the temple and dedicated the image to Minerva, and adorned the temple with pictures, which even to this day retain their lustre. But the Lacedæmonians and Athenians, each erected a trophy apart by themselves. On their consulting the oracle about offering sacrifice, Apollo answered, that they should dedicate an altar to Jupiter of freedom, but should not sacrifice till they had extinguished the fires throughout the country, as having been defiled by the barbarians, and had kindled unpolluted fire at the common altar at Delphi. The magistrates of Greece, therefore, went forthwith and compelled such as had fire to put it out; and Euchidas, a Platæan, promising to fetch fire, with all possible speed, from the altar of the god, went to Delphi, and having sprinkled and purified his body, crowned himself with laurel; and taking the fire from the altar ran back to Platæa, and got back there before sunset, performing in one day a journey of a thousand furlongs; and saluting his fellow-citizens and delivering them the fire, he immediately fell down, and in a short time after expired. But the Platæans, taking him up, interred him in the temple of Diana Euclia, setting this inscription over him: "Euchidas ran to Delphi and back again in one day." Most people believe that Euclia is Diana, and call her by that name. But some say she was the daughter of Hercules, by Myrto, the daughter of Menœtius, and sister of Patroclus, and, dying a virgin, was worshipped by the Bœotians and Locrians. Her altar and image are set up in all their market-places, and those of both sexes that are about marrying, sacrificed to her before the nuptials.

A general assembly of all the Greeks being called, Aristides proposed a decree, that the deputies and religious representatives of the Greek states should assemble annually at Platæa, and every fifth year celebrate the Eleutheria, or games of freedom. And that there should be a levy upon all Greece, for the war against the barbarians, of ten thousand spearmen, one thousand horse, and a hundred sail of ships; but the Platæans to be exempt, and sacred to the service of the gods, offering sacrifice for the welfare of Greece. These things being ratified, the Platæans undertook the performance of annual sacrifice to such as were slain and buried in that place; which they still perform in the following manner. On the sixteenth day of Mæmacterion (which with the Bœotians is Alalcomenus) they make their procession, which, beginning by break of day, is led by a trumpeter sounding for onset; then follow certain chariots loaded with myrrh and garlands; and then a black bull; then come the young men of free birth carrying libations of wine and milk in large two-handed vessels, and jars of oil and precious ointments, none of servile condition being permitted to have any hand in this ministration, because the men died in defence of freedom; after all comes the chief magistrate of Platæa, (for whom it is unlawful at other times either to touch iron, or wear any other colored garment but white), at that time apparelled in a purple robe; and, taking a water-pot out of the city record-office, he proceeds, bearing a sword in his hand, through the middle of the town to the sepulchres. Then drawing water out of a spring, he washes and anoints the monuments, and sacrificing the bull upon a pile of wood, and making supplication to Jupiter and Mercury of the earth, invites those valiant men who perished in the defence of Greece, to the banquet and the libations of blood. After this, mixing a bowl of wine, and pouring out for himself, he says, "I drink to those who lost their lives for the liberty of Greece." These solemnities the Platæans observe to this day.

Aristides perceived that the Athenians, after their return into the city, were eager for a democracy; and deeming the people to deserve consideration on account of their valiant behavior, as also that it was a matter of difficulty, they being well armed, powerful, and full of spirit with their victories, to oppose them by force, he brought forward a decree, that every one might share in the government, and the archons be chosen out of the whole body of the Athenians. And on Themistocles telling the people in assembly that he had some advice for them, which could not be given in public, but was most important for the advantage and security of the city, they appointed Aristides alone to hear and consider it with him. And on his acquainting Aristides that his intent was to set fire to the arsenal of the Greeks, for by that means should the Athenians become supreme masters of all Greece, Aristides, returning to the assembly, told them, that nothing was more advantageous than what Themistocles designed, and nothing more unjust. The Athenians, hearing this, gave Themistocles order to desist; such was the love of justice felt by the people, and such the credit and confidence they reposed in Aristides.

Being sent in joint commission with Cimon to the war, he took notice that Pausanias and the other Spartan captains made themselves offensive by imperiousness and harshness to the confederates; and by being himself gentle and considerate with them and by the courtesy and disinterested temper which Cimon after his example, manifested in the expeditions, he stole away the chief command from the Lacedæmonians, neither by weapons, ships, or horses, but by equity and wise policy. For the Athenians being endeared to the Greeks by the justice of Aristides and by Cimon's moderation, the tyranny and selfishness of Pausanias rendered them yet more desirable. He on all occasions treated the commanders of the confederates haughtily and roughly; and the common soldiers he punished with stripes, or standing under the iron anchor for a whole day together; neither was it permitted for any to provide straw for themselves to lie on, or forage for their horses, or to come near the springs to water before the Spartans were furnished, but servants with whips drove away such as approached. And when Aristides once was about to complain and expostulate with Pausanias, he told him, with an angry look, that he was not at leisure, and gave no attention to him. The consequence was that the sea captains and generals of the Greeks, in particular, the Chians, Samians, and Lesbians, came to Aristides and requested him to be their general, and to receive the confederates into his command, who had long desired to relinquish the Spartans and come over to the Athenians. But he answered, that he saw both equity and necessity in what they said, but their fidelity required the test of some action, the commission of which would make it impossible for the multitude to change their minds again. Upon which Uliades, the Samian, and Antagoras of Chios, conspiring together, ran in near Byzantium on Pausanias's galley, getting her between them as she was sailing before the rest. But when Pausanias, beholding them, rose up and furiously threatened soon to make them know that they had been endangering not his galley, but their own countries, they bid him go his way, and thank Fortune that fought for him at Platæa; for hitherto, in reverence to that, the Greeks had forborne from inflicting on him the punishment he deserved. In fine, they all went off and joined the Athenians. And here the magnanimity of the Lacedæmonians was wonderful. For when they perceived that their generals were becoming corrupted by the greatness of their authority, they voluntarily laid down the chief command, and left off sending any more of them to the wars, choosing rather to have citizens of moderation and consistent in the observance of their customs, than to possess the dominion of all Greece.

Even during the command of the Lacedæmonians, the Greeks paid a certain contribution towards the maintenance of the war; and being desirous to be rated city by city in their due proportion, they desired Aristides of the Athenians, and gave him command, surveying the country and revenue, to assess every one according to their ability and what they were worth. But he, being so largely empowered, Greece as it were submitting all her affairs to his sole management, went out poor, and returned poorer; laying the tax not only without corruption and injustice, but to the satisfaction and convenience of all. For as the ancients celebrated the age of Saturn, so did the confederates of Athens Aristides's taxation, terming it the happy time of Greece; and that more especially, as the sum was in a short time doubled, and afterwards trebled. For the assessment which Aristides made, was four hundred and sixty talents. But to this Pericles added very near one third part more; for Thucydides says, that in the beginning of the Peloponnesian war, the Athenians had coming in from their confederates six hundred talents. But after Pericles's death, the demagogues, increasing by little and little, raised it to the sum of thirteen hundred talents; not so much through the war's being so expensive and chargeable either by its length or ill success, as by their alluring the people to spend upon largesses and play-houses allowances, and in erecting statues and temples. Aristides, therefore, having acquired a wonderful and great reputation by this levy of the tribute, Themistocles is said to have derided him, as if this had been not the commendation of a man, but a money-bag; a retaliation, though not in the same kind, for some free words which Aristides had used. For he, when Themistocles once was saying that he thought the highest virtue of a general was to understand and foreknow the measures the enemy would take, replied, "This, indeed, Themistocles, is simply necessary, but the excellent thing in a general is to keep his hands from taking money."

Aristides, moreover, made all the people of Greece swear to keep the league, and himself took the oath in the name of the Athenians, flinging wedges of redhot iron into the sea, after curses against such as should make breach of their vow. But afterwards, it would seem, when things were in such a state as constrained them to govern with a stronger hand, he bade the Athenians to throw the perjury upon him, and manage affairs as convenience required. And, in general, Theophrastus tells us, that Aristides was, in his own private affairs, and those of his fellow-citizens, rigorously just, but that in public matters he acted often in accordance with his country's policy, which demanded, sometimes, not a little injustice. It is reported of him that he said in a debate, upon the motion of the Samians for removing the treasure from Delos to Athens, contrary to the league, that the thing indeed was not just, but was expedient.

In fine, having established the dominion of his city over so many people, he himself remained indigent; and always delighted as much in the glory of being poor, as in that of his trophies; as is evident from the following story. Callias, the torchbearer, was related to him: and was prosecuted by his enemies in a capital cause, in which, after they had slightly argued the matters on which they indicted him, they proceeded, beside the point, to address the judges: "You know," said they, "Aristides, the son of Lysimachus, who is the admiration of all Greece. In what a condition do you think his family is in at his house, when you see him appear in public in such a threadbare cloak? Is it not probable that one who, out of doors, goes thus exposed to the cold, must want food and other necessaries at home? Callias, the wealthiest of the Athenians, does nothing to relieve either him or his wife and children in their poverty, though he is his own cousin, and has made use of him in many cases, and often reaped advantage by his interest with you." But Callias, perceiving the judges were moved more particularly by this, and were exasperated against him, called in Aristides, requiring him to testify that when he frequently offered him divers presents, and entreated him to accept them, he had refused, answering, that it became him better to be proud of his poverty than Callias of his wealth: since there are many to be seen that make a good, or a bad use of riches, but it is difficult, comparatively, to meet with one who supports poverty in a noble spirit; those only should be ashamed of it who incurred it against their wills. On Aristides deposing these facts in favor of Callias, there was none who heard them, that went not away desirous rather to be poor like Aristides, than rich as Callias. Thus Æschines, the scholar of Socrates, writes. But Plato declares, that of all the great and renowned men in the city of Athens, he was the only one worthy of consideration; for Themistocles, Cimon, and Pericles filled the city with porticoes, treasure, and many other vain things, but Aristides guided his public life by the rule of justice. He showed his moderation very plainly in his conduct towards Themistocles himself. For though Themistocles had been his adversary in all his undertakings, and was the cause of his banishment, yet when he afforded a similar opportunity of revenge, being accused to the city, Aristides bore him no malice; but while Alcmæon, Cimon, and many others, were prosecuting and impeaching him, Aristides alone, neither did, nor said any ill against him, and no more triumphed over his enemy in his adversity, than he had envied him his prosperity.

Some say Aristides died in Pontus, during a voyage upon the affairs of the public. Others that he died of old age at Athens, being in great honor and veneration amongst his fellow-citizens. But Craterus, the Macedonian, relates his death as follows. After the banishment of Themistocles, he says, the people growing insolent, there sprung up a number of false and frivolous accusers, impeaching the best and most influential men and exposing them to the envy of the multitude, whom their good fortune and power had filled with self-conceit. Amongst these, Aristides was condemned of bribery, upon the accusation of Diophantus of Amphitrope, for taking money from the Ionians when he was collector of the tribute; and being unable to pay the fine, which was fifty minæ, sailed to Ionia, and died there. But of this Craterus brings no written proof, neither the sentence of his condemnation, nor the decree of the people; though in general it is tolerably usual with him to set down such things and to cite his authors. Almost all others who have spoken of the misdeeds of the people towards their generals, collect them all together, and tell us of the banishment of Themistocles, Miltiades's bonds, Pericles's fine, and the death of Paches in the judgment hall, who, upon receiving sentence, killed himself on the hustings, with many things of the like nature. They add the banishment of Aristides; but of this his condemnation, they make no mention.

Moreover, his monument is to be seen at Phalerum, which they say was built him by the city, he not having left enough even to defray funeral charges. And it is stated, that his two daughters were publicly married out of the prytaneum, or state-house, by the city, which decreed each of them three thousand drachmas for her portion; and that upon his son Lysimachus, the people bestowed a hundred minas of money, and as many acres of planted land, and ordered him besides, upon the motion of Alcibiades, four drachmas a day. Furthermore, Lysimachus leaving a daughter, named Polycrite, as Callisthenes says, the people voted her, also, the same allowance for food with those that obtained the victory in the Olympic Games. But Demetrius the Phalerian, Hieronymus the Rhodian, Aristoxenus the musician, and Aristotle, (if the Treatise of Nobility is to be reckoned among the genuine pieces of Aristotle), say that Myrto, Aristides's granddaughter, lived with Socrates the philosopher, who indeed had another wife, but took her into his house, being a widow, by reason of her indigence, and want of the necessaries of life. But Panætius sufficiently confutes this in his books concerning Socrates. Demetrius the Phalerian, in his Socrates, says he knew one Lysimachus, son to the daughter of Aristides, extremely poor, who used to sit near what is called the Iaccheum, and sustained himself by a table for interpreting dreams and that, upon his proposal and representations, a decree was passed by the people, to give the mother and aunt of this man half a drachma a day. The same Demetrius, when he was legislating himself, decreed each of these women a drachma *per diem*. And it is not to be wondered at, that the people of Athens should take such care of people living in the city, since hearing the granddaughter of Aristogiton was in a low condition in the isle of Lemnos, and so poor nobody would marry her, they brought her back to Athens, and, marrying her to a man of good birth, gave a farm at Potamus as her marriage-portion; and of similar humanity and bounty the city of Athens, even in our age, has given numerous proofs, and is justly admired and respected in consequence.

ALCIBIADES

ALCIBIADES, as it is supposed, was anciently descended from Eurysaces, the son of Ajax, by his father's side; and by his mother's side from Alcmæon. Dinomache, his mother, was the daughter of Megacles. His father, Clinias, having fitted out a galley at his own expense, gained great honor in the sea-fight at Artemisium, and was afterwards slain in the battle of Coronea, fighting against the Bœotians. Pericles and Ariphron, the sons of Xanthippus, nearly related to him, became the guardians of Alcibiades. It has been said not untruly that the friendship which Socrates felt for him has much contributed to his fame; and certain it is, that, though we have no account from any writer concerning the mother of Nicias or Demosthenes, of Lamachus or Phormion, of Thrasybulus or Theramenes, notwithstanding these were all illustrious men of the same period, yet we know even the nurse of Alcibiades, that her country was Lacedæmon, and her name Amycla; and that Zopyrus was his teacher and attendant; the one being recorded by Antisthenes, and the other by Plato.

It is not, perhaps, material to say any thing of the beauty of Alcibiades, only that it bloomed with him in all the ages of his life, in his infancy, in his youth, and in his manhood; and, in the peculiar character becoming to each of these periods, gave him, in every one of them, a grace and a charm. What Euripides says, that

"Of all fair things the autumn, too, is fair,"

is by no means universally true. But it happened so with Alcibiades, amongst few others, by reason of his happy constitution and natural vigor of body. It is said that his lisping, when he spoke, became him well, and gave a grace and persuasiveness to his rapid speech. Aristophanes takes notice of it in the verses in which he jests at

Theorus; "How like a *colax* he is," says Alcibiades, meaning a *corax*,[1] on which it is remarked,

> "How very happily he lisped the truth."

Archippus also alludes to it in a passage where he ridicules the son of Alcibiades;

> "That people may believe him like his father,
> He walks like one dissolved in luxury,
> Lets his robe trail behind him on the ground,
> Carelessly leans his head, and in his talk
> Affects to lisp."

His conduct displayed many great inconsistencies and variations, not unnaturally, in accordance with the many and wonderful vicissitudes of his fortunes; but among the many strong passions of his real character, the one most prevailing of all, was his ambition and desire of superiority, which appears in several anecdotes told of his sayings whilst he was a child. Once being hard pressed in wrestling, and fearing to be thrown, he got the hand of his antagonist to his mouth, and bit it with all his force; and when the other loosed his hold presently, and said, "You bite, Alcibiades, like a woman." "No," replied he, "like a lion." Another time as he played at dice in the street, being then but a child, a loaded cart came that way, when it was his turn to throw; at first he called to the driver to stop, because he was to throw in the way over which the cart was to pass; but the man giving him no attention and driving on, when the rest of the boys divided and gave way, Alcibiades threw himself on his face before the cart, and, stretching himself out, bade the carter pass on now if he would; which so startled the man, that he put back his horses, while all that saw it were terrified, and, crying out, ran to assist Alcibiades. When he began to study, he obeyed all his other masters fairly well, but refused to learn upon the flute, as a sordid thing, and not becoming a free citizen; saying, that to play on the lute or the harp does not in any way disfigure a man's body or face, but one is hardly to be known by the most intimate friends, when playing on the flute. Besides, one who plays on

[1] This fashionable Attic lisp, or slovenly articulation, turned the sound *r* into *l*. *Colax*, a flatterer; *Corax*, a crow.

the harp may speak or sing at the same time; but the use of the flute stops the mouth, intercepts the voice, and prevents all articulation. "Therefore," said he, "let the Theban youths pipe, who do not know how to speak, but we Athenians, as our ancestors have told us, have Minerva for our patroness, and Apollo for our protector, one of whom threw away the flute, and the other stripped the Flute-player of his skin." Thus, between raillery and good earnest, Alcibiades kept not only himself but others from learning, as it presently became the talk of the young boys, how Alcibiades despised playing on the flute, and ridiculed those who studied it. In consequence of which, it ceased to be reckoned amongst the liberal accomplishments, and became generally neglected.

It is stated in the invective which Antiphon wrote against Alcibiades, that once, when he was a boy, he ran away to the house of Democrates, one of those who made a favorite of him, and that Ariphron had determined to cause proclamation to be made for him, had not Pericles diverted him from it, by saying, that if he were dead, the proclaiming of him could only cause it to be discovered one day sooner, and if he were safe, it would be a reproach to him as long as he lived. Antiphon also says, that he killed one of his own servants with the blow of a staff in Sibyrtius's wrestling ground. But it is unreasonable to give credit to all that is objected by an enemy, who makes open profession of his design to defame him.

It was manifest that the many well-born persons who were continually seeking his company, and making their court to him, were attracted and captivated by his brilliant and extraordinary beauty only. But the affection which Socrates entertained for him is a great evidence of the natural noble qualities and good disposition of the boy, which Socrates, indeed, detected both in and under his personal beauty; and, fearing that his wealth and station, and the great number both of strangers and Athenians who flattered and caressed him, might at last corrupt him, resolved, if possible, to interpose, and preserve so hopeful a plant from perishing in the flower, before its fruit came to perfection. For never did fortune surround and enclose a man with so many of those things which we vulgarly call goods, or so protect him from every weapon of philosophy, and fence him from every access of free and searching words, as she did Alcibiades; who, from the beginning, was exposed to the flatteries of those who sought merely his gratification, such as might well unnerve him, and indispose him to listen to any real adviser or instructor. Yet such was the happiness of his genius, that he discerned Socrates from the rest, and admitted him, whilst he drove away the wealthy and the noble who made court to him. And, in a little time, they grew intimate, and Alcibiades, listening now to language entirely free from every thought of unmanly fondness and silly displays of affection, finding himself with one who sought to lay open to him the deficiencies of his mind, and repress his vain and foolish arrogance,

> "Dropped like the craven cock his conquered wing."

He esteemed these endeavors of Socrates as most truly a means which the gods made use of for the care and preservation of youth,[2] and began to think meanly of himself, and to admire him; to be pleased with his kindness, and to stand in awe of his virtue; and, unawares to himself, there became formed in his mind that reflex image and reciprocation of Love, or Anteros,[3] that Plato talks of. It was a matter of general wonder, when people saw him joining Socrates in his meals and his exercises, living with him in the same tent, whilst he was reserved and rough to all others who made their addresses to him, and acted, indeed, with great insolence to some of them. As in particular to Anytus, the son of Anthemion, one who was very fond of him, and invited him to an entertainment which he had prepared for some strangers. Alcibiades refused the invitation; but, having drunk to excess at his own house with some of his companions, went thither with them to play some frolic; and, standing at the door of the room where the guests were enjoying themselves, and seeing the tables covered with gold and silver cups, he commanded his servants to take away the one half of them, and carry them to his own house; and then, disdaining so much as to enter into the room himself, as soon as he had done this, went away. The company was indignant, and exclaimed at his

[2] In allusion to the philosophical theory which he quoted in the life of Theseus, that love is a divine provision for the care of the young.

[3] Eros and Anteros, Love and Love-again.

rude and insulting conduct; Anytus, however, said, on the contrary he had shown great consideration and tenderness in taking only a part, when he might have taken all.

He behaved in the same manner to all others who courted him, except only one stranger, who, as the story is told, having but a small estate, sold it all for about a hundred staters, which he presented to Alcibiades, and besought him to accept. Alcibiades, smiling and well pleased at the thing, invited him to supper, and, after a very kind entertainment, gave him his gold again, requiring him, moreover, not to fail to be present the next day, when the public revenue was offered to farm, and to outbid all others. The man would have excused himself, because the contract was so large, and would cost many talents; but Alcibiades, who had at that time a private pique against the existing farmers of the revenue, threatened to have him beaten if he refused. The next morning, the stranger, coming to the market-place, offered a talent more than the existing rate; upon which the farmers, enraged and consulting together, called upon him to name his sureties, concluding that he could find none. The poor man, being startled at the proposal, began to retire; but Alcibiades, standing at a distance, cried out to the magistrates, "Set my name down, he is a friend of mine; I will be security for him." When the other bidders heard this, they perceived that all their contrivance was defeated; for their way was, with the profits of the second year to pay the rent for the year preceding; so that, not seeing any other way to extricate themselves out of the difficulty, they began to entreat the stranger, and offered him a sum of money. Alcibiades would not suffer him to accept of less than a talent; but when that was paid down, he commanded him to relinquish the bargain, having by this device relieved his necessity.

Though Socrates had many and powerful rivals, yet the natural good qualities of Alcibiades gave his affection the mastery. His words overcame him so much, as to draw tears from his eyes, and to disturb his very soul. Yet sometimes he would abandon himself to flatterers, when they proposed to him varieties of pleasure, and would desert Socrates; who, then, would pursue him, as if he had been a fugitive slave. He despised every one else, and had no reverence or awe for any but him. Cleanthes, the philosopher, speaking of one to whom he was attached, says his only hold on him was by his ears, while his rivals had all the others offered them; and there is no question that Alcibiades was very easily caught by pleasures; and the expression used by Thucydides about the excesses of his habitual course of living gives occasion to believe so. But those who endeavored to corrupt Alcibiades, took advantage chiefly of his vanity and ambition, and thrust him on unseasonably to undertake great enterprises, persuading him, that as soon as he began to concern himself in public affairs, he would not only obscure the rest of the generals and statesmen, but outdo the authority and the reputation which Pericles himself had gained in Greece. But in the same manner as iron which is softened by the fire grows hard with the cold, and all its parts are closed again; so, as often as Socrates observed Alcibiades to be misled by luxury or pride, he reduced and corrected him by his addresses, and made him humble and modest, by showing him in how many things he was deficient, and how very far from perfection in virtue.

When he was past his childhood, he went once to a grammar-school, and asked the master for one of Homer's books; and he making answer that he had nothing of Homer's, Alcibiades gave him a blow with his fist, and went away. Another schoolmaster telling him that he had Homer corrected by himself; "How?" said Alcibiades, "and do you employ your time in teaching children to read? You, who are able to amend Homer, may well undertake to instruct men." Being once desirous to speak with Pericles, he went to his house, and was told there that he was not at leisure, but busied in considering how to give up his accounts to the Athenians; Alcibiades, as he went away, said, "It were better for him to consider how he might avoid giving up his accounts at all."

Whilst he was very young, he was a soldier in the expedition against Potidæa, where Socrates lodged in the same tent with him, and stood next him in battle. Once there happened a sharp skirmish, in which they both behaved with signal bravery; but Alcibiades receiving a wound, Socrates threw himself before him to defend him, and beyond any question saved him and his arms from the enemy, and so in all justice might have challenged the prize of valor. But the generals appearing eager to adjudge the honor to Alcibiades, because of his rank, Socrates, who desired to increase his thirst after glory of a noble kind, was the first to give evidence for him, and pressed them to crown him, and to decree to him the complete suit of armor. Afterwards, in the battle of Delium, when the Athenians were routed and Socrates with a few others was retreating on foot, Alcibiades, who was on horseback, observing it, would not pass on, but stayed to shelter him from the danger, and brought him safe off, though the enemy pressed hard upon them, and cut off many. But this happened some time after.

He gave a box on the ear to Hipponicus, the father of Callias, whose birth and wealth made him a person of great influence and repute. And this he did unprovoked by any passion or quarrel between them, but only because, in a frolic, he had agreed with his companions to do it. People were justly offended at this insolence, when it became known through the city; but early the next morning, Alcibiades went to his house and knocked at the door, and, being admitted to him, took off his outer garment, and, presenting his naked body, desired him to scourge and chastise him as he pleased. Upon this Hipponicus forgot all his resentment, and not only pardoned him, but soon after gave him his daughter Hipparete in marriage. Some say that it was not Hipponicus, but his son Callias, who gave Hipparete to Alcibiades, together with a portion of ten talents, and that after, when she had a child, Alcibiades forced him to give ten talents more, upon pretence that such was the agreement if she brought him any children. Afterwards, Callias, for fear of coming to his death by his means, declared, in a full assembly of the people, that if he should happen to die without children, the state should inherit his house and all his goods. Hipparete was a virtuous and dutiful wife, but, at last, growing impatient of the outrages done to her by her husband's continual entertaining of courtesans, as well strangers as Athenians, she departed from him and retired to her brother's house. Alcibiades seemed not at all concerned at this, and lived on still in the same luxury; but the law requiring that she should deliver to the archon in person, and not by proxy, the instrument by which she claimed a divorce, when, in obedience to the law, she presented herself before him to perform this, Alcibiades came in, caught her up, and carried her home through the market-place, no one daring to oppose him, nor to take her from him. She continued with him till her death, which happened not long after, when Alcibiades had gone to Ephesus. Nor is this violence to be thought so very enormous or unmanly. For the law, in making her who desires to be divorced appear in public, seems to design to give her husband an opportunity of treating with her, and of endeavoring to retain her.

Alcibiades had a dog which cost him seventy minas, and was a very large one, and very handsome. His tail, which was his principal ornament, he caused to be cut off, and his acquaintance exclaiming at him for it, and telling him that all Athens was sorry for the dog, and cried out upon him for this action, he laughed, and said, "Just what I wanted has happened, then. I wished the Athenians to talk about this, that they might not say something worse of me."

It is said that the first time he came into the assembly was upon occasion of a largess of money which he made to the people. This was not done by design, but as he passed along he heard a shout, and inquiring the cause, and having learned that there was a donative making to the people, he went in amongst them and gave money also. The multitude thereupon applauding him, and shouting, he was so transported at it, that he forgot a quail which he had under his robe, and the bird, being frighted with the noise, flew off; upon which the people made louder acclamations than before, and many of them started up to pursue the bird; and one Antiochus, a pilot, caught it and restored it to him, for which he was ever after a favorite with Alcibiades.

He had great advantages for entering public life; his noble birth, his riches, the personal courage he had shown in divers battles, and the multitude of his friends and dependents, threw open, so to say, folding doors for his admittance. But he did not consent to let his power with the people rest on any thing, rather than on his own gift of eloquence. That he was a master in the art of speaking, the comic poets bear him witness; and the most eloquent of public speakers, in his oration against Midias, allows that Alcibiades, among other perfections, was a most accomplished orator. If, however, we give credit to Theophrastus, who of all philosophers was the most curious inquirer, and the greatest lover of history, we are to understand that Alcibiades had the highest capacity for inventing, for discerning what was the right thing to be said for any purpose, and on any occasion; but, aiming not only at saying what was required, but also at saying it well, in respect, that is, of words and phrases, when these did not readily occur, he would often pause in the middle of his discourse for want of the apt word, and would be silent and stop till he could recollect himself, and had considered what to say.

His expenses in horses kept for the public games, and in the number of his chariots, were matter of great observation; never did any one but he, either private person or king, send seven chariots to the Olympic games. And to have carried away at once the first, the second, and the fourth prizes, as Thucydides says, or the third, as Euripides relates it, outdoes far away every distinction that ever was known or thought of in that kind. Euripides celebrates his success in this manner:

> "—But my song to you,
> Son of Clinias, is due.
> Victory is noble; how much more
> To do as never Greek before;
> To obtain in the great chariot race
> The first, the second, and third place;
> With easy step advanced to fame,
> To bid the herald three times claim
> The olive for one victor's name."

The emulation displayed by the deputations of various states, in the presents which they made to him, rendered this success yet more illustrious. The Ephesians erected a tent for him, adorned magnificently; the city of Chios furnished him with provender for his horses and with great numbers of beasts for sacrifice; and the Lesbians sent him wine and other provisions for the many great entertainments which he made. Yet in the midst of all this he escaped not without censure, occasioned either by the ill-nature of his enemies or by his own misconduct. For it is said, that one Diomedes, an Athenian, a worthy man and a friend to Alcibiades, passionately desiring to obtain the victory at the Olympic games, and having heard much of a chariot which belonged to the state at Argos, where he knew that Alcibiades had great power and many friends, prevailed with him to undertake to buy the chariot. Alcibiades did indeed buy it, but then claimed it for his own, leaving Diomedes to rage at him, and to call upon the gods and men to bear witness to the injustice. It would seem there was a suit at law commenced upon this occasion, and there is yet extant an oration concerning the chariot, written by Isocrates in defence of the son of Alcibiades. But the plaintiff in this action is named Tisias, and not Diomedes.

As soon as he began to intermeddle in the government, which was when he was very young, he quickly lessened the credit of all who aspired to the confidence of the people, except Phæax, the son of Erasistratus, and Nicias, the son of Niceratus, who alone could contest it with him. Nicias was arrived at a mature age, and was esteemed their first general. Phæax was but a rising statesman like Alcibiades; he was descended from noble ancestors, but was his inferior, as in many other things, so, principally in eloquence. He possessed rather the art of persuading in private conversation than of debate before the people, and was, as Eupolis said of him,

"The best of talkers, and of speakers worst."

There is extant an oration written by Phæax against Alcibiades, in which, amongst other things, it is said that Alcibiades made daily use at his table of many gold and silver vessels, which belonged to the commonwealth, as if they had been his own.

There was a certain Hyperbolus, of the township of Perithœdæ, whom Thucydides also speaks of as a man of bad character, a general butt for the mockery of all the comic writers of the time, but quite unconcerned at the worst things they could say, and, being careless of glory, also insensible of shame; a temper which some people call boldness and courage, whereas it is indeed impudence and recklessness. He was liked by nobody, yet the people made frequent use of him, when they had a mind to disgrace or calumniate any persons in authority. At this time, the people, by his persuasions, were ready to proceed to pronounce the sentence of ten years' banishment, called ostracism. This they made use of to humiliate and drive out of the city such citizens as outdid the rest in credit and power, indulging not so much perhaps their apprehensions as their jealousies in this way. And when, at this time, there was no doubt but that the ostracism would fall upon one of those three, Alcibiades contrived to form a coalition of parties, and, communicating his project to Nicias, turned the sentence upon Hyperbolus himself. Others say, that it was not with Nicias, but Phæax, that he consulted, and, by help of his party, procured the banishment of Hyperbolus, when he suspected nothing less. For, before that time, no mean or obscure person had ever fallen under that punishment, so that Plato, the comic poet, speaking of Hyperbolus, might well say,

> "The man deserved the fate; deny 't who can?
> Yes, but the fate did not deserve the man;
> Not for the like of him and his slave-brands
> Did Athens put the sherd into our hands."

But we have given elsewhere a fuller statement of what is known to us of the matter.

Alcibiades was not less disturbed at the distinctions which Nicias gained amongst the enemies of Athens, than at the honors which the Athenians themselves paid to him. For though Alcibiades was the proper appointed person[4] to receive all Lacedæmonians when they came to Athens, and had taken particular care of those that were made prisoners at Pylos, yet, after they had obtained the peace and restitution of the captives, by the procurement chiefly of Nicias, they paid him very special attentions. And it was commonly said in Greece, that the war was begun by Pericles, and that Nicias made an end of it, and the peace was generally called the peace of Nicias. Alcibiades was extremely annoyed at this, and, being full of envy, set himself to break the league. First, therefore, observing that the Argives, as well out of fear as hatred to the Lacedæmonians, sought for protection against them, he gave them a secret assurance of alliance with Athens. And communicating, as well in person as by letters, with the chief advisers of the people there, he

[4] The Proxenus, that is, who in the ancient cities exercised, in a private station, and as a matter of private magnificence and splendid hospitality (he being always a citizen of the state in which he resided) many of the duties of protection now officially committed to consuls and resident ministers.

encouraged them not to fear the Lacedæmonians, nor make concessions to them, but to wait a little, and keep their eyes on the Athenians, who, already, were all but sorry they had made peace, and would soon give it up. And, afterwards, when the Lacedæmonians had made a league with the Bœotians, and had not delivered up Panactum entire, as they ought to have done by the treaty, but only after first destroying it, which gave great offence to the people of Athens, Alcibiades laid hold of that opportunity to exasperate them more highly. He exclaimed fiercely against Nicias, and accused him of many things, which seemed probable enough: as that, when he was general, he made no attempt himself to capture their enemies that were shut up in the isle of Sphacteria, but, when they were afterwards made prisoners by others, he procured their release and sent them back to the Lacedæmonians, only to get favor with them; that he would not make use of his credit with them, to prevent their entering into this confederacy with the Bœotians and Corinthians, and yet, on the other side, that he sought to stand in the way of those Greeks who were inclined to make an alliance and friendship with Athens, if the Lacedæmonians did not like it.

It happened, at the very time when Nicias was by these arts brought into disgrace with the people, that ambassadors arrived from Lacedæmon, who, at their first coming, said what seemed very satisfactory, declaring that they had full powers to arrange all matters in dispute upon fair and equal terms. The council received their propositions, and the people was to assemble on the morrow to give them audience. Alcibiades grew very apprehensive of this, and contrived to gain a secret conference with the ambassadors. When they were met, he said: "What is it you intend, you men of Sparta? Can you be ignorant that the council always act with moderation and respect towards ambassadors, but that the people are full of ambition and great designs? So that, if you let them know what full powers your commission gives you, they will urge and press you to unreasonable conditions. Quit, therefore, this indiscreet simplicity, if you expect to obtain equal terms from the Athenians, and would not have things extorted from you contrary to your inclinations, and begin to treat with the people upon some reasonable articles, not avowing yourselves plenipotentiaries; and I will be ready to assist you, out of good-will to the Lacedæmonians." When he had said thus, he gave them his oath for the performance of what he promised, and by this way drew them from Nicias to rely entirely upon himself, and left them full of admiration of the discernment and sagacity they had seen in him. The next day, when the people were assembled and the ambassadors introduced, Alcibiades, with great apparent courtesy, demanded of them, With what powers they were come? They made answer that they were not come as plenipotentiaries.

Instantly upon that, Alcibiades, with a loud voice, as though he had received and not done the wrong, began to call them dishonest prevaricators, and to urge that such men could not possibly come with a purpose to say or do any thing that was sincere. The council was incensed, the people were in a rage, and Nicias, who knew nothing of the deceit and the imposture, was in the greatest confusion, equally surprised and ashamed at such a change in the men. So thus the Lacedæmonian ambassadors were utterly rejected, and Alcibiades was declared general, who presently united the Argives, the Eleans, and the people of Mantinea, into a confederacy with the Athenians.

No man commended the method by which Alcibiades effected all this, yet it was a great political feat thus to divide and shake almost all Peloponnesus, and to combine so many men in arms against the Lacedæmonians in one day before Mantinea; and, moreover, to remove the war and the danger so far from the frontier of the Athenians, that even success would profit the enemy but little, should they be conquerors, whereas, if they were defeated, Sparta itself was hardly safe.

After this battle at Mantinea, the select thousand of the army of the Argives attempted to overthrow the government of the people in Argos, and make themselves masters of the city; and the Lacedæmonians came to their aid and abolished the democracy. But the people took arms again, and gained the advantage, and Alcibiades came in to their aid and completed the victory, and persuaded them to build long walls, and by that means to join their city to the sea, and so to bring it wholly within the reach of the Athenian power. To this purpose, he procured them builders and masons from Athens, and displayed the greatest zeal for their service, and gained no less honor and power to himself than to the commonwealth of Athens. He also persuaded the people of Patræ to join their city to the sea, by building long walls; and when some one told them, by way of warning, that the Athenians would swallow them up at last, Alcibiades made answer, "Possibly it may be so, but it will be by little and little, and beginning at the feet, whereas the Lacedæmonians will begin at the head and devour you all at once." Nor did he neglect either to advise the Athenians to look to their interests by land, and often put the young men in mind of the oath which they had made at Agraulos to the effect that they would account wheat and barley, and vines and olives, to be the limits of Attica by which they were taught to claim a title to all land that was cultivated and productive.

But with all these words and deeds, and with all this sagacity and eloquence, he intermingled exorbitant luxury and wantonness in his eating and drinking and dissolute living; wore long purple robes like a woman, which dragged after him as he went through the market-place; caused the planks of his galley to be cut away, that so he might lie the softer, his bed not being placed on the boards, but hanging upon girths. His shield, again, which was richly gilded, had not the usual ensigns of the Athenians, but a Cupid, holding a thunderbolt in his hand, was painted upon it. The sight of all this made the people of good repute in the city feel disgust and abhorrence, and apprehension also, at his free-living, and his contempt of law, as things monstrous in themselves, and indicating designs of usurpation. Aristophanes has well expressed the people's feeling towards him:—

> "They love, and hate, and cannot do without him.

And still more strongly, under a figurative expression,

> "Best rear no lion in your state, 't is true;
> But treat him like a lion if you do."

The truth is, his liberalities, his public shows, and other munificence to the people, which were such as nothing could exceed, the glory of his ancestors, the force of his eloquence, the grace of his person, his strength of body, joined with his great courage and knowledge in military affairs, prevailed upon the Athenians to endure patiently his excesses, to indulge many things to him, and, according to their habit, to give the softest names to his faults, attributing them to youth and good nature. As, for example, he kept Agatharcus, the painter, a prisoner till he had painted his whole house, but then dismissed him with a reward. He publicly struck Taureas, who exhibited certain shows in opposition to him and contended with him for the prize. He selected for himself one of the captive Melian women, and had a son by her, whom he took care to educate. This the Athenians styled great humanity; and yet he was the principal cause of the slaughter of all the inhabitants of the isle of Melos who were of age to bear arms, having spoken in favor of that decree. When Aristophon, the painter, had drawn Nemea sitting and holding Alcibiades in her arms, the multitude seemed pleased with the piece, and thronged to see it, but older people disliked and disrelished it, and looked on these things as enormities, and movements towards tyranny. So that it was not said amiss by Archestratus, that Greece could not support a second Alcibiades. Once, when Alcibiades succeeded well in an oration which he made, and the whole assembly attended upon him to do him honor, Timon the misanthrope did not pass slightly by him, nor avoid him, as he did others, but purposely met him, and, taking him by the hand, said, "Go on boldly, my son, and increase in credit with the people, for thou wilt one day bring them calamities enough." Some that were present laughed at the saying, and some reviled Timon; but there were others upon whom it made a deep impression; so various was the judgment which was made of him, and so irregular his own character.

The Athenians, even in the lifetime of Pericles, had already cast a longing eye upon Sicily; but did not attempt any thing till after his death. Then, under pretence of aiding their confederates, they sent succors upon all occasions to those who were oppressed by the Syracusans, preparing the way for sending over a greater force. But Alcibiades was the person who inflamed this desire of theirs to the height, and prevailed with them no longer to proceed secretly, and by little and little, in their design, but to sail out with a great fleet, and undertake at once to make themselves masters of the island. He possessed the people with great hopes, and he himself entertained yet greater; and the conquest of Sicily, which was the utmost bound of their ambition, was but the mere outset of his expectation. Nicias endeavored to divert the people from the expedition, by representing to them that the taking of Syracuse would be a work of great difficulty; but Alcibiades dreamed of nothing less than the conquest of Carthage and Libya, and by the accession of these conceiving himself at once made master of Italy and of Peloponnesus, seemed to look upon Sicily as little more than a magazine for the war. The young men were soon elevated with these hopes, and listened gladly to those of riper years, who talked wonders of the countries they were going to; so that you might see great numbers sitting in the wrestling grounds and public places, drawing on the ground the figure of the island and the situation of Libya and Carthage. Socrates the philosopher and Meton the astrologer are said, however, never to have hoped for any good to the commonwealth from this war; the one, it is to be supposed, presaging what would ensue, by the intervention of his attendant Genius; and the other, either upon rational consideration of the project, or by use of the art of divination, conceived fears for its issue, and, feigning madness, caught up a burning torch, and seemed as if he would have set his own house on fire. Others report, that he did not take upon him to act the madman, but secretly in the night set his house on fire, and the next morning besought the people, that for his comfort, after such a calamity, they would spare his son from the expedition. By which artifice, he deceived his fellow-citizens, and obtained of them what he desired.

Together with Alcibiades, Nicias, much against his will, was appointed general: and he endeavored to avoid the command, not the less on account of his colleague. But the Athenians thought the war would proceed more prosperously, if they did not send Alcibiades free from all restraint, but tempered his heat with the caution of Nicias. This they chose the rather to do, because Lamachus, the third general, though he was of mature years, yet in several battles had appeared no less hot and rash than Alcibiades himself. When they began to deliberate of the number of forces, and of the manner of making the necessary provisions, Nicias made another attempt to oppose the design, and to prevent the war; but Alcibiades contradicted him, and carried his point with the people. And one Demostratus, an orator, proposing to give the generals absolute power over the preparations and the whole management of the war, it was presently decreed so. When all things were fitted for the voyage, many unlucky omens appeared. At that very time the feast of Adonis happened, in which the women were used to expose, in all parts of the city, images resembling dead men carried out to their burial, and to represent funeral solemnities by lamentations and mournful songs. The mutilation, however, of the images of Mercury, most of which, in one night, had their faces all disfigured, terrified many persons who were wont to despise most things of that nature. It was given out that it was done by the Corinthians, for the sake of the Syracusans, who were their colony, in hopes that the Athenians, by such prodigies, might be induced to delay or abandon the war. But the report gained no credit with the people, nor yet the opinion of those who would not believe that there was any thing ominous in the matter, but that it was only an extravagant action, committed, in that sort of sport which runs into license, by wild young men coming from a debauch. Alike enraged and terrified at the thing, looking upon it to proceed from a conspiracy of persons who designed some commotions in the state, the council, as well as the assembly of the people, which was held frequently in a few days' space, examined diligently every thing that might administer ground for suspicion. During this examination, Androcles, one of the demagogues, produced certain slaves and strangers before them, who accused Alcibiades and some of his friends of defacing other images in the same manner, and of having profanely acted the sacred mysteries at a drunken meeting, where one Theodorus represented the herald, Polytion the torch-bearer, and Alcibiades the chief priest, while the rest of the party appeared as candidates for initiation, and received the title of Initiates. These were the matters contained in the articles of information,[5] which Thessalus, the son of Cimon, exhibited against Alcibiades, for his

[5] *Eisangĕlia,* the technical term for an indictment before the legislature for misdemeanors not coming strictly under the letter of any written law.

impious mockery of the goddesses, Ceres and Proserpine. The people were highly exasperated and incensed against Alcibiades upon this accusation, which, being aggravated by Androcles, the most malicious of all his enemies, at first disturbed his friends exceedingly. But when they perceived that all the seamen designed for Sicily were for him, and the soldiers also, and when the Argive and Mantinean auxiliaries, a thousand men at arms, openly declared that they had undertaken this distant maritime expedition for the sake of Alcibiades, and that, if he was ill-used, they would all go home, they recovered their courage, and became eager to make use of the present opportunity for justifying him. At this his enemies were again discouraged, fearing lest the people should be more gentle to him in their sentence, because of the occasion they had for his service. Therefore, to obviate this, they contrived that some other orators, who did not appear to be enemies to Alcibiades, but really hated him no less than those who avowed it, should stand up in the assembly and say, that it was a very absurd thing that one who was created general of such an army with absolute power, after his troops were assembled, and the confederates were come, should lose the opportunity, whilst the people were choosing his judges by lot, and appointing times for the hearing of the cause. And, therefore, let him set sail at once; good fortune attend him; and when the war should be at an end, he might then in person make his defence according to the laws.

Alcibiades perceived the malice of this postponement, and, appearing in the assembly, represented that it was monstrous for him to be sent with the command of so large an army, when he lay under such accusations and calumnies; that he deserved to die, if he could not clear himself of the crimes objected to him; but when he had so done, and had proved his innocence, he should then cheerfully apply himself to the war, as standing no longer in fear of false accusers. But he could not prevail with the people who commanded him to sail immediately. So he departed, together with the other generals, having with them near 140 galleys, 5,100 men at arms, and about 1,300 archers, slingers, and light-armed men, and all the other provisions corresponding.

Arriving on the coast of Italy, he landed at Rhegium, and there stated his views of the manner in which they ought to conduct the war. He was opposed by Nicias; but Lamachus being of his opinion, they sailed for Sicily forthwith, and took Catana. This was all that was done while he was there, for he was soon after recalled by the Athenians to abide his trial. At first, as we before said, there were only some slight suspicions advanced against Alcibiades, and accusations by certain slaves and strangers. But afterwards, in his absence, his enemies attacked him more violently, and confounded together the breaking the images with the profanation of the mysteries, as though both had been committed in pursuance of the same conspiracy for changing the government. The people proceeded to imprison all that were accused, without distinction, and without hearing them, and repented now, considering the importance of the charge, that they had not immediately brought Alcibiades to his trial, and given judgment against him. Any of his friends or acquaintances who fell into the people's hands, whilst they were in this fury, did not fail to meet with very severe usage. Thucydides has omitted to name the informers, but others mention Dioclides and Teucer. Amongst whom is Phrynichus, the comic poet, in whom we find the following:—

"O dearest Hermes! only do take care,
And mind you do not miss your footing there;
Should you get hurt, occasion may arise
For a new Dioclides to tell lies."

To which he makes Mercury return this answer:—

"I will so, for I feel no inclination
To reward Teucer for more information."

The truth is, his accusers alleged nothing that was certain or solid against him. One of them, being asked how he knew the men who defaced the images, replying, that he saw them by the light of the moon, made a palpable misstatement, for it was just new moon when the fact was committed. This made all men of understanding cry out upon the thing; but the people were as eager as ever to receive further accusations, nor was their first heat at all abated, but they instantly seized and imprisoned every one that was accused. Amongst those who were detained in prison for their trials was Andocides the orator, whose descent the historian Hellanicus deduces from Ulysses. He was always supposed to hate popular government, and to support oligarchy. The chief ground of his being suspected of defacing the images was because the great Mercury, which stood near his house, and was an ancient monument of the tribe Ægeïs, was almost the only statue of all the remarkable ones, which remained entire. For this cause, it is now called the Mercury of Andocides, all men giving it that name, though the inscription is evidence to the contrary. It happened that Andocides, amongst the rest who were prisoners upon the same account, contracted particular acquaintance and intimacy with one Timæus, a person inferior to him in repute, but of remarkable dexterity and boldness. He persuaded Andocides to accuse himself and some few others of this crime, urging to him that, upon his confession, he would be, by the decree of the people, secure of his pardon, whereas the event of judgment is uncertain to all men, but to great persons, such as he was, most formidable. So that it was better for him, if he regarded himself, to save his life by a falsity, than to suffer an infamous death, as really guilty of the crime. And if he had regard to the public good, it was commendable to sacrifice a few suspected men, by that means to rescue many excellent persons from the fury of the people. Andocides was prevailed upon, and accused himself and some others, and, by the terms of the decree, obtained his pardon, while all the persons named by him, except some few who had saved themselves by flight, suffered death. To gain the greater credit to his information, he accused his own servants amongst others. But notwithstanding this, the people's anger was not wholly appeased; and being now no longer diverted by the mutilators, they were at leisure to pour out their whole rage upon Alcibiades. And, in conclusion, they sent the galley named the Salaminian, to recall him. But they expressly commanded those that were sent, to use no violence, nor seize upon his person, but address themselves to him in the mildest terms, requiring him to follow them to Athens in order to abide his trial, and clear himself before the people. For they feared mutiny and sedition in the army in an enemy's country, which indeed it would have been easy for

Alcibiades to effect, if he had wished it. For the soldiers were dispirited upon his departure, expecting for the future tedious delays, and that the war would be drawn out into a lazy length by Nicias, when Alcibiades, who was the spur to action, was taken away. For though Lamachus was a soldier, and a man of courage, poverty deprived him of authority and respect in the army. Alcibiades, just upon his departure, prevented Messena from falling into the hands of the Athenians. There were some in that city who were upon the point of delivering it up, but he, knowing the persons, gave information to some friends of the Syracusans, and so defeated the whole contrivance. When he arrived at Thurii, he went on shore, and, concealing himself there, escaped those who searched after him. But to one who knew him, and asked him if he durst not trust his own native country, he made answer, "In every thing else, yes; but in a matter that touches my life, I would not even my own mother, lest she might by mistake throw in the black ball instead of the white." When, afterwards, he was told that the assembly had pronounced judgment of death against him, all he said was "I will make them feel that I am alive."

The information against him was conceived in this form:—

"Thessalus, the son of Cimon, of the township of Lacia, lays information that Alcibiades, the son of Clinias, of the township of the Scambonidæ, has committed a crime against the goddesses Ceres and Proserpine, by representing in derision the holy mysteries, and showing them to his companions in his own house. Where, being habited in such robes as are used by the chief priest when he shows the holy things, he named himself the chief priest, Polytion the torch-bearer, and Theodorus, of the township of Phegæa, the herald; and saluted the rest of his company as Initiates and Novices. All which was done contrary to the laws and institutions of the Eumolpidæ, and the heralds and priests of the temple at Eleusis."

He was condemned as contumacious upon his not appearing, his property confiscated, and it was decreed that all the priests and priestesses should solemnly curse him. But one of them, Theano, the daughter of Menon, of the township of Agraule, is said to have opposed that part of the decree, saying that her holy office obliged her to make prayers, but not execrations.

Alcibiades, lying under these heavy decrees and sentences, when first he fled from Thurii, passed over into Peloponnesus, and remained some time at Argos. But being there in fear of his enemies, and seeing himself utterly hopeless of return to his native country, he sent to Sparta, desiring safe conduct, and assuring them that he would make them amends by his future services for all the mischief he had done them while he was their enemy. The Spartans giving him the security he desired, he went eagerly, was well received, and, at his very first coming, succeeded in inducing them, without any further caution or delay, to send aid to the Syracusans; and so roused and excited them, that they forthwith despatched Gylippus into Sicily, to crush the forces which the Athenians had in Sicily. A second point was to renew the war upon the Athenians at home. But the third thing, and the most important of all, was to make them fortify Decelea, which above every thing reduced and wasted the resources of the Athenians.

The renown which he earned by these public services was equalled by the admiration he attracted to his private life; he captivated and won over everybody by his conformity to Spartan habits. People who saw him wearing his hair close cut, bathing in cold water, eating coarse meal, and dining on black broth, doubted, or rather could not believe, that he ever had a cook in his house, or had ever seen a perfumer, or had worn a mantle of Milesian purple. For he had, as it was observed, this peculiar talent and artifice for gaining men's affections, that he could at once comply with and really embrace and enter into their habits and ways of life, and change faster than the chameleon. One color, indeed, they say the chameleon cannot assume; it cannot make itself appear white; but Alcibiades, whether with good men or with bad, could adapt himself to his company, and equally wear the appearance of virtue or vice. At Sparta, he was devoted to athletic exercises, was frugal and reserved; in Ionia, luxurious, gay, and indolent; in Thrace, always drinking; in Thessaly, ever on horseback; and when he lived with Tisaphernes, the Persian satrap, he exceeded the Persians themselves in magnificence and pomp. Not that his natural disposition changed so easily, nor that his real character was so very variable, but, whenever he was sensible that by pursuing his own inclinations he might give offence to those with whom he had occasion to converse, he transformed himself into any shape, and adopted any fashion, that he observed to be the most agreeable to them. So that to have seen him at Lacedæmon, a man, judging by the outward appearance, would have said, " 'Tis not Achilles's son, but he himself, the very man" that Lycurgus designed to form; while his real feelings and acts would have rather provoked the exclamation, " 'Tis the same woman still." For while king Agis was absent, and abroad with the army, he corrupted his wife Timæa, and had a child born by her. Nor did she even deny it, but when she was brought to bed of a son, called him in public Leotychides, but, amongst her confidants and attendants, would whisper that his name was Alcibiades. To such a degree was she transported by her passion for him. He, on the other side, would say, in his vain way, he had not done this thing out of mere wantonness of insult, nor to gratify a passion, but that his race might one day be kings over the Lacedæmonians.

There were many who told Agis that this was so, but time itself gave the greatest confirmation to the story. For Agis, alarmed by an earthquake, had quitted his wife, and, for ten months after, was never with her; Leotychides, therefore, being born after those ten months, he would not acknowledge him for his son; which was the reason that afterwards he was not admitted to the succession.

After the defeat which the Athenians received in Sicily, ambassadors were despatched to Sparta at once from Chios and Lesbos and Cyzicus, to signify their purpose of revolting from the Athenians. The Bœotians interposed in favor of the Lesbians, and Pharnabazus of the Cyzicenes, but the Lacedæmonians, at the persuasion of Alcibiades, chose to assist Chios before all others. He himself, also, went instantly to sea, procured the immediate revolt of almost all Ionia, and, coöperating with the Lacedæmonian generals, did great mischief to the Athenians. But Agis was his enemy, hating him for having dishonored his wife, and also impatient of his glory, as almost every enterprise and every success was ascribed to Alcibiades. Others, also, of the most powerful and ambitious amongst the Spartans, were possessed with jealousy of him, and, at last, prevailed with the magistrates in the city to send orders into Ionia that he should be killed. Alcibiades, however, had secret intelligence of this, and, in apprehension of the result, while he communicated all affairs to the Lacedæmonians, yet took care not to put himself into their power. At last he retired to Tisaphernes, the king of Persia's satrap, for his security, and immediately became the first and most influential person about him. For this barbarian, not being himself sincere, but a lover of guile and wickedness, admired his address and wonderful subtlety. And, indeed, the charm of daily intercourse with him was more than any character could resist or any disposition escape. Even those who feared and envied him could not but take delight, and have a sort of kindness for him, when they saw him and were in his company. So that Tisaphernes, otherwise a cruel character, and, above all other Persians, a hater of the Greeks, was yet so won by the flatteries of Alcibiades, that he set himself even to exceed him in responding to them. The most beautiful of his parks, containing salubrious streams and meadows, where he had built pavilions, and places of retirement royally and exquisitely adorned, received by his direction the name of Alcibiades, and was always so called and so spoken of.

Thus Alcibiades, quitting the interests of the Spartans, whom he could no longer trust, because he stood in fear of Agis, endeavored to do them ill offices, and render them odious to Tisaphernes, who, by his means, was hindered from assisting them vigorously, and from finally ruining the Athenians. For his advice was to furnish them but sparingly with money, and so wear them out, and consume them insensibly; when they had wasted their strength upon one another, they would both become ready to submit to the king. Tisaphernes readily pursued his counsel, and so openly expressed the liking and admiration which he had for him, that Alcibiades was looked up to by the Greeks of both parties, and the Athenians, now in their misfortunes, repented them of their severe sentence against him. And he, on the other side, began to be troubled for them, and to fear lest, if that commonwealth were utterly destroyed, he should fall into the hands of the Lacedæmonians, his enemies.

At that time the whole strength of the Athenians was in Samos. Their fleet maintained itself here, and issued from these headquarters to reduce such as had revolted, and protect the rest of their territories; in one way or other still contriving to be a match for their enemies at sea. What they stood in fear of, was Tisaphernes and the Phœnician fleet of one hundred and fifty galleys, which was said to be already under sail; if those came, there remained then no hopes for the commonwealth of Athens. Understanding this, Alcibiades sent secretly to the chief men of the Athenians, who were then at Samos, giving them hopes that he would make Tisaphernes their friend; he was willing, he implied, to do some favor, not to the people, nor in reliance upon them, but to the better citizens, if only, like brave men, they would make the attempt to put down the insolence of the people, and, by taking upon them the government, would endeavor to save the city from ruin. All of them gave a ready ear to the proposal made by Alcibiades, except only Phrynichus, of the township of Dirades, one of the generals, who suspected, as the truth was, that Alcibiades concerned not himself whether the government were in the people or the better citizens, but only sought by any means to make way for his return into his native country, and to that end inveighed against the people, thereby to gain the others, and to insinuate himself into their good opinion. But when Phrynichus found his counsel to be rejected, and that he was himself become a declared enemy of Alcibiades, he gave secret intelligence to Astyochus, the enemy's admiral, cautioning him to beware of Alcibiades, and to seize him as a double dealer, unaware that one traitor was making discoveries to another. For Astyochus, who was eager to gain the favor of Tisaphernes, observing the credit Alcibiades had with him, revealed to Alcibiades all that Phrynichus had said against him. Alcibiades at once despatched messengers to Samos, to accuse Phrynichus of the treachery. Upon this, all the commanders were enraged with Phrynichus, and set themselves against him, and he, seeing no other way to extricate himself from the present danger, attempted to remedy one evil by a greater. He sent to Astyochus to reproach him for betraying him, and to make an offer to him at the same time, to deliver into his hands both the army and the navy of the Athenians. This occasioned no damage to the Athenians, because Astyochus repeated his treachery, and revealed also this proposal to Alcibiades. But this again was foreseen by Phrynichus, who, expecting a second accusation from Alcibiades, to anticipate him, advertised the Athenians beforehand that the enemy was ready to sail in order to surprise them, and therefore advised them to fortify their camp, and to be in a readiness to go aboard their ships. While the Athenians were intent upon doing these things, they received other letters from Alcibiades, admonishing them to beware of Phrynichus, as one who designed to betray their fleet to the enemy, to which they then gave no credit at all, conceiving that Alcibiades, who knew perfectly the counsels and preparations of the enemy, was merely making use of that knowledge, in order to impose upon them in this false accusation of Phrynichus. Yet, afterwards, when Phrynichus was stabbed with a dagger in the market-place by Hermon, one of the guard, the Athenians, entering into an examination of the cause, solemnly condemned Phrynichus of treason, and decreed crowns to Hermon and his associates. And now the friends of Alcibiades, carrying all before them at Samos, despatched Pisander to Athens, to attempt a change of government, and to encourage the aristocratical citizens to take upon themselves the government, and overthrow the democracy, representing to them, that, upon these terms, Alcibiades would procure them the friendship and alliance of Tisaphernes.

This was the color and pretence made use of by those who desired to change the government of Athens to an oligarchy. But as soon as they prevailed, and had got the administration of affairs into their hands, under the name of the Five Thousand (whereas, indeed, they were but four hundred), they slighted Alcibiades altogether, and prosecuted the war with less vigor; partly because they durst not yet trust the citizens, who secretly detested this change, and partly because they thought the Lacedæmonians, who always befriended the government of the few, would be inclined to give them favorable terms.

The people in the city were terrified into submission, many of those who had dared openly to oppose the four hundred having been put to death. But those who were at Samos, indignant when they heard this news, were eager to set sail instantly for the Piræus; and, sending for Alcibiades, they declared him general, requiring him to lead them on to put down the tyrants. He, however, in that juncture, did not, as it might have been thought a man would, on being suddenly exalted by the favor of a multitude, think himself under an obligation to gratify and submit to all the wishes of those who, from a fugitive and an exile, had created him general of so great an army, and given him the command of such a fleet. But, as became a great captain, he opposed himself to the precipitate resolutions which their rage led them to, and, by restraining them from the great error they were about to commit, unequivocally saved the commonwealth. For if they then had sailed to Athens, all Ionia and the islands and the Hellespont would have fallen into the enemies' hands without opposition, while the Athenians, involved in civil war, would have been fighting with one another within the circuit of their own walls. It was Alcibiades alone, or, at least, principally, who prevented all this mischief; for he not only used persuasion to the whole army, and showed them the danger, but applied himself to them, one by one, entreating some, and constraining others. He was much assisted, however, by Thrasybulus of Stiria, who, having the loudest voice, as we are told, of all the Athenians, went along with him, and cried out to those who were ready to be gone. A second great service which Alcibiades did for them was, his undertaking that the Phœnician fleet, which the Lacedæmonians expected to be sent to them by the king of Persia, should either come in aid of the Athenians, or otherwise should not come at all. He sailed off with all expedition in order to perform this, and the ships, which had already been seen as near as Aspendus, were not brought any further by Tisaphernes, who thus deceived the Lacedæmonians; and it was by both sides believed that they had been diverted by the procurement of Alcibiades. The Lacedæmonians, in particular, accused him, that he had advised the Barbarian to stand still, and suffer the Greeks to waste and destroy one another, as it was evident that the accession of so great a force to either party would enable them to take away the entire dominion of the sea from the other side.

Soon after this, the four hundred usurpers were driven out, the friends of Alcibiades vigorously assisting those who were for the popular government. And now the people in the city not only desired, but commanded Alcibiades to return home from his exile.

He, however, desired not to owe his return to the mere grace and commiseration of the people, and resolved to come back, not with empty hands, but with glory, and after some service done. To this end, he sailed from Samos with a few ships, and cruised on the sea of Cnidos, and about the isle of Cos; but receiving intelligence there that Mindarus, the Spartan admiral, had sailed with his whole army into the Hellespont, and that the Athenians had followed him, he hurried back to succor the Athenian commanders, and, by good fortune, arrived with eighteen galleys at a critical time. For both the fleets having engaged near Abydos, the fight between them had lasted till night, the one side having the advantage on one quarter, and the other on another. Upon his first appearance, both sides formed a false impression; the enemy was encouraged, and the Athenians terrified. But Alcibiades suddenly raised the Athenian ensign in the admiral ship, and fell upon those galleys of the Peloponnesians which had the advantage and were in pursuit. He soon put these to flight, and followed them so close that he forced them on shore, and broke the ships in pieces, the sailors abandoning then and swimming away, in spite of all the efforts of Pharnabazus, whc had come down to their assistance by land, and did what he coulc to protect them from the shore. In fine, the Athenians, having taken thirty of the enemy's ships, and recovered all their own, erected a trophy. After the gaining of so glorious a victory, his vanity made him eager to show himself to Tisaphernes, and, having furnished himself with gifts and presents, and an equipage suitable to his dignity, he set out to visit him. But the thing did not succeed as he had imagined, for Tisaphernes had been long suspected by the Lacedæmonians, and was afraid to fall into disgrace with his king upon that account, and therefore thought that Alcibiades arrived very opportunely, and immediately caused him to be seized, and sent away prisoner to Sardis; fancying, by this act of injustice, to clear himself from all former imputations.

But about thirty days after, Alcibiades escaped from his keepers, and, having got a horse, fled to Clazomenæ, where he procured Tisaphernes additional disgrace by professing he was a party to his escape. From there he sailed to the Athenian camp, and, being informed there that Mindarus and Pharnabazus were together at

Cyzicus, he made a speech to the soldiers, telling them that sea-fighting, land-fighting, and, by the gods, fighting against fortified cities too, must be all one for them, as, unless they conquered everywhere, there was no money for them. As soon as ever he got them on ship-board, he hasted to Proconnesus, and gave command to seize all the small vessels they met, and guard them safely in the interior of the fleet, that the enemy might have no notice of his coming; and a great storm of rain, accompanied with thunder and darkness, which happened at the same time, contributed much to the concealment of his enterprise. Indeed, it was not only undiscovered by the enemy, but the Athenians themselves were ignorant of it, for he commanded them suddenly on board, and set sail when they had abandoned all intention of it. As the darkness presently passed away, the Peloponnesian fleet were seen riding out at sea in front of the harbor of Cyzicus. Fearing, if they discovered the number of his ships, they might endeavor to save themselves by land, he commanded the rest of the captains to slacken, and follow him slowly, whilst he, advancing with forty ships, showed himself to the enemy, and provoked them to fight. The enemy, being deceived as to their numbers, despised them, and, supposing they were to contend with those only, made themselves ready and began the fight. But as soon as they were engaged, they perceived the other part of the fleet coming down upon them, at which they were so terrified that they fled immediately. Upon that, Alcibiades, breaking through the midst of them with twenty of his best ships, hastened to the shore, disembarked, and pursued those who abandoned their ships and fled to land, and made a great slaughter of them. Mindarus and Pharnabazus, coming to their succor, were utterly defeated. Mindarus was slain upon the place, fighting valiantly; Pharnabazus saved himself by flight. The Athenians slew great numbers of their enemies, won much spoil, and took all their ships. They also made themselves masters of Cyzicus, which was deserted by Pharnabazus, and destroyed its Peloponnesian garrison, and thereby not only secured to themselves the Hellespont, but by force drove the Lacedæmonians from out of all the rest of the sea. They intercepted some letters written to the ephors, which gave an account of this fatal overthrow, after their short laconic manner. "Our hopes are at an end. Mindarus is slain. The men starve. We know not what to do."

The soldiers who followed Alcibiades in his last fight were so exalted with their success, and felt that degree of pride, that, looking on themselves as invincible, they disdained to mix with the other soldiers, who had been often overcome. For it happened not long before, Thrasyllus had received a defeat near Ephesus, and, upon that occasion, the Ephesians erected their brazen trophy to the disgrace of the Athenians. The soldiers of Alcibiades reproached those who were under the command of Thrasyllus with this misfortune, at the same time magnifying themselves and their own commander, and it went so far that they would not exercise with them, nor lodge in the same quarters. But soon after, Pharnabazus, with a great force of horse and foot, falling upon the soldiers of Thrasyllus, as they were laying waste the territory of Abydos, Alcibiades came to their aid, routed Pharnabazus, and, together with Thrasyllus, pursued him till it was night; and in this action the troops united, and returned together to the camp, rejoicing and congratulating one another. The next day he erected a trophy, and then proceeded to lay waste with fire and sword the whole province which was under Pharnabazus, where none ventured to resist; and he took divers priests and priestesses, but released them without ransom. He prepared next to attack the Chalcedonians, who had revolted from the Athenians, and had received a Lacedæmonian governor and garrison. But having intelligence that they had removed their corn and cattle out of the fields, and were conveying it all to the Bithynians, who were their friends, he drew down his army to the frontier of the Bithynians, and then sent a herald to charge them with this proceeding. The Bithynians, terrified at his approach, delivered up to him the booty, and entered into alliance with him.

Afterwards he proceeded to the siege of Chalcedon, and enclosed it with a wall from sea to sea. Pharnabazus advanced with his forces to raise the siege, and Hippocrates, the governor of the town, at the same time, gathering together all the strength he had, made a sally upon the Athenians. Alcibiades divided his army so as to engage them both at once, and not only forced Pharnabazus to a dishonorable flight, but defeated Hippocrates, and killed him and a number of the soldiers with him. After this he sailed into the Hellespont, in order to raise supplies of money, and took the city of Selymbria, in which action, through his precipitation, he exposed himself to great danger. For some within the town had undertaken to betray it into his hands, and, by agreement, were to give him a signal by a lighted torch about midnight. But one of the conspirators beginning to repent himself of the design, the rest, for fear of being discovered, were driven to give the signal before the appointed hour. Alcibiades, as soon as he saw the torch lifted up in the air, though his army was not in readiness to march, ran instantly towards the walls, taking with him about thirty men only, and commanding the rest of the army to follow him with all possible speed. When he came thither, he found the gate opened for him, and entered with his thirty men, and about twenty more light-armed men, who were come up to them. They were no sooner in the city, but he perceived the Selymbrians all armed, coming down upon him; so that there was no hope of escaping if he stayed to receive them; and, on the other hand, having been always successful till that day, wherever he commanded, he could not endure to be defeated and fly. So, requiring silence by sound of a trumpet, he commanded one of his men to make proclamation that the Selymbrians should not take arms against the Athenians. This cooled such of the inhabitants as were fiercest for the fight, for they supposed that all their enemies were within the walls, and it raised the hopes of others who were disposed to an accommodation. Whilst they were parleying, and propositions making on one side and the other, Alcibiades's whole army came up to the town. And now, conjecturing rightly, that the Selymbrians were well inclined to peace, and fearing lest the city might be sacked by the Thracians, who came in great numbers to his army to serve as volunteers, out of kindness for him, he commanded them all to retreat without the walls. And upon the submission of the Selymbrians, he saved them from being pillaged, only taking of them a sum of money, and, after placing an Athenian garrison in the town, departed.

During this action, the Athenian captains who besieged Chalcedon concluded a treaty with Pharnabazus upon these articles: That he should give them a sum of money; that the Chalcedonians should return to the subjection of Athens; and that the Athenians should make no inroad into the province whereof Pharnabazus was governor; and Pharnabazus was also to provide safe conducts for the Athenian ambassadors to the king of Persia. Afterwards, when Alcibiades returned thither, Pharnabazus required that he also should be sworn to the treaty; but he refused it, unless Pharnabazus would swear at the same time. When the treaty was sworn to on both sides Alcibiades went against the Byzantines, who had revolted from the Athenians, and drew a line of circumvallation about the city. But Anaxilaus and Lycurgus, together with some others, having undertaken to betray the city to him upon his engagement to preserve the lives and property of the inhabitants, he caused a report to be spread abroad, as if, by reason of some unexpected movement in Ionia, he should be obliged to raise the siege. And, accordingly, that day he made a show to depart with his whole fleet; but returned the same night, and went ashore with all his men at arms, and, silently and undiscovered, marched up to the walls. At the same time, his ships rowed into the harbor with all possible violence, coming on with much fury, and with great shouts and outcries. The Byzantines, thus surprised and astonished, while they all hurried to the defence of their port and shipping, gave opportunity to those who favored the Athenians, securely to receive Alcibiades into the city. Yet the enterprise was not accomplished without fighting, for the Peloponnesians, Bœotians, and Megarians not only repulsed those who came out of the ships, and forced them on board again, but, hearing that the Athenians were entered on the other side, drew up in order, and went to meet them. Alcibiades, however, gained the victory after some sharp fighting, in which he himself had the command of the right wing, and Theramenes of the left, and took about three hundred, who survived of the enemy, prisoners of war. After the battle, not one of the Byzantines was slain, or driven out of the city, according to the terms upon which the city was put into his hands, that they should receive no prejudice in life or property. And thus Anaxilaus, being afterwards accused at Lacedæmon for this treason, neither disowned nor professed to be ashamed of the action; for he urged that he was not a Lacedæmonian, but a Byzantine, and saw not Sparta, by Byzantium, in extreme danger; the city so blockaded that it was not possible to bring in any new provisions, and the Peloponnesians and Bœotians, who were in garrison, devouring the old stores, whilst the Byzantines, with their wives and children, were starving; that he had not, therefore, betrayed his country to enemies, but had delivered it from the calamities of war, and had but followed the example of the most worthy Lacedæmonians, who esteemed nothing to be honorable and just, but what was profitable for their country. The Lacedæmonians, upon hearing his defence, respected it, and discharged all that were accused.

And now Alcibiades began to desire to see his native country again, or rather to show his fellow-citizens a person who had gained so many victories for them. He set sail for Athens, the ships that accompanied him, being adorned with great numbers of shields and other spoils, and towing after them many galleys taken from the enemy, and the ensigns and ornaments of many others which he had sunk and destroyed; all of them together amounting to two hundred. Little credit, perhaps, can be given to what Duris the Samian, who professed to be descended from Alcibiades, adds, that Chrysogonus, who had gained a victory at the Pythian games, played upon his flute for the galleys, whilst the oars kept time with the music; and that Callippides, the tragedian, attired in his buskins, his purple robes, and other ornaments used in the theatre, gave the word to the rowers, and that the admiral galley entered into the port with a purple sail. Neither Theopompus, nor Ephorus, nor Xenophon, mentioned them. Nor, indeed, is it credible, that one who returned from so long an exile, and such variety of misfortunes, should come home to his countrymen in the style of revellers breaking up from a drinking-party. On the contrary, he entered the harbor full of fear, nor would he venture to go on shore, till, standing on the deck, he saw Euryptolemus, his cousin, and others of his friends and acquaintance, who were ready to receive him, and invited him to land. As soon as he was landed, the multitude who came out to meet him scarcely seemed so much as to see any of the other captains, but came in throngs about Alcibiades, and saluted him with loud acclamations, and still followed him; those who could press near him crowned him with garlands, and they who could not come up so close yet stayed to behold him afar off, and the old men pointed him out, and showed him to the young ones. Nevertheless, this public joy was mixed with some tears, and the present happiness was allayed by the remembrance of the miseries they had endured. They made reflections, that they could not have so unfortunately miscarried in Sicily, or been defeated in any of their other expectations, if they had left the management of their affairs formerly, and the command of their forces, to Alcibiades, since, upon his undertaking the administration, when they were in a manner driven from the sea, and could scarce defend the suburbs of their city by land, and, at the same time, were miserably distracted with intestine factions, he had raised them up from this low and deplorable condition, and had not only restored them to their ancient dominion of the sea, but had also made them everywhere victorious over their enemies on land.

There had been a decree for recalling him from his banishment already passed by the people, at the instance of Critias, the son of Callæschrus, as appears by his elegies, in which he puts Alcibiades in mind of this service:—

> "From my proposal did that edict come,
> Which from your tedious exile brought you home,
> The public vote at first was moved by me,
> And my voice put the seal to the decree."

The people being summoned to an assembly, Alcibiades came in amongst them, and first bewailed and lamented his own sufferings, and, in gentle terms complaining of the usage he had received, imputed all to his hard fortune, and some ill genius that attended him: then he spoke at large of their prospects, and exhorted them to courage and good hope. The people crowned him with crowns of gold, and created him general, both at land and sea, with absolute power. They also made a decree that his estate should be restored to him, and that the Eumolpidæ and the holy heralds should absolve him from the curses which they had solemnly pronounced against him by sentence of the people. Which when all the rest obeyed, Theodorus, the high-priest, excused himself, "For," said he, "if he is innocent, I never cursed him."

But notwithstanding the affairs of Alcibiades went so prosperously, and so much to his glory, yet many were still somewhat disturbed, and looked upon the time of his arrival to be ominous. For on the day that he came into the port, the feast of the goddess Minerva, which they call the Plynteria, was kept. It is the twenty-fifth day of Thargelion, when the Praxiergidæ solemnize their secret rites, taking all the ornaments from off her image, and keeping the part of the temple where it stands close covered. Hence the Athenians esteem this day most inauspicious, and never undertake any thing of importance upon it; and, therefore, they imagined that the goddess did not receive Alcibiades graciously and propitiously, thus hiding her face and rejecting him. Yet, notwithstanding, every thing succeeded according to his wish. When the one hundred galleys, that were to return with him, were fitted out and ready to sail, an honorable zeal detained him till the celebration of the mysteries was over. For ever since Decelea had been occupied, as the enemy commanded the roads leading from Athens to Eleusis, the procession, being conducted by sea, had not been performed with any proper solemnity; they were forced to omit the sacrifices and dances and other holy ceremonies, which had usually been performed in the way, when they led forth Iacchus. Alcibiades, therefore, judged it would be a glorious action, which would do honor to the gods and gain him esteem with men, if he restored the ancient splendor to these rites, escorting the procession again by land, and protecting it with his army in the face of the enemy. For either, if Agis stood still and did not oppose, it would very much diminish and obscure his reputation, or, in the other alternative, Alcibiades would engage in a holy war, in the cause of the gods, and in defence of the most sacred and solemn ceremonies; and this in the sight of his country, where he should have all his fellow-citizens witnesses of his valor. As soon as he had resolved upon this design, and had communicated it to the Eumolpidæ and heralds, he placed sentinels on the tops of the hills, and at the break of day sent forth his scouts. And then taking with him the priests and Initiates[6] and the Initiators, and encompassing them with his soldiers, he conducted them with great order and profound silence; an august and venerable procession,

[6] Mystæ and Mystagogi.

wherein all who did not envy him said, he performed at once the office of a high-priest and of a general. The enemy did not dare to attempt any thing against them, and thus he brought them back in safety to the city. Upon which, as he was exalted in his own thought, so the opinion which the people had of his conduct was raised to that degree, that they looked upon their armies as irresistible and invincible while he commanded them; and he so won, indeed, upon the lower and meaner sort of people, that they passionately desired to have him "tyrant" over them, and some of them did not scruple to tell him so, and to advise him to put himself out of the reach of envy, by abolishing the laws and ordinances of the people, and suppressing the idle talkers that were ruining the state, that so he might act and take upon him the management of affairs, without standing in fear of being called to an account.

How far his own inclinations led him to usurp sovereign power, is uncertain, but the most considerable persons in the city were so much afraid of it, that they hastened him on ship-board as speedily as they could, appointing the colleagues whom he chose, and allowing him all other things as he desired. Thereupon he set sail with a fleet of one hundred ships, and, arriving at Andros, he there fought with and defeated as well the inhabitants as the Lacedæmonians who assisted them. He did not, however, take the city; which gave the first occasion to his enemies for all their accusations against him. Certainly, if ever man was ruined by his own glory, it was Alcibiades. For his continual success had produced such an idea of his courage and conduct, that, if he failed in any thing he undertook, it was imputed to his neglect, and no one would believe it was through want of power. For they thought nothing was too hard for him, if he went about it in good earnest. They fancied, every day, that they should hear news of the reduction of Chios, and of the rest of Ionia, and grew impatient that things were not effected as fast and as rapidly as they could wish for them. They never considered how extremely money was wanting, and that, having to carry on war with an enemy who had supplies of all things from a great king, he was often forced to quit his armament, in order to procure money and provisions for the subsistence of his soldiers. This it was which gave occasion for the last accusation which was made against him. For Lysander, being sent from Lacedæmon with a commission to be admiral of their fleet, and being furnished by Cyrus with a great sum of money, gave every sailor four obols a day, whereas before they had but three. Alcibiades could hardly allow his men three obols, and therefore was constrained to go into Caria to furnish himself with money. He left the care of the fleet, in his absence, to Antiochus, an experienced seaman, but rash and inconsiderate, who had express orders from Alcibiades not to engage, though the enemy provoked him. But he slighted and disregarded these directions to that degree, that, having made ready his own galley and another, he stood for Ephesus, where the enemy lay, and, as he sailed before the heads of their galleys, used every provocation possible, both in words and deeds. Lysander at first manned out a few ships, and pursued him. But all the Athenian ships coming in to his assistance, Lysander, also, brought up his whole fleet, which gained an entire victory. He slew Antiochus himself, took many men and ships, and erected a trophy.

As soon as Alcibiades heard this news, he returned to Samos, and loosing from thence with his whole fleet, came and offered battle to Lysander. But Lysander, content with the victory he had gained, would not stir. Amongst others in the army who hated Alcibiades, Thrasybulus, the son of Thrason, was his particular enemy, and went purposely to Athens to accuse him, and to exasperate his enemies in the city against him. Addressing the people, he represented that Alcibiades had ruined their affairs and lost their ships by mere self-conceited neglect of his duties, committing the government of the army, in his absence, to men who gained his favor by drinking and scurrilous talking, whilst he wandered up and down at pleasure to raise money, giving himself up to every sort of luxury and excess amongst the courtesans of Abydos and Ionia, at a time when the enemy's navy were on the watch close at hand. It was also objected to him, that he had fortified a castle near Bisanthe in Thrace, for a safe retreat for himself, as one that either could not, or would not, live in his own country. The Athenians gave credit to these informations, and showed the resentment and displeasure which they had conceived against him, by choosing other generals.

As soon as Alcibiades heard of this, he immediately forsook the army, afraid of what might follow; and, collecting a body of mercenary soldiers, made war upon his own account against those Thracians who called themselves free, and acknowledged no king. By this means he amassed to himself a considerable treasure, and, at the same time, secured the bordering Greeks from the incursions of the barbarians.

Tydeus, Menander, and Adimantus, the new-made generals, were at that time posted at Ægospotami, with all the ships which the Athenians had left. From whence they were used to go out to sea every morning, and offer battle to Lysander, who lay near Lampsacus; and when they had done so, returning back again, lay, all the rest of the day, carelessly and without order, in contempt of the enemy. Alcibiades, who was not far off, did not think so slightly of their danger, nor neglect to let them know it, but, mounting his horse, came to the generals, and represented to them that they had chosen a very inconvenient station, where there was no safe harbor, and where they were distant from any town; so that they were constrained to send for their necessary provisions as far as Sestos. He also pointed out to them their carelessness in suffering the soldiers, when they went ashore, to disperse and wander up and down at their pleasure, while the enemy's fleet, under the command of one general, and strictly obedient to discipline, lay so very near them. He advised them to remove the fleet to Sestos. But the admirals not only disregarded what he said, but Tydeus, with insulting expressions, commanded him to be gone, saying, that now not he, but others, had the command of the forces. Alcibiades, suspecting something of treachery in them, departed, and told his friends, who accompanied him out of the camp, that if the generals had not used him with such insupportable contempt, he would within a few days have forced the Lacedæmonians, however unwilling, either to have fought the Athenians at sea, or to have deserted their ships. Some looked upon this as a piece of ostentation only; others said, the thing was probable, for that he might have brought down by land great numbers of the Thracian cavalry and archers, to assault and disorder them in their camp. The event, however, soon made it evident how rightly he had judged of the errors which the Athenians committed. For Lysander fell upon them on a sudden, when they least suspected it, with such fury that Conon alone, with eight galleys, escaped him; all the rest, which were about two hundred, he took and carried away, together with three thousand prisoners, whom he put to death. And within a short time after, he took Athens itself, burnt all the ships which he found there, and demolished their long walls.

After this Alcibiades, standing in dread of the Lacedæmonians, who were now masters both at sea and land, retired into Bithynia. He sent thither great treasure before him, took much with him, but left much more in the castle where he had before resided. But he lost great part of his wealth in Bithynia, being robbed by some Thracians who lived in those parts, and thereupon determined to go to the court of Artaxerxes, not doubting but that the king, if he would make trial of his abilities, would find him not inferior to Themistocles, besides that he was recommended by a more honorable cause. For he went, not as Themistocles did, to offer his services against his fellow-citizens, but against their enemies, and to implore the king's aid for the defence of his country. He concluded that Pharnabazus would most readily procure him a safe conduct, and therefore went into Phrygia to him, and continued to dwell there some time, paying him great respect, and being honorably treated by him. The Athenians, in the mean time, were miserably afflicted at their loss of empire, but when they were deprived of liberty also, and Lysander set up thirty despotic rulers in the city, in their ruin now they began to turn to those thoughts which, while safety was yet possible, they would not entertain; they acknowledged and bewailed their former errors and follies, and judged this second ill-usage of Alcibiades to be of all the most inexcusable. For he was rejected, without any fault committed by himself; and only because they were incensed against his subordinate for having shamefully lost a few ships, they much more shamefully deprived the commonwealth of its most valiant and accomplished general. Yet in this sad state of affairs, they had still some faint hopes left them, nor would they utterly despair of the Athenian commonwealth, while Alcibiades was safe. For they persuaded themselves that if before, when he was an exile, he could not content himself to live idly and at ease, much less now, if he could find any favorable opportunity, would he endure the insolence of the Lacedæmonians, and the outrages of the Thirty. Nor was it an absurd thing in the people to entertain such imaginations, when the Thirty themselves were so very solicitous to be informed and to get intelligence of all his actions and designs. In fine, Critias represented to Lysander that the Lacedæmonians could never securely enjoy the dominion of Greece, till the Athenian democracy was absolutely destroyed; and though now the people of Athens seemed quietly and patiently to submit to so small a number of governors, yet so long as Alcibiades lived, the knowledge of this fact would never suffer them to acquiesce in their present circumstances.

Yet Lysander would not be prevailed upon by these representations, till at last he received secret orders from the magistrates of Lacedæmon, expressly requiring him to get Alcibiades despatched: whether it was that they feared his energy and boldness in enterprising what was hazardous, or that it was done to gratify king Agis. Upon receipt of this order, Lysander sent away a messenger to Pharnabazus, desiring him to put it in execution. Pharnabazus committed the affair to Magæus, his brother, and to his uncle Susamithres. Alcibiades resided at that time in a small village in Phrygia, together with Timandra, a mistress of his. As he slept, he had this dream: he thought himself attired in his mistress's habit, and that she, holding him in her arms, dressed his head and painted his face as if he had been a woman; others say, he dreamed that he saw Magæus cut off his head and burn his body; at any rate, it was but a little while before his death that he had these visions. Those who were sent to assassinate him had not courage enough to enter the house, but surrounded it first, and set it on fire. Alcibiades, as soon as he perceived it, getting together great quantities of clothes and furniture, threw them upon the fire to choke it, and, having wrapped his cloak about his left arm, and holding his naked sword in his right, he cast himself into the middle of the fire, and escaped securely through it, before his clothes were burnt. The barbarians, as soon as they saw him, retreated, and none of them durst stay to expect him, or to engage with him, but, standing at a distance, they slew him with their darts and arrows. When he was dead, the barbarians departed, and Timandra took up his dead body, and, covering and wrapping it up in her own robes, she buried it as decently and as honorably as her circumstances would allow. It is said, that the famous Lais, who was called the Corinthian, though she was a native of Hyccara, a small town in Sicily, from whence she was brought a captive, was the daughter of this Timandra. There are some who agree with this account of Alcibiades's death in all points, except that they impute the cause of it neither to Pharnabazus, nor Lysander, nor the Lacedæmonians: but, they say, he was keeping with him a young lady of a noble house, whom he had debauched, and that her brothers, not being able to endure the indignity, set fire by night to the house where he was living, and, as he endeavored to save himself from the flames, slew him with their darts, in the manner just related.

CORIOLANUS

THE patrician house of the Marcii in Rome produced many men of distinction, and among the rest, Ancus Marcius, grandson to Numa by his daughter, and king after Tullus Hostilius. Of the same family were also Publius and Quintus Marcius, which two conveyed into the city the best and most abundant supply of water they have at Rome. As likewise Censorinus, who, having been twice chosen censor by the people, afterwards himself induced them to make a law that nobody should bear that office twice. But Caius Marcius, of whom I now write, being left an orphan, and brought up under the widowhood of his mother, has shown us by experience, that, although the early loss of a father may be attended with other disadvantages, yet it can hinder none from being either virtuous or eminent in the world, and that it is no obstacle to true goodness and excellence; however bad men may be pleased to lay the blame of their corruptions upon that misfortune and the neglect of them in their minority. Nor is he less an evidence to the truth of their opinion, who conceive that a generous and worthy nature without proper discipline, like a rich soil without culture, is apt, with its better fruits, to produce also much that is bad and faulty. While the force and vigor of his soul, and a persevering constancy in all he undertook, led him successfully into many noble achievements, yet, on the other side, also, by indulging the vehemence of his passion, and through an obstinate reluctance to yield or accommodate his humors and sentiments to those of people about him, he rendered himself incapable of acting and associating with others. Those who saw with admiration how proof his nature was against all the softnesses of pleasure, the hardships of service and the allurements of gain, while allowing to that universal firmness of his the respective names of temperance, fortitude, and justice, yet, in the life of the citizen and the statesman, could not choose but be disgusted at the severity and ruggedness of his deportment, and with his overbearing, haughty, and imperious temper. Education and study, and the favors of the muses, confer no greater benefit on those that seek them, than these humanizing and civilizing lessons, which teach our natural qualities to submit to the limitations prescribed by reason, and to avoid the wildness of extremes.

Those were times at Rome in which that kind of worth was most esteemed which displayed itself in military achievements; one evidence of which we find in the Latin word for virtue, which is properly equivalent to manly courage. As if valor and all virtue had been the same thing, they used as the common term the name of the particular excellence. But Marcius, having a more passionate inclination than any of that age for feats of war, began at once, from his very childhood, to handle arms; and feeling that adventitious implements and artificial arms would effect little, and be of small use to such as have not their native and natural weapons well fixed and prepared for service, he so exercised and inured his body to all sorts of activity and encounter, that, besides the lightness of a racer, he had a weight in close seizures and wrestlings with an enemy, from which it was hard for any to disengage himself; so that his competitors at home in displays of bravery, loath to own themselves inferior in that respect, were wont to ascribe their deficiencies to his strength of body, which they said no resistance and no fatigue could exhaust.

The first time he went out to the wars, being yet a stripling, was when Tarquinius Superbus, who had been king of Rome and was afterwards expelled, after many unsuccessful attempts, now entered upon his last effort, and proceeded to hazard all as it were upon a single throw. A great number of the Latins and other people of Italy joined their forces, and were marching with him toward the city, to procure his restoration; not, however, so much out of a desire to serve and oblige Tarquin, as to gratify their own fear and envy at the increase of the Roman greatness, which they were anxious to check and reduce. The armies met and engaged in a decisive battle, in the vicissitudes of which, Marcius, while fighting bravely in the dictator's presence, saw a Roman soldier struck down at a little distance, and immediately stepped in and stood before him, and slew his assailant. The general, after having gained the victory, crowned him for this act, one of the first, with a garland of oaken branches; it being the Roman custom thus to adorn those who had saved the life of a citizen; whether that the law intended some special honor to the oak, in memory of the Arcadians, a people the oracle had made famous by the name of acorn-eaters;[1] or whether the reason of it was because they might easily, and in all places where they fought, have plenty of oak for that purpose; or, finally, whether the oaken wreath, being sacred to Jupiter, the guardian of the city, might, therefore, be thought a proper ornament for one who preserved a citizen. And the oak, in truth, is the tree which bears the most and the prettiest fruit of any that grow wild, and is the strongest of all that are under cultivation; its acorns were the principal diet of the first mortals, and the honey found in it gave them drink. I may say, too, it furnished fowl and other creatures as dainties, in producing mistletoe for birdlime to ensnare them. In this battle, meantime, it is stated that Castor and Pollux appeared, and, immediately after the battle, were seen at Rome just by the fountain where their temple now stands, with their horses foaming with sweat, and told the news of the victory to the people in the Forum. The fifteenth of July, being the day of this conquest, became consequently a solemn holiday sacred to the Twin Brothers.

It may be observed, in general, that when young men arrive early at fame and repute, if they are of a nature but slightly touched with emulation, this early attainment is apt to extinguish their thirst and satiate their small appetite; whereas the first distinctions of more solid and weighty characters do but stimulate and quicken them and take them away, like a wind, in the pursuit of honor; they look upon these marks and testimonies to their virtue not as a recompense received for what they have already done, but as a pledge given by themselves of what they will perform hereafter, ashamed now to forsake or underlive the credit they have won, or, rather, not to exceed and obscure all that is gone before by the lustre of their following actions. Marcius, having a spirit of this noble make, was ambitious always to surpass himself, and did nothing, how extraor-

[1] "You ask me for Arcadia," said the oracle to the Spartans, when designing their early invasion. "You ask a great thing, I will not grant it. There are in Arcadia many acorn-eaters ready to prevent you. I, however, grudge you nothing. I grant you to dance about Tegea, and measure out the fair plain by the line."

dinary soever, but he thought he was bound to outdo it at the next occasion; and ever desiring to give continual fresh instances of his prowess, he added one exploit to another, and heaped up trophies upon trophies, so as to make it matter of contest also among his commanders, the later still vying with the earlier, which should pay him the greatest honor and speak highest in his commendation. Of all the numerous wars and conflicts in those days, there was not one from which he returned without laurels and rewards. And, whereas others made glory the end of their daring, the end of his glory was his mother's gladness; the delight she took to hear him praised and to see him crowned, and her weeping for joy in his embraces, rendered him, in his own thoughts, the most honored and most happy person in the world. Epaminondas is similarly said to have acknowledged his feeling, that it was the greatest felicity of his whole life that his father and mother survived to hear of his successful generalship and his victory at Leuctra. And he had the advantage, indeed, to have both his parents partake with him, and enjoy the pleasure of his good fortune. But Marcius, believing himself bound to pay his mother Volumnia all that gratitude and duty which would have belonged to his father, had he also been alive, could never satiate himself in his tenderness and respect to her. He took a wife, also, at her request and wish, and continued, even after he had children, to live still with his mother, without parting families.

The repute of his integrity and courage had, by this time, gained him a considerable influence and authority in Rome, when the senate, favoring the wealthier citizens, began to be at variance with the common people, who made sad complaints of the rigorous and inhuman usage they received from the money-lenders. For as many as were behind with them, and had any sort of property, they stripped of all they had, by the way of pledges and sales; and such as through former exactions were reduced already to extreme indigence, and had nothing more to be deprived of, these they led away in person and put their bodies under constraint, notwithstanding the scars and wounds that they could show in attestation of their public services in numerous campaigns; the last of which had been against the Sabines, which they undertook upon a promise made by their rich creditors that they would treat them with more gentleness for the future, Marcus Valerius, the consul, having, by order from the senate, engaged also for the performance of it. But when, after they had fought courageously and beaten the enemy, there was, nevertheless, no moderation or forbearance used, and the senate also professed to remember nothing of that agreement, and sat without testifying the least concern to see them dragged away like slaves and their goods seized upon as formerly, there began now to be open disorders and dangerous meetings in the city; and the enemy, also, aware of the popular confusion, invaded and laid waste the country. And when the consuls now gave notice, that all who were of an age to bear arms should make their personal appearance, but found no one regard the summons, the members of the government, then coming to consult what course should be taken, were themselves again divided in opinion: some thought it most advisable to comply a little in favor of the poor, by relaxing their overstrained rights, and mitigating the extreme rigor of the law, while others withstood this proposal; Marcius in particular, with more vehemence than the rest, alleging that the business of money on either side was not the main thing in question, urged that this disorderly proceeding was but the first insolent step towards open revolt against the laws, which it would become the wisdom of the government to check at the earliest moment.

There had been frequent assemblies of the whole senate, within a small compass of time, about this difficulty, but without any certain issue; the poor commonalty, therefore, perceiving there was likely to be no redress of their grievances, on a sudden collected in a body, and, encouraging each other in their resolution, forsook the city with one accord, and seizing the hill which is now called the Holy Mount, sat down by the river Anio, without committing any sort of violence or seditious outrage, but merely exclaiming, as they went along, that they had this long time past been, in fact, expelled and excluded from the city by the cruelty of the rich; that Italy would everywhere afford them the benefit of air and water and a place of burial, which was all they could expect in the city, unless it were, perhaps, the privilege of being wounded and killed in time of war for the defence of their creditors. The senate, apprehending the consequences, sent the most moderate and popular men of their own order to treat with them.

Menenius Agrippa, their chief spokesman, after much entreaty to the people, and much plain speaking on behalf of the senate, concluded, at length, with the celebrated fable. "It once happened," he said, "that all the other members of a man mutinied against the stomach, which they accused as the only idle, uncontributing part in the whole body, while the rest were put to hardships and the expense of much labor to supply and minister to its appetites. The stomach, however, merely ridiculed the silliness of the members, who appeared not to be aware that the stomach certainly does receive the general nourishment, but only to return it again, and redistribute it amongst the rest. Such is the case," he said, "ye citizens, between you and the senate. The counsels and plans that are there duly digested, convey and secure to all of you, your proper benefit and support."

A reconciliation ensued, the senate acceding to the request of the people for the annual election of five protectors for those in need of succor, the same that are now called the tribunes of the people; and the first two they pitched upon were Junius Brutus and Sicinnius Vellutus, their leaders in the secession.

The city being thus united, the commons stood presently to their arms, and followed their commanders to the war with great alacrity. As for Marcius, though he was not a little vexed himself to see the populace prevail so far, and gain ground of the senators, and might observe many other patricians have the same dislike of the late concessions, he yet besought them not to yield at least to the common people in the zeal and forwardness they now showed for their country's service, but to prove that they were superior to them, not so much in power and riches, as in merit and worth.

The Romans were now at war with the Volscian nation, whose principal city was Corioli; when, therefore, Cominius the consul had invested this important place, the rest of the Volscians, fearing it would be taken, mustered up whatever force they could from all parts, to relieve it, designing to give the Romans battle before the city, and so attack them on both sides. Cominius, to avoid this inconvenience, divided his army, marching himself with one body to encounter the Volscians on their approach from without, and leaving Titus Lartius, one of the bravest Romans of his time, to command the other and continue the siege. Those within Corioli, despising now the smallness of their number, made a sally upon them, and prevailed at first, and pursued the Romans into their trenches. Here it was that Marcius, flying out with a slender company, and cutting those in pieces that first engaged him, obliged the other assailants to slacken their speed; and then, with loud cries, called upon the Romans to renew the battle. For he had, what Cato thought a great point in a soldier, not only strength of hand and stroke, but also a voice and look that of themselves were a terror to an enemy. Divers of his own party now rallying and making up to him, the enemies soon retreated; but Marcius, not content to see them draw off and retire, pressed hard upon the rear, and drove them, as they fled away in haste, to the very gates of their city; where, perceiving the Romans to fall back from their pursuit, beaten off by the multitude of darts poured in upon them from the walls, and that none of his followers had the hardiness to think of falling in pellmell among the fugitives and so entering a city full of enemies in arms, he, nevertheless, stood and urged them to the attempt, crying out, that fortune had now set open Corioli, not so much to shelter the vanquished, as to receive the conquerors. Seconded by a few that were willing to venture with him, he bore along through the crowd, made good his passage, and thrust himself into the gate through the midst of them, nobody at first daring to resist him. But when the citizens, on looking about, saw that a very small number had entered, they now took courage, and came up and attacked them. A combat ensued of the most extraordinary description, in which Marcius, by strength of hand, and swiftness of foot, and daring of soul, overpowering every one that he assailed, succeeded in driving the enemy to seek refuge, for the most part, in the interior of the town, while the remainder submitted, and threw down their arms; thus affording Lartius abundant opportunity to bring in the rest of the Romans with ease and safety.

Corioli being thus surprised and taken, the greater part of the soldiers employed themselves in spoiling and pillaging it, while Marcius indignantly reproached them, and exclaimed that it was a dishonorable and unworthy thing, when the consul and their fellow-citizens had now perhaps encountered the other Volscians, and were hazarding their lives in battle, basely to misspend the time in running up and down for booty, and, under a pretence of enriching themselves, keep out of danger. Few paid him any attention, but, putting himself at the head of these, he took the road by which the consul's army had marched before him, encouraging his companions, and beseeching them, as they went along, not to give up, and praying often to the gods, too, that he might be so happy as to arrive before the fight was over, and come seasonably up to assist Cominius, and partake in the peril of the action.

It was customary with the Romans of that age, when they were moving into battle array, and were on the point of taking up their bucklers, and girding their coats about them, to make at the same time an unwritten will, or verbal testament, and to name who should be their heirs, in the hearing of three or four witnesses. In this precise posture Marcius found them at his arrival, the enemy being advanced within view.

They were not a little disturbed by his first appearance, seeing him covered with blood and sweat, and attended with a small train; but when he hastily made up to the consul with gladness in his looks, giving him his hand, and recounting to him how the city had been taken, and when they saw Cominius also embrace and salute him, every one took fresh heart; those that were near enough hearing, and those that were at a distance guessing, what had happened; and all cried out to be led to battle. First, however, Marcius desired to know of him how the Volscians had arrayed their army, and where they had placed their best men, and on his answering that he took the troops of the Antiates in the centre to be their prime warriors, that would yield to none in bravery, "Let me then demand and obtain of you," said Marcius, "that we may be posted against them." The consul granted the request, with much admiration of his gallantry. And when the conflict began by the soldiers darting at each other, and Marcius sallied out before the rest, the Volscians opposed to him were not able to make head against him; wherever he fell in, he broke their ranks, and made a lane through them; but the parties turning again, and enclosing him on each side with their weapons, the consul, who observed the danger he was in, despatched some of the choicest men he had for his rescue. The conflict then growing warm and sharp about Marcius, and many falling dead in a little space, the Romans bore so hard upon the enemies, and pressed them with such violence, that they forced them at length to abandon their ground, and to quit the field. And, going now to prosecute the victory, they besought Marcius, tired out with his toils, and faint and heavy through the loss of blood, that he would retire to the camp. He replied, however, that weariness was not for conquerors, and joined with them in the pursuit. The rest of the Volscian army was in like manner defeated, great numbers killed, and no less taken captive.

The day after, when Marcius, with the rest of the army, presented themselves at the consul's tent, Cominius rose, and having rendered all due acknowledgment to the gods for the success of that enterprise, turned next to Marcius, and first of all delivered the strongest encomium upon his rare exploits, which he had partly been an eye-witness of himself, in the late battle, and had partly learned from the testimony of Lartius. And then he required him to choose a tenth part of all the treasure and horses and captives that had fallen into their hands, before any division should be made to others; besides which, he made him the special present of a horse with trappings and ornaments, in honor of his actions. The whole army applauded; Marcius, however, stepped forth, and declaring his thankful acceptance of the horse, and his gratification at the praises of his general, said, that all other things, which he could only regard rather as mercenary advantages than any significations of honor, he must waive, and should be content with the ordinary proportion of such rewards. "I have only," said he, "one special grace to beg, and this I hope you will not deny me. There was a certain hospitable friend of mine among the Volscians, a man of probity and virtue, who is become a prisoner, and from former wealth and freedom is now reduced to servitude. Among his many misfortunes let my intercession redeem him from the one of being sold as a common slave." Such a refusal and such a request on the part of Marcius were followed with yet louder acclamations; and he had many more admirers of this generous superiority to avarice, than of the bravery he had shown in battle. The very persons who conceived some envy and despite to see him so specially honored, could not but acknowledge, that one who so nobly could refuse reward, was beyond others worthy to receive it; and were more charmed with that virtue which made him despise advantage, than with any of those former actions that had gained him his title to it. It is the higher accomplishment to use money well than to use arms; but not to need it is more noble than to use it.

When the noise of approbation and applause ceased, Cominius, resuming, said, "It is idle, fellow-soldiers, to force and obtrude those other gifts of ours on one who is unwilling to accept them; let us, therefore, give him one of such a kind that he cannot well reject it; let us pass a vote, I mean, that he shall hereafter be called Coriolanus, unless you think that his performance at Corioli has itself anticipated any such resolution." Hence, therefore, he had his third name of Coriolanus, making it all the plainer that Caius was a personal proper name, and the second, or surname, Marcius, one common to his house and family; the third being a subsequent addition which used to be imposed either from some particular act or fortune, bodily characteristic, or good quality of the bearer. Just as the Greeks, too, gave additional names in old time, in some cases from some achievement, Soter, for example, and Callinicus; or personal appearance, as Physcon and Grypus; good qualities, Euergetes and Philadelphus; good fortune, Eudæmon, the title of the second Battus.[2] Several monarchs have also had names given them in mockery, as Antigonus was called Doson, and Ptolemy, Lathyrus. This sort of title was yet more common among the Romans. One of the Metelli was surnamed Diadematus, because he walked about for a long time with a bandage on his head, to conceal a scar; and another, of the same family, got the name of Celer, from the rapidity he displayed in giving a funeral entertainment of gladiators within a few days after his father's death, his speed and energy in doing which was thought extraordinary. There are some, too, who even at this day take names from certain casual incidents at their nativity; a child that is born when his father is away from home is called Proculus;

[2] Soter, Saviour; Callinīcus, Victorious; Physcon, Fat-paunch; Grypus, Hook-nose; Euergetes, Benefactor; Philadelphus, Brotherly; Eudæmon, Fortunate; Doson, Going-to-give; Lathyrus is not certain.

or Postumus, if after his decease; and when twins come into the world, and one dies at the birth, the survivor has the name of Vopiscus. From bodily peculiarities they derive not only their Syllas and Nigers, but their Cæci and Claudii; wisely endeavoring to accustom their people not to reckon either the loss of sight, or any other bodily misfortune, as a matter of disgrace to them, but to answer to such names without shame, as if they were really their own. But this discussion better befits another place.

The war against the Volscians was no sooner at an end, than the popular orators revived domestic troubles, and raised another sedition, without any new cause of complaint or just grievance to proceed upon, but merely turning the very mischiefs that unavoidably ensued from their former contests into a pretext against the patricians. The greatest part of their arable land had been left unsown and without tillage, and the time of war allowing them no means or leisure to import provision from other countries, there was an extreme scarcity. The movers of the people then observing, that there was no corn to be bought, and that, if there had been, they had no money to buy it, began to calumniate the wealthy with false stories, and whisper it about, as if they, out of malice, had purposely contrived the famine. Meanwhile, there came an embassy from the Velitrani, proposing to deliver up their city to the Romans, and desiring they would send some new inhabitants to people it, as a late pestilential disease had swept away so many of the natives, that there was hardly a tenth part remaining of their whole community. This necessity of the Velitrani was considered by all more prudent people as most opportune in the present state of affairs; since the dearth made it needful to ease the city of its superfluous members, and they were in hope also, at the same time, to dissipate the gathering sedition by ridding themselves of the more violent and heated partisans, and discharging, so to say, the elements of disease and disorder in the state. The consuls, therefore, singled out such citizens to supply the desolation at Velitræ, and gave notice to others, that they should be ready to march against the Volscians, with the politic design of preventing intestine broils by employment abroad, and in the hope, that when rich as well as poor, plebeians and patricians, should be mingled again in the same army and the same camp, and engage in one common service for the public, it would mutually dispose them to reconciliation and friendship.

But Sicinnius and Brutus, the popular orators, interposed, crying out, that the consuls disguised the most cruel and barbarous action in the world under that mild and plausible name of a colony, and were simply precipitating so many poor citizens into a mere pit of destruction, bidding them settle down in a country where the air was charged with disease, and the ground covered with dead bodies, and expose themselves to the evil influence of a strange and angered deity. And then, as if it would not satisfy their hatred to destroy some by hunger, and offer others to the mercy of a plague, they must proceed to involve them also in a needless war of their own making, that no calamity might be wanting to complete the punishment of the citizens for refusing to submit to that of slavery to the rich.

By such addresses, the people were so possessed, that none of them would appear upon the consular summons to be enlisted for the war; and they showed entire aversion to the proposal for a new plantation; so that the senate was at a loss what to say or do. But Marcius, who began now to bear himself higher and to feel confidence in his past actions, conscious, too, of the admiration of the best and greatest men of Rome, openly took the lead in opposing the favorers of the people. The colony was despatched to Velitræ, those that were chosen by lot being compelled to depart upon high penalties; and when they obstinately persisted in refusing to enroll themselves for the Volscian service, he mustered up his own clients, and as many others as could be wrought upon by persuasion, and with these made an inroad into the territories of the Antiates, where, finding a considerable quantity of corn, and collecting much booty, both of cattle and prisoners, he reserved nothing for himself in private, but returned safe to Rome, while those that ventured out with him were seen laden with pillage, and driving their prey before them. This sight filled those that had stayed at home with regret for their perverseness, with envy at their fortunate fellow-citizens, and with feelings of dislike to Marcius, and hostility to his growing reputation and power, which might probably be used against the popular interest.

Not long after he stood for the consulship; when, however, the people began to relent and incline to favor him, being sensible what a shame it would be to repulse and affront a man of his birth and merit, after he had done them so many signal services. It was usual for those who stood for offices among them to solicit and address themselves personally to the citizens, presenting themselves in the forum with the toga on alone, and no tunic under it; either to promote their supplications by the humility of their dress, or that such as had received wounds might more readily display those marks of their fortitude. Certainly, it was not out of suspicion of bribery and corruption that they required all such petitioners for their favor to appear ungirt and open, without any close garment; as it was much later, and many ages after this, that buying and selling crept in at their elections, and money became an ingredient in the public suffrages; proceeding thence to attempt their tribunals, and even attack their camps, till, by hiring the valiant, and enslaving iron to silver, it grew master of the state and turned their commonwealth into a monarchy. For it was well and truly said that the first destroyer of the liberties of a people is he who first gave them bounties and largesses. At Rome the mischief seems to have stolen secretly in, and by little and little, not being at once discerned and taken notice of. It is not certainly known who the man was that did there first either bribe the citizens, or corrupt the courts; whereas, in Athens, Anytus, the son of Anthemion, is said to have been the first that gave money to the judges, when on his trial, toward the latter end of the Peloponnesian war, for letting the fort of Pylos fall into the hands of the enemy; in a period while the pure and golden race of men were still in possession of the Roman forum.

Marcius, therefore, as the fashion of candidates was showing the scars and gashes that were still visible on his body, from the many conflicts in which he had signalized himself during a service of seventeen years together they were, so to say, put out of countenance at this display of merit, and told one another that they ought in common modesty to create him consul. But when the day of election was now come, and Marcius appeared in the forum, with a pompous train of senators attending him, and the patricians all manifested greater concern, and seemed to be exerting greater efforts than they had ever done before on the like occasion, the commons then fell off again from the kindness they had conceived for him, and in the place of their late benevolence, began to feel something of indignation and envy; passions assisted by the fear they entertained, that if a man of such aristocratic temper, and so influential among the patricians, should be invested with the power which that office would give him, he might employ it to deprive the people of all that liberty which was yet left them. In conclusion, they rejected Marcius. Two other names were announced, to the great mortification of the senators, who felt as if the indignity reflected rather upon themselves than on Marcius. He, for his part, could not bear the affront with any patience. He had always indulged his temper, and had regarded the proud and contentious element of human nature as a sort of nobleness and magnanimity; reason and discipline had not imbued him with that solidity and equanimity which enters so largely into the virtues of the statesman. He had never learned how essential it is for any one who undertakes public business, and desires to deal with mankind, to avoid above all things that self-will, which, as Plato says, belongs to the family of solitude; and to pursue, above all things, that capacity so generally ridiculed, of submission to ill-treatment. Marcius, straightforward and direct, and possessed with the idea that to vanquish and overbear all opposition is the true part of bravery, and never imagining that it was the weakness and womanishness of his nature that broke out, so to say, in these ulcerations of anger, retired, full of fury and bitterness against the people. The young patricians, too, all that were proudest and most conscious of their noble birth, had always been devoted to his interest, and, adhering to him now, with a fidelity that did him no good, aggravated his resentment with the expression of their indignation and condolence. He had been their captain, and their willing instructor in the arts of war, when out upon expeditions, and their model in that true emulation and love of excellence which makes men extol, without envy or jealousy, each other's brave achievements.

In the midst of these distempers a large quantity of corn reached Rome, a great part bought up in Italy, but an equal amount sent as a present from Syracuse, from Gelo, then reigning there. Many began now to hope well of their affairs, supposing the city, by this means, would be delivered at once, both of its want and discord. A council, therefore, being presently held, the people came flocking about the senate-house, eagerly awaiting the issue of that deliberation, expecting that the market-prices would now be less cruel, and that what had come as a gift would be distributed as such. There were some within who so advised the senate; but Marcius, standing up, sharply inveighed against those who spoke in favor of the multitude, calling them flatterers of the rabble, traitors to the nobility, and alleging, that, by such gratifications, they did but cherish those ill seeds of boldness and petulance that had been sown among the people, to their own prejudice, which they should have done well to observe and stifle at their first appearance, and not have suffered the plebeians to grow so strong, by granting them magistrates of such authority as the tribunes. They were, indeed, even now formidable to the state, since every thing they desired was granted them; no constraint was put on their will; they refused obedience to the consuls, and, overthrowing all law and magistracy, gave the title of magistrate to their private factious leaders. "When things are come to such a pass, for us to sit here and decree largesses and bounties for them, like those Greeks where the populace is supreme and absolute, what would it be else," said he, "but to take their disobedience into pay, and maintain it for the common ruin of us all? They certainly cannot look upon these liberalities as a reward of public service, which they know they have so often deserted; nor yet of those secessions, by which they openly renounced their country; much less of the calumnies and slanders they have been always so ready to entertain against the senate; but will rather conclude that a bounty which seems to have no other visible cause or reason, must needs be the effect of our fear and flattery; and will, therefore, set no limit to their disobedience, nor ever cease from disturbances and sedition. Concession is mere madness; if we have any wisdom and resolution at all, we shall, on the contrary, never rest till we have recovered from them that tribunician power they have extorted from us; as being a plain subversion of the consulship, and a perpetual ground of separation in our city, that is no longer one, as heretofore, but has in this received such a wound and rupture, as is never likely to close and unite again, or suffer us to be of one mind, and to give over inflaming our distempers, and being a torment to each other."

Marcius, with much more to this purpose, succeeded, to an extraordinary degree, in inspiring the younger men with the same furious sentiments, and had almost all the wealthy on his side, who cried him up as the only person their city had, superior alike to force and flattery; some of the older men, however, opposed him, suspecting the consequences. As, indeed, there came no good of it; for the tribunes, who were present, perceiving how the proposal of Marcius took, ran out into the crowd with exclamations, calling on the plebeians to stand together, and come in to their assistance. The assembly met and soon became tumultuous. The sum of what Marcius had spoken, having been reported to the people, excited them to such fury, that they were ready to break in upon the senate. The tribunes prevented this, by laying all the blame on Coriolanus, whom, therefore, they cited by their messengers to come before them, and defend himself. And when he contemptuously repulsed the officers who brought him the summons, they came themselves, with the Ædiles, or overseers of the market, proposing to carry him away by force, and, accordingly, began to lay hold on his person. The patricians, however, coming to his rescue, not only thrust off the tribunes, but also beat the Ædiles, that were their seconds in the quarrel; night, approaching, put an end to the contest. But as soon as it was day, the consuls, observing the people to be highly exasperated, and that they ran from all quarters and gathered in the forum, were afraid for the whole city, so that, convening the senate afresh, they desired them to advise how they might best compose and pacify the incensed multitude by equitable language and indulgent decrees; since, if they wisely considered the state of things, they would find that it was no time to stand upon terms of honor, and a mere point of glory; such a critical conjuncture called for gentle methods, and for temperate and humane counsels. The majority, therefore, of the senators giving way, the consuls proceeded to pacify the people in the best manner they were able, answering gently to such imputations and charges as had been cast upon the senate, and using much tenderness and moderation in the admonitions and reproofs they gave them. On the point of the price of provisions, they said, there should be no difference at all between them. When a great part of the commonalty was grown cool, and it appeared from their orderly and peaceful behavior that they had been very much appeased by what they had heard, the tribunes, standing up, declared, in the name of the people, that since the senate was pleased to act soberly and do them reason, they, likewise, should be ready to yield in all that was fair and equitable on their side; they must insist, however, that Marcius should give in his answer to the several charges as follows: first, could he deny that he instigated the senate to overthrow the government and annul the privileges of the people? and, in the next place, when called to account for it, did he not disobey their summons? and, lastly, by the blows and other public affronts to the Ædiles, had he not done all he could to commence a civil war?

These articles were brought in against him, with a design either to humble Marcius, and show his submission, if, contrary to his nature, he should now court and sue the people; or, if he should follow his natural disposition, which they rather expected from their judgment of his character, then that he might thus make the breach final between himself and the people.

He came, therefore, as it were, to make his apology, and clear himself; in which belief the people kept silence, and gave him a quiet hearing. But when, instead of the submissive and deprecatory language expected from him, he began to use not only an offensive kind of freedom, seeming rather to accuse than apologize, but, as well by the tone of his voice as the air of his countenance, displayed a security that was not far from disdain and contempt of them, the whole multitude then became angry, and gave evident signs of impatience and disgust; and Sicinnius, the most violent of the tribunes, after a little private conference with his colleagues, proceeded solemnly to pronounce before them all, that Marcius was condemned to die by the tribunes of the people, and bid the Ædiles take him to the Tarpeian rock, and without delay throw him headlong from the precipice. When they, however, in compliance with the order, came to seize upon his body, many, even of the plebeian party, felt it to be a horrible and extravagant act; the patricians, meantime, wholly beside themselves with distress and horror, hurried up with cries to the rescue; and while some made actual use of their hands to hinder the arrest, and,surrounding Marcius, got him in among them, others, as in so great a tumult no good could be done by words, stretched out theirs, beseeching the multitude that they would not proceed to such furious extremities; and at length, the friends and acquaintance of the tribunes, wisely perceiving how impossible it would be to carry off Marcius to punishment without much bloodshed and slaughter of the nobility, persuaded them to forbear every thing unusual and odious; not to despatch him by any sudden violence, or without regular process, but refer the cause to the general suffrage of the people. Sicinnius then, after a little pause, turning to the patricians, demanded what their meaning was, thus forcibly to rescue Marcius out of the people's hands, as they were going to punish him; when it was replied by them, on the other side, and the question put, "Rather, how came it into your minds, and what is it you design, thus to drag one of the worthiest men of Rome, without trial, to a barbarous and illegal execution?" "Very well," said Sicinnius, "you shall have no ground in this respect for quarrel or complaint against the people. The people grant your request, and your partisan shall be tried. We appoint you, Marcius," directing his speech to him, "the third market-day ensuing, to appear and defend yourself, and to try if you can satisfy the Roman citizens of your innocence, who will then judge your case by vote." The patricians were content with such a truce and respite for that time, and gladly returned home, having for the present brought off Marcius in safety.

During the interval before the appointed time (for the Romans hold their sessions every ninth day, which from that cause are called *nundinæ* in Latin), a war fell out with the Antiates, likely to be of some continuance, which gave them hope they might one way or other elude the judgment. The people, they presumed, would become tractable, and their indignation lessen and languish by degrees in so long a space, if occupation and war did not wholly put it out of their mind. But when, contrary to expectation, they made a speedy agreement with the people of Antium, and the army came back to Rome, the patricians were again in great perplexity, and had frequent meetings to consider how things might be arranged, without either abandoning Marcius, or yet giving occasion to the popular orators to create new disorders. Appius Claudius, whom they counted among the senators most averse to the popular interest, made a solemn declaration, and told them beforehand, that the senate would utterly destroy itself and betray the government, if they should once suffer the people to assume the authority of pronouncing sentence upon any of the patricians; but the oldest senators and most favorable to the people maintained, on the other side, that the people would not be so harsh and severe upon them, as some were pleased to imagine, but rather become more gentle and humane upon the concession of that power, since it was not contempt of the senate, but the impression of being contemned by it, which made them pretend to such a prerogative. Let that be once allowed them as a mark of respect and kind feeling, and the mere possession of this power of voting would at once dispossess them of their animosity.

When, therefore, Marcius saw that the senate was in pain and suspense upon his account, divided, as it were, betwixt their kindness for him and their apprehensions from the people, he desired to know of the tribunes what the crimes were they intended to charge him with, and what the heads of the indictment they would oblige him to plead to before the people; and being told by them that he was to be impeached for attempting usurpation, and that they would prove him guilty of designing to establish arbitrary government, stepping forth upon this, "Let me go then," he said, "to clear myself from that imputation before an assembly of them; I freely offer myself to any sort of trial, nor do I refuse any kind of punishment whatsoever; only," he continued, "let what you now mention be really made my accusation, and do not you play false with the senate." On their consenting to these terms, he came to his trial. But when the people met together, the tribunes, contrary to all former practice, extorted first, that votes should be taken, not by centuries, but tribes; a change, by which the indigent and factious rabble, that had no respect for honesty and justice, would be sure to carry it against those who were rich and well known, and accustomed to serve the state in war. In the next place, whereas they had engaged to prosecute Marcius upon no other head but that of tyranny, which could never be made out against him, they relinquished this plea, and urged instead, his language in the senate against an abatement of the price of corn, and for the overthrow of the tribunician power; adding further, as a new impeachment the distribution that was made by him of the spoil and booty he had taken from the Antiates, when he overran their country, which he had divided among those that had followed him, whereas it ought rather to have been brought into the public treasury; which last accusation did, they say, more discompose Marcius than all the rest, as he had not anticipated he should ever be questioned on that subject, and, therefore, was less provided with any satisfactory answer to it on the sudden. And when, by way of excuse, he began to magnify the merits of those who had been partakers with him in the action, those that had stayed at home, being more numerous than the other, interrupted him with outcries. In conclusion, when they came to vote, a majority of three tribes condemned him; the penalty being perpetual banishment. The sentence of his condemnation being pronounced, the people went away with greater triumph and exultation than they had ever shown for any victory over enemies; while the senate was in grief and deep dejection, repenting now and vexed to the soul that they had not done and suffered all things rather than give way to the insolence of the people, and permit them to assume and abuse so great an authority. There was no need then to look at men's dresses, or other marks of distinction to know one from another: any one who was glad was, beyond all doubt, a plebeian; any one who looked sorrowful, a patrician.

Marcius alone, himself, was neither stunned nor humiliated. In mien, carriage, and countenance, he bore the appearance of entire composure, and while all his friends were full of distress, seemed the only man that was not touched with his misfortune. Not that either reflection taught him, or gentleness of temper made it natural for him, to submit: he was wholly possessed, on the contrary, with a profound and deep-seated fury, which passes with many for no pain at all. And pain, it is true, transmuted, so to say, by its own fiery heat into anger, loses every appearance of depression and feebleness; the angry man makes a show of energy, as the man in a high fever does of natural heat, while, in fact, all this action of the soul is but mere diseased palpitation, distention, and inflammation. That such was his distempered state appeared presently plainly enough in his actions. On his return home, after saluting his mother and his wife, who were all in tears and full of loud lamentations, and exhorting them to moderate the sense they had of his calamity, he proceeded at once to the city gates, whither all the nobility came to attend him; and so, not so much as taking any thing with him, or making any request to the company, he departed from them, having only three or four clients with him. He continued solitary for a few days in a place in the country, distracted with a variety of counsels, such as rage and indignation suggested to him; and proposing to himself no honorable or useful end, but only how he might best satisfy his revenge on the Romans, he resolved at length to raise up a heavy war against them from their nearest neighbors. He determined, first to make trial of the Volscians, whom he knew to be still vigorous and flourishing, both in men and treasure, and he imagined their force and power was not so much abated, as their spite and anger increased, by the late overthrows they had received from the Romans.

There was a man of Antium, called Tullus Aufidius, who, for his wealth and bravery and the splendor of his family, had the respect and privilege of a king among the Volscians, but whom Marcius knew to have a particular hostility to himself, above all other Romans. Frequent menaces and challenges had passed in battle between them, and those exchanges of defiance to which their hot and eager emulation is apt to prompt young soldiers had added private animosity to their national feelings of opposition. Yet for all this, considering Tullus to have a certain generosity of temper, and knowing that no Volscian, so much as he, desired an occasion to requite upon the Romans the evils they had done, he did what much confirms the saying, that

> "Hard and unequal is with wrath the strife,
> Which makes us buy its pleasure with our life."

Putting on such a dress as would make him appear to any whom he might meet most unlike what he really was, thus, like Ulysses,—

> "The town he entered of his mortal foes."

His arrival at Antium was about evening, and though several met him in the streets, yet he passed along without being known to any, and went directly to the house of Tullus, and, entering undiscovered, went up to the fire-hearth, and seated himself there without speaking a word, covering up his head. Those of the family could not but wonder, and yet they were afraid either to raise or question him, for there was a certain air of majesty both in his posture and silence, but they recounted to Tullus, being then at supper, the strangeness of this accident. He immediately rose from table and came in, and asked him who he was, and for what business he came thither; and then Marcius, unmuffling himself, and pausing awhile, "If," said he, "you cannot yet call me to mind, Tullus, or do not believe your eyes concerning me, I must of necessity be my own accuser. I am Caius Marcius, the author of so much mischief to the Volscians; of which, were I seeking to deny it, the surname of Coriolanus I now bear would be sufficient evidence against me. The one recompense I received for all the hardships and perils I have gone through, was the title that proclaims my enmity to your nation, and this is the only thing which is still left me. Of all other advantages, I have been stripped and deprived by the envy and outrage of the Roman people, and the cowardice and treachery of the magistrates and those of my own order. I am driven out as an exile, and become an humble suppliant at your hearth, not so much for safety and protection (should I have come hither, had I been afraid to die?), as to seek vengeance against those that expelled me; which, methinks, I have already obtained, by putting myself into your hands. If, therefore, you have really a mind to attack your enemies, come then, make use of that affliction you see me in to assist the enterprise, and convert my personal infelicity into a common blessing to the Volscians; as, indeed, I am likely to be more serviceable in fighting for than against you, with the advantage, which I now possess, of knowing all the secrets of the enemy that I am attacking. But if you decline to make any further attempts, I am neither desirous to live myself, nor will it be well in you to preserve a person who has been your rival and adversary of old, and now, when he offers you his service, appears unprofitable and useless to you."

Tullus on hearing this, was extremely rejoiced, and giving him his right hand, exclaimed, "Rise, Marcius, and be of good courage; it is a great happiness you bring to Antium, in the present you make us of yourself; expect every thing that is good from the Volscians." He then proceeded to feast and entertain him with every display of kindness, and for several days after they were in close deliberation together on the prospects of a war.

While this design was forming, there were great troubles and commotions at Rome, from the animosity of the senators against the people, heightened just now by the late condemnation of Marcius. Besides that, their soothsayers and priests, and even private persons, reported signs and prodigies not to be neglected; one of which is stated to have occurred as follows: Titus Latinus,[3] a man of ordinary condition, but of a quiet and virtuous character, free from all superstitious fancies, and yet more from vanity and exaggeration, had an apparition in his sleep, as if Jupiter came and bade him tell the senate, that it was with a bad and unacceptable dancer that they had headed his procession. Having beheld the vision, he said, he did not much attend to it at the first appearance; but after he had seen and slighted it a second and third time, he had lost a hopeful son, and was himself struck with a palsy. He was brought into the senate on a litter to tell this, and the story goes, that he had no sooner delivered his message there, but he at once felt his strength return, and got upon his legs, and went home alone, without need of any support. The senators, in wonder and surprise, made a diligent search into the matter. That which his dream alluded to was this: some citizen had, for some heinous offence, given up a servant of his to the rest of his fellows, with charge to whip him first through the market, and then to kill him; and while they were executing this command, and scourging the wretch, who screwed and turned himself into all manner of shapes and unseemly motions, through the pain he was in, the solemn procession in honor of Jupiter chanced to follow at their heels. Several of the attendants on which were, indeed, scandalized at the sight, yet no one of them interfered, or acted further in the matter than merely to utter some common reproaches and execrations on a master who inflicted so

[3] The correct name is probably Titus Latinius, for which Tiberius Atinius, in Livy, is merely a misreading.

cruel a punishment. For the Romans treated their slaves with great humanity in these times, when, working and laboring themselves, and living together among them they naturally were more gentle and familiar with them. It was one of the severest punishments for a slave who had committed a fault, to have to take the piece of wood which supports the pole of a wagon, and carry it about through the neighborhood; a slave who had once undergone the shame of this, and been thus seen by the household and the neighbors, had no longer any trust or credit among them, and had the name of *furcifer; furca* being the Latin word for a prop, or support.

When, therefore, Latinus had related his dream, and the senators were considering who this disagreeable and ungainly dancer could be, some of the company, having been struck with the strangeness of the punishment, called to mind and mentioned the miserable slave who was lashed through the streets and afterward put to death. The priests, when consulted confirmed the conjecture; the master was punished; and orders given for a new celebration of the procession and the spectacles in honor of the god. Numa, in other respects also a wise arranger of religious offices, would seem to have been especially judicious in his direction, with a view to the attentiveness of the people, that, when the magistrates or priests performed any divine worship, a herald should go before, and proclaim with a loud voice, *Hoc age*. Do this you are about, and so warn them to mind whatever sacred action they were engaged in, and not suffer any business or worldly avocation to disturb and interrupt it; most of the things which men do of this kind, being in a manner forced from them, and effected by constraint. It is usual with the Romans to recommence their sacrifices and processions and spectacles, not only upon such a cause as this, but for any slighter reason. If but one of the horses which drew the chariots called Tensæ, upon which the images of their gods were placed, happened to fail and falter, or if the driver took hold of the reins with his left hand, they would decree that the whole operation should commence anew; and, in latter ages, one and the same sacrifice was performed thirty times over, because of the occurrence of some defect or mistake or accident in the service. Such was the Roman reverence and caution in religious matters.

Marcius and Tullus were now secretly discoursing of their project with the chief men of Antium, advising them to invade the Romans while they were at variance among themselves. And when shame appeared to hinder them from embracing the motion, as they had sworn to a truce and cessation of arms for the space of two years, the Romans themselves soon furnished them with a pretence, by making proclamation, out of some jealousy or slanderous report, in the midst of the spectacles, that all the Volscians who had come to see them should depart the city before sunset. Some affirm that this was a contrivance of Marcius, who sent a man privately to the consuls, falsely to accuse the Volscians of intending to fall upon the Romans during the games, and to set the city on fire. This public affront roused and inflamed their hostility to the Romans; and Tullus, perceiving it, made his advantage of it, aggravating the fact, and working on their indignation, till he persuaded them, at last, to despatch ambassadors to Rome, requiring the Romans to restore that part of their country and those towns which they had taken from the Volscians in the late war. When the Romans heard the message, they indignantly replied, that the Volscians were the first that took up arms, but the Romans would be the last to lay them down. This answer being brought back, Tullus called a general assembly of the Volscians; and the vote passing for a war, he then proposed that they should call in Marcius, laying aside the remembrance of former grudges, and assuring themselves that the services they should now receive from him as a friend and associate, would abundantly outweigh any harm or damage he had done them when he was their enemy. Marcius was accordingly summoned, and having made his entrance, and spoken to the people, won their good opinion of his capacity, his skill, counsel, and boldness, not less by his present words than by his past actions. They joined him in commission with Tullus, to have full power as general of their forces in all that related to the war. And he, fearing lest the time that would be requisite to bring all the Volscians together in full preparation might be so long as to lose him the opportunity of action, left order with the chief persons and magistrates of the city to provide other things, while he himself, prevailing upon the most forward to assemble and march out with him as volunteers without staying to be enrolled, made a sudden inroad into the Roman confines, when nobody expected him, and possessed himself of so much booty, that the Volscians found they had more than they could either carry away or use in the camp. The abundance of provision which he gained, and the waste and havoc of the country which he made, were, however, of themselves and in his account, the smallest results of that invasion; the great mischief he intended, and his special object in all, was to increase at Rome the suspicions entertained of the patricians, and to make them upon worse terms with the people. With this view, while spoiling all the fields and destroying the property of other men, he took special care to preserve their farms and lands untouched, and would not allow his soldiers to ravage there, or seize upon any thing which belonged to them. From hence their invectives and quarrels against one another broke out afresh, and rose to a greater height than ever; the senators reproaching those of the commonalty with their late injustice to Marcius; while the plebeians, on their side, did not hesitate to accuse them of having, out of spite and revenge, solicited him to this enterprise, and thus, when others were involved in the miseries of a war by their means, they sat like unconcerned spectators, as being furnished with a guardian and protector abroad of their wealth and fortunes, in the very person of the public enemy. After this incursion and exploit, which was of great advantage to the Volscians, as they learned by it to grow more hardy and to contemn their enemy, Marcius drew them off, and returned in safety.

But when the whole strength of the Volscians was brought together into the field, with great expedition and alacrity, it appeared so considerable a body, that they agreed to leave part in garrison, for the security of their towns, and with the other part to march against the Romans. Marcius now desired Tullus to choose which of the two charges would be most agreeable to him. Tullus answered, that since he knew Marcius to be equally valiant with himself, and far more fortunate, he would have him take the command of those that were going out to the war, while he made it his care to defend their cities at home, and provide all conveniences for the army abroad. Marcius thus reinforced, and much stronger than before, moved first towards the city called Circæum, a Roman colony. He received its surrender, and did the inhabitants no injury; passing thence, he entered and laid waste the country of the Latins, where he expected the Romans would meet him, as the Latins were their confederates and allies, and had often sent to demand succors from them. The people, however, on their part, showing little inclination for the service, and the consuls themselves being unwilling to run the hazard of a battle, when the time of their office was almost ready to expire, they dismissed the Latin ambassadors without any effect; so that Marcius, finding no army to oppose him, marched up to their cities, and, having taken by force Toleria, Lavici, Peda, and Bola, all of which offered resistance, not only plundered their houses, but made a prey likewise of their persons. Meantime, he showed particular regard for all such as came over to his party, and, for fear they might sustain any damage against his will, encamped at the greatest distance he could, and wholly abstained from the lands of their property.

After, however, that he had made himself master of Bola, a town not above ten miles from Rome, where he found great treasure, and put almost all the adults to the sword; and when, on this, the other Volscians that were ordered to stay behind and protect their cities, hearing of his achievements and success, had not patience to remain any longer at home, but came hastening in their arms to Marcius, saying that he alone was their general and the sole commander they would own; with all this, his name and renown spread throughout all Italy, and universal wonder prevailed at the sudden and mighty revolution in the fortunes of two nations which the loss and the accession of a single man had effected.

All at Rome was in great disorder; they were utterly averse from fighting, and spent their whole time in cabals and disputes and reproaches against each other; until news was brought that the enemy had laid close siege to Lavinium, where were the images and sacred things of their tutelar gods, and from whence they derived the origin of their nation, that being the first city which Æneas built in Italy. These tidings produced a change as universal as it was extraordinary in the thoughts and inclinations of the people, but occasioned a yet stranger revulsion of feeling among the patricians. The people now were for repealing the sentence against

Marcius, and calling him back into the city; whereas the senate, being assembled to preconsider the decree, opposed and finally rejected the proposal, either out of the mere humor of contradicting and withstanding the people in whatever they should desire, or because they were unwilling, perhaps, that he should owe his restoration to their kindness; or having now conceived a displeasure against Marcius himself, who was bringing distress upon all alike, though he had not been ill treated by all, and was become a declared enemy to his whole country, though he knew well enough that the principal and all the better men condoled with him, and suffered in his injuries.

This resolution of theirs being made public, the people could proceed no further, having no authority to pass any thing by suffrage, and enact it for a law, without a previous decree from the senate. When Marcius heard of this, he was more exasperated than ever, and, quitting the siege of Lavinium, marched furiously towards Rome, and encamped at a place called the Cluilian ditches, about five miles from the city. The nearness of his approach did, indeed, create much terror and disturbance, yet it also ended their dissensions for the present; as nobody now, whether consul or senator, durst any longer contradict the people in their design of recalling Marcius; but, seeing their women running affrighted up and down the streets, and the old men at prayer in every temple with tears and supplications, and that, in short, there was a general absence among them both of courage and wisdom to provide for their own safety, they came at last to be all of one mind, that the people had been in the right to propose as they did a reconciliation with Marcius, and that the senate was guilty of a fatal error to begin a quarrel with him when it was a time to forget offences, and they should have studied rather to appease him. It was therefore, unanimously agreed by all parties, that ambassadors should be despatched, offering him return to his country, and desiring he would free them from the terrors and distresses of the war. The persons sent by the senate with this message were chosen out of his kindred and acquaintance, who naturally expected a very kind reception at their first interview, upon the score of that relation and their old familiarity and friendship with him; in which, however, they were much mistaken. Being led through the enemy's camp, they found him sitting in state amidst the chief men of the Volscians, looking insupportably proud and arrogant. He bade them declare the cause of their coming, which they did in the most gentle and tender terms, and with a behavior suitable to their language. When they had made an end of speaking, he returned them a sharp answer, full of bitterness and angry resentment, as to what concerned himself, and the ill usage he had received from them; but as general of the Volscians, he demanded restitution of the cities and the lands which had been seized upon during the late war, and that the same rights and franchises should be granted them at Rome, which had been before accorded to the Latins; since there could be no assurance that a peace would be firm and lasting, without fair and just conditions on both sides. He allowed them thirty days to consider and resolve.

The ambassadors being departed, he withdrew his forces out of the Roman territory. This, those of the Volscians who had long envied his reputation, and could not endure to see the influence he had with the people, laid hold of, as the first matter of complaint against him. Among them was also Tullus himself, not for any wrong done him personally by Marcius, but through the weakness incident to human nature. He could not help feeling mortified to find his own glory thus totally obscured, and himself overlooked and neglected now by the Volscians, who had so great an opinion of their new leader, that he alone was all to them, while other captains, they thought, should be content with that share of power, which he might think fit to accord. From hence the first seeds of complaint and accusation were scattered about in secret, and the malcontents met and heightened each other's indignation, saying, that to retreat as he did, was in effect to betray and deliver up, though not their cities and arms, yet what was as bad, the critical times and opportunities for action, on which depend the preservation or the loss of every thing else; since in less than thirty days' space, for which he had given a respite from the war, there might happen the greatest changes in the world. Yet Marcius spent not any part of the time idly, but attacked the confederates of the enemy, ravaged their land, and took from them seven great and populous cities in that interval. The Romans, in the meanwhile, durst not venture out to their relief; but were utterly fearful, and showed no more disposition or capacity for action, than if their bodies had been struck with a palsy, and become destitute of sense and motion. But when the thirty days were expired, and Marcius appeared again with his whole army, they sent another embassy to beseech him that he would moderate his displeasure, and would withdraw the Volscian army, and then make any proposals he thought best for both parties; the Romans would make no concessions to menaces, but if it were his opinion that the Volscians ought to have any favor shown them, upon laying down their arms they might obtain all they could in reason desire.

The reply of Marcius was, that he should make no answer to this as general of the Volscians, but, in the quality still of a Roman citizen, he would advise and exhort them, as the case stood, not to carry it so high, but think rather of just compliance, and return to him, before three days were at an end, with a ratification of his previous demands; otherwise, they must understand that they could not have any further freedom of passing through his camp upon idle errands.

When the ambassadors were come back, and had acquainted the senate with the answer, seeing the whole state now threatened as it were by a tempest, and the waves ready to overwhelm them, they were forced, as we say in extreme perils, to let down the sacred anchor. A decree was made, that the whole order of their priests, those who initiated in the mysteries or had the custody of them, and those who, according to the ancient practice of the country, divined from birds, should all and every one of them go in full procession to Marcius with their pontifical array, and the dress and habit which they respectively used in their several functions, and should urge him, as before, to withdraw his forces, and then treat with his countrymen in favor of the Volscians. He consented so far, indeed, as to give the deputation an admittance into his camp, but granted nothing at all, nor so much as expressed himself more mildly; but, without capitulating or receding, bade them once for all choose whether they would yield or fight, since the old terms were the only terms of peace. When this solemn application proved ineffectual, the priests, too, returning unsuccessful, they determined to sit still within the city, and keep watch about their walls, intending only to repulse the enemy, should he offer to attack them, and placing their hopes chiefly in time and in extraordinary accidents of fortune; as to themselves, they felt incapable of doing any thing for their own deliverance; mere confusion and terror and ill-boding reports possessed the whole city; till at last a thing happened not unlike what we so often find represented, without, however, being accepted as true by people in general, in Homer. On some great and unusual occasion we find him say:—

"But him the blue-eyed goddess did inspire;"

and elsewhere:—

"But some immortal turned my mind away,
To think what others of the deed would say;"

and again:—

"Were 't his own thought or were 't a god's command."

People are apt, in such passages, to censure and disregard the poet, as if, by the introduction of mere impossibilities and idle fictions, he were denying the action of a man's own deliberate thought and free choice; which is not, in the least, the case in Homer's representation, where the ordinary, probable, and habitual conclusions that common reason leads to are continually ascribed to our own direct agency. He certainly says frequently enough:—

"But I consulted with my own great soul;"

or, as in another passage:—

"He spoke. Achilles, with quick pain possessed,
Revolved two purposes in his strong breast;"

and in a third:—

"—Yet never to her wishes won
The just mind of the brave Bellerophon."

But where the act is something out of the way and extraordinary, and seems in a manner to demand some impulse of divine possession and sudden inspiration to account for it, here he does introduce divine agency, not to destroy, but to prompt the human will;

not to create in us another agency, but offering images to stimulate our own; images that in no sort or kind make our action involuntary, but give occasion rather to spontaneous action, aided and sustained by feelings of confidence and hope. For either we must totally dismiss and exclude divine influences from every kind of causality and origination in what we do, or else what other way can we conceive in which divine aid and coöperation can act? Certainly we cannot suppose that the divine beings actually and literally turn our bodies and direct our hands and our feet this way or that, to do what is right: it is obvious that they must actuate the practical and elective element of our nature, by certain initial occasions, by images presented to the imagination, and thoughts suggested to the mind, such either as to excite it to, or avert and withhold it from, any particular course.

In the perplexity which I have described, the Roman women went, some to other temples, but the greater part, and the ladies of highest rank, to the altar of Jupiter Capitolinus. Among these suppliants was Valeria, sister to the great Poplicola, who did the Romans eminent service both in peace and war. Poplicola himself was now deceased, as is told in the history of his life; but Valeria lived still, and enjoyed great respect and honor at Rome, her life and conduct no way disparaging her birth. She, suddenly seized with the sort of instinct or emotion of mind which I have described, and happily lighting, not without divine guidance, on the right expedient, both rose herself, and bade the others rise, and went directly with them to the house of Volumnia, the mother of Marcius. And coming in and finding her sitting with her daughter-in-law, and with her little grandchildren on her lap, Valeria, then surrounded by her female companions, spoke in the name of them all:—

"We that now make our appearance, O Volumnia, and you, Vergilia, are come as mere women to women, not by direction of the senate, or an order from the consuls, or the appointment of any other magistrate; but the divine being himself, as I conceive, moved to compassion by our prayers, prompted us to visit you in a body, and request a thing on which our own and the common safety depends, and which, if you consent to it, will raise your glory above that of the daughters of the Sabines, who won over their fathers and their husbands from mortal enmity to peace and friendship. Arise and come with us to Marcius; join in our supplication, and bear for your country this true and just testimony on her behalf: that notwithstanding the many mischiefs that have been done her, yet she has never outraged you, nor so much as thought of treating you ill, in all her resentment, but does now restore you safe into his hands, though there be small likelihood she should obtain from him any equitable terms."

The words of Valeria were seconded by the acclamations of the other women, to which Volumnia made answer:—

"I and Vergilia, my countrywomen, have an equal share with you all in the common miseries, and we have the additional sorrow, which is wholly ours, that we have lost the merit and good fame of Marcius, and see his person confined, rather than protected, by the arms of the enemy. Yet I account this the greatest of all misfortunes, if indeed the affairs of Rome be sunk to so feeble a state as to have their last dependence upon us. For it is hardly imaginable he should have any consideration left for us, when he has no regard for the country which he was wont to prefer before his mother and wife and children. Make use, however, of our service; and lead us, if you please, to him; we are able, if nothing more, at least to spend our last breath in making suit to him for our country."

Having spoken thus, she took Vergilia by the hand, and the young children, and so accompanied them to the Volscian camp. So lamentable a sight much affected the enemies themselves, who viewed them in respectful silence. Marcius was then sitting in his place, with his chief officers about him, and, seeing the party of women advance toward him, wondered what should be the matter; but perceiving at length that his mother was at the head of them, he would fain have hardened himself in his former inexorable temper, but, overcome by his feelings, and confounded at what he saw, he did not endure they should approach him sitting in state, but came down hastily to meet them, saluting his mother first, and embracing her a long time, and then his wife and children, sparing neither tears nor caresses, but suffering himself to be borne away and carried headlong, as it were, by the impetuous violence of his passion.

When he had satisfied himself, and observed that his mother Volumnia was desirous to say something, the Volscian council being first called in, he heard her to the following effect: "Our dress and our very persons, my son, might tell you, though we should say nothing ourselves, in how forlorn a condition we have lived at home since your banishment and absence from us; and now consider with yourself, whether we may not pass for the most unfortunate of all women, to have that sight, which should be the sweetest that we could see, converted, through I know not what fatality, to one of all others the most formidable and dreadful,—Volumnia to behold her son, and Vergilia her husband, in arms against the walls of Rome. Even prayer itself, whence others gain comfort and relief in all manner of misfortunes, is that which most adds to our confusion and distress; since our best wishes are inconsistent with themselves, nor can we at the same time petition the gods for Rome's victory and your preservation, but what the worst of our enemies would imprecate as a curse, is the very object of our vows. Your wife and children are under the sad necessity, that they must either be deprived of you, or of their native soil. As for myself, I am resolved not to wait till war shall determine this alternative for me; but if I cannot prevail with you to prefer amity and concord to quarrel and hostility, and to be the benefactor to both parties, rather than the destroyer of one of them, be assured of this from me, and reckon steadfastly upon it, that you shall not be able to reach your country, unless you trample first upon the corpse of her that brought you into life. For it will be ill in me to wait and loiter in the world till the day come wherein I shall see a child of mine, either led in triumph by his own countrymen, or triumphing over them. Did I require you to save your country by ruining the Volscians, then, I confess, my son, the case would be hard for you to solve. It is base to bring destitution on our fellow-citizens; it is unjust to betray those who have placed their confidence in us. But, as it is, we do but desire a deliverance equally expedient for them and us: only more glorious and honorable on the Volscian side, who as superior in arms, will be thought freely to bestow the two greatest of blessings, peace and friendship, even when they themselves receive the same. If we obtain these, the common thanks will be chiefly due to you as the principal cause; but if they be not granted, you alone must expect to bear the blame from both nations. The chance of all war is uncertain, yet thus much is certain in the present, that you, by conquering Rome, will only get the reputation of having undone your country; but if the Volscians happen to be defeated under your conduct, then the world will say, that, to satisfy a revengeful humor, you brought misery on your friends and patrons."

Marcius listened to his mother while she spoke, without answering her a word; and Volumnia, seeing him stand mute also for a long time after she had ceased, resumed: "O my son," said she, "what is the meaning of this silence? Is it a duty to postpone every thing to a sense of injuries, and wrong to gratify a mother in a request like this? Is it the characteristic of a great man to remember wrongs that have been done him, and not the part of a great and good man to remember benefits such as those that children receive from parents, and to requite them with honor and respect? You, methinks, who are so relentless in the punishment of the ungrateful, should not be more careless than others to be grateful yourself. You have punished your country already; you have not yet paid your debt to me. Nature and religion, surely, unattended by any constraint, should have won your consent to petitions so worthy and so just as these; but if it must be so, I will even use my last resource." Having said this, she threw herself down at his feet, as did also his wife and children; upon which Marcius, crying out, "O, mother! what is it you have done to me?" raised her up from the ground, and pressing her right hand with more than ordinary vehemence, "You have gained a victory," said he, "fortunate enough for the Romans, but destructive to your son; whom you, though none else, have defeated." After which, and a little private conference with his mother and his wife, he sent them back again to Rome, as they desired of him.

The next morning, he broke up his camp, and led the Volscians homeward, variously affected with what he had done; some of them complaining to him and condemning his act, others, who were inclined to a peaceful conclusion, unfavorable to neither. A third party, while much disliking his proceedings, yet could not look upon Marcius as a treacherous person, but thought it pardonable in him to be thus shaken and driven to surrender at last, under such compulsion. None, however, opposed his commands; they all obediently followed him, though rather from admiration of his virtue, than any regard they now had to his authority. The Roman people, meantime, more effectually manifested how much fear and danger they had been in while the war lasted, by their deportment after they were freed from it. Those that guarded the walls had no sooner given notice that the Volscians were dislodged and drawn off, but they set open all their temples in a moment, and began to crown themselves with garlands and prepare for sacrifice, as they were wont to do upon tidings brought of any signal victory. But the joy and transport of the whole city was chiefly remarkable in the honors and marks of affection paid to the women, as well by the senate as the people in general; every one declaring that they were, beyond all question, the instruments of the public safety. And the senate having passed a decree that whatsoever they would ask in the way of any favor or honor should be allowed and done for them by the magistrates, they demanded simply that a temple might be erected to Female Fortune, the expense of which they offered to defray out of their own contributions, if the city would be at the cost of sacrifices, and other matters pertaining to the due honor of the gods, out of the common treasury. The senate, much commending their public spirit, caused the temple to be built and a statue set up in it at the public charge; they, however, made up a sum among themselves, for a second image of Fortune, which the Romans say uttered, as it was putting up, words to this effect, "Blessed of the gods, O women, is your gift."

These words they profess were repeated a second time, expecting our belief for what seems pretty nearly an impossibility. It may be possible enough, that statues may seem to sweat, and to run with tears, and to stand with certain dewy drops of a sanguine color; for timber and stones are frequently known to contract a kind of scurf and rottenness productive of moisture; and various tints may form on the surfaces, both from within and from the action of the air outside; and by these signs it is not absurd to imagine that the deity may forewarn us. It may happen, also, that images and statues may sometimes make a noise not unlike that of a moan or groan, through a rupture or violent internal separation of the parts; but that an articulate voice and such express words, and language so clear and exact and elaborate, should proceed from inanimate things, is, in my judgment, a thing utterly out of possibility. For it was never known that either the soul of man, or the deity himself, uttered vocal sounds and language, alone, without an organized body and members fitted for speech. But where history seems in a manner to force our assent by the concurrence of numerous and credible witnesses, we are to conclude that an impression distinct from sensation affects the imaginative part of our nature, and then carries away the judgment, so as to believe it to be a sensation: just as in sleep we fancy we see and hear, without really doing either. Persons, however, whose strong feelings of reverence to the deity, and tenderness for religion, will not allow them to deny or invalidate any thing of this kind, have certainly a strong argument for their faith, in the wonderful and transcendent character of the divine power; which admits no manner of comparison with ours, either in its nature or its action, the modes or the strength of its operations. It is no contradiction to reason that it should do things that we cannot do, and effect what for us is impracticable: differing from us in all respects, in its acts yet more than in other points we may well believe it to be unlike us and remote from us. Knowledge of divine things for the most part, as Heraclitus says, is lost to us by incredulity.

When Marcius came back to Antium, Tullus, who thoroughly hated and greatly feared him, proceeded at once to contrive how he might immediately despatch him; as, if he escaped now, he was never likely to give him such another advantage. Having, therefore, got together and suborned several partisans against him, he required Marcius to resign his charge, and give the Volscians an account of his administration. He, apprehending the danger of a private condition, while Tullus held the office of general and exercised the greatest power among his fellow-citizens, made answer, that he was ready to lay down his commission, whenever those from whose common authority he had received it, should think fit to recall it, and that in the mean time he was ready to give the Antiates satisfaction, as to all particulars of his conduct, if they were desirous of it.

An assembly was called, and popular speakers, as had been concerted, came forward to exasperate and incense the multitude; but when Marcius stood up to answer, the more unruly and tumultuous part of the people became quiet on a sudden, and out of reverence allowed him to speak without the least disturbance; while all the better people, and such as were satisfied with a peace, made it evident by their whole behavior, that they would give him a favorable hearing, and judge and pronounce according to equity.

Tullus, therefore, began to dread the issue of the defence he was going to make for himself; for he was an admirable speaker, and the former services he had done the Volscians had procured and still preserved for him greater kindness than could be outweighed by any blame for his late conduct. Indeed, the very accusation itself was a proof and testimony of the greatness of his merits, since people could never have complained or thought themselves wronged, because Rome was not brought into their power, but that by his means they had come so near to taking it. For these reasons, the conspirators judged it prudent not to make any further delays, nor to test the general feeling; but the boldest of their faction, crying out that they ought not to listen to a traitor, nor allow him still to retain office and play the tyrant among them, fell upon Marcius in a body, and slew him there, none of those that were present offering to defend him. But it quickly appeared that the action was in nowise approved by the majority of the Volscians. who hurried out of their several cities to show respect to his corpse; to which they gave honorable interment, adorning his sepulchre with arms and trophies, as the monument of a noble hero and a famous general. When the Romans heard tidings of his death, they gave no other signification either of honor or of anger towards him, but simply granted the request of the women, that they might put themselves into mourning and bewail him for ten months, as the usage was upon the loss of a father or a son or a brother; that being the period fixed for the longest lamentation by the laws of Numa Pompilius, as is more amply told in the account of him.

Marcius was no sooner deceased, but the Volscians felt the need of his assistance. They quarrelled first with the Æquians, their confederates and their friends, about the appointment of the general of their joint forces, and carried their dispute to the length of bloodshed and slaughter; and were then defeated by the Romans in a pitched battle, where not only Tullus lost his life, but the principal flower of their whole army was cut in pieces; so that they were forced to submit and accept of peace upon very dishonorable terms, becoming subjects of Rome, and pledging themselves to submission.

COMPARISON OF ALCIBIADES WITH CORIOLANUS

HAVING described all their actions that seem to deserve commemoration, their military ones, we may say, incline the balance very decidedly upon neither side. They both, in pretty equal measure, displayed on numerous occasions the daring and courage of the soldier, and the skill and foresight of the general; unless, indeed, the fact that Alcibiades was victorious and successful in many contests both by sea and land, ought to gain him the title of a more complete commander. That so long as they remained and held command in their respective countries, they eminently sustained, and when they were driven into exile, yet more eminently damaged the fortunes of those countries, is common to both. All the sober citizens felt disgust at the petulance, the low flattery, and base seductions which Alcibiades, in his public life, allowed himself to employ with the view of winning the people's favor; and the ungraciousness, pride, and oligarchical haughtiness which Marcius, on the other hand, displayed in his, were the abhorrence of the Roman populace. Neither of these courses can be called commendable; but a man who ingratiates himself by indulgence and flattery, is hardly so censurable as one who, to avoid the appearance of flattering, insults. To seek power by servility to the people is a disgrace, but to maintain it by terror, violence, and oppression, is not a disgrace only, but an injustice.

Marcius, according to our common conceptions of his character, was undoubtedly simple and straightforward; Alcibiades, unscrupulous as a public man, and false. He is more especially blamed for the dishonorable and treacherous way in which, as Thucydides relates, he imposed upon the Lacedæmonian ambassadors, and disturbed the continuance of the peace. Yet this policy, which engaged the city again in war, nevertheless placed it in a powerful and formidable position, by the accession, which Alcibiades obtained for it, of the alliance of Argos and Mantinea. And Coriolanus also, Dionysius relates, used unfair means to excite war between the Romans and the Volscians, in the false report which he spread about the visitors at the Games; and the motive of this action seems to make it the worse of the two; since it was not done, like the other, out of ordinary political jealousy, strife, and competition. Simply to gratify anger, from which, as Ion says, no one ever yet got any return, he threw whole districts of Italy into confusion, and sacrificed to his passion against his country numerous innocent cities. It is true, indeed, that Alcibiades also, by his resentment, was the occasion of great disasters to his country, but he relented as soon as he found their feelings to be changed; and after he was driven out a second time, so far from taking pleasure in the errors and inadvertencies of their commanders, or being indifferent to the danger they were thus incurring, he did the very thing that Aristides is so highly commended for doing to Themistocles: he came to the generals who were his enemies, and pointed out to them what they ought to do. Coriolanus, on the other hand, first of all attacked the whole body of his countrymen, though only one portion of them had done him any wrong, while the other, the better and nobler portion, had actually suffered, as well as sympathized, with him. And, secondly, by the obduracy with which he resisted numerous embassies and supplications, addressed in propitiation of his single anger and offence, he showed that it had been to destroy and overthrow, not to recover and regain his country, that he had excited bitter and implacable hostilities against it. There is, indeed, one distinction that may be drawn. Alcibiades, it may be said, was not safe among the Spartans, and had the inducements at once of fear and of hatred to lead him again to Athens; whereas Marcius could not honorably have left the Volscians, when they were behaving so well to him: he, in the command of their forces and the enjoyment of their entire confidence, was in a very different position from Alcibiades, whom the Lacedæmonians did not so much wish to adopt into their service, as to use, and then abandon. Driven about from house to house in the city, and from general to general in the camp, the latter had no resort but to place himself in the hands of Tisaphernes; unless, indeed, we are to suppose that his object in courting favor with him was to avert the entire destruction of his native city, whither he wished himself to return.

As regards money, Alcibiades, we are told, was often guilty of procuring it by accepting bribes, and spent it ill in luxury and dissipation. Coriolanus declined to receive it, even when pressed upon him by his commanders as an honor; and one great reason for the odium he incurred with the populace in the discussions about their debts was, that he trampled upon the poor, not for money's sake, but out of pride and insolence.

Antipater, in a letter written upon the death of Aristotle the philosopher, observes, "Amongst his other gifts he had that of persuasiveness"; and the absence of this in the character of Marcius made all his great actions and noble qualities unacceptable to those whom they benefited: pride, and self-will, the consort, as Plato calls it, of solitude, made him insufferable. With the skill which Alcibiades, on the contrary, possessed to treat every one in the way most agreeable to him, we cannot wonder that all his successes were attended with the most exuberant favor and honor; his very errors, at times, being accompanied by something of grace and felicity. And so, in spite of great and frequent hurt that he had done the city, he was repeatedly appointed to office and command; while Coriolanus stood in vain for a place which his great services had made his due. The one, in spite of the harm he occasioned, could not make himself hated, nor the other, with all the admiration he attracted, succeed in being beloved by his countrymen.

Coriolanus, moreover, it should be said, did not as a general obtain any successes for his country, but only for his enemies against his country. Alcibiades was often of service to Athens, both as a soldier and as a commander. So long as he was personally present, he had the perfect mastery of his political adversaries; calumny only succeeded in his absence. Coriolanus was condemned in person at Rome; and in like manner killed by the Volscians, not indeed with any right or justice, yet not without some pretext occasioned by his own acts; since, after rejecting all conditions of peace in public, in private he yielded to the solicitations of the women, and, without establishing peace, threw up the favorable chances of war. He ought, before retiring, to have obtained the consent of those who had placed their trust in him; if indeed he considered their claims on him to be the strongest. Or, if we say that he did not care about the Volscians, but merely had prosecuted the war, which he now abandoned, for the satisfaction of his own resentment, then the noble thing would have been, not to spare his country for his mother's sake, but his mother in and with his country; since both his mother and his wife were part and parcel of that endangered country. After harshly repelling public supplications, the entreaties of ambassadors, and the prayers of priests, to concede all as a private favor to his mother was less an honor to her than a dishonor to the city which thus escaped, in spite, it would seem, of its own demerits, through the intercession of a single woman. Such a grace could, indeed, seem merely invidious, ungracious, and unreasonable in the eyes of both parties; he retreated without listening to the persuasions of his opponents, or asking the consent of his friends. The origin of all lay in his unsociable, supercilious, and self-willed disposition, which, in all cases, is offensive to most people; and when combined with a passion for distinction, passes into absolute savageness and mercilessness. Men decline to ask favors of the people, professing not to need any honors from them; and then are indignant if they do not obtain them. Metellus, Aristides, and Epaminondas certainly did not beg favors of the multitude; but that was because they, in real truth, did not value the gifts which a popular body can either confer or refuse; and when they were more than once driven into exile, rejected at elections, and condemned in courts of justice, they showed no resentment at the ill-humor of their fellow-citizens, but were willing and contented to return and be reconciled when the feeling altered and they were wished for. He who least likes courting favor, ought also least to think of resenting neglect: to feel wounded at being refused a distinction can only arise from an overweening appetite to have it.

Alcibiades never professed to deny that it was pleasant to him to be honored, and distasteful to him to be overlooked; and, accordingly, he always tried to place himself upon good terms with all that he met; Coriolanus's pride forbade him to pay attentions to those who could have promoted his advancement, and yet his love of distinction made him feel hurt and angry when he was disregarded. Such are the faulty parts of his character, which in all other respects was a noble one. For his temperance, continence, and probity, he might claim to be compared with the best and purest of the Greeks; not in any sort or kind with Alcibiades, the least scrupulous and most entirely careless of human beings in all these points.

DEMOSTHENES

WHOEVER it was, Sosius, that wrote the poem in honor of Alcibiades, upon his winning the chariot-race at the Olympian Games, whether it were Euripides, as is most commonly thought, or some other person, he tells us, that to a man's being happy it is in the first place requisite he should be born in "some famous city." But for him that would attain to true happiness, which for the most part is placed in the qualities and disposition of the mind, it is, in my opinion, of no other disadvantage to be of a mean, obscure country, than to be born of a small or plain-looking woman. For it were ridiculous to think that Iulis, a little part of Ceos, which itself is no great island, and Ægina, which an Athenian once said ought to be removed, like a small eye-sore, from the port of Piræus, should breed good actors and poets,[1] and yet should never be able to produce a just, temperate, wise, and high-minded man. Other arts, whose end it is to acquire riches or honor, are likely enough to wither and decay in poor and undistinguished towns; but virtue, like a strong and durable plant, may take root and thrive in any place where it can lay hold of an ingenuous nature, and a mind that is industrious. I, for my part, shall desire that for any deficiency of mine in right judgment or action, I myself may be, as in fairness, held accountable, and shall not attribute it to the obscurity of my birthplace.

But if any man undertake to write a history, that has to be collected from materials gathered by observation and the reading of works not easy to be got in all places, nor written always in his own language, but many of them foreign and dispersed in other hands, for him, undoubtedly, it is in the first place and above all things most necessary, to reside in some city of good note, addicted to liberal arts, and populous; where he may have plenty of all sorts

[1] Simonides, the lyric poet, was born at Iulis in Ceos; and Polus, the celebrated actor, who is mentioned in the account, further on, of Demosthenes's death, was a native of Ægina.

of books, and upon inquiry may hear and inform himself of such particulars as, having escaped the pens of writers, are more faithfully preserved in the memories of men, lest his work be deficient in many things, even those which it can least dispense with.

But for me, I live in a little town, where I am willing to continue, lest it should grow less; and having had no leisure, while I was in Rome and other parts of Italy, to exercise myself in the Roman language, on account of public business and of those who came to be instructed by me in philosophy, it was very late, and in the decline of my age, before I applied myself to the reading of Latin authors. Upon which that which happened to me, may seem strange, though it be true; for it was not so much by the knowledge of words, that I came to the understanding of things, as by my experience of things I was enabled to follow the meaning of words. But to appreciate the graceful and ready pronunciation of the Roman tongue, to understand the various figures and connection of words, and such other ornaments, in which the beauty of speaking consists, is, I doubt not, an admirable and delightful accomplishment; but it requires a degree of practice and study which is not easy, and will better suit those who have more leisure, and time enough yet before them for the occupation.

And so in this fifth book of my Parallel Lives, in giving an account of Demosthenes and Cicero, my comparison of their natural dispositions and their characters will be formed upon their actions and their lives as statesmen, and I shall not pretend to criticize their orations one against the other, to show which of the two was the more charming or the more powerful speaker. For there, as Ion says,

"We are but like a fish upon dry land;"

a proverb which Cæcilius perhaps forgot, when he employed his always adventurous talents in so ambitious an attempt as a comparison of Demosthenes and Cicero: and, possibly, if it were a thing obvious and easy for every man *to know himself*, the precept had not passed for an oracle.

The divine power seems originally to have designed Demosthenes and Cicero upon the same plan, giving them many similarities in their natural characters, as their passion for distinction and their love of liberty in civil life, and their want of courage in dangers and war, and at the same time also to have added many accidental resemblances. I think there can hardly be found two other orators, who, from small and obscure beginnings, became so great and mighty; who both contested with kings and tyrants; both lost their daughters, were driven out of their country, and returned with honor; who, flying from thence again, were both seized upon by their enemies, and at last ended their lives with the liberty of their countrymen. So that if we were to suppose there had been a trial of skill between nature and fortune, as there is sometimes between artists, it would be hard to judge, whether that succeeded best in making them alike in their dispositions and manners, or this, in the coincidences of their lives. We will speak of the eldest first.

Demosthenes, the father of Demosthenes, was a citizen of good rank and quality, as Theopompus informs us, surnamed the Sword-maker, because he had a large work-house, and kept servants skilful in that art at work. But of that which Æschines, the orator, said of his mother, that she was descended of one Gylon, who fled his country upon an accusation of treason, and of a barbarian woman, I can affirm nothing, whether he spoke true, or slandered and maligned her. This is certain, that Demosthenes, being as yet but seven years old, was left by his father in affluent circumstances, the whole value of his estate being little short of fifteen talents, and that he was wronged by his guardians, part of his fortune being embezzled by them, and the rest neglected; insomuch that even his teachers were defrauded of their salaries. This was the reason that he did not obtain the liberal education that he should have had; besides that on account of weakness and delicate health, his mother would not let him exert himself, and his teachers forbore to urge him. He was meagre and sickly from the first, and hence had his nickname of Batalus, given him, it is said, by the boys, in derision of his appearance; Batalus being, as some tell us, a certain enervated flute-player, in ridicule of whom Antiphanes wrote a play. Others speak of Batalus as a writer of wanton verses and drinking songs. And it would seem that some part of the body, not decent to be named, was at that time called *batalus* by the Athenians. But the name of Argas, which also they say was a nickname of Demosthenes, was given him for his behavior, as being savage and spiteful, *argas* being one of the poetical words for a snake; or for his disagreeable way of speaking, Argas being the name of a poet, who composed very harshly and disagreeably. So much, as Plato says, for such matters.

The first occasion of his eager inclination to oratory, they say, was this. Callistratus, the orator, being to plead in open court for Oropus, the expectation of the issue of that cause was very great, as well for the ability of the orator, who was then at the height of his reputation, as also for the fame of the action itself. Therefore, Demosthenes, having heard the tutors and schoolmasters agreeing among themselves to be present at this trial, with much importunity persuades his tutor to take him along with him to the hearing; who, having some acquaintance with the door-keepers, procured a place where the boy might sit unseen, and hear what was said. Callistratus having got the day, and being much admired, the boy began to look upon his glory with a kind of emulation, observing how he was courted on all hands, and attended on his way by the multitude; but his wonder was more than all excited by the power of his eloquence, which seemed able to subdue and win over any thing. From this time, therefore, bidding farewell to other sorts of learning and study, he now began to exercise himself, and to take pains in declaiming, as one that meant to be himself also an orator. He made use of Isæus as his guide to the art of speaking, though Isocrates at that time was giving lessons; whether, as some say, because he was an orphan, and was not able to pay Isocrates his appointed fee of ten minæ, or because he preferred Isæus's speaking, as being more business-like and effective in actual use. Hermippus says, that he met with certain memoirs without any author's name, in which it was written that Demosthenes was a scholar to Plato, and learnt much of his eloquence from him; and he also mentions Ctesibius, as reporting from Callias of Syracuse and some others, that Demosthenes secretly obtained a knowledge of the systems of Isocrates and Alcidamas, and mastered them thoroughly.

As soon, therefore, as he was grown up to man's estate, he began to go to law with his guardians, and to write orations against them;

who, in the mean time, had recourse to various subterfuges and pleas for new trials, and Demosthenes, though he was thus, as Thucydides says, taught his business in dangers, and by his own exertions was successful in his suit, was yet unable for all this to recover so much as a small fraction of his patrimony. He only attained some degree of confidence in speaking, and some competent experience in it. And having got a taste of the honor and power which are acquired by pleadings, he now ventured to come forth, and to undertake public business. And, as it is said of Laomedon, the Orchomenian, that by advice of his physician, he used to run long distances to keep off some disease of his spleen, and by that means having, through labor and exercise, framed the habit of his body, he betook himself to the great garland games,[2] and became one of the best runners at the long race; so it happened to Demosthenes, who, first venturing upon oratory for the recovery of his own private property, by this acquired ability in speaking, and at length, in public business, as it were in the great games, came to have the preëminence of all competitors in the assembly. But when he first addressed himself to the people, he met with great discouragements, and was derided for his strange and uncouth style, which was cumbered with long sentences and tortured with formal arguments to a most harsh and disagreeable excess. Besides, he had, it seems, a weakness in his voice, a perplexed and indistinct utterance and a shortness of breath, which, by breaking and disjointing his sentences, much obscured the sense and meaning of what he spoke. So that in the end, being quite disheartened, he forsook the assembly; and as he was walking carelessly and sauntering about the Piræus, Eunomus, the Thriasian, then a very old man, seeing him, upbraided him, saying that his diction was very much like that of Pericles, and that he was wanting to himself through cowardice and meanness of spirit, neither bearing up with courage against popular outcry, nor fitting his body for action, but suffering it to languish through mere sloth and negligence.

Another time, when the assembly had refused to hear him, and he was going home with his head muffled up, taking it very heavily,

[2] The Olympic, Pythian, Isthmian and Nemean Games, where the victors were crowned with garlands.

they relate that Satyrus, the actor, followed him, and being his familiar acquaintance, entered into conversation with him. To whom, when Demosthenes bemoaned himself, that having been the most industrious of all the pleaders, and having almost spent the whole strength and vigor of his body in that employment, he could not yet find any acceptance with the people, that drunken sots, mariners, and illiterate fellows were heard, and had the hustings for their own, while he himself was despised. "You say true, Demosthenes," replies Satyrus, "but I will quickly remedy the cause of all this, if you will repeat to me some passage out of Euripides or Sophocles." Which when Demosthenes had pronounced, Satyrus presently taking it up after him, gave the same passage, in his rendering of it, such a new form, by accompanying it with the proper mien and gesture, that to Demosthenes it seemed quite another thing. By this being convinced how much grace and ornament language acquires from action, he began to esteem it a small matter, and as good as nothing for a man to exercise himself in declaiming, if he neglected enunciation and delivery. Hereupon he built himself a place to study in under ground, (which was still remaining in our time), and hither he would come constantly every day to form his action, and to exercise his voice; and here he would continue, oftentimes without intermission, two or three months together, shaving one half of his head, that so for shame he might not go abroad, though he desired it ever so much.

Nor was this all, but he also made his conversation with people abroad, his common speech, and his business, subservient to his studies, taking from hence occasions and arguments as matter to work upon. For as soon as he was parted from his company, down he would go at once into his study, and run over every thing in order that had passed, and the reasons that might be alleged for and against it. Any speeches also, that he was present at, he would go over again with himself, and reduce into periods; and whatever others spoke to him, or he to them, he would correct, transform, and vary several ways. Hence it was, that he was looked upon as a person of no great natural genius, but one who owed all the power and ability he had in speaking to labor and industry. Of the truth of which it was thought to be no small sign, that he was very rarely heard to speak upon the occasion, but though he were by name frequently called upon by the people, as he sat in the assembly, yet he would not rise unless he had previously considered the subject, and came prepared for it. So that many of the popular pleaders used to make it a jest against him; and Pytheas once, scoffing at him, said that his arguments smelt of the lamp. To which Demosthenes gave the sharp answer, "It is true, indeed, Pytheas, that your lamp and mine are not conscious of the same things." To others, however, he would not much deny it, but would admit frankly enough, that he neither entirely wrote his speeches beforehand, nor yet spoke wholly extempore. And he would affirm, that it was the more truly popular act to use premeditation, such preparation being a kind of respect to the people; whereas, to slight and take no care how what is said is likely to be received by the audience, shows something of an oligarchical temper, and is the course of one that intends force rather than persuasion. Of his want of courage and assurance to speak offhand, they make it also another argument, that when he was at a loss, and discomposed, Demades would often rise up on the sudden to support him, but he was never observed to do the same for Demades.

Whence then, may some say, was it, that Æschines speaks of him as a person so much to be wondered at for his boldness in speaking? Or, how could it be, when Python, the Byzantine, "with so much confidence and such a torrent of words inveighed against"[3] the Athenians, that Demosthenes alone stood up to oppose him? Or, when Lamachus, the Myrinæan, had written a panegyric upon king Philip and Alexander, in which he uttered many things in reproach of the Thebans and Olynthians, and at the Olympic Games recited it publicly, how was it, that he, rising up, and recounting historically and demonstratively what benefits and advantages all Greece had received from the Thebans and Chalcidians, and on the contrary, what mischiefs the flatterers of the Macedonians had brought upon it, so turned the minds of all that were present that the sophist, in alarm at the outcry against him, secretly made his way out of the assembly? But Demosthenes, it should seem, regarded other points in the character of Pericles to be unsuited to him; but his

[3] These are his own words, quoted from the Oration on the Crown.

reserve and his sustained manner, and his forbearing to speak on the sudden, or upon every occasion, as being the things to which principally he owed his greatness, these he followed, and endeavored to imitate, neither wholly neglecting the glory which present occasion offered, nor yet willing too often to expose his faculty to the mercy of chance. For, in fact, the orations which were spoken by him had much more of boldness and confidence in them than those that he wrote, if we may believe Eratosthenes, Demetrius the Phalerian, and the Comedians. Eratosthenes says that often in his speaking he would be transported into a kind of ecstasy, and Demetrius, that he uttered the famous metrical adjuration to the people,

> "By the earth, the springs, the rivers, and the streams,"

as a man inspired, and beside himself. One of the comedians calls him a *rhopoperperethras*,[4] and another scoffs at him for his use of antithesis:—

> "And what he took, took back; a phrase to please
> The very fancy of Demosthenes."

Unless, indeed, this also is meant by Antiphanes for a jest upon the speech on Halonesus, which Demosthenes advised the Athenians not to *take* at Philip's hands, but to *take back*.[5]

All, however, used to consider Demades, in the mere use of his natural gifts, an orator impossible to surpass, and that in what he spoke on the sudden, he excelled all the study and preparation of Demosthenes. And Ariston, the Chian, has recorded a judgment which Theophrastus passed upon the orators; for being asked what kind of orator he accounted Demosthenes, he answered, "Worthy of the city of Athens;" and then, what he thought of Demades, he answered, "Above it." And the same philosopher reports, that Polyeuctus, the Sphettian, one of the Athenian politicians about that

[4] A loud declaimer about petty matters; from *rhopos*, small wares, and *perperos*, a loud talker.

[5] Halonesus had belonged to Athens, but had been seized by pirates, from whom Philip took it. He was willing to make a present of it to the Athenians, but Demosthenes warned them not on any account to *take* it, unless it were expressly understood that they *took* it *back;* Philip had no right to give what it was his duty to give back. The distinction thus put was apparently the subject of a great deal of pleasantry. Athenæus quotes five other passages from the comic writers, playing upon it in the same way.

time, was wont to say, that Demosthenes was the greatest orator, but Phocion the ablest, as he expressed the most sense in the fewest words. And, indeed, it is related, that Demosthenes himself, as often as Phocion stood up to plead against him, would say to his acquaintance, "Here comes the knife to my speech." Yet it does not appear whether he had this feeling for his powers of speaking, or for his life and character, and meant to say that one word or nod from a man who was really trusted, would go further than a thousand lengthy periods from others.

Demetrius, the Phalerian, tells us, that he was informed by Demosthenes himself, now grown old, that the ways he made use of to remedy his natural bodily infirmities and defects were such as these; his inarticulate and stammering pronunciation he overcame and rendered more distinct by speaking with pebbles in his mouth; his voice he disciplined by declaiming and reciting speeches or verses when he was out of breath, while running or going up steep places; and that in his house he had a large looking-glass, before which he would stand and go through his exercises. It is told that some one once came to request his assistance as a pleader, and related how he had been assaulted and beaten. "Certainly," said Demosthenes, "nothing of the kind can have happened to you." Upon which the other, raising his voice, exclaimed loudly, "What, Demosthenes, nothing has been done to me?" "Ah," replied Demosthenes, "now I hear the voice of one that has been injured and beaten." Of so great consequence towards the gaining of belief did he esteem the tone and action of the speaker. The action which he used himself was wonderfully pleasing to the common people; but by well-educated people, as, for example, by Demetrius, the Phalerian, it was looked upon as mean, humiliating, and unmanly. And Hermippus says of Æsion, that, being asked his opinion concerning the ancient orators and those of his own time, he answered that it was admirable to see with what composure and in what high style they addressed themselves to the people; but that the orations of Demosthenes, when they are read, certainly appear to be superior in point of construction, and more effective.[6] His written speeches,

[6] Æsion was a fellow scholar with Demosthenes. The comparison in his remarks gives the superiority in manner to the old speakers, whom he remembered in his youth, but in construction, to Demosthenes, his contemporary.

beyond all question, are characterized by austere tone and by their severity. In his extempore retorts and rejoinders, he allowed himself the use of jest and mockery. When Demades said, "Demosthenes teach me! So might the sow teach Minerva!" he replied, "Was it this Minerva, that was lately found playing the harlot in Collytus?"[7] When a thief, who had the nickname of the Brazen, was attempting to upbraid him for sitting up late, and writing by candlelight, "I know very well," said he, "that you had rather have all lights out; and wonder not, O ye men of Athens, at the many robberies which are committed, since we have thieves of brass and walls of clay." But on these points, though we have much more to mention, we will add nothing at present. We will proceed to take an estimate of his character from his actions and his life as a statesman.

His first entering into public business was much about the time of the Phocian war, as himself affirms, and may be collected from his Philippic orations. For of these, some were made after that action was over, and the earliest of them refer to its concluding events. It is certain that he engaged in the accusation of Midias when he was but two and thirty years old, having as yet no interest or reputation as a politician. And this it was, I consider, that induced him to withdraw the action, and accept a sum of money as a compromise. For of himself

"He was no easy or good-natured man,"

but of a determined disposition, and resolute to see himself righted; however, finding it a hard matter and above his strength to deal with Midias, a man so well secured on all sides with money, eloquence, and friends, he yielded to the entreaties of those who interceded for him. But had he seen any hopes or possibility of prevailing, I cannot believe that three thousand drachmas could have taken off the edge of his revenge. The object which he chose for himself in the commonwealth was noble and just, the defence of the Grecians against Philip; and in this he behaved himself so

[7] "Sus Minervam," the proverb. Collytus, together with Melite, formed the southwest, and, apparently, the more agreeable part of Athens. Plutarch, consoling a friend who was banished from his native city, tells him people cannot all live where they like best; it is not every Athenian can live in Collytus, nor does a man consider himself a miserable exile, who has to leave a house in Melite and take one in Diomea.

worthily that he soon grew famous, and excited attention everywhere for his eloquence and courage in speaking. He was admired through all Greece, the king of Persia courted him, and by Philip himself he was more esteemed than all the other orators. His very enemies were forced to confess that they had to do with a man of mark; for such a character even Æschines and Hyperides give him, where they accuse and speak against him.

So that I cannot imagine what ground Theopompus had to say, that Demosthenes was of a fickle, unsettled disposition, and could not long continue firm either to the same men or the same affairs; whereas the contrary is most apparent, for the same party and post in politics which he held from the beginning, to these he kept constant to the end; and was so far from leaving them while he lived, that he chose rather to forsake his life than his purpose. He was never heard to apologize for shifting sides like Demades, who would say, he often spoke against himself, but never against the city; nor as Melanopus, who, being generally against Callistratus, but being often bribed off with money, was wont to tell the people, "The man indeed is my enemy, but we must submit for the good of our country;" nor again as Nicodemus, the Messenian, who having first appeared on Cassander's side and afterwards taken part with Demetrius, said the two things were not in themselves contrary, it being always most advisable to obey the conqueror. We have nothing of this kind to say against Demosthenes, as one who would turn aside or prevaricate, either in word or deed. There could not have been less variation in his public acts if they had all been played, so to say, from first to last, from the same score. Panætius, the philosopher, said, that most of his orations are so written, as if they were to prove this one conclusion, that what is honest and virtuous is for itself only to be chosen; as that of the Crown, that against Aristocrates, that for the Immunities, and the Philippics; in all which he persuades his fellow-citizens to pursue not that which seems most pleasant, easy, or profitable; but declares over and over again, that they ought in the first place to prefer that which is just and honorable, before their own safety and preservation. So that if he had kept his hands clean, if his courage for the wars had been answerable to the generosity of his principles, and the dignity of his orations, he might deservedly have his name placed, not in the number of such orators as Mœrocles, Polyeuctus, and Hyperides, but in the highest rank with Cimon, Thucydides, and Pericles.

Certainly amongst those who were contemporary with him, Phocion, though he appeared on the less commendable side in the commonwealth, and was counted as one of the Macedonian party, nevertheless, by his courage and his honesty, procured himself a name not inferior to those of Ephialtes, Aristides, and Cimon. But Demosthenes, being neither fit to be relied on for courage in arms, as Demetrius says, nor on all sides inaccessible to bribery (for how invincible soever he was against the gifts of Philip and the Macedonians, yet elsewhere he lay open to assault, and was overpowered by the gold which came down from Susa and Ecbatana), was therefore esteemed better able to recommend than to imitate the virtues of past times. And yet (excepting only Phocion), even in his life and manners, he far surpassed the other orators of his time. None of them addressed the people so boldly; he attacked the faults, and opposed himself to the unreasonable desires of the multitude, as may be seen in his orations. Theopompus writes, that the Athenians having by name selected Demosthenes, and called upon him to accuse a certain person, he refused to do it; upon which the assembly being all in an uproar, he rose up and said, "Your counsellor, whether you will or no, O ye men of Athens, you shall always have me; but a sycophant or false accuser, though you would have me, I shall never be." And his conduct in the case of Antiphon was perfectly aristocratical; whom, after he had been acquitted in the assembly, he took and brought before the court of Areopagus, and, setting at naught the displeasure of the people, convicted him there of having promised Philip to burn the arsenal; whereupon the man was condemned by that court, and suffered for it. He accused, also, Theoris, the priestess, amongst other misdemeanors, of having instructed and taught the slaves to deceive and cheat their masters, for which the sentence of death passed upon her, and she was executed.

The oration which Apollodorus made use of, and by it carried the cause against Timotheus, the general, in an action of debt, it is said was written for him by Demosthenes; as also those against Phormion and Stephanus, in which latter case he was thought to have acted dishonorably, for the speech which Phormion used against Apollodorus was also of his making; he, as it were, having simply furnished two adversaries out of the same shop with weapons to wound one another. Of his orations addressed to the public assemblies, that against Androtion, and those against Timocrates and Aristocrates, were written for others, before he had come forward himself as a politician. They were composed, it seems, when he was but seven or eight and twenty years old. That against Aristogiton, and that for the Immunities, he spoke himself, at the request, as he says, of Ctesippus, the son of Chabrias, but, as some say, out of courtship to the young man's mother. Though, in fact, he did not marry her, for his wife was a woman of Samos, as Demetrius, the Magnesian, writes, in his book on Persons of the same Name. It is not certain whether his oration against Æschines, for Misconduct as Ambassador, was ever spoken; although Idomeneus says that Æschines wanted only thirty voices to condemn him. But this seems not to be correct, at least so far as may be conjectured from both their orations concerning the Crown; for in these, neither of them speaks clearly or directly of it, as a cause that ever came to trial. But let others decide this controversy.

It was evident, even in time of peace, what course Demosthenes would steer in the commonwealth; for whatever was done by the Macedonian, he criticized and found fault with, and upon all occasions was stirring up the people of Athens, and inflaming them against him. Therefore, in the court of Philip, no man was so much talked of, or of so great account as he; and when he came thither, one of the ten ambassadors who were sent into Macedonia, though all had audience given them, yet his speech was answered with most care and exactness. But in other respects, Philip entertained him not so honorably as the rest, neither did he show him the same kindness and civility with which he applied himself to the party of Æschines and Philocrates. So that, when the others commended Philip for his able speaking, his beautiful person, nay, and also for his good companionship in drinking, Demosthenes could not refrain from cavilling at these praises; the first, he said, was a quality which might well enough become a rhetorician, the second a woman, and the last was only the property of a sponge; no one of them was the proper commendation of a prince.

But when things came at last to war, Philip on the one side being not able to live in peace, and the Athenians, on the other side, being stirred up by Demosthenes, the first action he put them upon was the reducing of Eubœa, which, by the treachery of the tyrants, was brought under subjection to Philip. And on his proposition, the decree was voted, and they crossed over thither and chased the Macedonians out of the island. The next, was the relief of the Byzantines and Perinthians, whom the Macedonians at that time were attacking. He persuaded the people to lay aside their enmity against these cities, to forget the offences committed by them in the Confederate War, and to send them such succors as eventually saved and secured them. Not long after, he undertook an embassy through the States of Greece, which he solicited and so far incensed against Philip, that, a few only excepted, he brought them all into a general league. So that, besides the forces composed of the citizens themselves, there was an army consisting of fifteen thousand foot and two thousand horse, and the money to pay these strangers was levied and brought in with great cheerfulness. On which occasion it was, says Theophrastus, on the allies requesting that their contributions for the war might be ascertained and stated, Crobylus, the orator, made use of the saying, "War can't be fed at so much a day." Now was all Greece up in arms, and in great expectation what would be the event. The Eubœans, the Achæans, the Corinthians, the Megarians, the Leucadians, and Corcyræans, their people and their cities, were all joined together in a league. But the hardest task was yet behind, left for Demosthenes, to draw the Thebans into this confederacy with the rest. Their country bordered next upon Attica, they had great forces for the war, and at that time they were accounted the best soldiers of all Greece, but it was no easy matter to make them break with Philip, who, by many good offices, had so lately obliged them in the Phocian war; especially considering how the subjects of dispute and variance between the two cities were continually renewed and exasperated by petty quarrels, arising out of the proximity of their frontiers.

But after Philip, being now grown high and puffed up with his good success at Amphissa, on a sudden surprised Elatea and possessed himself of Phocis, and the Athenians were in a great consternation, none durst venture to rise up to speak, no one knew what to say, all were at a loss, and the whole assembly in silence and perplexity, in this extremity of affairs, Demosthenes was the only man who appeared, his counsel to them being alliance with the Thebans. And having in other ways encouraged the people, and, as his manner was, raised their spirits up with hopes, he, with some others, was sent ambassador to Thebes. To oppose him, as Marsyas says, Philip also sent thither his envoys, Amyntas and Clearchus, two Macedonians, besides Daochus, a Thessalian, and Thrasydæus. Now the Thebans, in their consultations, were well enough aware what suited best with their own interest, but every one had before his eyes the terrors of war, and their losses in the Phocian troubles were still recent; but such was the force and power of the orator, fanning up, as Theopompus says, their courage, and firing their emulation, that casting away every thought of prudence, fear, or obligation, in a sort of divine possession, they chose the path of honor, to which his words invited them. And this success, thus accomplished by an orator, was thought to be so glorious and of such consequence, that Philip immediately sent heralds to treat and petition for a peace: all Greece was aroused, and up in arms to help. And the commanders-in-chief, not only of Attica, but of Bœotia, applied themselves to Demosthenes, and observed his directions. He managed all the assemblies of the Thebans, no less than those of the Athenians; he was beloved both by the one and by the other, and exercised the same supreme authority with both; and that not by unfair means, or without just cause, as Theopompus professes, but indeed it was no more than was due to his merit.

But there was, it should seem, some divinely-ordered fortune, commissioned, in the revolution of things, to put a period at this time to the liberty of Greece, which opposed and thwarted all their actions, and by many signs foretold what should happen. Such were the sad predictions uttered by the Pythian priestess, and this old oracle cited out of the Sibyl's verses,—

> "The battle on Thermodon that shall be
> Safe at a distance I desire to see,
> Far, like an eagle, watching in the air.
> Conquered shall weep, and conqueror perish there."

This Thermodon, they say, is a little rivulet here in our country in Chæronea, running into the Cephisus. But we know of none that is so called at the present time; and can only conjecture that the streamlet which is now called Hæmon, and runs by the Temple of Hercules, where the Grecians were encamped, might perhaps in those days be called Thermodon, and after the fight, being filled with blood and dead bodies, upon this occasion, as we guess, might change its old name for that which it now bears. Yet Duris says that this Thermodon was no river, but that some of the soldiers, as they were pitching their tents and digging trenches about them, found a small stone statue, which, by the inscription, appeared to be the figure of Thermodon, carrying a wounded Amazon in his arms; and that there was another oracle current about it, as follows:—

> "The battle on Thermodon that shall be,
> Fail not, black raven, to attend and see;
> The flesh of men shall there abound for thee."

In fine, it is not easy to determine what is the truth. But of Demosthenes it is said, that he had such great confidence in the Grecian forces, and was so excited by the sight of the courage and resolution of so many brave men ready to engage the enemy, that he would by no means endure they should give any heed to oracles, or hearken to prophecies, but gave out that he suspected even the prophetess herself, as if she had been tampered with to speak in favor of Philip. The Thebans he put in mind of Epaminondas, the Athenians, of Pericles who always took their own measures and governed their actions by reason, looking upon things of this kind as mere pretexts for cowardice. Thus far, therefore, Demosthenes acquitted himself like a brave man. But in the fight he did nothing honorable, nor was his performance answerable to his speeches.

For he fled, deserting his place disgracefully, and throwing away his arms, not ashamed, as Pytheas observed, to belie the inscription written on his shield, in letters of gold, "With good fortune."

In the mean time Philip, in the first moment of victory, was so transported with joy, that he grew extravagant, and going out, after he had drunk largely, to visit the dead bodies, he chanted the first words of the decree that had been passed on the motion of Demosthenes,

"The motion of Demosthenes, Demosthenes's son,"[8]

dividing it metrically into feet, and marking the beats.

But when he came to himself, and had well considered the danger he was lately under, he could not forbear from shuddering at the wonderful ability and power of an orator who had made him hazard his life and empire on the issue of a few brief hours. The fame of it also reached even to the court of Persia, and the king sent letters to his lieutenants, commanding them to supply Demosthenes with money, and to pay every attention to him, as the only man of all the Grecians who was able to give Philip occupation and find employment for his forces near home, in the troubles of Greece. This afterwards came to the knowledge of Alexander, by certain letters of Demosthenes which he found at Sardis, and by other papers of the Persian officers, stating the large sums which had been given him.

At this time, however, upon the ill success which now happened to the Grecians, those of the contrary faction in the commonwealth fell foul upon Demosthenes, and took the opportunity to frame several informations and indictments against him. But the people not only acquitted him of these accusations, but continued towards him their former respect, and still invited him, as a man that meant well, to take a part in public affairs. Insomuch that when the bones of those who had been slain at Chæronea were brought home to be solemnly interred, Demosthenes was the man they chose to make the funeral oration. They did not show, under the misfortunes which befell them, a base or ignoble mind, as Theopompus writes in his

[8] Demosthenes Demosthenous, Paianieus, tad' eipen. "Demosthenes, the son of Demosthenes, of the Pæanian township, made this motion,"—the usual form of the commencement of the Votes of the Athenian Assembly.

exaggerated style, but, on the contrary, by the honor and respect paid to their counsellor, they made it appear that they were noway dissatisfied with the counsels he had given them. The speech, therefore, was spoken by Demosthenes. But the subsequent decrees he would not allow to be passed in his own name, but made use of those of his friends, one after another, looking upon his own as unfortunate and inauspicious; till at length he took courage again after the death of Philip, who did not long outlive his victory at Chæronea. And this, it seems, was that which was foretold in the last verse of the oracle,

"Conquered shall weep, and conqueror perish there."

Demosthenes had secret intelligence of the death of Philip, and laying hold of this opportunity to prepossess the people with courage and better hopes for the future, he came into the assembly with a cheerful countenance pretending to have had a dream that presaged some great good fortune for Athens; and, not long after, arrived the messengers who brought the news of Philip's death. No sooner had the people received it, but immediately they offered sacrifice to the gods, and decreed that Pausanias should be presented with a crown. Demosthenes appeared publicly in a rich dress, with a chaplet on his head, though it were but the seventh day since the death of his daughter, as is said by Æschines, who upbraids him upon this account, and rails at him as one void of natural affection towards his children. Whereas, indeed, he rather betrays himself to be of a poor, low spirit, and effeminate mind, if he really means to make wailings and lamentation the only signs of a gentle and affectionate nature, and to condemn those who bear such accidents with more temper and less passion. For my own part, I cannot say that the behavior of the Athenians on this occasion was wise or honorable, to crown themselves with garlands and to sacrifice to the Gods for the death of a Prince who, in the midst of his success and victories, when they were a conquered people, had used them with so much clemency and humanity. For besides provoking fortune, it was a base thing, and unworthy in itself, to make him a citizen of Athens, and pay him honors while he lived, and yet as soon as he fell by another's hand, to set no bounds to their jollity, to insult over him dead, and to sing triumphant songs of victory, as if by their own valor they had vanquished him. I must at the same time commend the behavior of Demosthenes, who, leaving tears and lamentations and domestic sorrows to the women, made it his business to attend to the interests of the commonwealth. And I think it the duty of him who would be accounted to have a soul truly valiant, and fit for government, that, standing always firm to the common good, and letting private griefs and troubles find their compensation in public blessings, he should maintain the dignity of his character and station, much more than actors who represent the persons of kings and tyrants, who, we see, when they either laugh or weep on the stage, follow, not their own private inclinations, but the course consistent with the subject and with their position. And if, moreover, when our neighbor is in misfortune, it is not our duty to forbear offering any consolation, but rather to say whatever may tend to cheer him, and to invite his attention to any agreeable objects, just as we tell people who are troubled with sore eyes, to withdraw their sight from bright and offensive colors to green, and those of a softer mixture, from whence can a man seek, in his own case, better arguments of consolation for afflictions in his family, than from the prosperity of his country, by making public and domestic chances count, so to say, together, and the better fortune of the state obscure and conceal the less happy circumstances of the individual. I have been induced to say so much, because I have known many readers melted by Æschines's language into a soft and unmanly tenderness.

But now to return to my narrative. The cities of Greece were inspirited once more by the efforts of Demosthenes to form a league together. The Thebans, whom he had provided with arms, set upon their garrison, and slew many of them; the Athenians made preparations to join their forces with them; Demosthenes ruled supreme in the popular assembly, and wrote letters to the Persian officers who commanded under the king in Asia, inciting them to make war upon the Macedonian, calling him child and simpleton.[9] But as soon as Alexander had settled matters in his own country, and

[9] *Margites,* the name of the character held up to ridicule in an old poem ascribed to Homer,—the boy, who, though fully grown up, has never attained the sense or wits of a man.

came in person with his army into Bœotia, down fell the courage of the Athenians, and Demosthenes was hushed; the Thebans, deserted by them, fought by themselves, and lost their city. After which, the people of Athens, all in distress and great perplexity, resolved to send ambassadors to Alexander, and amongst others, made choice of Demosthenes for one; but his heart failing him for fear of the king's anger, he returned back from Cithæron, and left the embassy. In the mean time, Alexander sent to Athens, requiring ten of their orators to be delivered up to him, as Idomeneus and Duris have reported, but as the most and best historians say, he demanded these eight only,—Demosthenes, Polyeuctus, Ephialtes, Lycurgus, Mœrocles, Demon, Callisthenes, and Charidemus. It was upon this occasion that Demosthenes related to them the fable in which the sheep are said to deliver up their dogs to the wolves; himself and those who with him contended for the people's safety, being, in his comparison, the dogs that defended the flock, and Alexander "the Macedonian arch wolf." He further told them, "As we see corn-masters sell their whole stock but a few grains of wheat which they carry about with them in a dish, as a sample of the rest, so you, by delivering up us, who are but a few, do at the same time unawares surrender up yourselves all together with us;" so we find it related in the history of Aristobulus, the Cassandrian. The Athenians were deliberating, and at a loss what to do, when Demades, having agreed with the persons whom Alexander had demanded, for five talents, undertook to go ambassador, and to intercede with the king for them; and, whether it was that he relied on his friendship and kindness, or that he hoped to find him satiated, as a lion glutted with slaughter, he certainly went, and prevailed with him both to pardon the men, and to be reconciled to the city.

So he and his friends, when Alexander went away, were great men, and Demosthenes was quite put aside. Yet when Agis, the Spartan, made his insurrection, he also for a short time attempted a movement in his favor; but he soon shrunk back again, as the Athenians would not take any part in it, and, Agis being slain, the Lacedæmonians were vanquished. During this time it was that the indictment against Ctesiphon, concerning the Crown, was brought to trial. The action was commenced a little before the battle in

Chæronea, when Chærondas was archon, but it was not proceeded with till about ten years after, Aristophon being then archon. Never was any public cause more celebrated than this, alike for the fame of the orators, and for the generous courage of the judges, who, though at that time the accusers of Demosthenes were in the height of power, and supported by all the favor of the Macedonians, yet would not give judgment against him, but acquitted him so honorably, that Æschines did not obtain the fifth part of their suffrages on his side, so that, immediately after, he left the city, and spent the rest of his life in teaching rhetoric about the island of Rhodes, and upon the continent in Ionia.

It was not long after that Harpalus fled from Alexander, and came to Athens out of Asia; knowing himself guilty of many misdeeds into which his love of luxury had led him, and fearing the king, who was now grown terrible even to his best friends. Yet this man had no sooner addressed himself to the people, and delivered up his goods, his ships, and himself to their disposal, but the other orators of the town had their eyes quickly fixed upon his money, and came in to his assistance, persuading the Athenians to receive and protect their suppliant. Demosthenes at first gave advice to chase him out of the country, and to beware lest they involved their city in a war upon an unnecessary and unjust occasion. But some few days after, as they were taking an account of the treasure, Harpalus, perceiving how much he was pleased with a cup of Persian manufacture, and how curiously he surveyed the sculpture and fashion of it, desired him to poise it in his hand, and consider the weight of the gold. Demosthenes, being amazed to feel how heavy it was, asked him what weight it *came to*. "To you," said Harpalus, smiling, "it shall *come with* twenty talents." And presently after, when night drew on, he sent him the cup with so many talents. Harpalus, it seems, was a person of singular skill to discern a man's covetousness by the air of his countenance, and the look and movements of his eyes. For Demosthenes could not resist the temptation, but admitting the present, like an armed garrison, into the citadel of his house, he surrendered bimself up to the interest of Harpalus. The next day, he came into the assembly with his neck swathed about with wool and rollers, and when they called on him to rise up and speak, he made signs as if he had lost his voice. But the wits, turning the matter to ridicule, said that certainly the orator had been seized that night with no other than a silver quinsy. And soon after, the people, becoming aware of the bribery, grew angry, and would not suffer him to speak, or make any apology for himself, but ran him down with noise; and one man stood up, and cried out, "What, ye men of Athens, will you not hear the cup-bearer?" So at length they banished Harpalus out of the city; and fearing lest they should be called to account for the treasure which the orators had purloined, they made a strict inquiry, going from house to house; only Callicles, the son of Arrhenidas, who was newly married, they would not suffer to be searched, out of respect, as Theopompus writes, to the bride, who was within.

Demosthenes resisted the inquisition, and proposed a decree to refer the business to the court of Areopagus, and to punish those whom that court should find guilty. But being himself one of the first whom the court condemned, when he came to the bar, he was fined fifty talents, and committed to prison; where, out of shame of the crime for which he was condemned, and through the weakness of his body, growing incapable of supporting the confinement, he made his escape, by the carelessness of some and by the connivance of others of the citizens. We are told, at least, that he had not fled far from the city, when, finding that he was pursued by some of those who had been his adversaries, he endeavored to hide himself. But when they called him by name, and coming up nearer to him, desired he would accept from them some money which they had brought from home as a provision for his journey, and to that purpose only had followed him, when they entreated him to take courage, and to bear up against his misfortune, he burst out into much greater lamentation, saying, "But how is it possible to support myself under so heavy an affliction, since I leave a city in which I have such enemies, as in any other it is not easy to find friends." He did not show much fortitude in his banishment, spending his time for the most part in Ægina and Trœzen, and, with tears in his eyes, looking towards the country of Attica. And there remain upon record some sayings of his, little resembling those sentiments of generosity and bravery which he used to express when he had the management of the commonwealth. For, as he was departing out of the city, it is reported, he lifted up his hands towards the Acropolis, and said, "O Lady Minerva, how is it that thou takest delight in three such fierce untractable beasts, the owl, the snake, and the people?" The young men that came to visit and converse with him, he deterred from meddling with state affairs, telling them, that if at first two ways had been proposed to him, the one leading to the speaker's stand and the assembly, the other going direct to destruction, and he could have foreseen the many evils which attend those who deal in public business, such as fears, envies, calumnies, and contentions, he would certainly have taken that which led straight on to his death.

But now happened the death of Alexander, while Demosthenes was in this banishment which we have been speaking of. And the Grecians were once again up in arms, encouraged by the brave attempts of Leosthenes, who was then drawing a circumvallation about Antipater, whom he held close besieged in Lamia. Pytheas, therefore, the orator, and Callimedon, called the Crab, fled from Athens, and taking sides with Antipater, went about with his friends and ambassadors to keep the Grecians from revolting and taking part with the Athenians. But, on the other side, Demosthenes, associating himself with the ambassadors that came from Athens, used his utmost endeavors and gave them his best assistance in persuading the cities to fall unanimously upon the Macedonians, and to drive them out of Greece. Phylarchus says that in Arcadia there happened a rencounter between Pytheas and Demosthenes, which came at last to downright railing, while the one pleaded for the Macedonians, and the other for the Grecians. Pytheas said, that as we always suppose there is some disease in the family to which they bring asses' milk, so wherever there comes an embassy from Athens, that city must needs be indisposed. And Demosthenes answered him, retorting the comparison: "Asses' milk is brought to restore health, and the Athenians come for the safety and recovery of the sick." With this conduct the people of Athens were so well pleased, that they decreed the recall of Demosthenes from banishment. The decree was brought in by Demon the Pæanian, cousin to Demosthenes. So they sent him a ship to Ægina, and he landed at the port of Piræus, where he was met and joyfully received by all the citizens, not so much as an Archon or a priest staying behind. And Demetrius, the Magnesian, says, that he lifted up his hands towards heaven, and blessed this day of his happy return, as far more honorable than that of Alcibiades; since he was recalled by his countrymen, not through any force or constraint put upon them, but by their own good-will and free inclinations. There remained only his pecuniary fine, which, according to law, could not be remitted by the people. But they found out a way to elude the law. It was a custom with them to allow a certain quantity of silver to those who were to furnish and adorn the altar for the sacrifice of Jupiter Soter. This office, for that turn, they bestowed on Demosthenes, and for the performance of it ordered him fifty talents, the very sum in which he was condemned.

Yet it was no long time that he enjoyed his country after his return, the attempts of the Greeks being soon all utterly defeated. For the battle at Cranon happened in Metagitnion, in Boëdromion the garrison entered into Munychia, and in the Pyanepsion following died Demosthenes after this manner.

Upon the report that Antipater and Craterus were coming to Athens, Demosthenes with his party took their opportunity to escape privily out of the city; but sentence of death was, upon the motion of Demades, passed upon them by the people. They dispersed themselves, flying some to one place, some to another; and Antipater sent about his soldiers into all quarters to apprehend them. Archias was their captain, and was thence called the exile-hunter. He was a Thurian born, and is reported to have been an actor of tragedies, and they say that Polus, of Ægina, the best actor of his time, was his scholar; but Hermippus reckons Archias among the disciples of Lacritus, the orator, and Demetrius says, he spent some time with Anaximenes. This Archias finding Hyperides the orator, Aristonicus of Marathon, and Himeræus, the brother of Demetrius the Phalerian, in Ægina, took them by force out of the temple of Æacus, whither they were fled for safety, and sent them to Antipater, then at Cleonæ, where they were all put to death; and Hyperides, they say, had his tongue cut out.

Demosthenes, he heard, had taken sanctuary at the temple of

Neptune in Calauria, and, crossing over thither in some light vessels, as soon as he had landed himself, and the Thracian spear-men that came with him, he endeavored to persuade Demosthenes to accompany him to Antipater, as if he should meet with no hard usage from him. But Demosthenes, in his sleep the night before, had a strange dream. It seemed to him that he was acting a tragedy, and contended with Archias for the victory; and though he acquitted himself well, and gave good satisfaction to the spectators, yet for want of better furniture and provision for the stage, he lost the day. And so, while Archias was discoursing to him with many expressions of kindness, he sate still in the same posture, and looking up steadfastly upon him, "O Archias," said he, "I am as little affected by your promises now as I used formerly to be by your acting." Archias at this beginning to grow angry and to threaten him, "Now," said Demosthenes, "you speak like the genuine Macedonian oracle; before you were but acting a part. Therefore forbear only a little, while I write a word or two home to my family." Having thus spoken, he withdrew into the temple, and taking a scroll, as if he meant to write, he put the reed into his mouth, and biting it, as he was wont to do when he was thoughtful or writing, he held it there for some time. Then he bowed down his head and covered it. The soldiers that stood at the door, supposing all this to proceed from want of courage and fear of death, in derision called him effeminate, and faint-hearted, and coward. And Archias, drawing near, desired him to rise up, and repeating the same kind things he had spoken before, he once more promised him to make his peace with Antipater. But Demosthenes, perceiving that now the poison had pierced and seized his vitals, uncovered his head, and fixing his eyes upon Archias, "Now," said he, "as soon as you please you may commence the part of Creon in the tragedy, and cast out this body of mine unburied. But, O gracious Neptune, I, for my part, while I am yet alive, arise up and depart out of this sacred place; though Antipater and the Macedonians have not left so much as thy temple unpolluted." After he had thus spoken and desired to be held up, because already he began to tremble and stagger, as he was going forward, and passing by the altar, he fell down, and with a groan gave up the ghost.

Ariston says that he took the poison out of a reed, as we have shown before. But Pappus, a certain historian whose history was recovered by Hermippus, says, that as he fell near the altar, there was found in his scroll this beginning only of a letter, and nothing more, "Demosthenes to Antipater." And that when his sudden death was much wondered at, the Thracians who guarded the doors reported that he took the poison into his hand out of a rag, and put it into his mouth, and that they imagined it had been gold which he swallowed; but the maid that served him, being examined by the followers of Archias, affirmed that he had worn it in a bracelet for a long time, as an amulet. And Eratosthenes also says that he kept the poison in a hollow ring, and that that ring was the bracelet which he wore about his arm. There are various other statements made by the many authors who have related the story, but there is no need to enter into their discrepancies; yet I must not omit what is said by Demochares, the relation of Demosthenes, who is of opinion, it was not by the help of poison that he met with so sudden and so easy a death, but that by the singular favor and providence of the gods he was thus rescued from the cruelty of the Macedonians. He died on the sixteenth of Pyanepsion, the most sad and solemn day of the Thesmophoria, which the women observe by fasting in the temple of the goddess.

Soon after his death, the people of Athens bestowed on him such honors as he had deserved. They erected his statue of brass; they decreed that the eldest of his family should be maintained in the Prytaneum; and on the base of his statue was engraven the famous inscription,—

> "Had you for Greece been strong, as wise you were,
> The Macedonian had not conquered her."

For it is simply ridiculous to say, as some have related, that Demosthenes made these verses himself in Calauria, as he was about to take the poison.

A little before he went to Athens, the following incident was said to have happened. A soldier, being summoned to appear before his superior officer, and answer to an accusation brought against him, put that little gold which he had into the hands of Demosthenes's statue. The fingers of this statue were folded one within another, and near it grew a small plane-tree, from which many leaves, either accidentally blown thither by the wind, or placed so on purpose by the man himself, falling together, and lying round about the gold, concealed it for a long time. In the end, the soldier returned, and found his treasure entire, and the fame of this incident was spread abroad. And many ingenious persons of the city competed with each other, on this occasion, to vindicate the integrity of Demosthenes, in several epigrams which they made on the subject.

As for Demades, he did not long enjoy the new honors he now came in for, divine vengeance for the death of Demosthenes pursuing him into Macedonia, where he was justly put to death by those whom he had basely flattered. They were weary of him before, but at this time the guilt he lay under was manifest and undeniable. For some of his letters were intercepted, in which he had encouraged Perdiccas[10] to fall upon Macedonia, and to save the Grecians, who, he said, hung only by an old rotten thread, meaning Antipater. Of this he was accused by Dinarchus, the Corinthian, and Cassander was so enraged, that he first slew his son in his bosom, and then gave orders to execute him; who might now at last, by his own extreme misfortunes, learn the lesson, that traitors, who make sale of their country, sell themselves first; a truth which Demosthenes had often foretold him, and he would never believe. Thus, Sosius, you have the life of Demosthenes, from such accounts as we have either read or heard concerning him.

[10] This, apparently, is one of Plutarch's slips of memory. It was not Perdiccas, but Antigonus; and so he tells the story himself in the life of Phocion.

CICERO

IT is generally said, that Helvia, the mother of Cicero, was both well born and lived a fair life; but of his father nothing is reported but in extremes. For whilst some would have him the son of a fuller, and educated in that trade, others carry back the origin of his family to Tullus Attius, an illustrious king of the Volscians, who waged war not without honor against the Romans. However, he who first of that house was surnamed Cicero seems to have been a person worthy to be remembered; since those who succeeded him not only did not reject, but were fond of the name, though vulgarly made a matter of reproach. For the Latins call a vetch *Cicer,* and a nick or dent at the tip of his nose, which resembled the opening in a vetch, gave him the surname of *Cicero.*

Cicero, whose story I am writing, is said to have replied with spirit to some of his friends, who recommended him to lay aside or change the name when he first stood for office and engaged in politics, that he would make it his endeavor to render the name of Cicero more glorious than that of the Scauri and Catuli. And when he was quæstor in Sicily, and was making an offering of silver plate to the gods, and had inscribed his two names, Marcus and Tullius, instead of the third he jestingly told the artificer to engrave the figure of a vetch by them. Thus much is told us about his name.

Of his birth it is reported, that his mother was delivered without pain or labor, on the third of the new Calends,[1] the same day on which now the magistrates of Rome pray and sacrifice for the emperor. It is said, also, that a vision appeared to his nurse, and foretold the child she then suckled should afterwards become a great benefit to the Roman States. To such presages, which might in general be thought mere fancies and idle talk, he himself erelong gave the credit of true prophecies. For as soon as he was of an age

[1] The third of January.

to begin to have lessons, he became so distinguished for his talent, and got such a name and reputation amongst the boys, that their fathers would often visit the school, that they might see young Cicero, and might be able to say that they themselves had witnessed the quickness and readiness in learning for which he was renowned. And the more rude among them used to be angry with their children, to see them, as they walked together, receiving Cicero with respect into the middle place. And being, as Plato would have the scholar-like and philosophical temper, eager for every kind of learning, and indisposed to no description of knowledge or instruction, he showed, however, a more peculiar propensity to poetry; and there is a poem now extant, made by him when a boy, in tetrameter verse, called Pontius Glaucus. And afterwards, when he applied himself more curiously to these accomplishments, he had the name of being not only the best orator, but also the best poet of Rome. And the glory of his rhetoric still remains, notwithstanding the many new modes in speaking since his time; but his verses are forgotten and out of all repute, so many ingenious poets having followed him.

Leaving his juvenile studies, he became an auditor of Philo the Academic, whom the Romans, above all the other scholars of Clitomachus, admired for his eloquence and loved for his character. He also sought the company of the Mucii, who were eminent statesmen and leaders in the senate, and acquired from them a knowledge of the laws. For some short time he served in arms under Sylla, in the Marsian war. But perceiving the commonwealth running into factions, and from faction all things tending to an absolute monarchy, he betook himself to a retired and contemplative life, and conversing with the learned Greeks, devoted himself to study, till Sylla had obtained the government, and the commonwealth was in some kind of settlement.

At this time, Chrysogonus, Sylla's emancipated slave, having laid an information about an estate belonging to one who was said to have been put to death by proscription, had bought it himself for two thousand drachmas. And when Roscius, the son and heir of the dead, complained, and demonstrated the estate to be worth two hundred and fifty talents, Sylla took it angrily to have his actions questioned, and preferred a process against Roscius for the murder of his father, Chrysogonus managing the evidence. None of the advocates durst assist him, but fearing the cruelty of Sylla, avoided the cause. The young man, being thus deserted, came for refuge to Cicero. Cicero's friends encouraged him, saying he was not likely ever to have a fairer and more honorable introduction to public life; he therefore undertook the defence, carried the cause, and got much renown for it.

But fearing Sylla, he travelled into Greece, and gave it out that he did so for the benefit of his health. And indeed he was lean and meagre, and had such a weakness in his stomach, that he could take nothing but a spare and thin diet, and that not till late in the evening. His voice was loud and good, but so harsh and unmanaged that in vehemence and heat of speaking he always raised it to so high a tone, that there seemed to be reason to fear about his health.

When he came to Athens, he was a hearer of Antiochus of Ascalon, with whose fluency and elegance of diction he was much taken, although he did not approve of his innovations in doctrine. For Antiochus had now fallen off from the New Academy, as they call it, and forsaken the sect of Carneades, whether that he was moved by the argument of manifestness [2] and the senses, or, as some say, had been led by feelings of rivalry and opposition to the followers of Clitomachus and Philo to change his opinions, and in most things to embrace the doctrine of the Stoics. But Cicero rather affected and adhered to the doctrines of the New Academy; and purposed with himself, if he should be disappointed of any employment in the commonwealth, to retire hither from pleading and political affairs, and to pass his life with quiet in the study of philosophy.

But after he had received the news of Sylla's death, and his body, strengthened again by exercise, was come to a vigorous habit, his voice managed and rendered sweet and full to the ear and pretty well brought into keeping with his general constitution, his friends

[2] According to a proposed correction, "by the manifestness of the senses." But the *enargeia,* or *manifestness* of things seen and felt, seems to be the recognized name of the argument against the sceptical views of the New Academy as to the possibility of certain knowledge. See Cicero's Academics, II. 6.

at Rome earnestly soliciting him by letters, and Antiochus also urging him to return to public affairs, he again prepared for use his orator's instrument of rhetoric, and summoned into action his political faculties, diligently exercising himself in declamations, and attending the most celebrated rhetoricians of the time. He sailed from Athens for Asia and Rhodes. Amongst the Asian masters, he conversed with Xenocles of Adramyttium, Dionysius of Magnesia, and Menippus of Caria; at Rhodes, he studied oratory with Apollonius, the son of Molon, and philosophy with Posidonius. Apollonius, we are told, not understanding Latin, requested Cicero to declaim in Greek. He complied willingly, thinking that his faults would thus be better pointed out to him. And after he finished, all his other hearers were astonished, and contended who should praise him most, but Apollonius, who had shown no signs of excitement whilst he was hearing him, so also now, when it was over, sate musing for some considerable time, without any remark. And when Cicero was discomposed at this, he said, "You have my praise and admiration, Cicero, and Greece my pity and commiseration, since those arts and that eloquence which are the only glories that remain to her, will now be transferred by you to Rome."

And now when Cicero, full of expectation, was again bent upon political affairs, a certain oracle blunted the edge of his inclination; for consulting the god of Delphi how he should attain most glory, the Pythoness answered, by making his own genius and not the opinion of the people the guide of his life; and therefore at first he passed his time in Rome cautiously, and was very backward in pretending to public offices, so that he was at that time in little esteem, and had got the names, so readily given by low and ignorant people in Rome, of Greek and Scholar. But when his own desire of fame and the eagerness of his father and relations had made him take in earnest to pleading, he made no slow or gentle advance to the first place, but shone out in full lustre at once, and far surpassed all the advocates of the bar. At first, it is said, he, as well as Demosthenes, was defective in his delivery, and on that account paid much attention to the instructions, sometimes of Roscius the comedian, and sometimes of Æsop the tragedian. They tell of this Æsop, that whilst he was representing on the theatre Atreus deliberating the revenge of Thyestes, he was so transported beyond himself in the heat of action, that he struck with his sceptre one of the servants, who was running across the stage, so violently, that he laid him dead upon the place. And such afterwards was Cicero's delivery, that it did not a little contribute to render his eloquence persuasive. He used to ridicule loud speakers, saying that they shouted because they could not speak, like lame men who get on horseback because they cannot walk. And his readiness and address in sarcasm, and generally in witty sayings, was thought to suit a pleader very well, and to be highly attractive, but his using it to excess offended many, and gave him the repute of ill nature.

He was appointed quæstor in a great scarcity of corn, and had Sicily for his province, where, though at first he displeased many, by compelling them to send their provisions to Rome, yet after they had had experience of his care, justice, and clemency, they honored him more than ever they did any of their governors before. It happened, also, that some young Romans of good and noble families, charged with neglect of discipline and misconduct in military service, were brought before the prætor in Sicily. Cicero undertook their defence, which he conducted admirably, and got them acquitted. So returning to Rome with a great opinion of himself for these things, a ludicrous incident befell him, as he tells us himself. Meeting an eminent citizen in Campania, whom he accounted his friend, he asked him what the Romans said and thought of his actions, as if the whole city had been filled with the glory of what he had done. His friend asked him in reply, "Where is it you have been, Cicero?" This for the time utterly mortified and cast him down, to perceive that the report of his actions had sunk into the city of Rome as into an immense ocean, without any visible effect or result in reputation. And afterwards considering with himself that the glory he contended for was an infinite thing, and that there was no fixed end nor measure in its pursuit, he abated much of his ambitious thoughts. Nevertheless, he was always excessively pleased with his own praise, and continued to the very last to be passionately fond of glory; which often interfered with the prosecution of his wisest resolutions.

On beginning to apply himself more resolutely to public business, he remarked it as an unreasonable and absurd thing that artificers, using vessels and instruments inanimate, should know the name, place, and use of every one of them, and yet the statesman, whose instruments for carrying out public measures are men, should be negligent and careless in the knowledge of persons. And so he not only acquainted himself with the names, but also knew the particular place where every one of the more eminent citizens dwelt, what lands he possessed, the friends he made use of, and those that were of his neighborhood, and when he travelled on any road in Italy, he could readily name and show the estates and seats of his friends and acquaintances. Having so small an estate, though a sufficient competency for his own expenses, it was much wondered at that he took neither fees nor gifts from his clients, and more especially, that he did not do so when he undertook the prosecution of Verres. This Verres, who had been prætor of Sicily, and stood charged by the Sicilians of many evil practices during his government there, Cicero succeeded in getting condemned, not by speaking, but in a manner by holding his tongue. For the prætors, favoring Verres, had deferred the trial by several adjournments to the last day, in which it was evident there could not be sufficient time for the advocates to be heard, and the cause brought to an issue. Cicero, therefore, came forward, and said there was no need of speeches; and after producing and examining witnesses, he required the judges to proceed to sentence. However, many witty sayings are on record, as having been used by Cicero on the occasion. When a man named Cæcilius, one of the freed slaves, who was said to be given to Jewish practices, would have put by the Sicilians, and undertaken the prosecution of Verres himself, Cicero asked, "What has a Jew to do with swine?" *verres* being the Roman word for boar. And when Verres began to reproach Cicero with effeminate living, "You ought," replied he, "to use this language at home, to your sons;" Verres having a son who had fallen into disgraceful courses. Hortensius the orator, not daring directly to undertake the defence of Verres, was yet persuaded to appear for him at the laying on of the fine, and received an ivory sphinx for his reward; and when Cicero, in some passage of his speech, obliquely reflected on him, and Hortensius told him he was not skilful in solving riddles, "No," said Cicero, "and yet you have the Sphinx in your house!"

Verres was thus convicted; though Cicero, who set the fine at seventy-five myriads,[3] lay under the suspicion of being corrupted by bribery to lessen the sum. But the Sicilians, in testimony of their gratitude, came and brought him all sorts of presents from the island, when he was ædile; of which he made no private profit himself, but used their generosity only to reduce the public price of provisions.

He had a very pleasant seat at Arpi,[4] he had also a farm near Naples, and another about Pompeii, but neither of any great value. The portion of his wife, Terentia, amounted to ten myriads, and he had a bequest valued at nine myriads of denarii; upon these he lived in a liberal but temperate style, with the learned Greeks and Romans that were his familiars. He rarely, if at any time, sat down to meat till sunset, and that not so much on account of business, as for his health and the weakness of his stomach. He was otherwise in the care of his body nice and delicate, appointing himself, for example, a set number of walks and rubbings. And after this manner managing the habit of his body, he brought it in time to be healthful, and capable of supporting many great fatigues and trials. His father's house he made over to his brother, living himself near the Palatine hill, that he might not give the trouble of long journeys to those that made suit to him. And, indeed, there were not fewer daily appearing at his door, to do their court to him, than there were that came to Crassus for his riches, or to Pompey for his power amongst the soldiers, these being at that time the two men of the greatest repute and influence in Rome. Nay, even Pompey himself used to pay court to Cicero, and Cicero's public actions did much to establish Pompey's authority and reputation in the state.

Numerous distinguished competitors stood with him for the prætor's office; but he was chosen before them all, and managed the decision of causes with justice and integrity. It is related that Licinius Macer, a man himself of great power in the city, and supported also by the assistance of Crassus, was accused before him of extortion, and that, in confidence on his own interest and the dili-

[3] Seventy-five ten thousands, i. e. 750,000 drachmas; Plutarch most likely counting the drachma as equivalent to the denarius. But the sum does not agree with the figures given in Cicero's own orations, and must be regarded as quite uncertain.

[4] Plutarch calls it Arpi, which is far from Rome, in Apulia, but it is, of course, Arpinum, Cicero's native place.

gence of his friends, whilst the judges were debating about the sentence, he went to his house, where hastily trimming his hair and putting on a clean gown, as already acquitted, he was setting off again to go to the Forum; but at his hall door meeting Crassus, who told him that he was condemned by all the votes, he went in again, threw himself upon his bed, and died immediately. This verdict was considered very creditable to Cicero, as showing his careful management of the courts of justice. On another occasion, Vatinius, a man of rude manners and often insolent in court to the magistrates, who had large swellings on his neck, came before his tribunal and made some request, and on Cicero's desiring further time to consider it, told him that he himself would have made no question about it, had he been prætor. Cicero, turning quickly upon him, answered, "But I, you see, have not the neck that you have." [5]

When there were but two or three days remaining in his office, Manilius was brought before him, and charged with peculation. Manilius had the good opinion and favor of the common people, and was thought to be prosecuted only for Pompey's sake, whose particular friend he was. And therefore, when he asked a space of time before his trial, and Cicero allowed him but one day, and that the next only, the common people grew highly offended, because it had been the custom of the prætors to allow ten days at least to the accused: and the tribunes of the people having called him before the people, and accused him, he, desiring to be heard, said, that as he had always treated the accused with equity and humanity, as far as the law allowed, so he thought it hard to deny the same to Manilius, and that he had studiously appointed that day of which alone, as prætor, he was master, and that it was not the part of those that were desirous to help him, to cast the judgment of his cause upon another prætor. These things being said made a wonderful change in the people, and, commending him much for it, they desired that he himself would undertake the defence of Manilius; which he willingly consented to, and that principally for the sake of Pompey, who was absent. And, accordingly, taking

[5] The strong, thick neck was both in Greek and Latin the sign of the pushing, unscrupulous man, who would take no refusal and stick at no doubt or difficulty. So in the life of Marius.

his place before the people again, he delivered a bold invective upon the oligarchical party and on those who were jealous of Pompey.

Yet he was preferred to the consulship no less by the nobles than the common people, for the good of the city; and both parties jointly assisted his promotion, upon the following reasons. The change of government made by Sylla, which at first seemed a senseless one, by time and usage had now come to be considered by the people no unsatisfactory settlement. But there were some that endeavored to alter and subvert the whole present state of affairs, not from any good motives, but for their own private gain; and Pompey being at this time employed in the wars with the kings of Pontus and Armenia, there was no sufficient force at Rome to suppress any attempts at a revolution. These people had for their head a man of bold, daring, and restless character, Lucius Catiline, who was accused, besides other great offences, of deflouring his virgin daughter, and killing his own brother; for which latter crime, fearing to be prosecuted at law, he persuaded Sylla to set him down, as though he were yet alive, amongst those that were to be put to death by proscription. This man the profligate citizens choosing for their captain, gave faith to one another, amongst other pledges, by sacrificing a man and eating of his flesh; and a great part of the young men of the city were corrupted by him, he providing for every one pleasures, drink, and women, and profusely supplying the expense of these debauches. Etruria, moreover, had all been excited to revolt, as well as a great part of Gaul within the Alps. But Rome itself was in the most dangerous inclination to change, on account of the unequal distribution of wealth and property, those of highest rank and greatest spirit having impoverished themselves by shows, entertainments, ambition of offices, and sumptuous buildings, and the riches of the city having thus fallen into the hands of mean and low-born persons. So that there wanted but a slight impetus to set all in motion, it being in the power of every daring man to overturn a sickly commonwealth.

Catiline, however, being desirous of procuring a strong position to carry out his designs, stood for the consulship, and had great hopes of success, thinking he should be appointed, with Caius Antonius as his colleague, who was a man fit to lead neither in a good cause nor in a bad one, but might be a valuable accession to another's power. These things the greatest part of the good and honest citizens apprehending, put Cicero upon standing for the consulship; whom the people readily receiving, Catiline was put by, so that he and Caius Antonius were chosen, although amongst the competitors he was the only man descended from a father of the equestrian, and not of the senatorial order.

Though the designs of Catiline were not yet publicly known, yet considerable preliminary troubles immediately followed upon the consulship. For, on the one side, those who were disqualified by the laws of Sylla from holding any public offices, being neither inconsiderable in power nor in number, came forward as candidates and caressed the people for them; speaking many things truly and justly against the tyranny of Sylla, only that they disturbed the government at an improper and unseasonable time; on the other hand, the tribunes of the people proposed laws to the same purpose, constituting a commission of ten persons, with unlimited powers, in whom as supreme governors should be vested the right of selling the public lands of Italy and Syria and Pompey's new conquests, of judging and banishing whom they pleased, of planting colonies, of taking moneys out of the treasury, and of levying and paying what soldiers should be thought needful. And several of the nobility favored this law, but especially Caius Antonius, Cicero's colleague, in hopes of being one of the ten. But what gave the greatest fear to the nobles was, that he was thought privy to the conspiracy of Catiline, and not to dislike it, because of his great debts.

Cicero, endeavoring in the first place to provide a remedy against this danger, procured a decree assigning to him the province of Macedonia, he himself declining that of Gaul, which was offered to him. And this piece of favor so completely won over Antonius, that he was ready to second and respond to, like a hired player, whatever Cicero said for the good of the country. And now, having made his colleague thus tame and tractable, he could with greater courage attack the conspirators. And, therefore, in the senate, making an oration against the law of the ten commissioners, he so confounded those who proposed it, that they had nothing to reply. And when they again endeavored, and, having prepared things beforehand, had called the consuls before the assembly of the people, Cicero, fearing nothing, went first out, and commanded the senate to follow him, and not only succeeded in throwing out the law, but so entirely overpowered the tribunes by his oratory, that they abandoned all thought of their other projects.

For Cicero, it may be said, was the one man above all others, who made the Romans feel how great a charm eloquence lends to what is good, and how invincible justice is, if it be well spoken; and that it is necessary for him who would dexterously govern a commonwealth, in action, always to prefer that which is honest before that which is popular, and in speaking, to free the right and useful measure from every thing that may occasion offence. An incident occurred in the theatre, during his consulship, which showed what his speaking could do. For whereas formerly the knights of Rome were mingled in the theatre with the common people, and took their places amongst them as it happened, Marcus Otho, when he was prætor, was the first who distinguished them from the other citizens, and appointed them a proper seat, which they still enjoy as their special place in the theatre. This the common people took as an indignity done to them, and, therefore, when Otho appeared in the theatre, they hissed him; the knights, on the contrary, received him with loud clapping. The people repeated and increased their hissing; the knights continued their clapping. Upon this, turning upon one another, they broke out into insulting words, so that the theatre was in great disorder. Cicero, being informed of it, came himself to the theatre, and summoning the people into the temple of Bellona, he so effectually chid and chastised them for it, that, again returning into the theatre, they received Otho with loud applause, contending with the knights who should give him the greatest demonstrations of honor and respect.

The conspirators with Catiline, at first cowed and disheartened, began presently to take courage again. And assembling themselves together, they exhorted one another boldly to undertake the design before Pompey's return, who, as it was said, was now on his march with his forces for Rome. But the old soldiers of Sylla were Catiline's chief stimulus to action. They had been disbanded all about Italy, but the greatest number and the fiercest of them lay scattered among the cities of Etruria, entertaining themselves with dreams of new plunder and rapine amongst the hoarded riches of Italy. These, having for their leader Manlius, who had served with distinction in the wars under Sylla, joined themselves to Catiline, and came to Rome to assist him with their suffrages at the election. For he again pretended to the consulship, having resolved to kill Cicero in a tumult at the elections. Also, the divine powers seemed to give intimation of the coming troubles, by earthquakes, thunderbolts, and strange appearances. Nor was human evidence wanting, certain enough in itself, though not sufficient for the conviction of the noble and powerful Catiline. Therefore Cicero, deferring the day of election, summoned Catiline into the senate, and questioned him as to the charges made against him. Catiline, believing there were many in the senate desirous of change, and to give a specimen of himself to the conspirators present, returned an audacious answer, "What harm," said he, "when I see two bodies, the one lean and consumptive with a head, the other great and strong without one, if I put a head to that body which wants one?" This covert representation of the senate and the people excited yet greater apprehensions in Cicero. He put on armor, and was attended from his house by the noble citizens in a body; and a number of the young men went with him into the Plain. Here, designedly letting his tunic slip partly off from his shoulders, he showed his armor underneath, and discovered his danger to the spectators; who, being much moved at it, gathered round about him for his defence. At length, Catiline was by a general suffrage again put by, and Silanus and Murena chosen consuls.

Not long after this, Catiline's soldiers got together in a body in Etruria, and began to form themselves into companies, the day appointed for the design being near at hand. About midnight, some of the principal and most powerful citizens of Rome, Marcus Crassus, Marcus Marcellus, and Scipio Mettellus went to Cicero's house, where, knocking at the gate, and calling up the porter, they commanded him to awake Cicero, and tell him they were there. The business was this: Crassus's porter after supper had delivered to him letters brought by an unknown person. Some of them were directed to others, but one to Crassus, without a name; this only

Crassus read, which informed him that there was a great slaughter intended by Catiline, and advised him to leave the city. The others he did not open, but went with them immediately by Cicero, being affrighted at the danger, and to free himself of the suspicion he lay under for his familiarity with Catiline. Cicero, considering the matter, summoned the senate at break of day. The letters he brought with him, and delivered them to those to whom they were directed, commanding them to read them publicly; they all alike contained an account of the conspiracy. And when Quintus Arrius, a man of prætorian dignity, recounted to them, how soldiers were collecting in companies in Etruria, and Manlius stated to be in motion with a large force, hovering about those cities, in expectation of intelligence from Rome, the senate made a decree, to place all in the hands of the consuls, who should undertake the conduct of every thing, and do their best to save the state.[6] This was not a common thing, but only done by the senate in case of imminent danger.

After Cicero had received this power, he committed all affairs outside to Quintus Metellus, but the management of the city he kept in his own hands. Such a numerous attendance guarded him every day when he went abroad, that the greatest part of the market-place[7] was filled with his train when he entered it. Catiline, impatient of further delay, resolved himself to break forth and go to Manlius, but he commanded Marcius and Cethegus to take their swords, and go early in the morning to Cicero's gates, as if only intending to salute him, and then to fall upon him and slay him. This a noble lady, Fulvia, coming by night, discovered to Cicero, bidding him beware of Cethegus and Marcius. They came by break of day, and being denied entrance, made an outcry and disturbance at the gates, which excited all the more suspicion. But Cicero, going forth, summoned the senate into the temple of Jupiter Stator, which stands at the end of the Sacred Street, going up to the Palatine. And when Catiline with others of his party also came, as intending to make his defence, none of the senators would sit by him, but all of them left the bench where he had placed himself. And when he began

[6] Dent operam consules ne quid respublica detrimenti capiat," the usual form for suspending other authority, and arming the consuls with discretionary power; much the same as placing the town in a state of siege.

[7] The Forum.

to speak, they interrupted him with outcries. At length Cicero, standing up, commanded him to leave the city, for since one governed the commonwealth with words, the other with arms, it was necessary there should be a wall betwixt them. Catiline, therefore, immediately left the town, with three hundred armed men; and assuming, as if he had been a magistrate, the rods, axes, and military ensigns, he went to Manlius, and having got together a body of near twenty thousand men, with these he marched to the several cities, endeavoring to persuade or force them to revolt. So it being now come to open war, Antonius was sent forth to fight him.

The remainder of those in the city whom he had corrupted, Cornelius Lentulus kept together and encouraged. He had the surname Sura, and was a man of a noble family, but a dissolute liver, who for his debauchery was formerly turned out of the senate, and was now holding the office of prætor for the second time, as the custom is with those who desire to regain the dignity of senator. It is said that he got the surname Sura upon this occasion; being quæstor in the time of Sylla, he had lavished away and consumed a great quantity of the public moneys, at which Sylla being provoked, called him to give an account in the senate; he appeared with great coolness and contempt, and said he had no account to give, but they might take this, holding up the calf of his leg, as boys do at ball, when they have missed. Upon which he was surnamed *Sura, sura* being the Roman word for the calf of the leg. Being at another time prosecuted at law, and having bribed some of the judges, he escaped only by two votes, and complained of the needless expense he had gone to in paying for a second, as one would have sufficed to acquit him. This man, such in his own nature, and now inflamed by Catiline, false prophets and fortune-tellers had also corrupted with vain hopes, quoting to him fictitious verses and oracles, and proving from the Sibylline prophecies that there were three of the name Cornelius designed by fate to be monarchs of Rome; two of whom, Cinna and Sylla, had already fulfilled the decree, and that divine fortune was now advancing with the gift of monarchy for the remaining third Cornelius; and that therefore he ought by all means to accept it, and not lose opportunity by delay, as Catiline had done.

Lentulus, therefore, designed no mean or trivial matter, for he had resolved to kill the whole senate, and as many other citizens as he could, to fire the city, and spare nobody, except only Pompey's children, intending to seize and keep them as pledges of his reconciliation with Pompey. For there was then a common and strong report that Pompey was on his way homeward from his great expedition. The night appointed for the design was one of the Saturnalia: swords, flax, and sulphur they carried and hid in the house of Cethegus; and providing one hundred men, and dividing the city into as many parts, they had allotted to every one singly his proper place, so that in a moment many kindling the fire, the city might be in a flame all together. Others were appointed to stop up the aqueducts, and to kill those who should endeavor to carry water to put it out. Whilst these plans were preparing, it happened there were two ambassadors from the Allobroges staying in Rome; a nation at that time in a distressed condition, and very uneasy under the Roman government. These Lentulus and his party judging useful instruments to move and seduce Gaul to revolt, admitted into the conspiracy, and they gave them letters to their own magistrates, and letters to Catiline; in those they promised liberty, in these they exhorted Catiline to set all slaves free, and to bring them along with him to Rome. They sent also to accompany them to Catiline, one Titus, a native of Croton, who was to carry those letters to him.

These counsels of inconsidering men, who conversed together over wine and with women, Cicero watched with sober industry and forethought, and with most admirable sagacity, having several emissaries abroad, who observed and traced with him all that was done, and keeping also a secret correspondence with many who pretended to join in the conspiracy. He thus knew all the discourse which passed betwixt them and the strangers; and lying in wait for them by night, he took the Crotonian with his letters, the ambassadors of the Allobroges acting secretly in concert with him.

By break of day, he summoned the senate into the temple of Concord, where he read the letters and examined the informers. Junius Silanus further stated, that several persons had heard Cethegus say, that three consuls and four prætors were to be slain; Piso, also, a person of consular dignity testified other matters of the like nature; and Caius Sulpicius, one of the prætors, being sent to Cethegus's house, found there a quantity of darts and of armor, and a still greater number of swords and daggers, all recently whetted. At length, the senate decreeing indemnity to the Crotonian upon his confession of the whole matter, Lentulus was convicted, abjured his office (for he was then prætor), and put off his robe edged with purple in the senate, changing it for another garment more agreeable to his present circumstances. He, thereupon, with the rest of his confederates present, was committed to the charge of the prætors in free custody.

It being evening, and the common people in crowds expecting without, Cicero went forth to them, and told them what was done, and then, attended by them, went to the house of a friend and near neighbor; for his own was taken up by the women, who were celebrating with secret rites the feast of the goddess whom the Romans call the Good, and the Greeks, the Women's goddess. For a sacrifice is annually performed to her in the consul's house, either by his wife or mother, in the presence of the vestal virgins. And having got into his friend's house privately, a few only being present, he began to deliberate how he should treat these men. The severest, and the only punishment fit for such heinous crimes, he was somewhat shy and fearful of inflicting, as well from the clemency of his nature, as also lest he should be thought to exercise his authority too insolently, and to treat too harshly men of the noblest birth and most powerful friendships in the city; and yet, if he should use them more mildly, he had a dreadful prospect of danger from them. For there was no likelihood, if they suffered less than death, they would be reconciled, but rather, adding new rage to their former wickedness, they would rush into every kind of audacity, while he himself, whose character for courage already did not stand very high with the multitude, would be thought guilty of the greatest cowardice and want of manliness.

Whilst Cicero was doubting what course to take, a portent happened to the women in their sacrificing. For on the altar, where the fire seemed wholly extinguished, a great and bright flame issued forth from the ashes of the burnt wood; at which others were affrighted, but the holy virgins called to Terentia, Cicero's wife, and bade her haste to her husband, and command him to execute what he had resolved for the good of his country, for the goddess had sent a great light to the increase of his safety and glory. Terentia, therefore, as she was otherwise in her own nature neither tender-hearted nor timorous, but a woman eager for distinction (who, as Cicero himself says, would rather thrust herself into his public affairs, than communicate her domestic matters to him), told him these things, and excited him against the conspirators. So also did Quintus his brother, and Publius Nigidius, one of his philosophical friends, whom he often made use of in his greatest and most weighty affairs of state.

The next day, a debate arising in the senate about the punishment of the men, Silanus, being the first who was asked his opinion, said, it was fit they should be all sent to the prison, and there suffer the utmost penalty. To him all consented in order till it came to Caius Cæsar, who was afterwards dictator. He was then but a young man, and only at the outset of his career, but had already directed his hopes and policy to that course by which he afterwards changed the Roman state into a monarchy. Of this others foresaw nothing; but Cicero had seen reason for strong suspicion, though without obtaining any sufficient means of proof. And there were some indeed that said that he was very near being discovered, and only just escaped him; others are of opinion that Cicero voluntarily overlooked and neglected the evidence against him, for fear of his friends and power; for it was very evident to everybody, that if Cæsar was to be accused with the conspirators, they were more likely to be saved with him, than he to be punished with them.

When, therefore, it came to Cæsar's turn to give his opinion, he stood up and proposed that the conspirators should not be put to death, but their estates confiscated, and their persons confined in such cities in Italy as Cicero should approve, there to be kept in custody till Catiline was conquered. To this sentence, as it was the most moderate, and he that delivered it a most powerful speaker, Cicero himself gave no small weight, for he stood up and, turning the scale on either side, spoke in favor partly of the former, partly of Cæsar's sentence. And all Cicero's friends, judging Cæsar's sentence most expedient for Cicero. because he would incur the less blame if the conspirators were not put to death, chose rather the latter; so that Silanus, also, changing his mind, retracted his opinion, and said he had not declared for capital, but only the utmost punishment, which to a Roman senator is imprisonment. The first man who spoke against Cæsar's motion was Catulus Lutatius. Cato followed, and so vehemently urged in his speech the strong suspicion about Cæsar himself, and so filled the senate with anger and resolution, that a decree was passed for the execution of the conspirators. But Cæsar opposed the confiscation of their goods, not thinking it fair that those who had rejected the mildest part of his sentence should avail themselves of the severest. And when many insisted upon it, he appealed to the tribunes, but they would do nothing; till Cicero himself yielding, remitted that part of the sentence.

After this, Cicero went out with the senate to the conspirators; they were not all together in one place, but the several prætors had then, some one, some another, in custody. And first he took Lentulus from the Palatine, and brought him by the Sacred Street, through the middle of the market-place, a circle of the most eminent citizens encompassing and protecting him. The people, affrighted at what was doing, passed along in silence, especially the young men; as if, with fear and trembling, they were undergoing a rite of initiation into some ancient, sacred mysteries of aristocratic power. Thus passing from the market-place, and coming to the gaol, he delivered Lentulus to the officer, and commanded him to execute him; and after him Cethegus, and so all the rest in order, he brought and delivered up to execution. And when he saw many of the conspirators in the market-place, still standing together in companies, ignorant of what was done, and waiting for the night, supposing the men were still alive and in a possibility of being rescued, he called out in a loud voice, and said, *"They did live"*; for so the Romans, to avoid inauspicious language, name those that are dead.

It was now evening, when he returned from the market-place to his own house, the citizens no longer attending him with silence, nor in order, but receiving him, as he passed, with acclamations and applauses, and saluting him as the saviour and founder of his country. A bright light shone through the streets from the lamps and torches set up at the doors, and the women showed lights from the tops of the houses, to honor Cicero, and to behold him returning home with a splendid train of the most principal citizens; amongst whom were many who had conducted great wars, celebrated triumphs, and added to the possessions of the Roman empire, both by sea and land. These, as they passed along with him, acknowledged to one another, that though the Roman people were indebted to several officers and commanders of that age for riches, spoils, and power, yet to Cicero alone they owed the safety and security of all these, for delivering them from so great and imminent a danger. For though it might seem no wonderful thing to prevent the design, and punish the conspirators, yet to defeat the greatest of all conspiracies with so little disturbance, trouble, and commotion, was very extraordinary. For the greater part of those who had flocked in to Catiline, as soon as they heard the fate of Lentulus and Cethegus, left and forsook him, and he himself, with his remaining forces, joining battle with Antonius, was destroyed with his army.

And yet there were some who were very ready both to speak ill of Cicero, and to do him hurt for these actions; and they had for their leaders some of the magistrates of the ensuing year, as Cæsar, who was one of the prætors, and Metellus and Bestia, the tribunes. These, entering upon their office some few days before Cicero's consulate expired, would not permit him to make any address to the people, but, throwing the benches before the Rostra, hindered his speaking, telling him he might, if he pleased, make the oath of withdrawal from office, and then come down again. Cicero, accordingly, accepting the conditions, came forward to make his withdrawal; and silence being made, he recited his oath, not in the usual, but in a new and peculiar form, namely, that he had saved his country, and preserved the empire; the truth of which oath all the people confirmed with theirs. Cæsar and the tribunes, all the more exasperated by this, endeavored to create him further trouble, and for this purpose proposed a law for calling Pompey home with his army, to put an end to Cicero's usurpation. But it was a very great advantage for Cicero and the whole commonwealth that Cato was at that time one of the tribunes. For he, being of equal power with the rest, and of greater reputation, could oppose their designs. He easily defeated their other projects, and, in an oration to the people, so highly extolled Cicero's consulate, that the greatest honors were decreed him, and he was publicly declared the Father of his Country, which title he seems to have obtained, the first man who did so, when Cato gave it him in this address to the people.

At this time, therefore, his authority was very great in the city; but he created himself much envy, and offended very many, not by any evil action, but because he was always lauding and magnifying himself. For neither senate, nor assembly of the people, nor court of judicature could meet, in which he was not heard to talk of Catiline and Lentulus. Indeed, he also filled his books and writings with his own praises, to such an excess as to render a style, in itself most pleasant and delightful, nauseous and irksome to his hearers; this ungrateful humor, like a disease, always cleaving to him. Nevertheless, though he was intemperately fond of his own glory, he was very free from envying others, and was, on the contrary, most liberally profuse in commending both the ancients and his contemporaries, as any one may see in his writings. And many such sayings of his are also remembered; as that he called Aristotle a river of flowing gold, and said of Plato's Dialogues, that if Jupiter were to speak, it would be in language like theirs. He used to call Theophrastus his special luxury. And being asked which of Demosthenes's orations he liked best, he answered, the longest. And yet some affected imitators of Demosthenes have complained of some words that occur in one of his letters, to the effect that Demosthenes sometimes falls asleep in his speeches; forgetting the many high encomiums he continually passes upon him, and the compliment he paid him when he named the most elaborate of all his orations, those he wrote against Antony, Philippics. And as for the eminent men of his own time, either in eloquence or philosophy, there was not one of them whom he did not, by writing or speaking favorably of him, render more illustrious. He obtained of Cæsar, when in power, the Roman citizenship for Cratippus, the Peripatetic, and got the court of Areopagus, by public decree, to request his stay at Athens, for the instruction of their youth, and the honor of their city. There are letters extant from Cicero to Herodes, and others to his son, in which he recommends the study of philosophy under Cratippus. There is one in which he blames Gorgias, the rhetorician, for enticing his son into luxury and drinking, and, therefore, forbids him his company. And this, and one other to Pelops, the Byzantine, are the only two of his Greek epistles which seem to be written in anger. In the first, he justly reflects on Gorgias, if he were what he was thought to be, a dissolute and profligate character; but in the other, he rather meanly expostulates and complains with Pelops, for neglecting to procure him a decree of certain honors from the Byzantines.

Another illustration of his love of praise is the way in which sometimes, to make his orations more striking, he neglected decorum and dignity. When Munatius, who had escaped conviction by his advocacy, immediately prosecuted his friend Sabinus, he said in the warmth of his resentment, "Do you suppose you were acquitted for your own merits, Munatius, and was it not that I so darkened the case, that the court could not see your guilt?" When from the Rostra he had made an eulogy on Marcus Crassus, with much applause, and within a few days after again as publicly reproached him, Crassus called to him, and said, "Did not you yourself two days ago, in this same place, commend me?" "Yes," said Cicero, "I exercised my eloquence in declaiming upon a bad subject." At another time, Crassus had said that no one of his family had ever lived beyond sixty years of age, and afterwards denied it, and asked, "What should put it into my head to say so?" "It was to gain the people's favor," answered Cicero; "you knew how glad they would be to hear it." When Crassus expressed admiration of the Stoic doctrine, that *the good man is always rich,* "Do you not mean," said Cicero, "their doctrine that *all things belong to the wise?"* Crassus being generally accused of covetousness. One of Crassus's sons, who was thought so exceedingly like a man of the name of Axius as to throw some suspicion on his mother's honor, made a successful speech in the senate. Cicero on being asked how he liked it, replied with the Greek words, *Axios Crassou.*[8]

When Crassus was about to go into Syria, he desired to leave

[8] Which may mean, either *worthy of Crassus,* or *Crassus's son Axius.* The jest on the Stoic doctrines is also rather obscure. Crassus appears to have praised the first dictum in its proper philosophical sense; that the only truly rich man is he who is virtuous; Cicero suggests, that a text which is more to Crassus's purpose is the other, that the wise man is the possessor of all things, that is, may make himself as rich as he pleases.

Cicero rather his friend than his enemy, and, therefore, one day saluting him, told him he would come and sup with him, which the other as courteously received. Within a few days after, on some of Cicero's acquaintances interceding for Vatinius, as desirous of reconciliation and friendship, for he was then his enemy, "What," he replied, "does Vatinius also wish to come and sup with me?" Such was his way with Crassus. When Vatinius, who had swellings in his neck, was pleading a cause, he called him the *tumid* orator; and having been told by some one that Vatinius was dead, on hearing presently after that he was alive, "May the rascal perish," said he, "for his news not being true."

Upon Cæsar's bringing forward a law for the division of the lands in Campania amongst the soldiers, many in the senate opposed it; amongst the rest, Lucius Gellius, one of the oldest men in the house, said it should never pass whilst he lived. "Let us postpone it," said Cicero, "Gellius does not ask us to wait long." There was a man of the name of Octavius, suspected to be of African descent. He once said, when Cicero was pleading that he could not hear him; "Yet there are holes," said Cicero, "in your ears."[9] When Metellus Nepos told him, that he had ruined more as a witness, than he had saved as an advocate, "I admit," said Cicero, "that I have more truth than eloquence." To a young man who was suspected of having given a poisoned cake to his father, and who talked largely of the invectives he meant to deliver against Cicero, "Better these," replied he, "than your cakes." Publius Sextius, having amongst others retained Cicero as his advocate in a certain cause, was yet desirous to say all for himself, and would not allow anybody to speak for him; when he was about to receive his acquittal from the judges, and the ballots were passing, Cicero called to him, "Make haste, Sextius, and use your time; to-morrow you will be nobody." He cited Publius Cotta to bear testimony in a certain cause, one who affected to be thought a lawyer, though ignorant and unlearned; to whom, when he had said, "I know nothing of the matter," he answered, "You think, perhaps, we ask you about a point of law." To Metellus Nepos, who, in a dispute between them, repeated sev-

[9] The marks of the ears having been bored for ear-rings would be considered proof of his being of barbarian origin.

eral times, "Who was your father, Cicero?" he replied, "Your mother has made the answer to such a question in your case more difficult;" Nepos's mother having been of ill repute. The son, also, was of a giddy, uncertain temper. At one time, he suddenly threw up his office of tribune, and sailed off into Syria to Pompey; and immediately after, with as little reason, came back again. He gave his tutor, Philagrus, a funeral with more than necessary attention, and then set up the stone figure of a crow over his tomb. "This," said Cicero, "is really appropriate; as he did not teach you to speak, but to fly about." When Marcus Appius, in the opening of some speech in a court of justice, said that his friend had desired him to employ industry, eloquence, and fidelity in that cause, Cicero answered, "And how have you had the heart not to accede to any one of his requests?"

To use this sharp raillery against opponents and antagonists in judicial pleading seems allowable rhetoric. But he excited much ill feeling by his readiness to attack any one for the sake of a jest. A few anecdotes of this kind may be added. Marcus Aquinius, who had two sons-in-law in exile, received from him the name of king Adrastus.[10] Lucius Cotta, an intemperate lover of wine, was censor when Cicero stood for the consulship. Cicero, being thirsty at the election, his friends stood round about him while he was drinking. "You have reason to be afraid," he said, "lest the censor should be angry with me for drinking water." Meeting one day Voconius with his three very ugly daughters, he quoted the verse,

"He reared a race without Apollo's leave."

When Marcus Gellius, who was reputed the son of a slave, had read several letters in the senate with a very shrill, and loud voice, "Wonder not," said Cicero, "he comes of the criers." When Faustus Sylla, the son of Sylla the dictator, who had during his dictatorship, by public bills proscribed and condemned so many citizens, had so far wasted his estate, and got into debt, that he was forced to publish his bills of sale, Cicero told him that he liked these bills much better

[10] Adrastus, king of Argos, married his daughters to the exiles, Tydeus and Polynices. The verse below, quoted from a tragedy, must refer to Laius and his son, born against the warning of the oracle, Œdipus. "Without Apollo's leave" would be a phrase like "invita Minerva" applied to any unsuccessful, or infelicitous, or injudicious proceeding.

than those of his father. By this habit he made himself odious with many people.

But Clodius's faction conspired against him upon the following occasion. Clodius was a member of a noble family, in the flower of his youth, and of a bold and resolute temper. He, being in love with Pompeia, Cæsar's wife, got privately into his house in the dress and attire of a music-girl; the women being at that time offering there the sacrifice which must not be seen by men, and there was no man present. Clodius, being a youth and beardless, hoped to get to Pompeia among the women without being taken notice of. But coming into a great house by night, he missed his way in the passages, and a servant belonging to Aurelia, Cæsar's mother, spying him wandering up and down, inquired his name. Thus being necessitated to speak, he told her he was seeking for one of Pompeia's maids, Abra by name; and she, perceiving it not to be a woman's voice, shrieked out, and called in the women; who, shutting the gates, and searching every place, at length found Clodius hidden in the chamber of the maid with whom he had come in. This matter being much talked about, Cæsar put away his wife, Pompeia, and Clodius was prosecuted for profaning the holy rites.

Cicero was at this time his friend, for he had been useful to him in the conspiracy of Catiline, as one of his forwardest assistants and protectors. But when Clodius rested his defence upon this point, that he was not then at Rome, but at a distance in the country, Cicero testified that he had come to his house that day, and conversed with him on several matters; which thing was indeed true, although Cicero was thought to testify it not so much for the truth's sake as to preserve his quiet with Terentia his wife. For she bore a grudge against Clodius on account of his sister Clodia's wishing, as it was alleged, to marry Cicero, and having employed for this purpose the intervention of Tullus, a very intimate friend of Cicero's; and his frequent visits to Clodia, who lived in their neighborhood, and the attentions he paid to her had excited Terentia's suspicions, and, being a woman of a violent temper, and having the ascendant over Cicero, she urged him on to taking a part against Clodius, and delivering his testimony. Many other good and honest citizens also gave evidence against him, for perjuries, disorders, bribing the people, and debauching women. Lucullus proved, by his women-servants, that he had debauched his youngest sister when she was Lucullus's wife; and there was a general belief that he had done the same with his two other sisters, Tertia, whom Marcius Rex, and Clodia, whom Metellus Celer had married; the latter of whom was called Quadrantia, because one of her lovers had deceived her with a purse of small copper money instead of silver, the smallest copper coin being called a *quadrant*. Upon this sister's account, in particular, Clodius's character was attacked. Notwithstanding all this, when the common people united against the accusers and witnesses and the whole party, the judges were affrighted, and a guard was placed about them for their defence; and most of them wrote their sentences on the tablets in such a way, that they could not well be read. It was decided, however, that there was a majority for his acquittal, and bribery was reported to have been employed; in reference to which Catulus remarked, when he next met the judges, "You were very right to ask for a guard, to prevent your money being taken from you." And when Clodius upbraided Cicero that the judges had not believed his testimony, "Yes," said he, "five and twenty of them trusted me, and condemned you, and the other thirty did not trust you, for they did not acquit you till they had got your money."

Cæsar, though cited, did not give his testimony against Clodius, and declared himself not convinced of his wife's adultery, but that he had put her away because it was fit that Cæsar's house should not be only free of the evil fact, but of the fame too.

Clodius, having escaped this danger, and having got himself chosen one of the tribunes, immediately attacked Cicero, heaping up all matters and inciting all persons against him. The common people he gained over with popular laws; to each of the consuls he decreed large provinces, to Piso, Macedonia, and to Gabinius, Syria; he made a strong party among the indigent citizens, to support him in his proceedings, and had always a body of armed slaves about him. Of the three men then in greatest power, Crassus was Cicero's open enemy, Pompey indifferently made advances to both, and Cæsar was going with an army into Gaul. To him, though not his friend (what had occurred in the time of the conspiracy having created suspicions between them), Cicero applied, requesting an appointment as one of his lieutenants in the province. Cæsar accepted him, and Clodius, perceiving that Cicero would thus escape his tribunician authority, professed to be inclinable to a reconciliation, laid the greatest fault upon Terentia, made always a favorable mention of him, and addressed him with kind expressions, as one who felt no hatred or ill-will, but who merely wished to urge his complaints in a moderate and friendly way. By these artifices, he so freed Cicero of all his fears, that he resigned his appointment to Cæsar, and betook himself again to political affairs. At which Cæsar being exasperated, joined the party of Clodius against him, and wholly alienated Pompey from him; he also himself declared in a public assembly of the people, that he did not think Lentulus and Cethegus, with their accomplices, were fairly and legally put to death without being brought to trial. And this, indeed, was the crime charged upon Cicero, and this impeachment he was summoned to answer. And so, as an accused man, and in danger for the result, he changed his dress, and went round with his hair untrimmed, in the attire of a suppliant, to beg the people's grace. But Clodius met him in every corner, having a band of abusive and daring fellows about him, who derided Cicero for his change of dress and his humiliation, and often, by throwing dirt and stones at him, interrupted his supplication to the people.

However, first of all, almost the whole equestrian order changed their dress with him, and no less than twenty thousand young gentlemen followed him with their hair untrimmed, and supplicating with him to the people. And then the senate met, to pass a decree that the people should change their dress as in time of public sorrow. But the consuls opposing it, and Clodius with armed men besetting the senate-house, many of the senators ran out, crying out and tearing their clothes. But this sight moved neither shame nor pity; Cicero must either fly or determine it by the sword with Clodius. He entreated Pompey to aid him, who was on purpose gone out of the way, and was staying at his country-house in the Alban hills; and first he sent his son-in-law Piso to intercede with him, and afterwards set out to go himself. Of which Pompey being informed, would not stay to see him, being ashamed at the remembrance of the many conflicts in the commonwealth which Cicero had undergone in his behalf, and how much of his policy he had directed for his advantage. But being now Cæsar's son-in-law, at his instance he had set aside all former kindness, and, slipping out at another door, avoided the interview. Thus being forsaken by Pompey, and left alone to himself, he fled to the consuls. Gabinius was rough with him, as usual, but Piso spoke more courteously, desiring him to yield and give place for a while to the fury of Clodius, and await a change of times, and to be now, as before, his country's savior from the peril of these troubles and commotions which Clodius was exciting.

Cicero, receiving this answer, consulted with his friends. Lucullus advised him to stay, as being sure to prevail at last; others to fly, because the people would soon desire him again, when they should have enough of the rage and madness of Clodius. This last Cicero approved. But first he took a statue of Minerva, which had been long set up and greatly honored in his house, and carrying it to the capitol, there dedicated it, with the inscription, "To Minerva, Patroness of Rome." And receiving an escort from his friends, about the middle of the night he left the city, and went by land through Lucania, intending to reach Sicily.

But as soon as it was publicly known that he was fled, Clodius proposed to the people a decree of exile, and by his own order interdicted him fire and water, prohibiting any within five hundred miles in Italy to receive him into their houses. Most people, out of respect for Cicero, paid no regard to this edict, offering him every attention, and escorting him on his way. But at Hipponium, a city of Lucania, now called Vibo, one Vibius, a Sicilian by birth, who, amongst many other instances of Cicero's friendship, had been made head of the state engineers when he was consul, would not receive him into his house, sending him word he would appoint a place in the country for his reception. Caius Vergilius, the prætor of Sicily, who had been on the most intimate terms with him, wrote to him to forbear coming into Sicily. At these things Cicero being disheartened, went to Brundusium, whence putting forth with a prosperous wind, a contrary gale blowing from the sea carried him back to Italy the next day. He put again to sea. and having reached Dyrrachium, on his coming to shore there, it is reported that an earthquake and a convulsion in the sea happened at the same time, signs which the diviners said intimated that his exile would not be long, for these were prognostics of change. Although many visited him with respect, and the cities of Greece contended which should honor him most, he yet continued disheartened and disconsolate, like an unfortunate lover, often casting his looks back upon Italy; and, indeed, he was become so poor-spirited, so humiliated and dejected by his misfortunes, as none could have expected in a man who had devoted so much of his life to study and learning. And yet he often desired his friends not to call him orator, but philosopher, because he had made philosophy his business, and had only used rhetoric as an instrument for attaining his objects in public life. But the desire of glory[11] has great power in washing the tinctures of philosophy out of the souls of men, and in imprinting the passions of the common people, by custom and conversation, in the minds of those that take a part in governing them, unless the politician be very careful so to engage in public affairs as to interest himself only in the affairs themselves, but not participate in the passions that are consequent to them.

Clodius, having thus driven away Cicero, fell to burning his farms and villas, and afterwards his city house, and built on the site of it a temple to Liberty. The rest of his property he exposed to sale by daily proclamation, but nobody came to buy. By these courses he became formidable to the noble citizens, and, being followed by the commonalty, whom he had filled with insolence and licentiousness, he began at last to try his strength against Pompey, some of whose arrangements in the countries he conquered, he attacked. The disgrace of this made Pompey begin to reproach himself for his cowardice in deserting Cicero, and, changing his mind, he now wholly set himself with his friends to contrive his return. And when Clodius opposed it, the senate made a vote that no public measure

[11] *Doxa,* the Greek word for "the desire of glory," should, perhaps, be translated "opinion." It is, in its original sense, "what people think," and is commonly used for people's *good* opinion, "glory," or "reputation." On the other hand, the philosophers employ it to express *opinion,* which may be false, as opposed to *knowledge,* which must be of the truth. If a philosopher, engaged in politics, does not confine his attention strictly to definite objects and acts, but lets himself be affected by the results, by people's good or bad *opinion* about them, his real convictions and *knowledge* will soon be overpowered.

should be ratified or passed by them till Cicero was recalled. But when Lentulus was consul, the commotions grew so high upon this matter, that the tribunes were wounded in the Forum, and Quintus, Cicero's brother, was left as dead, lying unobserved amongst the slain. The people began to change in their feelings; and Annius Milo, one of their tribunes, was the first who took confidence to summon Clodius to trial for acts of violence. Many of the common people and out of the neighboring cities formed a party with Pompey, and he went with them, and drove Clodius out of the Forum, and summoned the people to pass their vote. And, it is said, the people never passed any suffrage more unanimously than this. The senate, also, striving to outdo the people, sent letters of thanks to those cities which had received Cicero with respect in his exile, and decreed that his house and his country-places, which Clodius had destroyed, should be rebuilt at the public charge.

Thus Cicero returned sixteen months after his exile, and the cities were so glad, and people so zealous to meet him, that what he boasted of afterwards, that Italy had brought him on her shoulders home to Rome, was rather less than the truth. And Crassus himself, who had been his enemy before his exile, went then voluntarily to meet him, and was reconciled, to please his son Publius, as he said, who was Cicero's affectionate admirer.

Cicero had not been long at Rome, when, taking the opportunity of Clodius's absence, he went, with a great company, to the capitol, and there tore and defaced the tribunician tables, in which were recorded the acts done in the time of Clodius. And on Clodius calling him in question for this, he answered, that he, being of the patrician order, had obtained the office of tribune against law, and, therefore, nothing done by him was valid. Cato was displeased at this, and opposed Cicero, not that he commended Clodius, but rather disapproved of his whole administration; yet, he contended, it was an irregular and violent course for the senate to vote the illegality of so many decrees and acts, including those of Cato's own government in Cyprus and at Byzantium. This occasioned a breach between Cato and Cicero, which though it came not to open enmity, yet made a more reserved friendship between them.

After this, Milo killed Clodius, and, being arraigned for the murder, he procured Cicero as his advocate. The senate, fearing lest the questioning of so eminent and high-spirited a citizen as Milo might disturb the peace of the city, committed the superintendence of this and of the other trials to Pompey, who should undertake to maintain the security alike of the city and of the courts of justice. Pompey, therefore, went in the night, and occupying the high grounds about it, surrounded the Forum with soldiers. Milo, fearing lest Cicero, being disturbed by such an unusual sight, should conduct his cause the less successfully, persuaded him to come in a litter into the Forum, and there repose himself till the judges were set, and the court filled. For Cicero, it seems, not only wanted courage in arms, but, in his speaking also, began with timidity, and in many cases scarcely left off trembling and shaking when he had got thoroughly into the current and substance of his speech. Being to defend Licinius Murena against the prosecution of Cato, and being eager to outdo Hortensius, who had made his plea with great applause, he took so little rest that night, and was so disordered with thought and over-watching, that he spoke much worse than usual. And so now, on quitting his litter to commence the cause of Milo, at the sight of Pompey, posted, as it were, and encamped with his troops above, and seeing arms shining round about the Forum, he was so confounded, that he could hardly begin his speech, for the trembling of his body, and hesitance of his tongue; whereas Milo, meantime, was bold and intrepid in his demeanor, disdaining either to let his hair grow, or to put on the mourning habit. And this, indeed, seems to have been one principal cause of his condemnation. Cicero, however, was thought not so much to have shown timidity for himself, as anxiety about his friend.

He was made one of the priests, whom the Romans call Augurs, in the room of Crassus the younger, dead in Parthia. Then he was appointed by lot, to the province of Cilicia, and set sail thither with twelve thousand foot and two thousand six hundred horse. He had orders to bring back Cappadocia to its allegiance to Ariobarzanes, its king; which settlement he effected very completely without recourse to arms. And perceiving the Cilicians, by the great loss the Romans had suffered in Parthia, and the commotions in Syria, to have become disposed to attempt a revolt, by a gentle course of government he soothed them back into fidelity. He would accept none of the presents that were offered him by the kings; he remitted the charge of public entertainments, but daily, at his own house, received the ingenious and accomplished persons of the province, not sumptuously, but liberally. His house had no porter, nor was he ever found in bed by any man, but early in the morning, standing or walking before his door, he received those who came to offer their salutations. He is said never once to have ordered any of those under his command to be beaten with rods, or to have their garments rent. He never gave contumelious language in his anger, nor inflicted punishment with reproach. He detected an embezzlement, to a large amount, in the public money, and thus relieved the cities from their burdens, and at the same time that he allowed those who made restitution, to retain without further punishment their rights as citizens. He engaged too, in war, so far as to give a defeat to the banditti who infested Mount Amanus, for which he was saluted by his army Imperator. To Cæcilius[12] the orator, who asked him to send him some panthers from Cilicia, to be exhibited on the theatre at Rome, he wrote, in commendation of his own actions, that there were no panthers in Cilicia, for they were all fled to Caria, in anger that in so general a peace they had become the sole objects of attack. On leaving his province, he touched at Rhodes, and tarried for some length at Athens, longing much to renew his old studies. He visited the eminent men of learning, and saw his former friends and companions; and after receiving in Greece the honors that were due to him, returned to the city, where every thing was now just as it were in a flame, breaking out into a civil war.

When the senate would have decreed him a triumph, he told them he had rather, so differences were accommodated, follow the triumphal chariot of Cæsar. In private, he gave advice to both, writing many letters to Cæsar, and personally entreating Pompey; doing his best to soothe and bring to reason both the one and the other. But when matters became incurable, and Cæsar was approaching Rome, and Pompey durst not abide it, but, with many honest citizens, left the city, Cicero, as yet, did not join in the flight, and was reputed to adhere to Cæsar. And it is very evident he was

[12] Probably Cælius.

in his thoughts much divided, and wavered painfully between both, for he writes in his epistles, "To which side should I turn? Pompey has the fair and honorable plea for war; and Cæsar, on the other hand, has managed his affairs better, and is more able to secure himself and his friends. So that I know whom I should fly, not whom I should fly to." But when Trebatius, one of Cæsar's friends, by letter signified to him that Cæsar thought it was his most desirable course to join his party, and partake his hopes, but if he considered himself too old a man for this, then he should retire into Greece, and stay quietly there, out of the way of either party, Cicero, wondering that Cæsar had not written himself, gave an angry reply that he should not do any thing unbecoming his past life. Such is the account to be collected from his letters.

But as soon as Cæsar was marched into Spain, he immediately sailed away to join Pompey. And he was welcomed by all but Cato; who, taking him privately, chid him for coming to Pompey. As for himself, he said, it had been indecent to forsake that part in the commonwealth which he had chosen from the beginning; but Cicero might have been more useful to his country and friends, if, remaining neuter, he had attended and used his influence to moderate the result, instead of coming hither to make himself, without reason or necessity, an enemy to Cæsar, and a partner in such great dangers. By this language, partly, Cicero's feelings were altered, and partly, also, because Pompey made no great use of him. Although, indeed, he was himself the cause of it by his not denying that he was sorry he had come, by his depreciating Pompey's resources, finding fault underhand with his counsels, and continually indulging in jests and sarcastic remarks on his fellow-soldiers. Though he went about in the camp with a gloomy and melancholy face himself, he was always trying to raise a laugh in others, whether they wished it or not. It may not be amiss to mention a few instances. To Domitius, on his preferring to a command one who was no soldier, and saying, in his defence, that he was a modest and prudent person, he replied, "Why did not you keep him for a tutor for your children?" On hearing Theophanes, the Lesbian, who was master of the engineers in the army, praised for the admirable way in which he had consoled the Rhodians for the loss of their fleet, "What a thing it is," he said, "to have a Greek in command!" When Cæsar had been acting successfully, and in a manner blockading Pompey, Lentulus was saying it was reported that Cæsar's friends were out of heart; "Because," said Cicero, "they do not wish Cæsar well." To one Marcius, who had just come from Italy, and told them that there was a strong report at Rome that Pompey was blocked up, he said, "And you sailed hither to see it with your own eyes." To Nonius, encouraging them after a defeat to be of good hope, because there were seven eagles still left in Pompey's camp, "Good reason for encouragement," said Cicero, "if we were going to fight with jack-daws." Labienus insisted on some prophecies to the effect that Pompey would gain the victory; "Yes," said Cicero, "and the first step in the campaign has been losing our camp."

After the battle of Pharsalia was over, at which he was not present for want of health, and Pompey was fled, Cato, having considerable forces and a great fleet at Dyrrachium, would have had Cicero commander-in-chief, according to law, and the precedence of his consular dignity. And on his refusing the command, and wholly declining to take part in their plans for continuing the war, he was in the greatest danger of being killed, young Pompey and his friends calling him traitor, and drawing their swords upon him; only that Cato interposed, and hardly rescued and brought him out of the camp.

Afterwards, arriving at Brundusium, he tarried there sometime in expectation of Cæsar, who was delayed by his affairs in Asia and Egypt. And when it was told him that he was arrived at Tarentum, and was coming thence by land to Brundusium, he hastened towards him, not altogether without hope, and yet in some fear of making experiment of the temper of an enemy and conqueror in the presence of many witnesses. But there was no necessity for him either to speak or do anything unworthy of himself; for Cæsar, as soon as he saw him coming a good way before the rest of the company, came down to meet him, saluted him, and, leading the way, conversed with him alone for some furlongs. And from that time forward he continued to treat him with honor and respect; so that, when Cicero wrote an oration in praise of Cato, Cæsar, in writing an answer to it, took occasion to commend Cicero's own life and eloquence, comparing him to Pericles and Theramenes. Cicero's oration was called Cato; Cæsar's, anti-Cato.

So also, it is related that when Quintus Ligarius was prosecuted for having been in arms against Cæsar, and Cicero had undertaken his defence, Cæsar said to his friends, "Why might we not as well once more hear a speech from Cicero? Ligarius, there is no question, is a wicked man and an enemy." But when Cicero began to speak, he wonderfully moved him, and proceeded in his speech with such varied pathos, and such a charm of language, that the color of Cæsar's countenance often changed, and it was evident that all the passions of his soul were in commotion. At length, the orator touching upon the Pharsalian battle, he was so affected that his body trembled, and some of the papers he held dropped out of his hands. And thus he was overpowered, and acquitted Ligarius.

Henceforth, the commonwealth being changed into a monarchy, Cicero withdrew himself from public affairs, and employed his leisure in instructing those young men that would, in philosophy; and by the near intercourse he thus had with some of the noblest and highest in rank, he again began to possess great influence in the city. The work and object which he set himself was to compose and translate philosophical dialogues and to render logical and physical terms into the Roman idiom. For he it was, as it is said, who first or principally gave Latin names to *phantasia, syncatathesis, epokhe, catalepsis,*[13] *atomon, ameres, kenon,* and other such technical terms, which, either by metaphors or other means of accommodation, he succeeded in making intelligible and expressible to the

[13] *Phantăsia,* sensation excited by some external object, "impulsione oblata extrinsecus," Cicero renders by *visum; syncătăthĕsis,* the act of acceptance on our part, he calls *assensio* or *assensus; epŏkhē* is the suspension of assent, "suspensio assensionis"; *catalepsis,* or *comprehensio,* is the next step in perception after *assensio; ătŏmŏn* has been turned, but not by Cicero, into *insecabile;* he calls atoms *individua corpora,* or *individua,* using the same word also for *ămĕrĕs; kĕnon* is *inane* or *vacuum.* Most of these terms are introduced in the Academics, see I. 11, II. 6 and 18, and the curious illustration from Zeno in 47. Pointing with his left hand to his right, as it lay open and outspread. Here, said he, is sensation, *visum, phantasia;* letting the fingers begin to close, this, he proceeded, is assent, *syncatathesis;* by closing his hand he exemplified comprehension or *catalepsis;* and, at last, seizing it with his left, such, he said, is knowledge. *Phantasia,* of course, is etymologically our *fancy,* and *epokhe,* in the sense of a point in time to pause at, our *epoch.*

Romans. For his recreation, he exercised his dexterity in poetry, and when he was set to it, would make five hundred verses in a night. He spent the greatest part of his time at his country house near Tusculum. He wrote to his friends that he led the life of Laertes,[14] either jestingly, as his custom was, or rather from a feeling of ambition for public employment, which made him impatient under the present state of affairs. He rarely went to the city, unless to pay his court to Cæsar. He was commonly the first amongst those who voted him honors, and sought out new terms of praise for himself and for his actions. As, for example, what he said of the statues of Pompey, which had been thrown down, and were afterwards by Cæsar's orders set up again: that Cæsar, by this act of humanity, had indeed set up Pompey's statues, but he had fixed and established his own.

He had a design, it is said, of writing the history of his country, combining with it much of that of Greece, and incorporating in it all the stories and legends of the past that he had collected. But his purposes were interfered with by various public and various private unhappy occurrences and misfortunes; for most of which he was himself in fault. For first of ali, he put away his wife Terentia, by whom he had been neglected in the time of the war, and sent away destitute of necessaries for his journey; neither did he find her kind when he returned from Italy, for she did not join him at Brundusium, where he staid a long time, nor would allow her young daughter, who undertook so long a journey, decent attendance, or the requisite expenses; besides, she left him a naked and empty house, and yet had involved him in many and great debts. These were alleged as the fairest reasons for the divorce. But Terentia, who denied them all, had the most unmistakable defence furnished her by her husband himself, who not long after married a young maiden for the love of her beauty, as Terentia upbraided him; or as Tiro, his emancipated slave, has written, for her riches to discharge his debts. For the young woman was very rich, and Cicero had the custody of her estate, being left guardian in trust; and being indebted many myriads of money, he was persuaded by his friends

[14] "Who," says the description in the first book of the Odyssey, "comes no more to the city, but lives away in pain and grief on his land, with one old woman to feed him, when he tires himself with tottering about his vineyard." So, also, when Ulysses goes to see him, in the last book.

and relations to marry her, notwithstanding his disparity of age, and to use her money to satisfy his creditors. Antony, who mentions this marriage in his answer to the Philippics, reproaches him for putting away a wife with whom he had lived to old age; adding some happy strokes of sarcasm on Cicero's domestic, inactive, unsoldier-like habits. Not long after this marriage, his daughter died in child-bed at Lentulus's house, to whom she had been married after the death of Piso, her former husband. The philosophers from all parts came to comfort Cicero; for his grief was so excessive, that he put away his new-married wife, because she seemed to be pleased at the death of Tullia. And thus stood Cicero's domestic affairs at this time.

He had no concern in the design that was now forming against Cæsar, although, in general, he was Brutus's most principal confidant, and one who was as aggrieved at the present, and as desirous of the former state of public affairs, as any other whatsoever. But they feared his temper, as wanting courage, and his old age, in which the most daring dispositions are apt to be timorous.

As soon, therefore, as the act was committed by Brutus and Cassius, and the friends of Cæsar were got together, so that there was fear the city would again be involved in a civil war, Antony, being consul, convened the senate, and made a short address recommending concord. And Cicero, following with various remarks such as the occasion called for, persuaded the senate to imitate the Athenians, and decree an amnesty for what had been done in Cæsar's case, and to bestow provinces on Brutus and Cassius. But neither of these things took effect. For as soon as the common people, of themselves inclined to pity, saw the dead body of Cæsar borne through the market-place, and Antony showing his clothes filled with blood, and pierced through in every part with swords, enraged to a degree of frenzy, they made a search for the murderers, and with firebrands in their hands ran to their houses to burn them. They, however, being forewarned, avoided this danger; and expecting many more and greater to come, they left the city.

Antony on this was at once in exultation, and every one was in alarm with the prospect that he would make himself sole ruler, and Cicero in more alarm than any one. For Antony, seeing his influence reviving in the commonwealth, and knowing how closely he was connected with Brutus, was ill-pleased to have him in the city. Besides, there had been some former jealousy between them, occasioned by the difference of their manners. Cicero, fearing the event, was inclined to go as lieutenant with Dolabella into Syria. But Hirtius and Pansa, consuls elect as successors of Antony, good men and lovers of Cicero, entreated him not to leave them, undertaking to put down Antony if he would stay in Rome. And he, neither distrusting wholly, nor trusting them, let Dolabella go without him, promising Hirtius that he would go and spend his summer at Athens, and return again when he entered upon his office. So he set out on his journey; but some delay occurring in his passage, new intelligence, as often happens, came suddenly from Rome, that Antony had made an astonishing change, and was doing all things and managing all public affairs at the will of the senate, and that there wanted nothing but his presence to bring things to a happy settlement. And therefore, blaming himself for his cowardice, he returned again to Rome, and was not deceived in his hopes at the beginning. For such multitudes flocked out to meet him, that the compliments and civilities which were paid him at the gates, and at his entrance into the city, took up almost one whole day's time.

On the morrow, Antony convened the senate, and summoned Cicero thither. He came not, but kept his bed, pretending to be ill with his journey; but the true reason seemed the fear of some design against him, upon a suspicion and intimation given him on his way to Rome. Antony, however, showed great offence at the affront, and sent soldiers, commanding them to bring him or burn his house; but many interceding and supplicating for him, he was contented to accept sureties. Ever after, when they met, they passed one another with silence, and continued on their guard, till Cæsar, the younger,[15] coming from Apollonia, entered on the first Cæsar's inheritance, and was engaged in a dispute with Antony about two thousand five hundred myriads of money, which Antony detained from the estate.

Upon this, Philippus, who married the mother, and Marcellus,

[15] Augustus.

who married the sister of young Cæsar, came with the young man to Cicero, and agreed with him that Cicero should give them the aid of his eloquence and political influence with the senate and people, and Cæsar give Cicero the defence of his riches and arms. For the young man had already a great party of the soldiers of Cæsar about him. And Cicero's readiness to join him was founded, it is said, on some yet stronger motives; for it seems, while Pompey and Cæsar were yet alive, Cicero, in his sleep, had fancied himself engaged in calling some of the sons of the senators into the capitol, Jupiter being about, according to the dream, to declare one of them the chief ruler of Rome. The citizens, running up with curiosity, stood about the temple, and the youths, sitting in their purple-bordered robes, kept silence. On a sudden the doors opened, and the youths, arising one by one in order, passed round the god, who reviewed them all, and, to their sorrow, dismissed them; but when this one was passing by, the god stretched forth his right hand and said, "O ye Romans, this young man, when he shall be lord of Rome, shall put an end to all your civil wars." It is said that Cicero formed from his dream a distinct image of the youth, and retained it afterwards perfectly, but did not know who it was. The next day, going down into the Campus Martius, he met the boys returning from their gymnastic exercises, and the first was he, just as he had appeared to him in his dream. Being astonished at it, he asked him who were his parents. And it proved to be this young Cæsar, whose father was a man of no great eminence, Octavius, and his mother, Attia, Cæsar's sister's daughter; for which reason, Cæsar, who had no children, made him by will the heir of his house and property. From that time, it is said that Cicero studiously noticed the youth whenever he met him, and he as kindly received the civility; and by fortune he happened to be born when Cicero was consul.

These were the reasons spoken of; but it was principally Cicero's hatred of Antony, and a temper unable to resist honor, which fastened him to Cæsar, with the purpose of getting the support of Cæsar's power for his own public designs. For the young man went so far in his court to him, that he called him Father; at which Brutus was so highly displeased that, in his epistles to Atticus he reflected on Cicero, saying, it was manifest, by his courting Cæsar for fear of Antony, he did not intend liberty to his country, but an indulgent master to himself. Notwithstanding, Brutus took Cicero's son, then studying philosophy at Athens, gave him a command, and employed him in various ways, with a good result. Cicero's own power at this time was at the greatest height in the city, and he did whatsoever he pleased; he completely overpowered and drove out Antony, and sent the two consuls, Hirtius and Pansa, with an army, to reduce him; and, on the other hand, persuaded the senate to allow Cæsar the lictors and ensigns of a prætor, as though he were his country's defender. But after Antony was defeated in battle, and the two consuls slain, the armies united, and ranged themselves with Cæsar. And the senate, fearing the young man, and his extraordinary fortune, endeavored, by honors and gifts, to call off the soldiers from him, and to lessen his power; professing there was no further need of arms, now Antony was put to flight.

This giving Cæsar an affright, he privately sends some friends to entreat and persuade Cicero to procure the consular dignity for them both together; saying he should manage the affairs as he pleased, should have the supreme power, and govern the young man who was only desirous of name and glory. And Cæsar himself confessed, that in fear of ruin, and in danger of being deserted, he had seasonably made use of Cicero's ambition, persuading him to stand with him, and to accept the offer of his aid and interest for the consulship.

And now, more than at any other time, Cicero let himself be carried away and deceived, though an old man, by the persuasions of a boy. He joined him in soliciting votes, and procured the goodwill of the senate, not without blame at the time on the part of his friends; and he, too, soon enough after, saw that he had ruined himself, and betrayed the liberty of his country. For the young man, once established, and possessed of the office of consul, bade Cicero farewell; and, reconciling himself to Antony and Lepidus, joined his power with theirs, and divided the government, like a piece of property, with them. Thus united, they made a schedule of above two hundred persons who were to be put to death. But the greatest contention in all their debates was on the question of

Cicero's case. Antony would come to no conditions, unless he should be the first man to be killed. Lepidus held with Antony, and Cæsar opposed them both. They met secretly and by themselves, for three days together, near the town of Bononia. The spot was not far from the camp, with a river surrounding it. Cæsar, it is said, contended earnestly for Cicero the first two days; but on the third day he yielded, and gave him up. The terms of their mutual concessions were these: that Cæsar should desert Cicero, Lepidus his brother Paulus, and Antony, Lucius Cæsar, his uncle by his mother's side. Thus they let their anger and fury take from them the sense of humanity, and demonstrated that no beast is more savage than man, when possessed with power answerable to his rage.

Whilst these things were contriving, Cicero was with his brother at his country-house near Tusculum; whence, hearing of the proscriptions, they determined to pass to Astura, a villa of Cicero's near the sea, and to take shipping from thence for Macedonia to Brutus, of whose strength in that province news had already been heard. They travelled together in their separate litters, overwhelmed with sorrow; and often stopping on the way till their litters came together, condoled with one another. But Quintus was the more disheartened, when he reflected on his want of means for his journey; for, as he said, he had brought nothing with him from home. And even Cicero himself had but a slender provision. It was judged, therefore, most expedient that Cicero should make what haste he could to fly, and Quintus return home to provide necessaries, and thus resolved, they mutually embraced, and parted with many tears.

Quintus, within a few days after, betrayed by his servants to those who came to search for him, was slain, together with his young son. But Cicero was carried to Astura, where, finding a vessel, he immediately went on board her, and sailed as far as Circæum with a prosperous gale; but when the pilots resolved immediately to set sail from thence, whether fearing the sea, or not wholly distrusting the faith of Cæsar, he went on shore, and passed by land a hundred furlongs, as if he was going for Rome. But losing resolution and changing his mind, he again returned to the sea, and there spent the night in fearful and perplexed thoughts. Sometimes he resolved to go into Cæsar's house privately, and there kill himself upon the altar of his household gods, to bring divine vengeance upon him; but the fear of torture put him off this course. And after passing through a variety of confused and uncertain counsels, at last he let his servants carry him by sea to Capitæ,[16] where he had a house, an agreeable place to retire to in the heat of summer, when the Etesian winds are so pleasant.

There was at that place a chapel of Apollo, not far from the sea-side, from which a flight of crows rose with a great noise, and made toward Cicero's vessel as it rowed to land, and lighting on both sides of the yard, some croaked, others pecked the ends of the ropes. This was looked upon by all as an ill omen; and, therefore, Cicero went again ashore, and entering his house, lay down upon his bed to compose himself to rest. Many of the crows settled about the window, making a dismal cawing; but one of them alighted upon the bed where Cicero lay covered up, and with its bill by little and little pecked off the clothes from his face. His servants, seeing this, blamed themselves that they should stay to be spectators of their master's murder, and do nothing in his defence, whilst the brute creatures came to assist and take care of him in his undeserved affliction; and, therefore, partly by entreaty, partly by force, they took him up, and carried him in his litter towards the sea-side.

But in the mean time the assassins were come with a band of soldiers, Herennius, a centurion, and Popillius, a tribune, whom Cicero had formerly defended when prosecuted for the murder of his father. Finding the doors shut, they broke them open, and Cicero not appearing, and those within saying they knew not where he was, it is stated that a youth, who had been educated by Cicero in the liberal arts and sciences, an emancipated slave of his brother Quintus, Philologus by name, informed the tribune that the litter was on its way to the sea through the close and shady walks. The tribune, taking a few with him, ran to the place where he was to come out. And Cicero, perceiving Herennius running in the walks, commanded his servants to set down the litter; and stroking his chin, as he used to do, with his left hand, he looked steadfastly upon his murderers, his person covered with dust, his beard and hair

[16] This, as we find from other authority, means Caieta, the present Gaeta. Nothing is known of any such place as Capitæ. Formiæ, the present Mola di Gaeta, is close by; and here Cicero is known to have had a villa, the Formianum.

untrimmed, and his face worn with his troubles. So that the greatest part of those that stood by covered their faces whilst Herennius slew him. And thus was he murdered, stretching forth his neck out of the litter, being now in his sixty-fourth year. Herennius cut off his head, and, by Antony's command, his hands also, by which his Philippics were written; for so Cicero styled those orations he wrote against Antony, and so they are called to this day.

When these members of Cicero were brought to Rome, Antony was holding an assembly for the choice of public officers; and when he heard it, and saw them, he cried out, "Now let there be an end of our proscriptions." He commanded his head and hands to be fastened up over the Rostra, where the orators spoke; a sight which the Roman people shuddered to behold, and they believed they saw there not the face of Cicero, but the image of Antony's own soul. And yet amidst these actions he did justice in one thing, by delivering up Philologus to Pomponia, the wife of Quintus, who, having got his body into her power, besides other grievous punishments, made him cut off his own flesh by pieces, and roast and eat it; for so some writers have related. But Tiro, Cicero's emancipated slave, has not so much as mentioned the treachery of Philologus.

Some long time after, Cæsar, I have been told, visiting one of his daughter's sons, found him with a book of Cicero's in his hand. The boy for fear endeavored to hide it under his gown; which Cæsar perceiving, took it from him, and turning over a great part of the book standing, gave it him again, and said, "My child, this was a learned man, and a lover of his country." [17] And immediately after he had vanquished Antony, being then consul, he made Cicero's son his colleague in the office; and under that consulship, the senate took down all the statues of Antony, and abolished all the other honors that had been given him, and decreed that none of that family should thereafter bear the name of Marcus; and thus the final acts of the punishment of Antony were, by the divine powers, devolved upon the family of Cicero.

[17] It is not easy to find any proper equivalent for the word here translated by "learned." *Logios,* derived from *logos,* which is indifferently *speech* and *reason* (thinking and speaking being both powers of *articulating*), may be one who has thought much and well, one who has much to say, and one who can say it well.

COMPARISON OF DEMOSTHENES AND CICERO

THESE are the most memorable circumstances recorded in history of Demosthenes and Cicero which have come to our knowledge. But omitting an exact comparison of their respective faculties in speaking, yet thus much seems fit to be said; that Demosthenes, to make himself a master in rhetoric, applied all the faculties he had, natural or acquired, wholly that way; that he far surpassed in force and strength of eloquence all his contemporaries in political and judicial speaking, in grandeur and majesty all the panegyrical orators, and in accuracy and science all the logicians and rhetoricians of his day;[1] that Cicero was highly educated, and by his diligent study became a most accomplished general scholar in all these branches, having left behind him numerous philosophical treatises of his own on Academic principles; as, indeed, even in his written speeches, both political and judicial, we see him continually trying to show his learning by the way. And one may discover the different temper of each of them in their speeches. For Demosthenes's oratory was without all embellishment and jesting, wholly composed for real effect and seriousness; not smelling of the lamp, as Pytheas scoffingly said, but of the temperance, thoughtfulness, austerity, and grave earnestness of his temper. Whereas Cicero's love of mockery often ran him into scurrility; and in his love of laughing away serious arguments in judicial cases by jests and facetious remarks, with a view to the advantage of his clients, he paid too little regard to what was decent; saying, for example, in his defence of Cælius, that he had done no absurd thing in such plenty and affluence to indulge himself in pleasures, it being a kind of madness not to enjoy the things we possess, especially since the most eminent philosophers have asserted pleasure to be the

[1] The political, the judicial, and the panegyrical departments were the three varieties of oratory. To the practitioners in these are added the *sophistæ,* the logic and rhetoric masters.

chiefest good. So also we are told, that when Cicero, being consul, undertook the defence of Murena against Cato's prosecution, by way of bantering Cato, he made a long series of jokes upon the absurd *paradoxes,* as they are called, of the Stoic sect; so that a loud laughter passing from the crowd to the judges, Cato, with a quiet smile, said to those that sat next to him, "My friends, what an amusing consul we have."

And, indeed, Cicero was by natural temper very much disposed to mirth and pleasantry, and always appeared with a smiling and serene countenance. But Demosthenes had constant care and thoughtfulness in his look, and a serious anxiety, which he seldom, if ever, laid aside; and, therefore, was accounted by his enemies, as he himself confessed, morose and ill-mannered.

Also, it is very evident, out of their several writings, that Demosthenes never touched upon his own praises but decently and without offence when there was need of it, and for some weightier end; but, upon other occasions modestly and sparingly. But Cicero's immeasurable boasting of himself in his orations argues him guilty of an uncontrollable appetite for distinction, his cry being evermore that arms should give place to the gown, and the soldier's laurel to the tongue.[2] And at last we find him extolling not only his deeds and actions, but his orations also, as well those that were only spoken, as those that were published; as if he were engaged in a boyish trial of skill, who should speak best, with the rhetoricians, Isocrates and Anaximenes, not as one who could claim the task to guide and instruct the Roman nation, the

"Soldier full-armed, terrific to the foe."

It is necessary, indeed, for a political leader to be an able speaker; but it is an ignoble thing for any man to admire and relish the glory of his own eloquence. And, in this matter, Demosthenes had a more than ordinary gravity and magnificence of mind, accounting his talent in speaking nothing more than a mere accomplishment and matter of practice, the success of which must depend greatly on the good-will and candor of his hearers, and regarding

[2] Translating Cicero's famous verse upon himself—

Cedant arma togæ, concedat laurea linguæ.

those who pride themselves on such accounts to be men of a low and petty disposition.

The power of persuading and governing the people did, indeed, equally belong to both, so that those who had armies and camps at command stood in need of their assistance; as Chares, Diopithes, and Leosthenes of Demosthenes's, Pompey and young Cæsar of Cicero's, as the latter himself admits in his Memoirs addressed to Agrippa and Mæcenas. But what are thought and commonly said most to demonstrate and try the tempers of men, namely, authority, and place, by moving every passion, and discovering every frailty, these are things which Demosthenes never received; nor was he ever in a position to give such proof of himself, having never obtained any eminent office, nor led any of those armies into the field against Philip which he raised by his eloquence. Cicero, on the other hand, was sent quæstor into Sicily, and proconsul into Cilicia and Cappadocia, at a time when avarice was at the height, and the commanders and governors who were employed abroad, as though they thought it a mean thing to steal, set themselves to seize by open force; so that it seemed no heinous matter to take bribes, but he that did it most moderately was in good esteem. And yet he, at this time, gave the most abundant proofs alike of his contempt of riches and of his humanity and good-nature. And at Rome, when he was created consul in name, but indeed received sovereign and dictatorial authority against Catiline and his conspirators, he attested the truth of Plato's prediction, that then the miseries of states would be at an end, when by a happy fortune supreme power, wisdom, and justice should be united in one.[3]

It is said, to the reproach of Demosthenes, that his eloquence was mercenary; that he privately made orations for Phormion and Apollodorus, though adversaries in the same cause; that he was charged with moneys received from the king of Persia, and condemned for bribes from Harpalus. And should we grant that all those (and they are not few) who have made these statements against him have spoken what is untrue, yet that Demosthenes was not the character to look without desire on the presents offered him out of respect and gratitude by royal persons, and that one who lent

[3] Or, as the dictum is in his Republic, "When the philosopher should be king."

money on maritime usury was likely to be thus indifferent, is what we cannot assert. But that Cicero refused, from the Sicilians when he was quæstor, from the king of Cappadocia when he was proconsul, and from his friends at Rome when he was in exile, many presents, though urged to receive them, has been said already.

Moreover, Demosthenes's banishment was infamous, upon conviction for bribery; Cicero's very honorable, for ridding his country of a set of villains. Therefore, when Demosthenes fled his country, no man regarded it; for Cicero's sake the senate changed their habit, and put on mourning, and would not be persuaded to make any act before Cicero's return was decreed. Cicero, however, passed his exile idly in Macedonia. But the very exile of Demosthenes made up a great part of the services he did for his country; for he went through the cities of Greece, and everywhere, as we have said, joined in the conflict on behalf of the Grecians, driving out the Macedonian ambassadors, and approving himself a much better citizen than Themistocles and Alcibiades did in the like fortune. And, after his return, he again devoted himself to the same public service, and continued firm to his opposition to Antipater and the Macedonians. Whereas Lælius reproached Cicero in the senate for sitting silent when Cæsar, a beardless youth, asked leave to come forward, contrary to the law, as a candidate for the consulship; and Brutus, in his epistles, charges him with nursing and rearing a greater and more heavy tyranny than that they had removed.

Finally, Cicero's death excites our pity; for an old man to be miserably carried up and down by his servants, flying and hiding himself from that death which was, in the course of nature, so near at hand; and yet at last to be murdered. Demosthenes, though he seemed at first a little to supplicate, yet, by his preparing and keeping the poison by him, demands our admiration; and still more admirable was his using it. When the temple of the god no longer afforded him a sanctuary, he took refuge, as it were, at a mightier altar, freeing himself from arms and soldiers, and laughing to scorn the cruelty of Antipater.

CÆSAR

AFTER Sylla became master of Rome, he wished to make Cæsar put away his wife Cornelia, daughter of Cinna, the late sole ruler of the commonwealth, but was unable to effect it either by promises or intimidation, and so contented himself with confiscating her dowry. The ground of Sylla's hostility to Cæsar, was the relationship between him and Marius; for Marius, the elder, married Julia, the sister of Cæsar's father, and had by her the younger Marius, who consequently was Cæsar's first cousin. And though at the beginning, while so many were to be put to death and there was so much to do, Cæsar was overlooked by Sylla, yet he would not keep quiet, but presented himself to the people as a candidate for the priesthood, though he was yet a mere boy. Sylla, without any open opposition, took measures to have him rejected, and in consultation whether he should be put to death, when it was urged by some that it was not worth his while to contrive the death of a boy, he answered, that they knew little who did not see more than one Marius in that boy. Cæsar, on being informed of this saying, concealed himself, and for a considerable time kept out of the way in the country of the Sabines, often changing his quarters, till one night, as he was removing from one house to another on account of his health, he fell into the hands of Sylla's soldiers, who were searching those parts in order to apprehend any who had absconded. Cæsar, by a bribe of two talents, prevailed with Cornelius, their captain, to let him go, and was no sooner dismissed but he put to sea, and made for Bithynia. After a short stay there with Nicomedes, the king, in his passage back he was taken near the island Pharmacusa by some of the pirates, who, at that time, with large fleets of ships and innumerable smaller vessels infested the seas everywhere.

When these men at first demanded of him twenty talents for his ransom, he laughed at them for not understanding the value of their prisoner, and voluntarily engaged to give them fifty. He presently despatched those about him to several places to raise the money, till at last he was left among a set of the most bloodthirsty people in the world, the Cilicians, only with one friend and two attendants. Yet he made so little of them, that when he had a mind to sleep, he would send to them, and order them to make no noise. For thirty-eight days, with all the freedom in the world, he amused himself with joining in their exercises and games, as if they had not been his keepers, but his guards. He wrote verses and speeches, and made them his auditors, and those who did not admire them, he called to their faces illiterate and barbarous, and would often, in raillery, threaten to hang them. They were greatly taken with this, and attributed his free talking to a kind of simplicity and boyish playfulness. As soon as his ransom was come from Miletus, he paid it, and was discharged, and proceeded at once to man some ships at the port of Miletus, and went in pursuit of the pirates, whom he surprised with their ships still stationed at the island, and took most of them. Their money he made his prize, and the men he secured in prison at Pergamus, and made application to Junius, who was then governor of Asia, to whose office it belonged, as prætor, to determine their punishment. Junius, having his eye upon the money, for the sum was considerable, said he would think at his leisure what to do with the prisoners, upon which Cæsar took his leave of him, and went off to Pergamus, where he ordered the pirates to be brought forth and crucified; the punishment he had often threatened them with whilst he was in their hands, and they little dreamed he was in earnest.

In the mean time Sylla's power being now on the decline, Cæsar's friends advised him to return to Rome, but he went to Rhodes, and entered himself in the school of Apollonius, Molon's son, a famous rhetorician, one who had the reputation of a worthy man, and had Cicero for one of his scholars. Cæsar is said to have been admirably fitted by nature to make a great statesman and orator, and to have taken such pains to improve his genius this way, that without dispute he might challenge the second place. More he did not aim at, as choosing to be first rather amongst men of arms and power, and, therefore, never rose to that height of eloquence to which nature would have carried him, his attention being diverted to those expeditions and designs which at length gained him the empire. And he himself, in his answer to Cicero's panegyric on Cato, desires his reader not to compare the plain discourse of a soldier with the harangues of an orator who had not only fine parts, but had employed his life in this study.

When he was returned to Rome, he accused Dolabella of maladministration, and many cities of Greece came in to attest it. Dolabella was acquitted, and Cæsar, in return for the support he had received from the Greeks, assisted them in their prosecution of Publius Antonius for corrupt practices, before Marcus Lucullus, prætor of Macedonia. In this cause he so far succeeded, that Antonius was forced to appeal to the tribunes at Rome, alleging that in Greece he could not have fair play against Grecians. In his pleadings at Rome, his eloquence soon obtained him great credit and favor, and he won no less upon the affections of the people by the affability of his manners and address, in which he showed a tact and consideration beyond what could have been expected at his age; and the open house he kept, the entertainments he gave, and the general splendor of his manner of life contributed little by little to create and increase his political influence. His enemies slighted the growth of it at first, presuming it would soon fail when his money was gone; whilst in the mean time it was growing up and flourishing among the common people. When his power at last was established and not to be overthrown, and now openly tended to the altering of the whole constitution, they were aware too late, that there is no beginning so mean, which continued application will not make considerable, and that despising a danger at first, will make it at last irresistible. Cicero was the first who had any suspicions of his designs upon the government, and, as a good pilot is apprehensive of a storm when the sea is most smiling, saw the designing temper of the man through this disguise of good-humor and affability, and said, that in general, in all he did and undertook, he detected the ambition for absolute power, "but when I see his hair so carefully arranged, and observe him adjusting it with one finger, I cannot imagine it should enter into such a man's thoughts to subvert the Roman state." But of this more hereafter.

The first proof he had of the people's good-will to him, was when he received by their suffrages a tribuneship in the army, and came out on the list with a higher place than Caius Popilius. A second and clearer instance of their favor appeared upon his making a magnificent oration in praise of his aunt Julia, wife to Marius, publicly in the forum, at whose funeral he was so bold as to bring forth the images of Marius, which nobody had dared to produce since the government came into Sylla's hands, Marius's party having from that time been declared enemies of the State. When some who were present had begun to raise a cry against Cæsar, the people answered with loud shouts and clapping in his favor, expressing their joyful surprise and satisfaction at his having, as it were, brought up again from the grave those honors of Marius, which for so long a time had been lost to the city. It had always been the custom at Rome to make funeral orations in praise of elderly matrons, but there was no precedent of any upon young women till Cæsar first made one upon the death of his own wife. This also procured him favor, and by this show of affection he won upon the feelings of the people, who looked upon him as a man of great tenderness and kindness of heart. After he had buried his wife, he went as quæstor into Spain under one of the prætors, named Vetus, whom he honored ever after, and made his son his own quæstor, when he himself came to be prætor. After this employment was ended, he married Pompeia, his third wife, having then a daughter by Cornelia, his first wife, whom he afterwards married to Pompey the Great. He was so profuse in his expenses, that before he had any public employment, he was in debt thirteen hundred talents, and many thought that by incurring such expense to be popular, he changed a solid good for what would prove but a short and uncertain return; but in truth he was purchasing what was of the greatest value at an inconsiderable rate. When he was made surveyor of the Appian Way, he disbursed, besides the public money, a great sum out of his private purse; and when he was ædile, he provided such a number of gladiators, that he entertained the people with three hundred and twenty single combats, and by his great liberality and magnificence in theatrical shows, in processions, and public feastings, he threw into the shade all the attempts that had been made before him, and gained so much upon the people, that every one was eager to find out new offices and new honors for him in return for his munificence.

There being two factions in the city, one that of Sylla, which was very powerful, the other that of Marius, which was then broken and in a very low condition, he undertook to revive this and to make it his own. And to this end, whilst he was in the height of his repute with the people for the magnificent shows he gave as ædile, he ordered images of Marius, and figures of Victory, with trophies in their hands, to be carried privately in the night and placed in the capitol. Next morning, when some saw them bright with gold and beautifully made, with inscriptions upon them, referring to Marius's exploits over the Cimbrians, they were surprised at the boldness of him who had set them up, nor was it difficult to guess who it was. The fame of this soon spread and brought together a great concourse of people. Some cried out that it was an open attempt against the established government thus to revive those honors which had been buried by the laws and decrees of the senate; that Cæsar had done it to sound the temper of the people whom he had prepared before, and to try whether they were tame enough to bear his humor, and would quietly give way to his innovations. On the other hand, Marius's party took courage, and it was incredible how numerous they were suddenly seen to be, and what a multitude of them appeared and came shouting into the capitol. Many, when they saw Marius's likeness, cried for joy, and Cæsar was highly extolled as the one man, in the place of all others, who was a relation worthy of Marius. Upon this the senate met, and Catulus Lutatius, one of the most eminent Romans of that time, stood up and inveighed against Cæsar, closing his speech with the remarkable saying, that Cæsar was now not working mines, but planting batteries to overthrow the state. But when Cæsar had made an apology for himself, and satisfied the senate, his admirers were very much animated, and advised him not to depart from his own thoughts for any one, since with the people's good favor he would erelong get the better of them all, and be the first man in the commonwealth.

At this time, Metellus, the High-Priest, died, and Catulus and Isauricus, persons of the highest reputation, and who had great influence in the senate, were competitors for the office; yet Cæsar would not give way to them, but presented himself to the people as a candidate against them. The several parties seeming very equal, Catulus, who, because he had the most honor to lose, was the most apprehensive of the event, sent to Cæsar to buy him off, with offers of a great sum of money. But his answer was, that he was ready to borrow a larger sum than that, to carry on the contest. Upon the day of election, as his mother conducted him out of doors with tears, after embracing her, "My mother," he said, "to-day you will see me either High-Priest, or an exile." When the votes were taken, after a great struggle, he carried it, and excited among the senate and nobility great alarm lest he might now urge on the people to every kind of insolence. And Piso and Catulus found fault with Cicero for having let Cæsar escape, when in the conspiracy of Catiline he had given the government such advantage against him. For Catiline, who had designed not only to change the present state of affairs, but to subvert the whole empire and confound all, had himself taken to flight, while the evidence was yet incomplete against him, before his ultimate purposes had been properly discovered. But he had left Lentulus and Cethegus in the city to supply his place in the conspiracy, and whether they received any secret encouragement and assistance from Cæsar is uncertain; all that is certain is, that they were fully convicted in the senate, and when Cicero, the consul, asked the several opinions of the senators, how they would have them punished, all who spoke before Cæsar sentenced them to death; but Cæsar stood up and made a set speech, in which he told them, that he thought it without precedent and not just to take away the lives of persons of their birth and distinction before they were fairly tried, unless there was an absolute necessity for it; but that if they were kept confined in any towns of Italy Cicero himself should choose, till Catiline was defeated, then the senate might in peace and at their leisure determine what was best to be done.

This sentence of his carried so much appearance of humanity, and he gave it such advantage by the eloquence with which he urged it, that not only those who spoke after him closed with it, but even they who had before given a contrary opinion, now came over to his, till it came about to Catulus's and Cato's turn to speak. They warmly opposed it, and Cato intimated in his speech the suspicion of Cæsar himself, and pressed the matter so strongly, that the criminals were given up to suffer execution. As Cæsar was going out of the senate, many of the young men who at that time acted as guards to Cicero, ran in with their naked swords to assault him. But Curio, it is said, threw his gown over him, and conveyed him away, and Cicero himself, when the young men looked up to see his wishes, gave a sign not to kill him, either for fear of the people, or because he thought the murder unjust and illegal. If this be true, I wonder how Cicero came to omit all mention of it in his book about his consulship. He was blamed, however, afterwards, for not having made use of so fortunate an opportunity against Cæsar, as if he had let it escape him out of fear of the populace, who, indeed, showed remarkable solicitude about Cæsar, and some time after, when he went into the senate to clear himself of the suspicions he lay under, and found great clamors raised against him, upon the senate in consequence sitting longer than ordinary, they went up to the house in a tumult, and beset it, demanding Cæsar, and requiring them to dismiss him. Upon this, Cato, much fearing some movement among the poor citizens, who were always the first to kindle the flame among the people, and placed all their hopes in Cæsar, persuaded the senate to give them a monthly allowance of corn, an expedient which put the commonwealth to the extraordinary charge of seven million five hundred thousand drachmas in the year, but quite succeeded in removing the great cause of terror for the present, and very much weakened Cæsar's power, who at that time was just going to be made prætor, and consequently would have been more formidable by his office.

But there was no disturbance during his prætorship, only what misfortune he met with in his own domestic affairs. Publius Clodius was a patrician by descent, eminent both for his riches and eloquence, but in licentiousness of life and audacity exceeded the most noted profligates of the day. He was in love with Pompeia, Cæsar's wife, and she had no aversion to him. But there was strict watch kept on her apartment, and Cæsar's mother, Aurelia, who was a discreet woman, being continually about her, made any interview very dangerous and difficult. The Romans have a goddess whom they call Bona, the same whom the Greeks call Gynæcea. The Phrygians, who claim a peculiar title to her, say she was mother to Midas. The Romans profess she was one of the Dryads, and married to Faunus. The Grecians affirm that she is the mother of Bacchus whose name is not to be uttered, and, for this reason, the women who celebrate her festival, cover the tents with vine-branches, and, in accordance with the fable, a consecrated serpent is placed by the goddess. It is not lawful for a man to be by, nor so much as in the house, whilst the rites are celebrated, but the women by themselves perform the sacred offices, which are said to be much the same with those used in the solemnities of Orpheus. When the festival comes, the husband, who is either consul or prætor, and with him every male creature, quits the house. The wife then taking it under her care, sets it in order, and the principal ceremonies are performed during the night, the women playing together amongst themselves as they keep watch, and music of various kinds going on.

As Pompeia was at that time celebrating this feast, Clodius, who as yet had no beard, and so thought to pass undiscovered, took upon him the dress and ornaments of a singing woman, and so came thither, having the air of a young girl. Finding the doors open, he was without any stop introduced by the maid, who was in the intrigue. She presently ran to tell Pompeia, but as she was away a long time, he grew uneasy waiting for her, and left his post and traversed the house from one room to another, still taking care to avoid the lights, till at last Aurelia's woman met him, and invited him to play with her, as the women did among themselves. He refused to comply, and she presently pulled him forward, and asked him who he was, and whence he came. Clodius told her he was waiting for Pompeia's own maid, Abra,[1] being in fact her own

[1] Abra was the Greek word for the favorite waiting-maid; and was, also, this girl's own proper name. Clodius said he was waiting for Pompeia's *Abra,* that being, also, as it happened, her name.

name also, and as he said so, betrayed himself by his voice. Upon which the woman shrieking, ran into the company where there were lights, and cried out, she had discovered a man. The women were all in a fright. Aurelia covered up the sacred things and stopped the proceedings, and having ordered the doors to be shut, went about with lights to find Clodius, who was got in the maid's room that he had come in with, and was seized there. The women knew him, and drove him out of doors, and at once, that same night, went home and told their husbands the story. In the morning, it was all about the town, what an impious attempt Clodius had made, and how he ought to be punished as an offender, not only against those whom he had affronted, but also against the public and the gods. Upon which one of the tribunes impeached him for profaning the holy rites, and some of the principal senators combined together and gave evidence against him, that besides many other horrible crimes, he had been guilty of incest with his own sister, who was married to Lucullus. But the people set themselves against this combination of the nobility, and defended Clodius, which was of great service to him with the judges, who took alarm and were afraid to provoke the multitude. Cæsar at once dismissed Pompeia, but being summoned as a witness against Clodius, said he had nothing to charge him with. This looking like a paradox, the accuser asked him why he parted with his wife. Cæsar replied, "I wished my wife to be not so much as suspected." Some say that Cæsar spoke this as his real thought; others, that he did it to gratify the people, who were earnest to save Clodius. Clodius, at any rate, escaped; most of the judges giving their opinions so written as to be illegible, that they might not be in danger from the people by condemning him, nor in disgrace with the nobility by acquitting him.

Cæsar, in the mean time, being out of his prætorship, had got the province of Spain, but was in great embarrassment with his creditors, who, as he was going off, came upon him, and were very pressing and importunate. This led him to apply himself to Crassus, who was the richest man in Rome, but wanted Cæsar's youthful vigor and heat to sustain the opposition against Pompey. Crassus took upon him to satisfy those creditors who were not uneasy to him, and would not be put off any longer, and engaged himself to the amount of eight hundred and thirty talents, upon which Cæsar was now at liberty to go to his province. In his journey, as he was crossing the Alps, and passing by a small village of the barbarians with but few inhabitants and those wretchedly poor, his companions asked the question among themselves by way of mockery, if there were any canvassing for offices there; any contention which should be uppermost, or feuds of great men one against another. To which Cæsar made answer seriously, "For my part, I had rather be the first man among these fellows, than the second man in Rome." It is said that another time, when free from business in Spain, after reading some part of the history of Alexander, he sat a great while very thoughtful, and at last burst out into tears. His friends were surprised, and asked him the reason of it. "Do you think," said he, "I have not just cause to weep, when I consider that Alexander at my age had conquered so many nations, and I have all this time done nothing that is memorable?" As soon as he came into Spain he was very active, and in a few days had got together ten new cohorts of foot in addition to the twenty which were there before. With these he marched against the Calaici and Lusitani and conquered them, and advancing as far as the ocean, subdued the tribes which never before had been subject to the Romans. Having managed his military affairs with good success, he was equally happy in the course of his civil government. He took pains to establish a good understanding amongst the several states, and no less care to heal the differences between debtors and creditors. He ordered that the creditor should receive two parts of the debtor's yearly income, and that the other part should be managed by the debtor himself, till by this method the whole debt was at last discharged. This conduct made him leave his province with a fair reputation; being rich himself, and having enriched his soldiers, and having received from them the honorable name of Imperator.

There is a law among the Romans, that whoever desires the honor of a triumph must stay without the city and expect his answer. And another, that those who stand for the consulship shall appear personally upon the place. Cæsar was come home at the very time of choosing consuls, and being in a difficulty between these two opposite laws, sent to the senate a desire that since he was obliged to be absent, he might sue for the consulship by his friends. Cato, being backed by the law, at first opposed his request; afterwards perceiving that Cæsar had prevailed with a great part of the senate to comply with it, he made it his business to gain time, and went on wasting the whole day in speaking. Upon which Cæsar thought fit to let the triumph fall, and pursued the consulship. Entering the town and coming forward immediately, he had recourse to a piece of state-policy by which everybody was deceived but Cato. This was the reconciling of Crassus and Pompey, the two men who then were most powerful in Rome. There had been a quarrel between them, which he now succeeded in making up, and by this means strengthened himself by the united power of both, and so under the cover of an action which carried all the appearance of a piece of kindness and good-nature, caused what was in effect a revolution in the government. For it was not the quarrel between Pompey and Cæsar, as most men imagine, which was the origin of the civil wars, but their union, their conspiring together at first to subvert the aristocracy, and so quarreling afterwards between themselves. Cato, who often foretold what the consequence of this alliance would be, had then the character of a sullen, interfering man, but in the end the reputation of a wise but unsuccessful counsellor.

Thus Cæsar being doubly supported by the interests of Crassus and Pompey, was promoted to the consulship, and triumphantly proclaimed with Calpurnius Bibulus. When he entered on his office, he brought in bills which would have been preferred with better grace by the most audacious of the tribunes than by a consul, in which he proposed the plantation of colonies and division of lands, simply to please the commonalty. The best and most honorable of the senators opposed it, upon which, as he had long wished for nothing more than for such a colorable pretext, he loudly protested how much against his will it was to be driven to seek support from the people, and how the senate's insulting and harsh conduct left no other course possible for him, than to devote himself henceforth to the popular cause and interest. And so he hurried out of the senate, and presenting himself to the people, and there placing Crassus and Pompey, one on each side of him, he asked them whether they consented to the bills he had proposed. They owned their assent, upon which he desired them to assist him against those who had threatened to oppose him with their swords. They engaged they would, and Pompey added further, that he would meet their swords with a sword and buckler too. These words the nobles much resented, as neither suitable to his own dignity, nor becoming the reverence due to the senate, but resembling rather the vehemence of a boy, or the fury of a madman. But the people were pleased with it. In order to get a yet firmer hold upon Pompey, Cæsar having a daughter, Julia, who had been before contracted to Servilius Cæpio, now betrothed her to Pompey, and told Servilius he should have Pompey's daughter, who was not unengaged either, but promised to Sylla's son, Faustus. A little time after, Cæsar married Calpurnia, the daughter of Piso, and got Piso made consul for the year following. Cato exclaimed loudly against this, and protested with a great deal of warmth, that it was intolerable the government should be prostituted by marriages, and that they should advance one another to the commands of armies, provinces, and other great posts, by means of women. Bibulus, Cæsar's colleague, finding it was to no purpose to oppose his bills, but that he was in danger of being murdered in the forum, as also was Cato, confined himself to his house, and there let the remaining part of his consulship expire. Pompey, when he was married, at once filled the forum with soldiers, and gave the people his help in passing the new laws, and secured Cæsar the government of all Gaul, both on this and the other side of the Alps, together with Illyricum and the command of four legions for five years. Cato made some attempts against these proceedings, but was seized and led off on the way to prison by Cæsar, who expected he would appeal to the tribunes. But when he saw that Cato went along without speaking a word, and not only the nobility were indignant, but that the people, also, out of respect for Cato's virtue, were following in silence, and with dejected looks, he himself privately desired one of the tribunes to rescue Cato. As for the other senators, some few of them attended the house, the rest being disgusted, absented themselves. Hence Considius, a very old man, took occasion one day to tell Cæsar, that the senators did not meet because they were afraid of his soldiers. Cæsar asked, "Why don't you then, out of the same fear, keep at home?" To which Considius replied, that age was his guard against fear, and that the small remains of his life were not worth much caution. But the most disgraceful thing that was done in Cæsar's consulship, was his assisting to gain the tribuneship for the same Clodius who had made the attempt upon his wife's chastity, and intruded upon the secret vigils. He was elected on purpose to effect Cicero's downfall; nor did Cæsar leave the city to join his army, till they two had overpowered Cicero, and driven him out of Italy.

Thus far we have followed Cæsar's actions before the wars of Gaul. After this, he seems to begin his course afresh, and to enter upon a new life and scene of action. And the period of those wars which he now fought, and those many expeditions in which he subdued Gaul, showed him to be a soldier and general not in the least inferior to any of the greatest and most admired commanders who had ever appeared at the head of armies. For if we compare him with the Fabii, the Metelli, the Scipios, and with those who were his contemporaries, or not long before him, Sylla Marius, the two Luculli, or even Pompey himself, whose glory, it may be said, went up at that time to heaven for every excellence in war, we shall find Cæsar's actions to have surpassed them all. One he may be held to have outdone in consideration of the difficulty of the country in which he fought, another in the extent of territory which he conquered; some, in the number and strength of the enemies whom he defeated; one man, because of the wildness and perfidiousness of the tribes whose good-will he conciliated, another in his humanity and clemency to those he overpowered; others, again in his gifts and kindnesses to his soldiers; all alike in the number of the battles which he fought and the enemies whom he killed. For he had not pursued the wars in Gaul full ten years, when he had taken by storm above eight hundred towns, subdued three hundred states, and of the three millions of men, who made up the gross sum of those with whom at several times he engaged, he had killed one million, and taken captive a second.

He was so much master of the good-will and hearty service of his soldiers, that those who in other expeditions were but ordinary men, displayed a courage past defeating or withstanding when they went upon any danger where Cæsar's glory was concerned. Such a one was Acilius, who, in the sea-fight before Marseilles, had his right hand struck off with a sword, yet did not quit his buckler out of his left, but struck the enemies in the face with it, till he drove them off, and made himself master of the vessel. Such another was Cassius Scæva, who, in a battle near Dyrrhachium, had one of his eyes shot out with an arrow, his shoulder pierced with one javelin, and his thigh with another; and having received one hundred and thirty darts upon his target, called to the enemy, as though he would surrender himself. But when two of them came up to him, he cut off the shoulder of one with a sword, and by a blow over the face forced the other to retire, and so with the assistance of his friends, who now came up, made his escape. Again, in Britain, when some of the foremost officers had accidentally got into a morass full of water, and there were assaulted by the enemy, a common soldier, whilst Cæsar stood and looked on, threw himself into the midst of them, and after many signal demonstrations of his valor, rescued the officers, and beat off the barbarians. He himself, in the end, took to the water, and with much difficulty, partly by swimming, partly by wading, passed it, but in the passage lost his shield. Cæsar and his officers saw it and admired, and went to meet him with joy and acclamation. But the soldier, much dejected and in tears, threw himself down at Cæsar's feet, and begged his pardon for having let go his buckler. Another time in Africa, Scipio having taken a ship of Cæsar's in which Granius Petro, lately appointed quæstor, was sailing, gave the other passengers as free prize to his soldiers, but thought fit to offer the quæstor his life. But he said it was not usual for Cæsar's soldiers to take, but give mercy, and having said so, fell upon his sword and killed himself.

This love of honor and passion for distinction were inspired into them and cherished in them by Cæsar himself, who, by his unsparing distribution of money and honors, showed them that he did not heap up wealth from the wars for his own luxury, or the gratifying his private pleasures, but that all he received was but a public fund laid by for the reward and encouragement of valor, and that he looked upon all he gave to deserving soldiers as so much increase to his own riches. Added to this, also, there was no danger to which he did not willingly expose himself, no labor from which he pleaded an exemption. His contempt of danger was not so much wondered at by his soldiers, because they knew how much he coveted honor. But his enduring so much hardship, which he did to all appearance beyond his natural strength, very much astonished them. For he was a spare man, had a soft and white skin, was distempered in the head, and subject to an epilepsy, which, it is said, first seized him at Corduba. But he did not make the weakness of his constitution a pretext for his ease, but rather used war as the best physic against his indispositions; whilst by indefatigable journeys, coarse diet, frequent lodging in the field, and continual laborious exercise, he struggled with his diseases, and fortified his body against all attacks. He slept generally in his chariots or litters, employing even his rest in pursuit of action. In the day he was thus carried to the forts, garrisons, and camps, one servant sitting with him, who used to write down what he dictated as he went, and a soldier attending behind with his sword drawn. He drove so rapidly, that when he first left Rome, he arrived at the river Rhone within eight days. He had been an expert rider from his childhood; for it was usual with him to sit with his hands joined together behind his back, and so to put his horse to its full speed. And in this war he disciplined himself so far as to be able to dictate letters from on horseback, and to give directions to two who took notes at the same time, or, as Oppius says, to more. And it is thought that he was the first who contrived means for communicating with friends by cipher, when either press of business, or the large extent of the city, left him no time for a personal conference about matters that required despatch. How little nice he was in his diet, may be seen in the following instance. When at the table of Valerius Leo, who entertained him at supper at Milan, a dish of asparagus was put before him, on which his host instead of oil had poured sweet ointment. Cæsar partook of it without any disgust, and reprimanded his friends for finding fault with it. "For it was enough," said he, "not to eat what you did not like; but he who reflects on another man's want of breeding, shows he wants it as much himself." Another time upon the road he was driven by a storm into a poor man's cottage, where he found but one room, and that such as would afford but a mean reception to a single person, and therefore told his companions, places of honor should be given up to the greater men, and necessary accommodations to the weaker, and accordingly ordered that Oppius, who was in bad health, should lodge within, whilst he and the rest slept under a shed at the door.

His first war in Gaul was against the Helvetians and Tigurini, who having burnt their own towns, twelve in number, and four hundred villages, would have marched forward through that part of Gaul which was included in the Roman province, as the Cimbrians and Teutons formerly had done. Nor were they inferior to these in courage; and in numbers they were equal, being in all three hundred thousand, of which one hundred and ninety thousand were fighting men. Cæsar did not engage the Tigurini in person, but Labienus, under his directions, routed them near the river Arar. The Helvetians surprised Cæsar, and unexpectedly set upon him as he was conducting his army to a confederate town. He succeeded, however, in making his retreat into a strong position, where, when he had mustered and marshalled his men, his horse was brought to him; upon which he said, "When I have won the battle, I will use my horse for the chase, but at present let us go against the enemy," and accordingly charged them on foot. After a long and severe combat, he drove the main army out of the field, but found the hardest work at their carriages and ramparts, where not only the men stood and fought but the women also and children defended themselves, till they were cut to pieces; insomuch that the fight was scarcely ended till midnight. This action, glorious in itself, Cæsar crowned with another yet more noble, by gathering in a body all the barbarians that had escaped out of the battle, above one hundred thousand in number, and obliging them to reoccupy the country which they had deserted, and the cities which they had burnt. This he did for fear the Germans should pass in and possess themselves of the land whilst it lay uninhabited.

His second war was in defence of the Gauls against the Germans, though some time before he had made Ariovistus, their king, recognized at Rome as an ally. But they were very insufferable neighbours to those under his government; and it was probable, when occasion offered, they would renounce the present arrangements, and march on to occupy Gaul. But finding his officers timorous, and especially those of the young nobility who came along with him in hopes of turning their campaigns with him into a means for their own pleasure or profit, he called them together, and advised them to march off, and not run the hazard of a battle against their inclinations, since they had such weak and unmanly feelings; telling them that he would take only the tenth legion, and march against the barbarians, whom he did not expect to find an enemy more formidable than the Cimbri, nor, he added, should they find him a general inferior to Marius. Upon this, the tenth legion deputed some of their body to pay him their acknowledgments and thanks, and the other legions blamed their officers, and all, with great vigor and zeal, followed him many days' journey till they encamped within two hundred furlongs of the enemy. Ariovistus's courage to some extent was cooled upon their very approach; for never expecting the Romans would attack the Germans, whom he had thought it more likely they would not venture to withstand even in defence of their own subjects, he was the more surprised at Cæsar's conduct, and saw his army to be in consternation. They were still more discouraged by the prophecies of their holy women, who foretell the future by observing the eddies of rivers, and taking signs from the windings and noise of streams, and who now warned them not to engage before the next new moon appeared. Cæsar having had intimation of this, and seeing the Germans lie still, thought it expedient to attack them whilst they were under these apprehensions, rather than sit still and wait their time. Accordingly he made his approaches to the strongholds and hills on which they lay encamped, and so galled and fretted them, that at last they came down with great fury to engage. But he gained a signal victory, and pursued them for four hundred furlongs, as far as the Rhine; all which space was covered with spoils and bodies of the slain. Ariovistus made shift to pass the Rhine with the small remains of an army, for it is said the number of the slain amounted to eighty thousand.

After this action, Cæsar left his army at their winter-quarters in the country of the Sequani, and in order to attend to affairs at Rome, went into that part of Gaul which lies on the Po, and was part of his province; for the river Rubicon divides Gaul, which is on this side the Alps, from the rest of Italy. There he sat down and employed himself in courting people's favor; great numbers coming to him continually, and always finding their requests answered; for he never failed to dismiss all with present pledges of his kindness in hand, and further hopes for the future. And during all this time of the war in Gaul, Pompey never observed how Cæsar was on the one hand using the arms of Rome to effect his conquests, and on the other was gaining over and securing to himself the favor of the Romans, with the wealth which those conquests obtained him. But when he heard that the Belgæ, who were the most powerful of all the Gauls, and inhabited a third part of the country, were revolted, and had got together a great many thousand men in arms, he immediately set out and took his way thither with great expedition, and falling upon the enemy as they were ravaging the Gauls, his allies, he soon defeated and put to flight the largest and least scattered division of them. For though their numbers were great, yet they made but a slender defence, and the marshes and deep rivers were made passable to the Roman foot by the vast quantity of dead bodies. Of those who revolted, all the tribes that lived near the ocean came over without fighting, and he, therefore, led his army against the Nervii, the fiercest and most warlike people of all in those parts. These live in a country covered with continuous woods, and having lodged their children and property out of the way in the depth of the forest, fell upon Cæsar with a body of sixty thousand men, before he was prepared for them, while he was making his encampment. They soon routed his cavalry, and having surrounded the twelfth and seventh legions, killed all the officers, and had not Cæsar himself snatched up a buckler, and forced his way through his own men to come up to the barbarians, or had not the tenth legion, when they saw him in danger, run in from the tops of the hills, where they lay, and broken through the enemy's ranks to rescue him, in all probability not a Roman would have been saved. But now, under the influence of Cæsar's bold example, they fought a battle, as the phrase is, of more than human courage, and yet with their utmost efforts they were not able to drive the enemy out of the field, but cut them down fighting in their defence. For out of sixty thousand men, it is stated that not above five hundred survived the battle, and of four hundred of their senators not above three.

When the Roman senate had received news of this, they voted sacrifices and festivals to the gods, to be strictly observed for the space of fifteen days, a longer space than ever was observed for any victory before. The danger to which they had been exposed by the joint outbreak of such a number of nations was felt to have been great; and the people's fondness for Cæsar gave additional lustre to successes achieved by him. He now, after settling everything in Gaul, came back again, and spent the winter by the Po, in order to carry on the designs he had in hand at Rome. All who were candidates for offices used his assistance, and were supplied with money from him to corrupt the people and buy their votes, in return of which, when they were chosen, they did all things to advance his power. But what was more considerable, the most eminent and powerful men in Rome in great numbers came to visit him at Lucca, Pompey, and Crassus, and Appius, the governor of Sardinia, and Nepos, the proconsul of Spain, so that there were in the place at one time one hundred and twenty lictors, and more than two hundred senators. In deliberation here held, it was determined that Pompey and Crassus should be consuls again for the following year; that Cæsar should have a fresh supply of money, and that his command should be renewed to him for five years more. It seemed very extravagant to all thinking men, that those very persons who had received so much money from Cæsar should persuade the senate to grant him more, as if he were in want. Though in truth it was not so much upon persuasion as compulsion, that, with sorrow and groans for their own acts, they passed the measure. Cato was not present, for they had sent him seasonably out of the way into Cyprus; but Favonius, who was a zealous imitator of Cato, when he found he could do no good by opposing it, broke out of the house, and loudly declaimed against these proceedings to the people, but none gave him any hearing; some slighting him out of respect to Crassus and Pompey, and the greater part to gratify Cæsar, on whom depended their hopes.

After this, Cæsar returned again to his forces in Gaul, where he found that country involved in a dangerous war, two strong nations of the Germans having lately passed the Rhine, to conquer it; one of them called the Usipes, the other the Tenteritæ.[2] Of the war with this people, Cæsar himself has given this account in his commentaries, that the barbarians, having sent ambassadors to treat with him, did, during the treaty, set upon him in his march, by which means with eight hundred men they routed five thousand of his horse, who did not suspect their coming; that afterwards they sent other ambassadors to renew the same fraudulent practices, whom he kept in custody, and led on his army against the barbarians, as judging it mere simplicity to keep faith with those who had so faithlessly broken the terms they had agreed to. But Tanusius states, that when the senate decreed festivals and sacrifices for this victory, Cato declared it to be his opinion that Cæsar ought to be given into the hands of the barbarians, that so the guilt which this breach of faith might otherwise bring upon the state, might be expiated by transferring the curse on him, who was the occasion of it. Of those who passed the Rhine, there were four hundred thousand cut off; those few who escaped were sheltered by the Sugambri, a people of Germany. Cæsar took hold of this pretence to invade the Germans, being at the same time ambitious of the honor of being the first man that should pass the Rhine with an army. He carried a bridge across it, though it was very wide, and the current at that particular point very full, strong, and violent, bringing down with its waters trunks of trees, and other lumber, which much shook and weakened the foundations of his bridge. But he drove great piles of wood into the bottom of the river above the passage, to catch and stop these as they floated down, and thus fixing his bridle upon the stream, successfully finished his bridge, which no one who saw could believe to be the work but of ten days.

In the passage of his army over it, he met with no opposition; the Suevi themselves, who are the most warlike people of all Ger-

[2] The Usipetes and Tencteri of Cæsar's own narrative. The Sugambri below are the same as the Sigambri or Sicambri in the neighborhood of the river Sieg. Tanusius was an historical writer, and is quoted by Suetonius. The bridge was probably a little below Coblenz.

many, flying with their effects into the deepest and most densely wooded valleys. When he had burnt all the enemy's country, and encouraged those who embraced the Roman interest, he went back into Gaul, after eighteen days' stay in Germany. But his expedition into Britain was the most famous testimony of his courage. For he was the first who brought a navy into the western ocean, or who sailed into the Atlantic with an army to make war; and by invading an island, the reported extent of which had made its existence a matter of controversy among historians, many of whom questioned whether it were not a mere name and fiction, not a real place, he might be said to have carried the Roman empire beyond the limits of the known world. He passed thither twice from that part of Gaul which lies over against it, and in several battles which he fought, did more hurt to the enemy than service to himself, for the islanders were so miserably poor, that they had nothing worth being plundered of. When he found himself unable to put such an end to the war as he wished, he was content to take hostages from the king, and to impose a tribute, and then quitted the island. At his arrival in Gaul, he found letters which lay ready to be conveyed over the water to him from his friends at Rome, announcing his daughter's death, who died in labor of a child by Pompey. Cæsar and Pompey both were much afflicted with her death, nor were their friends less disturbed, believing that the alliance was now broken, which had hitherto kept the sickly commonwealth in peace, for the child also died within a few days after the mother. The people took the body of Julia, in spite of the opposition of the tribunes, and carried it into the field of Mars, and there her funeral rites were performed, and her remains are laid.

Cæsar's army was now grown very numerous, so that he was forced to disperse them into various camps for their winter-quarters, and he having gone himself to Italy, as he used to do, in his absence a general outbreak throughout the whole of Gaul commenced, and large armies marched about the country, and attacked the Roman quarters, and attempted to make themselves masters of the forts where they lay. The greatest and strongest party of the rebels, under the command of Abriorix, cut off Cotta and Titurius with all their men, while a force of sixty thousand strong besieged the legion under the command of Cicero,[3] and had almost taken it by storm, the Roman soldiers being all wounded, and having quite spent themselves by a defence beyond their natural strength. But Cæsar, who was at a great distance, having received the news, quickly got together seven thousand men, and hastened to relieve Cicero. The besiegers were aware of it, and went to meet him, with great confidence that they should easily overpower such an handful of men. Cæsar, to increase their presumption, seemed to avoid fighting, and still marched off, till he found a place conveniently situated for a few to engage against many, where he encamped. He kept his soldiers from making any attack upon the enemy, and commanded them to raise the ramparts higher, and barricade the gates, that by show of fear, they might heighten the enemy's contempt of them. Till at last they came without any order in great security to make an assault, when he issued forth, and put them to flight with the loss of many men.

This quieted the greater part of the commotions in these parts of Gaul and Cæsar, in the course of the winter, visited every part of the country, and with great vigilance took precautions against all innovations. For there were three legions now come to him to supply the place of the men he had lost, of which Pompey furnished him with two, out of those under his command; the other was newly raised in the part of Gaul by the Po. But in a while the seeds of war, which had long since been secretly sown and scattered by the most powerful men in those warlike nations, broke forth into the greatest and most dangerous war that ever was in those parts, both as regards the number of men in the vigor of their youth who were gathered and armed from all quarters, the vast funds of money collected to maintain it, the strength of the towns, and the difficulty of the country where it was carried on. It being winter, the rivers were frozen, the woods covered with snow, and the level country flooded, so that in some places the ways were lost through the depth of the snow; in others, the overflowing of marshes and streams made every kind of passage uncertain. All which difficulties made it seem impracticable for Cæsar to make any attempt upon the insurgents. Many tribes had revolted together, the chief of them being the Ar-

[3] Quintus Cicero, the orator's brother. Abriorix is Ambiorix of the Commentaries.

verni and Carnutini;[4] the general who had the supreme command in war was Vergentorix, whose father the Gauls had put to death on suspicion of his aiming at absolute government.

He having disposed his army in several bodies, and set officers over them, drew over to him all the country round about as far as those that lie upon the Arar, and having intelligence of the opposition which Cæsar now experienced at Rome, thought to engage all Gaul in the war. Which if he had done a little later, when Cæsar was taken up with the civil wars, Italy had been put into as great a terror as before it was by the Cimbri. But Cæsar, who above all men was gifted with the faculty of making the right use of every thing in war, and most especially of seizing the right moment, as soon as he heard of the revolt, returned immediately the same way he went, and showed the barbarians, by the quickness of his march in such a severe season, that an army was advancing against them which was invincible. For in the time that one would have thought it scarce credible that a courier or express should have come with a message from him, he himself appeared with all his army, ravaging the country, reducing their posts, subduing their towns, receiving into his protection those who declared for him. Till at last the Edui, who hitherto had styled themselves brethren to the Romans, and had been much honored by them, declared against him, and joined the rebels, to the great discouragement of his army. Accordingly he removed thence, and passed the country of the Lingones, desiring to reach the territories of the Sequani, who were his friends, and who lay like a bulwark in front of Italy against the other tribes of Gaul. There the enemy came upon him, and surrounded him with many myriads, whom he also was eager to engage; and at last, after some time and with much slaughter, gained on the whole a complete victory; though at first he appears to have met with some reverse, and the Aruveni show you a small sword hanging up in a temple, which they say was taken from Cæsar. Cæsar saw this afterwards himself, and smiled, and when his friends

[4] The Arverni, the same people whom he presently calls the Aruveni, of the mountains of Auvergne, and the Carnutes of the country around Orleans. Vergentorix appears to be a Greek abbreviation of Vercingetorix, the full name given by Cæsar, which is itself conceived to have been not a proper name, but a title.

advised it should be taken down, would not permit it, because he looked upon it as consecrated.

After the defeat, a great part of those who had escaped, fled with their king into a town called Alesia, which Cæsar besieged, though the height of the walls, and number of those who defended them, made it appear impregnable; and meantime, from without the walls, he was assailed by a greater danger than can be expressed. For the choice men of Gaul, picked out of each nation, and well armed, came to relieve Alesia, to the number of three hundred thousand; nor were there in the town less than one hundred and seventy thousand. So that Cæsar being shut betwixt two such forces, was compelled to protect himself by two walls, one towards the town, the other against the relieving army, as knowing if these forces should join, his affairs would be entirely ruined. The danger that he underwent before Alesia,[5] justly gained him great honor on many accounts, and gave him an opportunity of showing greater instances of his valor and conduct than any other contest had done. One wonders much how he should be able to engage and defeat so many thousands of men without the town, and not be perceived by those within, but yet more, that the Romans themselves, who guarded their wall which was next the town, should be strangers to it. For even they knew nothing of the victory, till they heard the cries of the men and lamentations of the women who were in the town, and had from thence seen the Romans at a distance carrying into their camp a great quantity of bucklers, adorned with gold and silver, many breastplates stained with blood, besides cups and tents made in the Gallic fashion. So soon did so vast an army dissolve and vanish like a ghost or dream, the greatest part of them being killed upon the spot. Those who were in Alesia, having given themselves and Cæsar much trouble, surrendered at last; and Vergentorix, who was the chief spring of all the war, putting his best armor on, and adorning his horse, rode out of the gates, and made

[5] Alesia is identified with Alise, or with the summit of Mount Auxois, near Flavigny, not far from Dijon. The course of Roman occupation, interposing between Central Gaul and the German competitors for its possession, seems to follow the line of the Rhone and Saone upwards, and the Meuse and Moselle downwards, from Marseilles and Lyons to Treves and the Rhine. Alesia is near the head waters of the Saone.

a turn about Cæsar as he was sitting, then quitted his horse, threw off his armor, and remained seated quietly at Cæsar's feet until he was led away to be reserved for the triumph.

Cæsar had long ago resolved upon the overthrow of Pompey, as had Pompey, for that matter, upon his. For Crassus, the fear of whom had hitherto kept them in peace, having now been killed in Parthia, if the one of them wished to make himself the greatest man in Rome, he had only to overthrow the other; and if he again wished to prevent his own fall, he had nothing for it but to be beforehand with him whom he feared. Pompey had not been long under any such apprehensions, having till lately despised Cæsar, as thinking it no difficult matter to put down him whom he himself had advanced. But Cæsar had entertained this design from the beginning against his rivals, and had retired, like an expert wrestler, to prepare himself apart for the combat. Making the Gallic wars his exercise-ground, he had at once improved the strength of his soldiery, and had heightened his own glory by his great actions, so that he was looked on as one who might challenge comparison with Pompey. Nor did he let go any of those advantages which were now given him both by Pompey himself and the times, and the ill government of Rome, where all who were candidates for offices publicly gave money, and without any shame bribed the people, who having received their pay, did not contend for their benefactors with their bare suffrages, but with bows, swords, and slings. So that after having many times stained the place of election with the blood of men killed upon the spot, they left the city at last without a government at all, to be carried about like a ship without a pilot to steer her; while all who had any wisdom could only be thankful if a course of such wild and stormy disorder and madness might end no worse than in a monarchy. Some were so bold as to declare openly, that the government was incurable but by a monarchy, and that they ought to take that remedy from the hands of the gentlest physician, meaning Pompey, who, though in words he pretended to decline it, yet in reality made his utmost efforts to be declared dictator. Cato perceiving his design, prevailed with the senate to make him sole consul, that with the offer of a more legal sort of monarchy he might be withheld from demanding the dictatorship. They over and above voted him the continuance of his provinces, for he had two, Spain and all Africa, which he governed by his lieutenants, and maintained armies under him, at the yearly charge of a thousand talents out of the public treasury.

Upon this Cæsar also sent and petitioned for the consulship, and the continuance of his provinces. Pompey at first did not stir in it, but Marcellus and Lentulus opposed it, who had always hated Cæsar, and now did every thing, whether fit or unfit, which might disgrace and affront him. For they took away the privilege of Roman citizens from the people of New Comum, who were a colony that Cæsar had lately planted in Gaul; and Marcellus, who was then consul, ordered one of the senators of that town, then at Rome, to be whipped, and told him he laid that mark upon him to signify he was no citizen of Rome, bidding him, when he went back again, to show it to Cæsar. After Marcellus's consulship, Cæsar began to lavish gifts upon all the public men out of the riches he had taken from the Gauls; discharged Curio, the tribune, from his great debts; gave Paulus, then consul, fifteen hundred talents, with which he built the noble court of justice[6] adjoining the forum, to supply the place of that called the Fulvian. Pompey, alarmed at these preparations, now openly took steps, both by himself and his friends, to have a successor appointed in Cæsar's room, and sent to demand back the soldiers whom he had lent him to carry on the wars in Gaul. Cæsar returned them, and made each soldier a present of two hundred and fifty drachmas. The officer who brought them home to Pompey, spread amongst the people no very fair or favorable report of Cæsar, and flattered Pompey himself with false suggestions that he was wished for by Cæsar's army; and though his affairs here were in some embarrassment through the envy of some, and the ill state of the government, yet there the army was at his command, and if they once crossed into Italy, would presently declare for him; so weary were they of Cæsar's endless expeditions, and so suspicious of his designs for a monarchy. Upon this Pompey grew presumptuous, and neglected all warlike preparations, as fearing no danger, and used no other means against him than mere speeches and votes, for which Cæsar cared nothing. And one of

[6] Or basilica.

his captains, it is said, who was sent by him to Rome, standing before the senate-house one day, and being told that the senate would not give Cæsar a longer time in his government, clapped his hand on the hilt of his sword, and said, "But this shall."

Yet the demands which Cæsar made had the fairest colors of equity imaginable. For he proposed to lay down his arms, and that Pompey should do the same, and both together should become private men, and each expect a reward of his services from the public. For that those who proposed to disarm him, and at the same time to confirm Pompey in all the power he held, were simply establishing the one in the tyranny which they accused the other of aiming at. When Curio made these proposals to the people in Cæsar's name, he was loudly applauded, and some threw garlands towards him, and dismissed him as they do successful wrestlers, crowned with flowers. Antony, being tribune, produced a letter sent from Cæsar on this occasion, and read it, though the consuls did what they could to oppose it. But Scipio, Pompey's father-in-law, proposed in the senate, that if Cæsar did not lay down his arms within such a time, he should be voted an enemy; and the consuls putting it to the question, whether Pompey should dismiss his soldiers, and again, whether Cæsar should disband his, very few assented to the first, but almost all to the latter. But Antony proposing again, that both should lay down their commissions, all but a very few agreed to it. Scipio was upon this very violent, and Lentulus the consul cried aloud, that they had need of arms, and not of suffrages, against a robber; so that the senators for the present adjourned, and appeared in mourning as a mark of their grief for the dissension.

Afterwards there came other letters from Cæsar, which seemed yet more moderate, for he proposed to quit every thing else, and only to retain Gaul within the Alps, Illyricum, and two legions, till he should stand a second time for consul. Cicero, the orator, who was lately returned from Cilicia, endeavored to reconcile differences, and softened Pompey, who was willing to comply in other things, but not to allow him the soldiers. At last Cicero used his persuasions with Cæsar's friends to accept of the provinces, and six thousand soldiers only, and so to make up the quarrel. And Pompey was inclined to give way to this, but Lentulus, the consul, would not hearken to it, but drove Antony and Curio out of the senate-house with insults, by which he afforded Cæsar the most plausible pretence that could be, and one which he could readily use to inflame the soldiers, by showing them two persons of such repute and authority, who were forced to escape in a hired carriage in the dress of slaves. For so they were glad to disguise themselves, when they fled out of Rome.

There were not about him at that time above three hundred horse, and five thousand foot; for the rest of his army, which was left behind the Alps, was to be brought after him by officers who had received orders for that purpose. But he thought the first motion towards the design which he had on foot did not require large forces at present, and that what was wanted was to make this first step suddenly, and so as to astound his enemies with the boldness of it; as it would be easier, he thought, to throw them into consternation by doing what they never anticipated, than fairly to conquer them, if he had alarmed them by his preparations. And therefore, he commanded his captains and other officers to go only with their swords in their hands, without any other arms, and make themselves masters of Ariminum, a large city of Gaul, with as little disturbance and bloodshed as possible. He committed the care of these forces to Hortensius, and himself spent the day in public as a stander-by and spectator of the gladiators, who exercised before him. A little before night he attended to his person, and then went into the hall, and conversed for some time with those he had invited to supper, till it began to grow dusk, when he rose from table, and made his excuses to the company, begging them to stay till he came back, having already given private directions to a few immediate friends, that they should follow him, not all the same way, but some one way, some another. He himself got into one of the hired carriages, and drove at first another way, but presently turned towards Ariminum. When he came to the river Rubicon, which parts Gaul within the Alps from the rest of Italy, his thoughts began to work, now he was just entering upon the danger, and he wavered much in his mind, when he considered the greatness of the enterprise into which he was throwing himself. He checked his course, and ordered a halt, while he revolved with himself, and often changed his opinion one way and the other, without speaking a word. This was when his purposes fluctuated most; presently he also discussed the matter with his friends who were about him, (of which number Asinius Pollio was one), computing how many calamities his passing that river would bring upon mankind, and what a relation of it would be transmitted to posterity. At last, in a sort of passion, casting aside calculation, and abandoning himself to what might come, and using the proverb frequently in their mouths who enter upon dangerous and bold attempts, "The die is cast," with these words he took the river. Once over, he used all expedition possible, and before it was day reached Ariminum, and took it. It is said that the night before he passed the river, he had an impious dream, that he was unnaturally familiar with his own mother.

As soon as Ariminum was taken, wide gates, so to say, were thrown open, to let in war upon every land alike and sea, and with the limits of the province, the boundaries of the laws were transgressed. Nor would one have thought that, as at other times, the mere men and women fled from one town of Italy to another in their consternation, but that the very towns themselves left their sites, and fled for succor to each other. The city of Rome was overrun as it were with a deluge, by the conflux of people flying in from all the neighboring places. Magistrates could no longer govern, nor the eloquence of any orator quiet it; it was all but suffering shipwreck by the violence of its own tempestuous agitation. The most vehement contrary passions and impulses were at work every where. Nor did those who rejoiced at the prospect of the change altogether conceal their feelings, but when they met, as in so great a city they frequently must, with the alarmed and dejected of the other party, they provoked quarrels by their bold expressions of confidence in the event. Pompey, sufficiently disturbed of himself, was yet more perplexed by the clamors of others; some telling him that he justly suffered for having armed Cæsar against himself and the government; others blaming him for permitting Cæsar to be insolently used by Lentulus, when he made such ample concessions, and offered such reasonable proposals towards an accommodation. Favonius bade him now stamp upon the ground; for once talking big in the senate, he desired them not to trouble themselves about making any preparations for the war, for that he himself, with one stamp of his foot, would fill all Italy with soldiers. Yet still Pompey at that time had more forces than Cæsar; but he was not permitted to pursue his own thoughts, but being continually disturbed with false reports and alarms, as if the enemy was close upon him and carrying all before him, he gave way, and let himself be borne down by the general cry. He put forth an edict declaring the city to be in a state of anarchy, and left it with orders that the senate should follow him, and that no one should stay behind who did not prefer tyranny to their country and liberty.

The consuls at once fled, without making even the usual sacrifices; so did most of the senators, carrying off their own goods in as much haste as if they had been robbing their neighbors. Some, who had formerly much favored Cæsar's cause, in the prevailing alarm, quitted their own sentiments, and without any prospect of good to themselves, were carried along by the common stream. It was a melancholy thing to see the city tossed in these tumults, like a ship given up by her pilots, and left to run, as chance guides her, upon any rock in her way. Yet, in spite of their sad condition, people still esteemed the place of their exile to be their country for Pompey's sake, and fled from Rome, as if it had been Cæsar's camp. Labienus even, who had been one of Cæsar's nearest friends, and his lieutenant, and who had fought by him zealously in the Gallic wars, now deserted him, and went over to Pompey. Cæsar sent all his money and equipage after him, and then sat down before Corfinium, which was garrisoned with thirty cohorts under the command of Domitius. He, in despair of maintaining the defence, requested a physician, whom he had among his attendants, to give him poison; and taking the dose, drank it, in hopes of being dispatched by it. But soon after, when he was told that Cæsar showed the utmost clemency towards those he took prisoners, he lamented his misfortune, and blamed the hastiness of his resolution. His physician consoled him, by informing him that he had taken a sleeping draught, not a poison; upon which, much rejoiced, and rising from his bed, he went presently to Cæsar, and gave him the pledge of his hand, yet afterwards again went over to Pompey. The report of these actions at Rome, quieted those who were there, and some who had fled thence returned. Cæsar took into his army Domitius's soldiers, as he did all those whom he found in any town enlisted for Pompey's service. Being now strong and formidable enough, he advanced against Pompey himself, who did not stay to receive him, but fled to Brundisium, having sent the consuls before with a body of troops to Dyrrhachium. Soon after, upon Cæsar's approach, he set to sea, as shall be more particularly related in his Life. Cæsar would have immediately pursued him, but wanted shipping, and therefore went back to Rome, having made himself master of all Italy without bloodshed in the space of sixty days. When he came thither, he found the city more quiet than he expected, and many senators present, to whom he addressed himself with courtesy and deference, desiring them to send to Pompey about any reasonable accommodations towards a peace. But nobody complied with this proposal; whether out of fear of Pompey, whom they had deserted, or that they thought Cæsar did not mean what he said, but thought it his interest to talk plausibly. Afterwards, when Metellus, the tribune, would have hindered him from taking money out of the public treasure, and adduced some laws against it, Cæsar replied, that arms and laws had each their own time; "If what I do displeases you, leave the place; war allows no free talking. When I have laid down my arms, and made peace, come back and make what speeches you please. And this," he added, "I will tell you in diminution of my own just right, as indeed you and all others who have appeared against me and are now in my power, may be treated as I please." Having said this to Metellus, he went to the doors of the treasury, and the keys being not to be found, sent for smiths to force them open. Metellus again making resistance, and some encouraging him in it, Cæsar, in a louder tone, told him he would put him to death, if he gave him any further disturbance. "And this," said he, "you know, young man, is more disagreeable for me to say, than to do." These words made Metellus withdraw for fear, and obtained speedy execution henceforth for all orders that Cæsar gave for procuring necessaries for the war.

He was now proceeding to Spain, with the determination of first crushing Afranius and Varro, Pompey's lieutenants, and making himself master of the armies and provinces under them, that he might then more securely advance against Pompey, when he had no enemy left behind him. In this expedition his person was often in danger from ambuscades, and his army by want of provisions, yet he did not desist from pursuing the enemy, provoking them to fight, and hemming them with his fortifications, till by main force he made himself master of their camps and their forces. Only the generals got off, and fled to Pompey.

When Cæsar came back to Rome, Piso, his father-in-law, advised him to send men to Pompey, to treat of a peace; but Isauricus, to ingratiate himself with Cæsar, spoke against it. After this, being created dictator by the senate, he called home the exiles, and gave back their rights as citizens to the children of those who had suffered under Sylla; he relieved the debtors by an act remitting some part of the interest on their debts, and passed some other measures of the same sort, but not many. For within eleven days he resigned his dictatorship, and having declared himself consul, with Servilius Isauricus, hastened again to the war. He marched so fast, that he left all his army behind him, except six hundred chosen horse, and five legions, with which he put to sea in the very middle of winter, about the beginning of the month January, (which corresponds pretty nearly with the Athenian month Posideon), and having past the Ionian Sea, took Oricum and Apollonia, and then sent back the ships to Brundisium, to bring over the soldiers who were left behind in the march. They, while yet on the march, their bodies now no longer in the full vigor of youth, and they themselves weary with such a multitude of wars, could not but exclaim against Cæsar, "When at last, and where, will this Cæsar let us be quiet? He carries us from place to place, and uses us as if we were not to be worn out, and had no sense of labor. Even our iron itself is spent by blows, and we ought to have some pity on our bucklers and breastplates, which have been used so long. Our wounds, if nothing else, should make him see that we are mortal men, whom he commands, subject to the same pains and sufferings as other human beings. The very gods themselves cannot force the winter season, or hinder the storms in their time; yet he pushes forward, as if he were not pursuing, but flying from an enemy." So they talked as they marched leisurely towards Brundisium. But when they came thither, and found Cæsar gone off before them, their feelings changed, and they blamed themselves as traitors to their general. They now railed at their officers for marching so slowly, and placing themselves on the heights overlooking the sea towards Epirus, they kept watch to see if they could espy the vessels which were to transport them to Cæsar.

He in the mean time was posted in Apollonia, but had not an army with him able to fight the enemy, the forces from Brundisium being so long in coming, which put him to great suspense and embarrassment what to do. At last he resolved upon a most hazardous experiment, and embarked, without any one's knowledge, in a boat of twelve oars, to cross over to Brundisium, though the sea was at that time covered with a vast fleet of the enemies. He got on board in the night time, in the dress of a slave, and throwing himself down like a person of no consequence, lay along at the bottom of the vessel. The river Anius[7] was to carry them down to sea, and there used to blow a gentle gale every morning from the land, which made it calm at the mouth of the river, by driving the waves forward; but this night there had blown a strong wind from the sea, which overpowered that from the land, so that where the river met the influx of the sea-water and the opposition of the waves, it was extremely rough and angry; and the current was beaten back with such a violent swell, that the master of the boat could not make good his passage, but ordered his sailors to tack about and return. Cæsar, upon this, discovers himself, and taking the man by the hand, who was surprised to see him there, said, "Go on, my friend, and fear nothing; you carry Cæsar and his fortune in your boat." The mariners, when they heard that, forgot the storm, and laying all their strength to their oars, did what they could to force their way down the river. But when it was to no purpose, and the vessel now took in much water, Cæsar finding himself in such danger in the very mouth of the river, much against his will permitted the master to turn back. When he was come to land, his soldiers ran to him in a multitude, reproaching him for what he had done, and indignant that he should think himself not strong

[7] The Aöus or Æas.

enough to get a victory by their sole assistance, but must disturb himself, and expose his life for those who were absent, as if he could not trust those who were with him.

After this, Antony came over with the forces from Brundisium, which encouraged Cæsar to give Pompey battle, though he was encamped very advantageously, and furnished with plenty of provisions both by sea and land, whilst he himself was at the beginning but ill-supplied, and before the end was extremely pinched for want of necessaries, so that his soldiers were forced to dig up a kind of root which grew there, and tempering it with milk, to feed on it. Sometimes they made a kind of bread of it, and advancing up to the enemy's outposts, would throw in these loaves, telling them, that as long as the earth produced such roots they would not give up blockading Pompey. But Pompey took what care he could, that neither the loaves nor the words should reach his men, who were out of heart and despondent, through terror at the fierceness and hardiness of their enemies, whom they looked upon as a sort of wild beasts. There were continual skirmishes about Pompey's outworks, in all which Cæsar had the better, except one, when his men were forced to fly in such a manner that he had like to have lost his camp. For Pompey made such a vigorous sally on them that not a man stood his ground; the trenches were filled with the slaughter, many fell upon their own ramparts and bulwarks, whither they were driven in flight by the enemy. Cæsar met them, and would have turned them back, but could not. When he went to lay hold of the ensigns, those who carried them threw them down, so that the enemies took thirty-two of them. He himself narrowly escaped; for taking hold of one of his soldiers, a big and strong man, that was flying by him, he bade him stand and face about; but the fellow, full of apprehensions from the danger he was in, laid hold of his sword, as if he would strike Cæsar, but Cæsar's armor-bearer cut off his arm. Cæsar's affairs were so desperate at that time, that when Pompey, either through over-cautiousness, or his ill fortune, did not give the finishing stroke to that great success, but retreated after he had driven the routed enemy within their camp, Cæsar, upon seeing his withdrawal, said to his friends, "The victory to-day had been on the enemies' side, if they had had a general who knew how to gain it." When he was retired into his tent, he laid himself down to sleep, but spent that night as miserably as ever he did any, in perplexity and consideration with himself, coming to the conclusion that he had conducted the war amiss. For when he had a fertile country before him, and all the wealthy cities of Macedonia and Thessaly, he had neglected to carry the war thither, and had sat down by the seaside, where his enemies had such a powerful fleet, so that he was in fact rather besieged by the want of necessaries, than besieging others with his arms. Being thus distracted in his thoughts with the view of the difficulty and distress he was in, he raised his camp, with the intention of advancing towards Scipio, who lay in Macedonia; hoping either to entice Pompey into a country where he should fight without the advantage he now had of supplies from the sea, or to overpower Scipio, if not assisted.

This set all Pompey's army and officers on fire to hasten and pursue Cæsar, whom they concluded to be beaten and flying. But Pompey was afraid to hazard a battle on which so much depended, and being himself provided with all necessaries for any length of time, thought to tire out and waste the vigor of Cæsar's army, which could not last long. For the best part of his men, though they had great experience, and showed an irresistible courage in all engagements, yet by their frequent marches, changing their camps,[8] attacking fortifications, and keeping long night-watches, were getting worn-out and broken; they being now old, their bodies less fit for labor, and their courage, also, beginning to give way with the failure of their strength. Besides, it was said that an infectious disease, occasioned by their irregular diet, was prevailing in Cæsar's army, and what was of greatest moment, he was neither furnished with money nor provisions, so that in a little time he must needs fall of himself.

For these reasons Pompey had no mind to fight him, but was thanked for it by none but Cato, who rejoiced at the prospect of sparing his fellow-citizens. For he when he saw the dead bodies of those who had fallen in the last battle on Cæsar's side, to the num-

[8] Or, perhaps more probably, "raising fortifications," which had been very much their occupation latterly. Up to this point the campaign had been a war of intrenchments.

ber of a thousand, turned away, covered his face, and shed tears. But every one else upbraided Pompey for being reluctant to fight, and tried to goad him on by such nicknames as Agamemnon, and king of kings, as if he were in no hurry to lay down his sovereign authority, but was pleased to see so many commanders attending on him, and paying their attendance at his tent. Favonius, who affected Cato's free way of speaking his mind, complained bitterly that they should eat no figs even this year at Tusculum, because of Pompey's love of command. Afranius, who was lately returned out of Spain, and on account of his ill success there, labored under the suspicion of having been bribed to betray the army, asked why they did not fight this purchaser of provinces. Pompey was driven, against his own will, by this kind of language, into offering battle, and proceeded to follow Cæsar. Cæsar had found great difficulties in his march, for no country would supply him with provisions, his reputation being very much fallen since his late defeat. But after he took Gomphi, a town of Thessaly, he not only found provisions for his army, but physic too. For there they met with plenty of wine, which they took very freely, and heated with this, sporting and revelling on their march in bacchanalian fashion, they shook off the disease, and their whole constitution was relieved and changed into another habit.

When the two armies were come into Pharsalia,[9] and both encamped there, Pompey's thoughts ran the same way as they had done before, against fighting, and the more because of some unlucky presages, and a vision he had in a dream.[10] But those who were about him were so confident of success, that Domitius, and Spinther, and Scipio, as if they had already conquered, quarrelled which should succeed Cæsar in the pontificate. And many sent to Rome to take houses fit to accommodate consuls and prætors, as being sure of entering upon those offices, as soon as the battle was over. The cavalry especially were obstinate for fighting, being splen-

[9] "Into Pharsalia," is properly "into the territory of the town of Pharsalus," and in other passages where the battle is mentioned in the translation by the name, as the Romans use it, of *Pharsalia*, the Greek is *Pharsalus*.

[10] Here follows the words, "He fancied he saw himself in the theatre, receiving the plaudits of the people." Either the text is incomplete, and the remainder of the description has been lost, or else it is the imperfect explanation added in the margin by an annotator. The full account is given in the Life of Pompey.

didly armed and bravely mounted, and valuing themselves upon the fine horses they kept, and upon their own handsome persons; as also upon the advantage of their numbers, for they were five thousand against one thousand of Cæsar's. Nor were the numbers of the infantry less disproportionate, there being forty-five thousand of Pompey's, against twenty-two thousand of the enemy.

Cæsar, collecting his soldiers together, told them that Corfinius[11] was coming up to them with two legions, and that fifteen cohorts more under Calenus were posted at Megara and Athens; he then asked them whether they would stay till these joined them, or would hazard the battle by themselves. They all cried out to him not to wait, but on the contrary to do whatever he could to bring about an engagement as soon as possible. When he sacrificed to the gods for the lustration of his army, upon the death of the first victim, the augur told him, within three days he should come to a decisive action. Cæsar asked him whether he saw any thing in the entrails, which promised an happy event. "That," said the priest, "you can best answer yourself; for the gods signify a great alteration from the present posture of affairs. If, therefore, you think yourself well off now, expect worse fortune; if unhappy, hope for better." The night before the battle, as he walked the rounds about midnight, there was a light seen in the heaven, very bright and flaming, which seemed to pass over Cæsar's camp, and fall into Pompey's. And when Cæsar's soldiers came to relieve the watch in the morning, they perceived a panic disorder among the enemies. However, he did not expect to fight that day, but set about raising his camp with the intention of marching towards Scotussa.

But when the tents were now taken down, his scouts rode up to him, and told him the enemy would give him battle. With this news he was extremely pleased, and having performed his devotions to the gods, set his army in battle array, dividing them into three bodies. Over the middlemost he placed Domitius Calvinus; Antony commanded the left wing, and he himself the right, being resolved to fight at the head of the tenth legion. But when he saw the enemy's cavalry taking position against him, being struck with their fine appearance and their number, he gave private orders that

[11] Cornificius.

six cohorts from the rear of the army should come round and join him, whom he posted behind the right wing, and instructed them what they should do, when the enemy's horse came to charge. On the other side, Pompey commanded the right wing, Domitius the left, and Scipio, Pompey's father-in-law, the centre. The whole weight of the cavalry was collected on the left wing, with the intent that they should outflank the right wing of the enemy, and rout that part where the general himself commanded. For they thought no phalanx of infantry could be solid enough to sustain such a shock, but that they must necessarily be broken and shattered all to pieces upon the onset of so immense a force of cavalry. When they were ready on both sides to give the signal for battle, Pompey commanded his foot who were in the front, to stand their ground, and without breaking their order, receive quietly the enemy's first attack, till they came within javelin's cast. Cæsar, in this respect, also, blames Pompey's generalship, as if he had not been aware how the first encounter, when made with an impetus and upon the run, gives weight and force to the strokes, and fires the men's spirits into a flame, which the general concurrence fans to full heat. He himself was just putting the troops into motion and advancing to the action, when he found one of his captains, a trusty and experienced soldier, encouraging his men to exert their utmost. Cæsar called him by his name, and said, "What hopes, Caius Crassinius, and what grounds for encouragement?" Crassinius stretched out his hand, and cried in a loud voice, "We shall conquer nobly, Cæsar; and I this day will deserve your praises, either alive or dead." So he said, and was the first man to run in upon the enemy, followed by the hundred and twenty soldiers about him, and breaking through the first rank, still pressed on forwards with much slaughter of the enemy, till at last he was struck back by the wound of a sword, which went in at his mouth with such force that it came out at his neck behind.

Whilst the foot was thus sharply engaged in the main battle, on the flank Pompey's horse rode up confidently, and opened their ranks very wide, that they might surround the right wing of Cæsar. But before they engaged, Cæsar's cohorts rushed out and attacked them, and did not dart their javelins at a distance, nor strike at the thighs and legs, as they usually did in close battle, but aimed at their faces. For thus Cæsar had instructed them, in hopes that young gentlemen, who had not known much of battles and wounds, but came wearing their hair long, in the flower of their age and height of their beauty, would be more apprehensive of such blows, and not care for hazarding both a danger at present and a blemish for the future. And so it proved, for they were so far from bearing the stroke of the javelins, that they could not stand the sight of them, but turned about, and covered their faces to secure them. Once in disorder, presently they turned about to fly; and so most shamefully ruined all. For those who had beat them back, at once outflanked the infantry, and falling on their rear, cut them to pieces. Pompey, who commanded the other wing of the army, when he saw his cavalry thus broken and flying, was no longer himself, nor did he now remember that he was Pompey the Great, but like one whom some god had deprived of his senses, retired to his tent without speaking a word, and there sat to expect the event, till the whole army was routed, and the enemy appeared upon the works which were thrown up before the camp, where they closely engaged with his men, who were posted there to defend it. Then first he seemed to have recovered his senses, and uttering, it is said, only these words, "What, into the camp too?" he laid aside his general's habit, and putting on such clothes as might best favor his flight, stole off. What fortune he met with afterwards, how he took shelter in Egypt, and was murdered there, we tell you in his Life.

Cæsar, when he came to view Pompey's camp, and saw some of his opponents dead upon the ground, others dying, said, with a groan, "This they would have; they brought me to this necessity. I, Caius Cæsar, after succeeding in so many wars, had been condemned, had I dismissed my army."[12] These words, Pollio says, Cæsar spoke in Latin at that time, and that he himself wrote them in Greek; adding, that those who were killed at the taking of the camp, were most of them servants; and that not above six thousand soldiers fell. Cæsar incorporated most of the foot whom he took prisoners, with his own legions, and gave a free pardon to many

[12] "Hoc voluerunt; tantis rebus gestis C. Cæsar condemnatus essem, nisi ab exercitu auxilium petissem," quoted from Asinius Pollio, by Suetonius.

of the distinguished persons, and amongst the rest, to Brutus, who afterwards killed him. He did not immediately appear after the battle was over, which put Cæsar, it is said, into great anxiety for him; nor was his pleasure less when he saw him present himself alive.

There were many prodigies that foreshowed this victory, but the most remarkable that we are told of, was that at Tralles. In the temple of Victory stood Cæsar's statue. The ground on which it stood was naturally hard and solid, and the stone with which it was paved still harder; yet it is said that a palm-tree shot itself up near the pedestal of this statue. In the city of Padua, one Caius Cornelius, who had the character of a good augur, the fellow-citizen and acquaintance of Livy, the historian, happened to be making some augural observations that very day when the battle was fought. And first, as Livy tells us, he pointed out the time of the fight, and said to those who were by him, that just then the battle was begun, and the men engaged. When he looked a second time, and observed the omens, he leaped up as if he had been inspired, and cried out, "Cæsar, you are victorious." This much surprised the standers by, but he took the garland which he had on from his head, and swore he would never wear it again till the event should give authority to his art. This Livy positively states for a truth.

Cæsar, as a memorial of his victory, gave the Thessalians their freedom, and then went in pursuit of Pompey. When he was come into Asia, to gratify Theopompus, the author of the collection of fables, he enfranchised the Cnidians, and remitted one third of their tribute to all the people of the province of Asia. When he came to Alexandria, where Pompey was already murdered, he would look upon Theodotus, who presented him with his head, but taking only his signet, shed tears. Those of Pompey's friends who had been arrested by the king of Egypt, as they were wandering in those parts, he relieved, and offered them his own friendship. In his letter to his friends at Rome, he told them that the greatest and most signal pleasure his victory had given him, was to be able continually to save the lives of fellow-citizens who had fought against him. As to the war in Egypt, some say it was at once dangerous and dishonorable, and noways necessary, but occasioned only by his passion for Cleopatra. Others blame the ministers of the king, and especially the eunuch Pothinus, who was the chief favorite, and had lately killed Pompey, who had banished Cleopatra, and was now secretly plotting Cæsar's destruction, (to prevent which, Cæsar from that time began to sit up whole nights, under pretence of drinking, for the security of his person), while openly he was intolerable in his affronts to Cæsar, both by his words and actions. For when Cæsar's soldiers had musty and unwholesome corn measured out to them, Pothinus told them they must be content with it, since they were fed at another's cost. He ordered that his table should be served with wooden and earthen dishes, and said Cæsar had carried off all the gold and silver plate, under pretence of arrears of debt. For the present king's father owed Cæsar one thousand seven hundred and fifty myriads of money; Cæsar had formerly remitted to his children the rest, but thought fit to demand the thousand myriads at that time, to maintain his army. Pothinus told him that he had better go now and attend to his other affairs of greater consequence, and that he should receive his money at another time with thanks. Cæsar replied that he did not want Egyptians to be his counsellors, and soon after privately sent for Cleopatra from her retirement.

She took a small boat, and one only of her confidents, Apollodorus, the Sicilian, along with her, and in the dusk of the evening landed near the palace. She was at a loss how to get in undiscovered, till she thought of putting herself into the coverlet of a bed and lying at length, whilst Apollodorus tied up the bedding and carried it on his back through the gates to Cæsar's apartment. Cæsar was first captivated by this proof of Cleopatra's bold wit, and was afterwards so overcome by the charm of her society, that he made a reconciliation between her and her brother, on condition that she should rule as his colleague in the kingdom. A festival was kept to celebrate this reconciliation, where Cæsar's barber, a busy, listening fellow, whose excessive timidity made him inquisitive into every thing, discovered that there was a plot carrying on against Cæsar by Achillas, general of the king's forces, and Pothinus, the eunuch. Cæsar, upon the first intelligence of it, set a guard upon the hall where the feast was kept, and killed Pothinus. Achillas escaped to the army, and raised a troublesome and embarrassing war against Cæsar, which it was not easy for him to manage with his few soldiers against so powerful a city and so large an army. The first difficulty he met with was want of water, for the enemies had turned the canals.[13] Another was, when the enemy endeavored to cut off his communication by sea, he was forced to divert that danger by setting fire to his own ships, which, after burning the docks, thence spread on and destroyed the great library. A third was, when in an engagement near Pharos, he leaped from the mole into a small boat, to assist his soldiers who were in danger, and when the Egyptians pressed him on every side, he threw himself into the sea, and with much difficulty swam off. This was the time when, according to the story, he had a number of manuscripts in his hand, which, though he was continually darted at, and forced to keep his head often under water, yet he did not let go, but held them up safe from wetting in one hand, whilst he swam with the other. His boat, in the mean time, was quickly sunk. At last, the king having gone off to Achillas and his party, Cæsar engaged and conquered them. Many fell in that battle, and the king himself was never seen after. Upon this, he left Cleopatra queen of Egypt, who soon after had a son by him, whom the Alexandrians called Cæsarion, and then departed for Syria.

Thence he passed to Asia, where he heard that Domitius was beaten by Pharnaces, son of Mithridates, and had fled out of Pontus with a handful of men; and that Pharnaces pursued the victory so eagerly, that though he was already master of Bithynia and Cappadocia, he had a further design of attempting the Lesser Armenia, and was inviting all the kings and tetrarchs there to rise. Cæsar immediately marched against him with three legions, fought him near Zela, drove him out of Pontus, and totally defeated his army. When he gave Amantius, a friend of his at Rome, an account of this action, to express the promptness and rapidity of it, he used three words, I came, saw, and conquered, which in Latin[14] having

[13] By which Alexandria, there being no springs, was wholly supplied.

[14] Veni, Vidi, Vici. A tablet with this inscription was displayed in the triumph which was afterwards celebrated for this war. Amantius does not seem to be a true Roman name. It has been corrected into Caius Matius, a well-known friend of Cæsar's.

all the same cadence, carry with them a very suitable air of brevity.

Hence he crossed into Italy, and come to Rome at the end of that year, for which he had been a second time chosen dictator, though that office had never before lasted a whole year, and was elected consul for the next. He was ill spoken of, because upon a mutiny of some soldiers, who killed Cosconius and Galba, who had been prætors, he gave them only the slight reprimand of calling them *Citizens,* instead of *Fellow-Soldiers,* and afterwards assigned to each man a thousand drachmas, besides a share of lands in Italy. He was also reflected on for Dolabella's extravagance, Amantius's covetousness, Antony's debauchery, and Corfinius's profuseness, who pulled down Pompey's house, and rebuilt it, as not magnificent enough; for the Romans were much displeased with all these. But Cæsar, for the prosecution of his own scheme of government, though he knew their characters and disapproved them, was forced to make use of those who would serve him.

After the battle of Pharsalia, Cato and Scipio fled into Africa, and there, with the assistance of king Juba, got together a considerable force, which Cæsar resolved to engage. He, accordingly, passed into Sicily about the winter-solstice, and to remove from his officers' minds all hopes of delay there, encamped by the sea-shore, and as soon as ever he had a fair wind, put to sea with three thousand foot and a few horse. When he had landed them, he went back secretly, under some apprehensions for the larger part of his army, but met them upon the sea, and brought them all to the same camp. There he was informed that the enemies relied much upon an ancient oracle, that the family of the Scipios should be always victorious in Africa. There was in his army a man, otherwise mean and contemptible, but of the house of the Africani, and his name Scipio Sallutio. This man Cæsar, (whether in raillery, to ridicule Scipio, who commanded the enemy, or seriously to bring over the omen to his side, it were hard to say), put at the head of his troops, as if he were general, in all the frequent battles which he was compelled to fight. For he was in such want both of victualling for his men, and forage for his horses, that he was forced to feed the horses with sea-weed, which he washed thoroughly to take off its saltness, and mixed with a little grass, to give it a more agreeable taste. The

Numidians, in great numbers, and well horsed, whenever he went, came up and commanded the country. Cæsar's cavalry being one day unemployed, diverted themselves with seeing an African, who entertained them with dancing and at the same time playing upon the pipe to admiration. They were so taken with this, that they alighted, and gave their horses to some boys, when on a sudden the enemy surrounded them, killed some, pursued the rest, and fell in with them into their camp; and had not Cæsar himself and Asinius Pollio come to their assistance, and put a stop to their flight, the war had been then at an end. In another engagement, also, the enemy had again the better, when Cæsar, it is said, seized a standard-bearer, who was running away, by the neck, and forcing him to face about, said, "Look, that is the way to the enemy."

Scipio, flushed with this success at first, had a mind to come to one decisive action. He therefore left Afranius and Juba in two distinct bodies not far distant, and marched himself towards Thapsus, where he proceeded to build a fortified camp above a lake, to serve as a centre-point for their operations, and also as a place of refuge. Whilst Scipio was thus employed, Cæsar with incredible despatch made his way through thick woods, and a country supposed to be impassable, cut off one party of the enemy, and attacked another in the front. Having routed these, he followed up his opportunity and the current of his good fortune, and on the first onset carried Afranius's camp, and ravaged that of the Numidians, Juba, their king, being glad to save himself by flight; so that in a small part of a single day he made himself master of three camps, and killed fifty thousand of the enemy, with the loss only of fifty of his own men. This is the account some give of that fight. Others say, he was not in the action, but that he was taken with his usual distemper just as he was setting his army in order. He perceived the approaches of it, and before it had too far disordered his senses, when he was already beginning to shake under its influence, withdrew into a neighboring fort, where he reposed himself. Of the men of consular and prætorian dignity that were taken after the fight, several Cæsar put to death, others anticipated him by killing themselves.

Cato had undertaken to defend Utica, and for that reason was not in the battle. The desire which Cæsar had to take him alive, made him hasten thither; and upon the intelligence that he had despatched himself, he was much discomposed, for what reason is not so well agreed. He certainly said, "Cato, I must grudge you your death, as you grudged me the honor of saving your life." Yet the discourse he wrote against Cato after his death, is no great sign of his kindness, or that he was inclined to be reconciled to him. For how is it probable that he would have been tender of his life, when he was so bitter against his memory? But from his clemency to Cicero, Brutus, and many others who fought against him, it may be divined that Cæsar's book was not written so much out of animosity to Cato, as in his own vindication. Cicero had written an encomium upon Cato, and called it by his name. A composition by so great a master upon so excellent a subject, was sure to be in every one's hands. This touched Cæsar, who looked upon a panegyric on his enemy, as no better than an invective against himself; and therefore he made in his Anti-Cato, a collection of whatever could be said in his derogation. The two compositions, like Cato and Cæsar themselves, have each of them their several admirers.

Cæsar, upon his return to Rome, did not omit to pronounce before the people a magnificent account of his victory, telling them that he had subdued a country which would supply the public every year with two hundred thousand attic bushels of corn, and three million pounds weight of oil. He then led three triumphs for Egypt, Pontus, and Africa, the last for the victory over, not Scipio, but king Juba, as it was professed, whose little son was then carried in the triumph, the happiest captive that ever was, who of a barbarian Numidian, came by this means to obtain a place among the most learned historians of Greece. After the triumphs, he distributed rewards to his soldiers, and treated the people with feasting and shows. He entertained the whole people together at one feast, where twenty-two thousand dining couches were laid out; and he made a display of gladiators, and of battles by sea, in honor, as he said, of his daughter Julia, though she had been long since dead. When these shows were over, an account was taken of the people, who, from three hundred and twenty thousand, were now reduced to one hundred and fifty thousand. So great a waste had the civil war made in

Rome alone, not to mention what the other parts of Italy and the provinces suffered.

He was now chosen a fourth time consul, and went into Spain against Pompey's sons. They were but young, yet had gathered together a very numerous army, and showed they had courage and conduct to command it, so that Cæsar was in extreme danger. The great battle was near the town of Munda, in which Cæsar seeing his men hard pressed, and making but a weak resistance, ran through the ranks among the soldiers, and crying out, asked them whether they were not ashamed to deliver him into the hands of boys? At last, with great difficulty, and the best efforts he could make, he forced back the enemy, killing thirty thousand of them, though with the loss of one thousand of his best men. When he came back from the fight, he told his friends that he had often fought for victory, but this was the first time that he had ever fought for life. This battle was won on the feast of Bacchus, the very day in which Pompey, four years before, had set out for the war. The younger of Pompey's sons escaped; but Didius, some days after the fight, brought the head of the elder to Cæsar. This was the last war he was engaged in. The triumph which he celebrated for this victory, displeased the Romans beyond any thing. For he had not defeated foreign generals, or barbarian kings, but had destroyed the children and family of one of the greatest men of Rome, though unfortunate; and it did not look well to lead a procession in celebration of the calamities of his country, and to rejoice in those things for which no other apology could be made either to gods or men, than their being absolutely necessary. Besides that, hitherto he had never sent letters or messengers to announce any victory over his fellow-citizens, but had seemed rather to be ashamed of the action, than to expect honor from it.

Nevertheless his countrymen, conceding all to his fortune, and accepting the bit, in the hope that the government of a single person would give them time to breathe after so many civil wars and calamities, made him dictator for life. This was indeed a tyranny avowed, since his power now was not only absolute, but perpetual too. Cicero made the first proposals to the senate for conferring honors upon him, which might in some sort be said not to exceed the limits of ordinary human moderation. But others, striving which should deserve most, carried them so excessively high, that they made Cæsar odious to the most indifferent and moderate sort of men, by the pretension and the extravagance of the titles which they decreed him. His enemies, too, are thought to have had some share in this, as well as his flatterers. It gave them advantage against him, and would be their justification for any attempt they should make upon him; for since the civil wars were ended, he had nothing else that he could be charged with. And they had good reason to decree a temple to Clemency, in token of their thanks for the mild use he made of his victory. For he not only pardoned many of those who fought against him, but, further, to some gave honors and offices; as particularly to Brutus and Cassius, who both of them were prætors. Pompey's images that were thrown down, he set up again, upon which Cicero also said that by raising Pompey's statues he had fixed his own. When his friends advised him to have a guard, and several offered their service, he would not hear of it; but said it was better to suffer death once, than always to live in fear of it. He looked upon the affections of the people to be the best and surest guard, and entertained them again with public feasting, and general distributions of corn; and to gratify his army, he sent out colonies to several places, of which the most remarkable were Carthage and Corinth; which as before they had been ruined at the same time, so now were restored and repeopled together.

As for the men of high rank, he promised to some of them future consulships and prætorships, some he consoled with other offices and honors, and to all held out hopes of favor by the solicitude he showed to rule with the general goodwill; insomuch that upon the death of Maximus one day before his consulship was ended, he made Caninius Revilius consul for that day. And when many went to pay the usual compliments and attentions to the new consul, "Let us make haste," said Cicero, "lest the man be gone out of his office before we come."

Cæsar was born to do great things, and had a passion after honor, and the many noble exploits he had done did not now serve as an inducement to him to sit still and reap the fruit of his past labors, but were incentives and encouragements to go on, and raised in him ideas of still greater actions, and a desire of new glory, as if the present were all spent. It was in fact a sort of emulous struggle with himself, as it had been with another, how he might outdo his past actions by his future. In pursuit of these thoughts, he resolved to make war upon the Parthians, and when he had subdued them, to pass through Hyrcania; thence to march along by the Caspian Sea to Mount Caucasus, and so on about Pontus, till he came into Scythia; then to overrun all the countries bordering upon Germany, and Germany itself; and so to return through Gaul into Italy, after completing the whole circle of his intended empire, and bounding it on every side by the ocean. While preparations were making for this expedition, he proposed to dig through the isthmus on which Corinth stands; and appointed Anienus to superintend the work. He had also a design of diverting the Tiber, and carrying it by a deep channel directly from Rome to Circeii, and so into the sea near Tarracina, that there might be a safe and easy passage for all merchants who traded to Rome. Besides this, he intended to drain all the marshes by Pomentium and Setia, and gain ground enough from the water to employ many thousands of men in tillage. He proposed further to make great mounds on the shore nearest Rome, to hinder the sea from breaking in upon the land, to clear the coast at Ostia of all the hidden rocks and shoals that made it unsafe for shipping, and to form ports and harbors fit to receive the large number of vessels that would frequent them.

These things were designed without being carried into effect; but his reformation of the calendar, in order to rectify the irregularity of time, was not only projected with great scientific ingenuity, but was brought to its completion, and proved of very great use. For it was not only in ancient times that the Romans had wanted a certain rule to make the revolutions of their months fall in with the course of the year, so that their festivals and solemn days for sacrifice were removed by little and little, till at last they came to be kept at seasons quite the contrary to what was at first intended, but even at this time the people had no way of computing the solar year; only the priests could say the time, and they, at their pleasure, without giving any notice, slipped in the intercalary month, which they called Mercedonius. Numa was the first who put in this month, but his expedient was but a poor one and quite inadequate to correct all the errors that arose in the returns of the annual cycles, as we have shown in his Life. Cæsar called in the best philosophers and mathematicians of his time to settle the point, and out of the systems he had before him, formed a new and more exact method of correcting the calendar, which the Romans use to this day, and seem to succeed better than any nation in avoiding the errors occasioned by the inequality of the cycles. Yet even this gave offence to those who looked with an evil eye on his position, and felt oppressed by his power. Cicero, the orator, when some one in his company chanced to say, the next morning Lyra would rise, replied, "Yes, in accordance with the edict," as if even this were a matter of compulsion.

But that which brought upon him the most apparent and mortal hatred, was his desire of being king; which gave the common people the first occasion to quarrel with him, and proved the most specious pretence to those who had been his secret enemies all along. Those, who would have procured him that title, gave it out, that it was foretold in the Sybils' books that the Romans should conquer the Parthians when they fought against them under the conduct of a king, but not before. And one day, as Cæsar was coming down from Alba to Rome, some were so bold as to salute him by the name of king; but he finding the people disrelish it, seemed to resent it himself, and said his name was Cæsar, not king. Upon this, there was a general silence, and he passed on looking not very well pleased or contented. Another time, when the senate had conferred on him some extravagant honors, he chanced to receive the message as he was sitting on the rostra, where, though the consuls and prætors themselves waited on him, attended by the whole body of the senate, he did not rise, but behaved himself to them as if they had been private men, and told them his honors wanted rather to be retrenched than increased. This treatment offended not only the senate, but the commonalty, too, as if they thought the affront upon the senate equally reflected upon the whole republic; so that all who could decently leave him went off, looking much discomposed. Cæsar, perceiving the false step he had made, immediately retired home; and laying his throat bare, told his friends that he was ready to offer this to any one who would give the stroke. But afterwards he made the malady from which he suffered, the excuse for his sitting, saying that those who are attacked by it, lose their presence of mind, if they talk much standing; that they presently grow giddy, fall into convulsions, and quite lose their reason. But this was not the reality, for he would willingly have stood up to the senate, had not Cornelius Balbus, one of his friends, or rather flatterers, hindered him. "Will you not remember," said he, "you are Cæsar, and claim the honor which is due to your merit?"

He gave a fresh occasion of resentment by his affront to the tribunes. The Lupercalia were then celebrated, a feast at the first institution belonging, as some writers say, to the shepherds, and having some connection with the Arcadian Lycæa. Many young noblemen and magistrates run up and down the city with their upper garments off, striking all they meet with thongs of hide, by way of sport; and many women, even of the highest rank, place themselves in the way, and hold out their hands to the lash, as boys in a school do to the master, out of a belief that it procures an easy labor to those who are with child, and makes those conceive who are barren. Cæsar, dressed in a triumphal robe, seated himself in a golden chair at the rostra, to view this ceremony. Antony, as consul, was one of those who ran this course, and when he came into the forum, and the people made way for him, he went up and reached to Cæsar a diadem wreathed with laurel. Upon this, there was a shout, but only a slight one, made by the few who were planted there for that purpose; but when Cæsar refused it, there was universal applause. Upon the second offer, very few, and upon the second refusal, all again applauded. Cæsar finding it would not take, rose up, and ordered the crown to be carried into the capitol. Cæsar's statues were afterwards found with royal diadems on their heads. Flavius and Marullus, two tribunes of the people, went presently and pulled them off, and having apprehended those who first saluted Cæsar as king, committed them to prison. The people followed them with acclamations, and called them by the name of Brutus, because Brutus was the first who ended the succession of kings, and transferred the power which before was lodged in one man into the hands of the senate and people. Cæsar so far resented this, that he displaced Marullus and Flavius; and in urging his charges against them, at the same time ridiculed the people, by himself giving the men more than once the names of Bruti, and Cumæi.[15]

This made the multitude turn their thoughts to Marcus Brutus, who, by his father's side, was thought to be descended from that first Brutus, and by his mother's side from the Servilii, another noble family, being besides nephew and son-in-law to Cato. But the honors and favors he had received from Cæsar, took off the edge from the desires he might himself have felt for overthrowing the new monarchy. For he had not only been pardoned himself after Pompey's defeat at Pharsalia, and had procured the same grace for many of his friends, but was one in whom Cæsar had a particular confidence. He had at that time the most honorable prætorship of the year, and was named for the consulship four years after, being preferred before Cassius, his competitor. Upon the question as to the choice, Cæsar, it is related, said that Cassius had the fairer pretensions, but that he could not pass by Brutus. Nor would he afterwards listen to some who spoke against Brutus, when the conspiracy against him was already afoot, but laying his hand on his body, said to the informers, "Brutus will wait for this skin of mine," intimating that he was worthy to bear rule on account of his virtue, but would not be base and ungrateful to gain it. Those who desired a change, and looked on him as the only, or at least the most proper, person to effect it, did not venture to speak with him; but in the night-time laid papers about his chair of state, where he used to sit and determine causes, with such sentences in them as, "You are asleep, Brutus," "You are no longer Brutus." Cassius, when he perceived his ambition a little raised upon this, was more instant than before to work him yet further, having himself a private grudge against Cæsar, for some reasons that we have mentioned in the Life of Brutus. Nor was Cæsar without suspicions of him, and said once to his friends, "What do you think Cassius is aiming at? I don't like him, he looks so pale." And when it was told him that Antony and Dolabella were in a plot against him, he said he did not

[15] Brutus, in Latin, means heavy, stupid; and the Cumæans were for one reason or other proverbial for dulness.

fear such fat, luxurious men, but rather the pale, lean fellows, meaning Cassius and Brutus.

Fate, however, is to all appearances more unavoidable than unexpected. For many strange prodigies and apparitions are said to have been observed shortly before the event. As to the lights in the heavens, the noises heard in the night, and the wild birds which perched in the forum, these are not perhaps worth taking notice of in so great a case as this. Strabo, the philosopher, tells us that a number of men were seen, looking as if they were heated through with fire, contending with each other; that a quantity of flame issued from the hand of a soldier's servant, so that they who saw it thought he must be burnt, but that after all he had no hurt. As Cæsar was sacrificing, the victim's heart was missing, a very bad omen, because no living creature can subsist without a heart. One finds it also related by many, that a soothsayer bade him prepare for some great danger on the ides of March. When the day was come, Cæsar, as he went to the senate, met this soothsayer, and said to him by way of raillery, "The ides of March are come;" who answered him calmly, "Yes, they are come, but they are not past." The day before this assassination, he supped with Marcus Lepidus; and as he was signing some letters, according to his custom, as he reclined at table, there arose a question what sort of death was the best. At which he immediately, before any one could speak, said, "A sudden one."

After this, as he was in bed with his wife, all the doors and windows of the house flew open together; he was startled at the noise, and the light which broke into the room, and sat up in his bed, where by the moonshine he perceived Calpurnia fast asleep, but heard her utter in her dream some indistinct words and inarticulate groans. She fancied at that time she was weeping over Cæsar, and holding him butchered in her arms. Others say this was not her dream, but that she dreamed that a pinnacle which the senate, as Livy relates, had ordered to be raised on Cæsar's house by way of ornament and grandeur, was tumbling down, which was the occasion of her tears and ejaculations. When it was day, she begged of Cæsar, if it were possible, not to stir out, but to adjourn the senate to another time; and if he slighted her dreams, that he would be pleased to consult his fate by sacrifices, and other kinds of divination. Nor was he himself without some suspicion and fears; for he never before discovered any womanish superstition in Calpurnia, whom he now saw in such great alarm. Upon the report which the priests made to him, that they had killed several sacrifices, and still found them inauspicious, he resolved to send Antony to dismiss the senate.

In this juncture, Decimus Brutus, surnamed Albinus, one whom Cæsar had such confidence in that he made him his second heir, who nevertheless was engaged in the conspiracy with the other Brutus and Cassius, fearing lest if Cæsar should put off the senate to another day, the business might get wind, spoke scoffingly and in mockery of the diviners, and blamed Cæsar for giving the senate so fair an occasion of saying he had put a slight upon them, for that they were met upon his summons, and were ready to vote unanimously, that he should be declared king of all the provinces out of Italy, and might wear a diadem in any other place but Italy, by sea or land. If any one should be sent to tell them they might break up for the present, and meet again when Calpurnia should chance to have better dreams, what would his enemies say? Or who would with any patience hear his friends, if they should presume to defend his government as not arbitrary and tyrannical? But if he was possessed so far as to think this day unfortunate, yet it were more decent to go himself to the senate, and to adjourn it in his own person. Brutus, as he spoke these words, took Cæsar by the hand, and conducted him forth. He was not gone far from the door, when a servant of some other person's made towards him, but not being able to come up to him, on account of the crowd of those who pressed about him, he made his way into the house, and committed himself to Calpurnia, begging of her to secure him till Cæsar returned, because he had matters of great importance to communicate to him.

Artemidorus, a Cnidian, a teacher of Greek logic, and by that means so far acquainted with Brutus and his friends as to have got into the secret, brought Cæsar in a small written memorial, the heads of what he had to depose. He had observed that Cæsar, as he received any papers, presently gave them to the servants who attended on him; and therefore came as near to him as he could, and said,

"Read this, Cæsar, alone, and quickly, for it contains matter of great importance which nearly concerns you." Cæsar received it, and tried several times to read it, but was still hindered by the crowd of those who came to speak to him. However, he kept it in his hand by itself till he came into the senate. Some say it was another who gave Cæsar this note, and that Artemidorus could not get to him, being all along kept off by the crowd.

All these things might happen by chance. But the place which was destined for the scene of this murder, in which the senate met that day, was the same in which Pompey's statue stood and was one of the edifices which Pompey had raised and dedicated with his theatre to the use of the public, plainly showing that there was something of a supernatural influence which guided the action, and ordered it to that particular place. Cassius, just before the act, is said to have looked towards Pompey's statue, and silently implored his assistance, though he had been inclined to the doctrines of Epicurus. But this occasion and the instant danger, carried him away out of all his reasonings, and filled him for the time with a sort of inspiration. As for Antony, who was firm to Cæsar, and a strong man, Brutus Albinus kept him outside the house, and delayed him with a long conversation contrived on purpose. When Cæsar entered, the senate stood up to show their respect to him, and of Brutus's confederates, some came about his chair and stood behind it, others met him, pretending to add their petitions to those of Tillius Cimber, in behalf of his brother, who was in exile; and they followed him with their joint supplications till he came to his seat. When he was sat down, he refused to comply with their requests, and upon their urging him further, began to reproach them severally for their importunities, when Tillius, laying hold of his robe with both his hands, pulled it down from his neck, which was the signal for the assault. Casca gave him the first cut, in the neck, which was not mortal nor dangerous, as coming from one who at the beginning of such a bold action was probably very much disturbed. Cæsar immediately turned about, and laid his hand upon the dagger and kept hold of it. And both of them at the same time cried out, he that received the blow, in Latin, "Vile Casca, what does this mean?" and he that gave it, in Greek, to his brother, "Brother, help!" Upon this first onset, those who were not privy to the design were astonished, and their horror and amazement at what they saw were so great, that they durst not fly nor assist Cæsar, nor so much as speak a word. But those who came prepared for the business inclosed him on every side, with their naked daggers in their hands. Which way soever he turned, he met with blows, and saw their swords levelled at his face and eyes, and was encompassed, like a wild beast in the toils, on every side. For it had been agreed they should each of them make a thrust at him, and flesh themselves with his blood; for which reason Brutus also gave him one stab in the groin. Some say that he fought and resisted all the rest, shifting his body to avoid the blows, and calling out for help, but that when he saw Brutus's sword drawn, he covered his face with his robe and submitted, letting himself fall, whether it were by chance, or that he was pushed in that direction by his murderers, at the foot of the pedestal on which Pompey's statue stood, and which was thus wetted with his blood. So that Pompey himself seemed to have presided, as it were, over the revenge done upon his adversary, who lay here at his feet, and breathed out his soul through his multitude of wounds, for they say he received three and twenty. And the conspirators themselves were many of them wounded by each other, whilst they all levelled their blows at the same person.

When Cæsar was dispatched, Brutus stood forth to give a reason for what they had done, but the senate would not hear him, but flew out of doors in all haste, and filled the people with so much alarm and distraction that some shut up their houses, others left their counters and shops. All ran one way or the other, some to the place to see the sad spectacle, others back again after they had seen it. Antony and Lepidus, Cæsar's most faithful friends, got off privately, and hid themselves in some friends' houses. Brutus and his followers, being yet hot from the deed, marched in a body from the senate-house to the capitol with their drawn swords, not like persons who thought of escaping, but with an air of confidence and assurance, and as they went along, called to the people to resume their liberty, and invited the company of any more distinguished people whom they met. And some of these joined the procession and went up along with them, as if they also had been of the con-

Brutus, being to pass his army from Abydos to the continent on the other side, laid himself down one night, as he used to do, in his tent, and was not asleep, but thinking of his affairs, and what events he might expect. For he is related to have been the least inclined to sleep of all men who have commanded armies, and to have had the greatest natural capacity for continuing awake, and employing himself without need of rest. He thought he heard a noise at the door of his tent, and looking that way, by the light of his lamp, which was almost out, saw a terrible figure, like that of a man, but of unusual stature and severe countenance. He was somewhat frightened at first, but seeing it neither did nor spoke any thing to him, only stood silently by his bedside, he asked who it was. The spectre answered him, "Thy evil genius, Brutus, thou shalt see me at Philippi." Brutus answered courageously, "Well, I shall see you," and immediately the appearance vanished. When the time was come, he drew up his army near Philippi against Antony and Cæsar, and in the first battle won the day, routed the enemy, and plundered Cæsar's camp. The night before the second battle, the same phantom appeared to him again, but spoke not a word. He presently understood his destiny was at hand, and exposed himself to all the danger of the battle. Yet he did not die in the fight, but seeing his men defeated, got up to the top of a rock, and there presenting his sword to his naked breast, and assisted, as they say, by a friend, who helped him to give the thrust, met his death.

ANTONY

THE grandfather of Antony was the famous pleader, whom Marius put to death for having taken part with Sylla. His father was Antony, surnamed of Crete, not very famous or distinguished in public life, but a worthy, good man, and particularly remarkable for his liberality, as may appear from a single example. He was not very rich, and was for that reason checked in the exercise of his good-nature by his wife. A friend that stood in need of money came to borrow of him. Money he had none, but he bade a servant bring him water in a silver basin, with which, when it was brought, he wetted his face, as if he meant to shave; and, sending away the servant upon another errand, gave his friend the basin, desiring him to turn it to his purpose. And when there was, afterwards, a great inquiry for it in the house, and his wife was in a very ill humor, and was going to put the servants one by one to the search, he acknowledged what he had done, and begged her pardon.

His wife was Julia, of the family of the Cæsars, who, for her discretion and fair behavior, was not inferior to any of her time. Under her, Antony received his education, she being, after the death of his father, remarried to Cornelius Lentulus, who was put to death by Cicero for having been of Catiline's conspiracy. This, probably, was the first ground and occasion of that mortal grudge that Antony bore Cicero. He says, even, that the body of Lentulus was denied burial, till, by application made to Cicero's wife, it was granted to Julia. But this seems to be a manifest error, for none of those that suffered in the consulate of Cicero had the right of burial denied them. Antony grew up a very beautiful youth, but, by the worst of misfortunes, he fell into the acquaintance and friendship of Curio, a man abandoned to his pleasures; who, to make Antony's dependence upon him a matter of greater necessity, plunged him into a life of drinking and dissipation, and led him through a course of such extravagance, that he ran, at that early age, into debt to the amount of two hundred and fifty talents. For this sum, Curio became his surety; on hearing which, the elder Curio, his father, drove Antony out of his house. After this, for some short time, he took part with Clodius, the most insolent and outrageous demagogue of the time, in his course of violence and disorder; but, getting weary, before long, of his madness, and apprehensive of the powerful party forming against him, he left Italy, and travelled into Greece, where he spent his time in military exercises and in the study of eloquence. He took most to what was called the Asiatic taste in speaking, which was then at its height, and was, in many ways, suitable to his ostentatious, vaunting temper, full of empty flourishes and unsteady efforts for glory.

After some stay in Greece, he was invited by Gabinius, who had been consul, to make a campaign with him in Syria, which at first he refused, not being willing to serve in a private character, but, receiving a commission to command the horse, he went along with him. His first service was against Aristobulus, who had prevailed with the Jews to rebel. Here he was himself the first man to scale the largest of the works, and beat Aristobulus out of all of them; after which he routed, in a pitched battle, an army many times over the number of his, killed almost all of them, and took Aristobulus and his son prisoners. This war ended, Gabinius was solicited by Ptolemy to restore him to his kingdom of Egypt, and a promise made of ten thousand talents reward. Most of the officers were against this enterprise, and Gabinius himself did not much like it, though sorely tempted by the ten thousand talents. But Antony, desirous of brave actions, and willing to please Ptolemy, joined in persuading Gabinius to go. And whereas all were of opinion that the most dangerous thing before them was the march to Pelusium, in which they would have to pass over a deep sand, where no fresh water was to be hoped for, along the Ecregma and the Serbonian marsh (which the Egyptians call Typhon's breathing-hole, and which is, in probability, water left behind by, or making its way through from, the Red Sea, which is here divided from the Mediterranean by a narrow isthmus), Antony, being ordered thither with the horse, not only made himself master of the passes, but won

Pelusium itself, a great city, took the garrison prisoners, and, by this means, rendered the march secure to the army, and the way to victory not difficult for the general to pursue. The enemy, also, reaped some benefit of his eagerness for honor. For when Ptolemy, after he had entered Pelusium, in his rage and spite against the Egyptians, designed to put them to the sword, Antony withstood him, and hindered the execution. In all the great and frequent skirmishes and battles, he gave continual proofs of his personal valor and military conduct; and once in particular, by wheeling about and attacking the rear of the enemy, he gave the victory to the assailants in the front, and received for this service signal marks of distinction. Nor was his humanity towards the deceased Archelaus less taken notice of. He had been formerly his guest and acquaintance, and, as he was now compelled, he fought him bravely while alive, but, on his death, sought out his body and buried it with royal honors. The consequence was that he left behind him a great name among the Alexandrians, and all who were serving in the Roman army looked upon him as a most gallant soldier.

He had also a very good and noble appearance; his beard was well grown, his forehead large, and his nose aquiline, giving him altogether a bold, masculine look, that reminded people of the faces of Hercules in paintings and sculptures. It was, moreover, an ancient tradition, that the Antonys were descended from Hercules, by a son of his called Anton; and this opinion he thought to give credit to, by the similarity of his person just mentioned, and also by the fashion of his dress. For, whenever he had to appear before large numbers, he wore his tunic girt low about the hips, a broadsword on his side, and over all a large, coarse mantle. What might seem to some very insupportable, his vaunting, his raillery, his drinking in public, sitting down by the men as they were taking their food, and eating, as he stood, off the common soldiers' tables, made him the delight and pleasure of the army. In love affairs, also, he was very agreeable; he gained many friends by the assistance he gave them in theirs, and took other people's raillery upon his own with good-humor. And his generous ways, his open and lavish hand in gifts and favors to his friends and fellow-soldiers, did a great deal for him in his first advance to power, and, after he had become great, long maintained his fortunes, when a thousand follies were hastening their overthrow. One instance of his liberality I must relate. He had ordered payment to one of his friends of twenty-five myriads of money, or *decies,* as the Romans call it, and his steward, wondering at the extravagance of the sum, laid all the silver in a heap, as he should pass by. Antony, seeing the heap, asked what it meant; his steward replied, "The money you have ordered to be given to your friend." So, perceiving the man's malice, said he, "I thought the *decies* had been much more; 't is too little; let it be doubled." This, however, was at a later time.

When the Roman state finally broke up into two hostile factions, the aristocratical party joining Pompey, who was in the city, and the popular side seeking help from Cæsar, who was at the head of an army in Gaul, Curio, the friend of Antony, having changed his party and devoted himself to Cæsar, brought over Antony also to his service. And the influence which he gained with the people by his eloquence and by the money which was supplied by Cæsar enabled him to make Antony, first, tribune of the people, and then, augur. And Antony's accession to office was at once of the greatest advantage to Cæsar. In the first place, he resisted the consul Marcellus, who was putting under Pompey's orders the troops who were already collected, and was giving him power to raise new levies; he, on the other hand, making an order that they should be sent into Syria to reinforce Bibulus, who was making war with the Parthians, and that no one should give in his name to serve under Pompey. Next, when the senators would not suffer Cæsar's letters to be received or read in the senate, by virtue of his office he read them publicly, and succeeded so well, that many were brought to change their mind; Cæsar's demands, as they appeared in what he wrote, being but just and reasonable. At length, two questions being put in the senate, the one, whether Pompey should dismiss his army, the other, if Cæsar his, some were for the former, for the latter all, except some few, when Antony stood up and put the question, if it would be agreeable to them that both Pompey and Cæsar should dismiss their armies. This proposal met with the greatest approval, they gave him loud acclamations, and called for it to be put to the vote. But when the consuls would not have it so, Cæsar's friends again made some new offers, very fair and equitable, but were strongly opposed by Cato, and Antony himself was commanded to leave the senate by the consul Lentulus. So, leaving them with execrations, and disguising himself in a servant's dress, hiring a carriage with Quintus Cassius, he went straight away to Cæsar, declaring at once, when they reached the camp, that affairs at Rome were conducted without any order or justice, that the privilege of speaking in the senate was denied the tribunes, and that he who spoke for common fair dealing was driven out and in danger of his life.

Upon this, Cæsar set his army in motion, and marched into Italy; and for this reason it is that Cicero writes in his Philippics, that Antony was as much the cause of the civil war, as Helen was of the Trojan. But this is but a calumny. For Cæsar was not of so slight or weak a temper as to suffer himself to be carried away, by the indignation of the moment, into a civil war with his country, upon the sight of Antony and Cassius seeking refuge in his camp, meanly dressed and in a hired carriage, without ever having thought of it or taken any such resolution long before. This was to him, who wanted a pretence of declaring war, a fair and plausible occasion; but the true motive that led him was the same that formerly led Alexander and Cyrus against all mankind, the unquenchable thirst of empire, and the distracted ambition of being the greatest man in the world, which was impracticable for him, unless Pompey were put down. So soon, then, as he had advanced and occupied Rome, and driven Pompey out of Italy, he purposed first to go against the legions that Pompey had in Spain, and then cross over and follow him with the fleet that should be prepared during his absence, in the mean time leaving the government of Rome to Lepidus, as prætor, and the command of the troops and of Italy to Antony, as tribune of the people. Antony was not long in getting the hearts of the soldiers, joining with them in their exercises, and for the most part living amongst them, and making them presents to the utmost of his abilities; but with all others he was unpopular enough. He was too lazy to pay attention to the complaints of persons who were injured; he listened impatiently to petitions; and he had an ill name for familiarity with other people's wives. In short, the government of Cæsar (which, so far as he was concerned himself, had the appearance of any thing rather than a tyranny), got a bad repute through his friends. And of these friends, Antony, as he had the largest trust, and committed the greatest errors, was thought the most deeply in fault.

Cæsar, however, at his return from Spain, overlooked the charges against him, and had no reason ever to complain, in the employments he gave him in the war, of any want of courage, energy, or military skill. He himself, going aboard at Brundusium, sailed over the Ionian Sea with a few troops, and sent back the vessels with orders to Antony and Gabinius to embark the army, and come over with all speed into Macedonia. Gabinius, having no mind to put to sea in the rough, dangerous weather of the winter season, was for marching the army round by the long land route; but Antony, being more afraid lest Cæsar might suffer from the number of his enemies, who pressed him hard, beat back Libo, who was watching with a fleet at the mouth of the haven of Brundusium, by attacking his galleys with a number of small boats, and, gaining thus an opportunity, put on board twenty thousand foot and eight hundred horse, and so set out to sea. And, being espied by the enemy and pursued, from this danger he was rescued by a strong south wind, which sprang up and raised so high a sea, that the enemy's galleys could make little way. But his own ships were driving before it upon a lee shore of cliffs and rocks running sheer to the water, where there was no hope of escape, when all of a sudden the wind turned about to south-west, and blew from land to the main sea, where Antony, now sailing in security, saw the coast all covered with the wreck of the enemy's fleet. For hither the galleys in pursuit had been carried by the gale, and not a few of them dashed to pieces. Many men and much property fell into Antony's hands; he took also the town of Lissus, and, by the seasonable arrival of so large a reinforcement, gave Cæsar great encouragement.

There was not one of the many engagements that now took place one after another in which he did not signalize himself; twice he stopped the army in its full flight, led them back to a charge, and gained the victory. So that not without reason his reputation, next to Cæsar's, was greatest in the army. And what opinion Cæsar himself had of him well appeared when for the final battle in Pharsalia, which was to determine every thing, he himself chose to lead the right wing, committing the charge of the left to Antony, as to the best officer of all that served under him. After the battle, Cæsar, being created dictator, went in pursuit of Pompey, and sent Antony to Rome, with the character of Master of the Horse, who is in office and power next to the dictator, when present, and in his absence is the first, and pretty nearly indeed the sole magistrate. For on the appointment of a dictator, with the one exception of the tribunes, all other magistrates cease to exercise any authority in Rome.

Dolabella, however, who was tribune, being a young man and eager for change, was now for bringing in a general measure for cancelling debts, and wanted Antony, who was his friend, and forward enough to promote any popular project, to take part with him in this step. Asinius and Trebellius were of the contrary opinion, and it so happened at the same time, Antony was crossed by a terrible suspicion that Dolabella was too familiar with his wife; and in great trouble at this, he parted with her (she being his cousin, and daughter to Caius Antonius, the colleague of Cicero), and, taking part with Asinius, came to open hostilities with Dolabella, who had seized on the forum, intending to pass his law by force. Antony, backed by a vote of the senate that Dolabella should be put down by force of arms, went down and attacked him, killing some of his, and losing some of his own men; and by this action lost his favor with the commonalty, while with the better class and with all well conducted people his general course of life made him, as Cicero says, absolutely odious, utter disgust being excited by his drinking bouts at all hours, his wild expenses, his gross amours, the day spent in sleeping or walking off his debauches, and the night in banquets and at theatres, and in celebrating the nuptials of some comedian or buffoon. It is related that, drinking all night at the wedding of Hippias, the comedian, on the morning, having to harangue the people, he came forward, overcharged as he was, and vomited before them all, one of his friends holding his gown for him. Sergius, the player, was one of the friends who could do most with him; also Cytheris, a woman of the same trade, whom he made much of, and who, when he went his progress, accompanied him in a litter, and had her equipage, not in any thing inferior to his mother's;

while every one, moreover, was scandalized at the sight of the golden cups that he took with him, fitter for the ornaments of a procession than the uses of a journey, at his having pavilions set up, and sumptuous morning repasts laid out by river sides and in groves, at his having chariots drawn by lions, and common women and singing girls quartered upon the houses of serious fathers and mothers of families. And it seemed very unreasonable that Cæsar, out of Italy, should lodge in the open field, and, with great fatigue and danger, pursue the remainder of a hazardous war, whilst others, by favor of his authority, should insult the citizens with their impudent luxury.

All this appears to have aggravated party quarrels in Rome, and to have encouraged the soldiers in acts of license and rapacity. And, accordingly, when Cæsar came home, he acquitted Dolabella, and, being created the third time consul, took, not Antony, but Lepidus, for his colleague. Pompey's house being offered for sale, Antony bought it, and, when the price was demanded of him, loudly complained. This, he tells us himself, and because he thought his former services had not been recompensed as they deserved, made him not follow Cæsar with the army into Libya. However, Cæsar, by dealing gently with his errors, seems to have succeeded in curing him of a good deal of his folly and extravagance. He gave up his former courses, and took a wife, Fulvia, the widow of Clodius the demagogue, a woman not born for spinning or housewifery, nor one that could be content with ruling a private husband, but prepared to govern a first magistrate, or give orders to a commander-in-chief. So that Cleopatra had great obligations to her for having taught Antony to be so good a servant, he coming to her hands tame and broken into entire obedience to the commands of a mistress. He used to play all sorts of sportive, boyish tricks, to keep Fulvia in good-humor. As, for example, when Cæsar, after his victory in Spain, was on his return, Antony, among the rest, went out to meet him; and, a rumor being spread that Cæsar was killed and the enemy marching into Italy, he returned to Rome, and, disguising himself, came to her by night muffled up as a servant that brought letters from Antony. She, with great impatience, before she received the letter, asks if Antony were well, and instead of an answer he gives her the letter; and, as she was opening it, took her about the neck and kissed her. This little story of many of the same nature, I give as a specimen.

There was nobody of any rank in Rome that did not go some days' journey to meet Cæsar on his return from Spain; but Antony was the best received of any, admitted to ride the whole journey with him in his carriage, while behind came Brutus Albinus, and Octavian, his niece's son, who afterwards bore his name and reigned so long over the Romans. Cæsar being created, the fifth time, consul, without delay chose Antony for his colleague, but, designing himself to give up his own consulate to Dolabella, he acquainted the senate with his resolution. But Antony opposed it with all his might, saying much that was bad against Dolabella, and receiving the like language in return, till Cæsar could bear with the indecency no longer, and deferred the matter to another time. Afterwards, when he came before the people to proclaim Dolabella, Antony cried out that the auspices were unfavorable, so that at last Cæsar, much to Dolabella's vexation, yielded and gave it up. And it is credible that Cæsar was about as much disgusted with the one as the other. When some one was accusing them both to him, "It is not," said he, "these well-fed, long-haired men that I fear, but the pale and the hungry looking;" meaning Brutus and Cassius, by whose conspiracy he afterwards fell.

And the fairest pretext for that conspiracy was furnished, without his meaning it, by Antony himself. The Romans were celebrating their festival, called the Lupercalia, when Cæsar, in his triumphal habit, and seated above the Rostra in the market-place, was a spectator of the sports. The custom is, that many young noblemen and of the magistracy, anointed with oil and having straps of hide in their hands, run about and strike, in sport, at every one they meet. Antony was running with the rest; but, omitting the old ceremony, twining a garland of bay round a diadem, he ran up to the Rostra, and, being lifted up by his companions, would have put it upon the head of Cæsar, as if by that ceremony he were declared king. Cæsar seemingly refused, and drew aside to avoid it, and was applauded by the people with great shouts. Again Antony pressed it, and again he declined its acceptance. And so the dispute

While matters went thus in Rome, the young Cæsar, Cæsar's niece's son, and by testament left his heir, arrived at Rome from Apollonia, where he was when his uncle was killed. The first thing he did was to visit Antony, as his father's friend. He spoke to him concerning the money that was in his hands, and reminded him of the legacy Cæsar had made of seventy-five drachmas to every Roman citizen. Antony, at first, laughing at such discourse from so young a man, told him he wished he were in his health, and that he wanted good counsel and good friends, to tell him the burden of being executor to Cæsar would sit very uneasily upon his young shoulders. This was no answer to him; and, when he persisted in demanding the property, Antony went on treating him injuriously both in word and deed, opposed him when he stood for the tribune's office, and, when he was taking steps for the dedication of his father's golden chair, as had been enacted, he threatened to send him to prison if he did not give over soliciting the people. This made the young Cæsar apply himself to Cicero, and all those that hated Antony; by them he was recommended to the senate, while he himself courted the people, and drew together the soldiers from their settlements, till Antony got alarmed, and gave him a meeting in the Capitol, where, after some words, they came to an accommodation.

That night Antony had a very unlucky dream, fancying that his right hand was thunderstruck. And, some few days after, he was informed that Cæsar was plotting to take his life. Cæsar explained, but was not believed, so that the breach was now made as wide as ever; each of them hurried about all through Italy to engage, by great offers, the old soldiers that lay scattered in their settlements, and to be the first to secure the troops that still remained undischarged.

Cicero was at this time the man of greatest influence in Rome. He made use of all his art to exasperate people against Antony, and at length persuaded the senate to declare him a public enemy, to send Cæsar the rods and axes and other marks of honor usually given to prætors, and to issue orders to Hirtius and Pansa, who were the consuls, to drive Antony out of Italy. The armies engaged near Modena, and Cæsar himself was present and took part in the battle. Antony was defeated, but both the consuls were slain. Antony, in his flight, was overtaken by distresses of every kind, and the worst of all of them was famine. But it was his character in calamities to be better than at any other time. Antony, in misfortune, was most nearly a virtuous man. It is common enough for people, when they fall into great disasters, to discern what is right, and what they ought to do; but there are but few who in such extremities have the strength to obey their judgment, either in doing what it approves or avoiding what it condemns; and a good many are so weak as to give way to their habits all the more, and are incapable of using their minds. Antony, on this occasion, was a most wonderful example to his soldiers. He, who had just quitted so much luxury and sumptuous living, made no difficulty now of drinking foul water and feeding on wild fruits and roots. Nay, it is related they ate the very bark of trees, and, in passing over the Alps, lived upon creatures that no one before had ever been willing to touch.

The design was to join the army on the other side the Alps, commanded by Lepidus, who he imagined would stand his friend, he having done him many good offices with Cæsar. On coming up and encamping near at hand, finding he had no sort of encouragement offered him, he resolved to push his fortune and venture all. His hair was long and disordered, nor had he shaved his beard since his defeat; in this guise, and with a dark colored cloak flung over him, he came into the trenches of Lepidus, and began to address the army. Some were moved at his habit, others at his words, so that Lepidus, not liking it, ordered the trumpets to sound, that he might be heard no longer. This raised in the soldiers yet a greater pity, so that they resolved to confer secretly with him, and dressed Lælius and Clodius in women's clothes, and sent them to see him. They advised him without delay to attack Lepidus's trenches, assuring him that a strong party would receive him, and, if he wished it, would kill Lepidus. Antony, however, had no wish for this, but next morning marched his army to pass over the river that parted the two camps. He was himself the first man that stepped in, and, as he went through towards the other bank, he saw Lepidus's soldiers in great numbers reaching out their hands to help him, and beating down the works to make him way. Being entered into the camp, and finding himself absolute master, he nevertheless treated Lepidus with the greatest civility, and gave him the title of Father, when he spoke to him, and, though he had everything at his own command, he left him the honor of being called the general. This fair usage brought over to him Munatius Plancus, who was not far off with a considerable force. Thus in great strength he repassed the Alps, leading with him into Italy seventeen legions and ten thousand horse, besides six legions which he left in garrison under the command of Varius, one of his familiar friends and boon companions, whom they used to call by the nickname of Cotylon.[2]

Cæsar, perceiving that Cicero's wishes were for liberty, had ceased to pay any further regard to him, and was now employing the mediation of his friends to come to a good understanding with Antony. They both met together with Lepidus in a small island, where the conference lasted three days. The empire was soon determined of, it being divided amongst them as if it had been their paternal inheritance. That which gave them all the trouble was to agree who should be put to death, each of them desiring to destroy his enemies and to save his friends. But, in the end, animosity to those they hated carried the day against respect for relations and affection for friends; and Cæsar sacrificed Cicero to Antony, Antony gave up his uncle Lucius Cæsar, and Lepidus received permission to murder his brother Paulus, or, as others say, yielded his brother to them. I do not believe anything ever took place more truly savage or barbarous than this composition, for, in this exchange of blood for blood, they were equally guilty of the lives they surrendered and of those they took; or, indeed more guilty in the case of their friends, for whose deaths they had not even the justification of hatred. To complete the reconciliation, the soldiery, coming about them, demanded that confirmation should be given to it by some alliance of marriage; Cæsar should marry Clodia, the daughter of Fulvia, wife to Antony. This also being agreed to, three hundred persons were put to death by proscription. Antony gave orders to those that were to kill Cicero, to cut off his head and right hand, with which he had written his invectives against him; and, when they were brought before him, he regarded them joyfully, actually bursting out more than once into laughter, and, when he had satiated

[2] From *Cotyle,* a cup.

himself with the sight of them, ordered them to be hung up above the speaker's place in the forum, thinking thus to insult the dead, while in fact he only exposed his own wanton arrogance, and his unworthiness to hold the power that fortune had given him. His uncle Lucius Cæsar, being closely pursued, took refuge with his sister, who, when the murderers had broken into her house and were pressing into her chamber, met them at the door, and, spreading out her hands, cried out several times, "You shall not kill Lucius Cæsar till you first dispatch me, who gave your general his birth;" and in this manner she succeeded in getting her brother out of the way, and saving his life.

This triumvirate was very hateful to the Romans, and Antony most of all bore the blame, because he was older than Cæsar, and had greater authority than Lepidus, and withal he was no sooner settled in his affairs, but he returned to his luxurious and dissolute way of living. Besides the ill reputation he gained by his general behavior, it was some considerable disadvantage to him his living in the house of Pompey the Great, who had been as much admired for his temperance and his sober, citizen-like habits of life, as ever he was for having triumphed three times. They could not without anger see the doors of that house shut against magistrates, officers, and envoys, who were shamefully refused admittance, while it was filled inside with players, jugglers, and drunken flatterers, upon whom were spent the greatest part of the wealth which violence and cruelty procured. For they did not limit themselves to the forfeiture of the estates of such as were proscribed, defrauding the widows and families, nor were they contented with laying on every possible kind of tax and imposition; but, hearing that several sums of money were, as well by strangers as citizens of Rome, deposited in the hands of the vestal virgins, they went and took the money away by force. When it was manifest that nothing would ever be enough for Antony, Cæsar at last called for a division of property. The army was also divided between them, upon their march into Macedonia to make war with Brutus and Cassius, Lepidus being left with the command of the city.

However, after they had crossed the sea and engaged in operations of war, encamping in front of the enemy, Antony opposite

Cassius, and Cæsar opposite Brutus, Cæsar did nothing worth relating, and all the success and victory were Antony's. In the first battle, Cæsar was completely routed by Brutus, his camp taken, he himself very narrowly escaping by flight. As he himself writes in his Memoirs, he retired before the battle, on account of a dream which one of his friends had. But Antony, on the other hand, defeated Cassius; though some have written that he was not actually present in the engagement, and only joined afterwards in the pursuit. Cassius was killed, at his own entreaty and order, by one of his most trusted freedmen, Pindarus, not being aware of Brutus's victory. After a few days' interval, they fought another battle, in which Brutus lost the day, and slew himself; and Cæsar being sick, Antony had almost all the honor of the victory. Standing over Brutus's dead body, he uttered a few words of reproach upon him for the death of his brother Caius, who had been executed by Brutus's order in Macedonia in revenge of Cicero; but, saying presently that Hortensius was most to blame for it, he gave order for his being slain upon his brother's tomb, and, throwing his own scarlet mantle, which was of great value, upon the body of Brutus, he gave charge to one of his own freedmen to take care of his funeral. This man, as Antony came to understand, did not leave the mantle with the corpse, but kept both it and a good part of the money that should have been spent in the funeral for himself; for which he had him put to death.

But Cæsar was conveyed to Rome, no one expecting that he would long survive. Antony, proposing to go to the eastern provinces to lay them under contribution, entered Greece with a large force. The promise had been made that every common soldier should receive for his pay five thousand drachmas; so it was likely there would be need of pretty severe taxing and levying to raise money. However, to the Greeks he showed at first reason and moderation enough; he gratified his love of amusement by hearing the learned men dispute, by seeing the games, and undergoing initiation; and in judicial matters he was equitable, taking pleasure in being styled a lover of Greece, but, above all, in being called a lover of Athens, to which city he made very considerable presents. The people of Megara wished to let him know that they also had something to show him, and invited him to come and see their senate-house. So he went and examined it, and on their asking him how he liked it, told them it was "not very large, but extremely *ruinous.*" At the same time, he had a survey made of the temple of the Pythian Apollo, as if he had designed to repair it, and indeed he had declared to the senate his intention so to do.

However, leaving Lucius Censorinus in Greece, he crossed over into Asia, and there laid his hands on the stores of accumulated wealth, while kings waited at his door, and queens were rivalling one another, who should make him the greatest presents or appear most charming in his eyes. Thus, whilst Cæsar in Rome was wearing out his strength amidst seditions and wars, Antony, with nothing to do amidst the enjoyments of peace, let his passions carry him easily back to the old course of life that was familiar to him. A set of harpers and pipers, Anaxenor and Xuthus, the dancing-man Metrodorus, and a whole Bacchic rout of the like Asiatic exhibitors, far outdoing in license and buffoonery the pests that had followed out of Italy, came in and possessed the court; the thing was past patience, wealth of all kinds being wasted on objects like these. The whole of Asia was like the city in Sophocles, loaded, at one time,

> "——— with incense in the air,
> Jubilant songs, and outcries of despair."

When he made his entry into Ephesus, the women met him dressed up like Bacchantes, and the men and boys like Satyrs and Fauns, and throughout the town nothing was to be seen but spears wreathed about with ivy, harps, flutes, and psaltries, while Antony in their songs was Bacchus the Giver of Joy and the Gentle. And so indeed he was to some, but to far more the Devourer and the Savage;[3] for he would deprive persons of worth and quality of their fortunes to gratify villains and flatterers, who would sometimes beg the estates of men yet living, pretending they were dead, and, obtaining a grant, take possession. He gave his cook the house of a Magnesian citizen, as a reward for a single highly successful supper, and, at last,

[3] "*Charidotes* and *Meilichius* in their songs, but too often, in reality, *Omestes* and *Agrionius.*" These are all epithets applied in various forms of worship to the Greek Dionysus or Bacchus. It was to Bacchus Omestes, the Devourer, that the Greeks, in the battle of Salamis, offered the Persian princes. See the story in the lives of Themistocles and Aristides.

when he was proceeding to lay a second whole tribute on Asia, Hybreas, speaking on behalf of the cities, took courage, and told him broadly, but aptly enough for Antony's taste, "If you can take two yearly tributes, you can doubtless give us a couple of summers, and a double harvest time;" and put it to him in the plainest and boldest way, that Asia had raised two hundred thousand talents for his service: "If this has not been paid to you, ask your collectors for it; if it has, and is all gone, we are ruined men." These words touched Antony to the quick, who was simply ignorant of most things that were done in his name; not that he was so indolent, as he was prone to trust frankly in all about him. For there was much simplicity in his character; he was slow to see his faults, but, when he did see them, was extremely repentant, and ready to ask pardon of those he had injured; prodigal in his acts of reparation, and severe in his punishments, but his generosity was much more extravagant than his severity; his raillery was sharp and insulting, but the edge of it was taken off by his readiness to submit to any kind of repartee; for he was as well contented to be rallied, as he was pleased to rally others. And this freedom of speech was, indeed, the cause of many of his disasters. He never imagined that those who used so much liberty in their mirth would flatter or deceive him in business of consequence, not knowing how common it is with parasites to mix their flattery with boldness, as confectioners do their sweetmeats with something biting, to prevent the sense of satiety. Their freedoms and impertinences at table were designed expressly to give to their obsequiousness in council the air of being not complaisance, but conviction.

Such being his temper, the last and crowning mischief that could befall him came in the love of Cleopatra, to awaken and kindle to fury passions that as yet lay still and dormant in his nature, and to stifle and finally corrupt any elements that yet made resistance in him, of goodness and a sound judgment. He fell into the snare thus. When making preparation for the Parthian war, he sent to command her to make her personal appearance in Cilicia, to answer an accusation, that she had given great assistance, in the late wars, to Cassius. Dellius, who was sent on this message, had no sooner seen her face, and remarked her adroitness and subtlety in speech, but he felt convinced that Antony would not so much as think of giving any molestation to a woman like this; on the contrary, she would be the first in favor with him. So he set himself at once to pay his court to the Egyptian, and gave her his advice, "to go," in the Homeric style, to Cilicia, "in her best attire,"[4] and bade her fear nothing from Antony, the gentlest and kindest of soldiers. She had some faith in the words of Dellius, but more in her own attractions, which, having formerly recommended her to Cæsar and the young Cnæus Pompey, she did not doubt might prove yet more successful with Antony. Their acquaintance was with her when a girl, young, and ignorant of the world, but she was to meet Antony in the time of life when women's beauty is most splendid, and their intellects are in full maturity.[5] She made great preparation for her journey, of money, gifts, and ornaments of value, such as so wealthy a kingdom might afford, but she brought with her her surest hopes in her own magic arts and charms.

She received several letters, both from Antony and from his friends, to summon her, but she took no account of these orders; and at last, as if in mockery of them, she came sailing up the river Cydnus, in a barge with gilded stern and outspread sails of purple, while oars of silver beat time to the music of flutes and fifes and harps. She herself lay all along, under a canopy of cloth of gold, dressed as Venus in a picture, and beautiful young boys, like painted Cupids, stood on each side to fan her. Her maids were dressed like Sea Nymphs and Graces, some steering at the rudder, some working at the ropes. The perfumes diffused themselves from the vessel to the shore, which was covered with multitudes, part following the galley up the river on either bank, part running out of the city to see the sight. The market-place was quite emptied, and Antony at last was left alone sitting upon the tribunal; while the word went through all the multitude, that Venus was come to feast with Bacchus, for the common good of Asia. On her arrival, Antony sent to invite her to supper. She thought it fitter he should come to her; so,

[4] "To go to Ida in her best attire" is the verse, in which Plutarch merely substitutes Cilicia for Ida. See the Iliad Book, XIV. 162, where Juno is described as setting forth to beguile Jupiter from his watch on Mount Ida, while Neptune shall check the Trojans.

[5] She was now about twenty-eight years old.

willing to show his good-humor and courtesy, he complied, and went. He found the preparation to receive him magnificent beyond expression, but nothing so admirable as the great number of lights; for on a sudden there was let down altogether so great a number of branches with lights in them so ingeniously disposed, some in squares, and some in circles, that the whole thing was a spectacle that has seldom been equalled for beauty.

The next day, Antony invited her to supper, and was very desirous to outdo her as well in magnificence as contrivance; but he found he was altogether beaten in both, and was so well convinced of it, that he was himself the first to jest and mock at his poverty of wit, and his rustic awkwardness. She, perceiving that his raillery was broad and gross, and savored more of the soldier than the courtier, rejoined in the same taste, and fell into it at once, without any sort of reluctance or reserve. For her actual beauty, it is said, was not in itself so remarkable that none could be compared with her, or that no one could see her without being struck by it, but the contact of her presence, if you lived with her, was irresistible; the attraction of her person, joining with the charm of her conversation, and the character that attended all she said or did, was something bewitching. It was a pleasure merely to hear the sound of her voice, with which, like an instrument of many strings, she could pass from one language to another; so that there were few of the barbarian nations that she answered by an interpreter; to most of them she spoke herself, as to the Æthiopians, Troglodytes, Hebrews, Arabians, Syrians, Medes, Parthians, and many others, whose language she had learnt; which was all the more surprising, because most of the kings her predecessors scarcely gave themselves the trouble to acquire the Egyptian tongue, and several of them quite abandoned the Macedonian.

Antony was so captivated by her, that, while Fulvia his wife maintained his quarrels in Rome against Cæsar by actual force of arms, and the Parthian troops, commanded by Labienus (the king's generals having made him commander-in-chief), were assembled in Mesopotamia, and ready to enter Syria, he could yet suffer himself to be carried away by her to Alexandria, there to keep holiday, like a boy, in play and diversion, squandering and fooling away in enjoyments that most costly, as Antiphon says, of all valuables, time. They had a sort of company, to which they gave a particular name, calling it that of the Inimitable Livers. The members entertained one another daily in turn, with an extravagance of expenditure beyond measure or belief. Philotas, a physician of Amphissa, who was at that time a student of medicine in Alexandria, used to tell my grandfather Lamprias, that, having some acquaintance with one of the royal cooks, he was invited by him, being a young man, to come and see the sumptuous preparations for supper. So he was taken into the kitchen, where he admired the prodigious variety of all things; but particularly, seeing eight wild boars roasting whole, says he, "Surely you have a great number of guests." The cook laughed at his simplicity, and told him there were not above twelve to sup, but that every dish was to be served up just roasted to a turn, and if any thing was but one minute ill-timed, it was spoiled; "And," said he, "maybe Antony will sup just now, maybe not this hour, maybe he will call for wine, or begin to talk, and will put it off. So that," he continued, "it is not one, but many suppers must be had in readiness, as it is impossible to guess at his hour." This was Philotas's story; who related besides, that he afterwards came to be one of the medical attendants of Antony's eldest son by Fulvia, and used to be invited pretty often, among other companions, to his table, when he was not supping with his father. One day another physician had talked loudly, and given great disturbance to the company, whose mouth Philotas stopped with this sophistical syllogism: "In some states of fever the patient should take cold water; every one who has a fever is in some state of fever; therefore in a fever cold water should always be taken." The man was quite struck dumb, and Antony's son, very much pleased, laughed aloud, and said, "Philotas, I make you a present of all you see there," pointing to a sideboard covered with plate. Philotas thanked him much, but was far enough from ever imagining that a boy of his age could dispose of things of that value. Soon after, however, the plate was all brought to him, and he was desired to set his mark upon it; and when he put it away from him, and was afraid to accept the present, "What ails the man?" said he that brought it; "do you know that he who gives you this is Antony's son, who is free to give it, if it were all gold? but if you will be advised by me, I would counsel you to accept of the value in money from us; for there may be amongst the rest some antique or famous piece of workmanship, which Antony would be sorry to part with." These anecdotes my grandfather told us Philotas used frequently to relate.

To return to Cleopatra; Plato admits four sorts of flattery,[6] but she had a thousand. Were Antony serious or disposed to mirth, she had at any moment some new delight or charm to meet his wishes; at every turn she was upon him, and let him escape her neither by day nor by night. She played at dice with him, drank with him, hunted with him; and when he exercised in arms, she was there to see. At night she would go rambling with him to disturb and torment people at their doors and windows, dressed like a servant-woman, for Antony also went in servant's disguise, and from these expeditions he often came home very scurvily answered, and sometimes even beaten severely, though most people guessed who it was. However, the Alexandrians in general liked it all well enough, and joined good humoredly and kindly in his frolic and play, saying they were much obliged to Antony for acting his tragic parts at Rome, and keeping his comedy for them. It would be trifling without end to be particular in his follies, but his fishing must not be forgotten. He went out one day to angle with Cleopatra, and, being so unfortunate as to catch nothing in the presence of his mistress, he gave secret orders to the fishermen to dive under water, and put fishes that had been already taken upon his hooks; and these he drew so fast that the Egyptian perceived it. But, feigning great admiration, she told everybody how dexterous Antony was, and invited them next day to come and see him again. So, when a number of them had come on board the fishing boats, as soon as he had let down his hook, one of her servants was beforehand with his divers, and fixed upon his hook a salted fish from Pontus. Antony,

[6] See the Gorgias, chapter 19. The four Flatteries are the four Counterfeit Arts, which profess to do good to men's bodies and souls, and in reality only gratify their pleasures. The legislator's place is thus usurped by the sophist, the false reasoner, in deliberative assemblies; that of the judge by the rhetorician or pleader; the medical adviser is supplanted by the purveyor of luxuries, and the gymnastic teacher by the adorner of the person. The four genuine Arts are *nomothetike, dicanike, iatrike,* and *gymnastike;* the four corresponding Flatteries are *sophistike, rhetorike, opsopoiike,* and *kommotike.*

feeling his line give drew up the prey, and when, as may be imagined, great laughter ensued, "Leave," said Cleopatra, "the fishing-rod, general, to us poor sovereigns of Pharos and Canopus; your game is cities, provinces, and kingdoms."

Whilst he was thus diverting himself and engaged in this boys' play, two despatches arrived; one from Rome, that his brother Lucius and his wife Fulvia, after many quarrels among themselves, had joined in war against Cæsar, and, having lost all, had fled out of Italy; the other bringing little better news, that Labienus, at the head of the Parthians, was overrunning Asia, from Euphrates and Syria as far as Lydia and Ionia. So, scarcely at last rousing himself from sleep, and shaking off the fumes of wine, he set out to attack the Parthians, and went as far as Phœnicia; but, upon the receipt of lamentable letters from Fulvia, turned his course with two hundred ships to Italy. And, in his way, receiving such of his friends as fled from Italy, he was given to understand that Fulvia was the sole cause of the war, a woman of a restless spirit and very bold, and withal her hopes were that commotions in Italy would force Antony from Cleopatra. But it happened that Fulvia, as she was coming to meet her husband, fell sick by the way, and died at Sicyon, so that an accommodation was the more easily made. For when he reached Italy, and Cæsar showed no intention of laying any thing to his charge, and he on his part shifted the blame of every thing on Fulvia, those that were friends to them would not suffer that the time should be spent in looking narrowly into the plea, but made a reconciliation first, and then a partition of the empire between them, taking as their boundary the Ionian Sea, the eastern provinces falling to Antony, to Cæsar the western, and Africa being left to Lepidus. And an agreement was made, that every one in their turn, as they thought fit, should make their friends consuls, when they did not choose to take the offices themselves.

These terms were well approved of, but yet it was thought some closer tie would be desirable; and for this, fortune offered occasion. Cæsar had an elder sister, not of the whole blood, for Attia was his mother's name, hers Ancharia. This sister, Octavia, he was extremely attached to, as, indeed, she was, it is said, quite a wonder of a woman. Her husband, Caius Marcellus, had died not long before, and Antony was now a widower by the death of Fulvia; for, though he did not disavow the passion he had for Cleopatra, yet he disowned any thing of marriage, reason, as yet, upon this point, still maintaining the debate against the charms of the Egyptian. Everybody concurred in promoting this new alliance, fully expecting that with the beauty, honor, and prudence of Octavia, when her company should, as it was certain it would, have engaged his affections, all would be kept in the safe and happy course of friendship. So, both parties being agreed, they went to Rome to celebrate the nuptials, the senate dispensing with the law by which a widow was not permitted to marry till ten months after the death of her husband.

Sextus Pompeius was in possession of Sicily, and with his ships, under the command of Menas, the pirate, and Menecrates, so infested the Italian coast, that no vessels durst venture into those seas. Sextus had behaved with much humanity towards Antony, having received his mother when she fled with Fulvia, and it was therefore judged fit that he also should be received into the peace. They met near the promontory of Misenum, by the mole of the port, Pompey having his fleet at anchor close by, and Antony and Cæsar their troops drawn up all along the shore. There it was concluded that Sextus should quietly enjoy the government of Sicily and Sardinia, he conditioning to scour the seas of all pirates, and to send so much corn every year to Rome.

This agreed on, they invited one another to supper, and by lot it fell to Pompey's turn to give the first entertainment, and Antony, asking where it was to be, "There," said he, pointing to the admiral-galley, a ship of six banks of oars, "that is the only house that Pompey is heir to of his father's."[7] And this he said, reflecting upon Antony, who was then in possession of his father's house. Having fixed the ship on her anchors, and formed a bridgeway from the promontory to conduct on board of her, he gave them a cordial welcome. And when they began to grow warm, and jests were passing freely on Antony and Cleopatra's loves, Menas, the pirate, whispered Pompey in the ear, "Shall I," said he, "cut the cables, and make you master not of Sicily only and Sardinia, but of the whole Roman

[7] "In Carinis," according to Dion Cassius, was the answer. "In the Carinæ," which might mean either the ships, or the quarter called the Carinæ, at Rome, in which stood his father's house.

empire?" Pompey, having considered a little while, returned him answer, "Menas, this might have been done without acquainting me; now we must rest content; I do not break my word." And so, having been entertained by the other two in their turns, he set sail for Sicily.

After the treaty was completed, Antony despatched Ventidius into Asia, to check the advance of the Parthians, while he, as a compliment to Cæsar, accepted the office of priest to the deceased Cæsar. And in any state affair and matter of consequence, they both behaved themselves with much consideration and friendliness for each other. But it annoyed Antony, that in all their amusements, on any trial of skill or fortune, Cæsar should be constantly victorious. He had with him an Egyptian diviner, one of those who calculate nativities, who, either to make his court to Cleopatra, or that by the rules of his art he found it to be so, openly declared to him, that though the fortune that attended him was bright and glorious, yet it was overshadowed by Cæsar's; and advised him to keep himself as far distant as he could from that young man; "for your Genius," said he, "dreads his; when absent from him yours is proud and brave, but in his presence unmanly and dejected;" and incidents that occurred appeared to show that the Egyptian spoke truth. For whenever they cast lots for any playful purpose, or threw dice, Antony was still the loser; and repeatedly, when they fought game-cocks or quails, Cæsar's had the victory. This gave Antony a secret displeasure, and made him put the more confidence in the skill of his Egyptian. So, leaving the management of his home affairs to Cæsar, he left Italy, and took Octavia, who had lately borne him a daughter, along with him into Greece.

Here, whilst he wintered in Athens, he received the first news of Ventidius's successes over the Parthians, of his having defeated them in a battle, having slain Labienus and Pharnapates, the best general their king, Hyrodes, possessed. For the celebrating of which he made a public feast through Greece, and for the prizes which were contested at Athens he himself acted as steward, and, leaving at home the ensigns that are carried before the general, he made his public appearance in a gown and white shoes, with the steward's wands marching before; and he performed his duty in taking the combatants by the neck, to part them, when they had fought enough.

When the time came for him to set out for the war, he took a garland from the sacred olive, and, in obedience to some oracle, he filled a vessel with the water of the Clepsydra,[8] to carry along with him. In this interval, Pacorus, the Parthian king's son, who was marching into Syria with a large army, was met by Ventidius, who gave him battle in the country of Cyrrhestica, slew a large number of his men, and Pacorus among the first. This victory was one of the most renowned achievements of the Romans, and fully avenged their defeats under Crassus, the Parthians being obliged, after the loss of three battles successively, to keep themselves within the bounds of Media and Mesopotamia. Ventidius was not willing to push his good fortune further, for fear of raising some jealousy in Antony, but, turning his arms against those that had quitted the Roman interest, he reduced them to their former obedience. Among the rest, he besieged Antiochus, king of Commagene, in the city of Samosata, who made an offer of a thousand talents for his pardon, and a promise of submission to Antony's commands. But Ventidius told him that he must send to Antony, who was already on his march, and had sent word to Ventidius to make no terms with Antiochus, wishing that at any rate this one exploit might be ascribed to him, and that people might not think that all his successes were won by his lieutenants. The siege, however, was long protracted; for when those within found their offers refused, they defended themselves stoutly, till, at last, Antony, finding he was doing nothing, in shame and regret for having refused the first offer, was glad to make an accommodation with Antiochus for three hundred talents. And, having given some orders for the affairs of Syria, he returned to Athens; and, paying Ventidius the honors he well deserved, dismissed him to receive his triumph. He is the only man that has ever yet triumphed for victories obtained over the Parthians; he was of obscure birth, but, by means of Antony's friendship, obtained an opportunity of showing his capacity, and doing great things; and his making such glorious use of it gave new credit to the current observation about Cæsar and Antony, that they were more fortu-

[8] The Clepsydra was a sacred spring, still to be found, inclosed in a chapel in the rock, on the north side of the Acropolis, near the cave of Apollo and Pan.

nate in what they did by their lieutenants than in their own persons. For Sossius, also, had great success, and Canidius, whom he left in Armenia, defeated the people there, and also the kings of the Albanians and Iberians, and marched victorious as far as Caucasus, by which means the fame of Antony's arms had become great among the barbarous nations.

He, however, once more, upon some unfavorable stories, taking offence against Cæsar, set sail with three hundred ships for Italy, and, being refused admittance to the port of Brundusium, made for Tarentum. There his wife Octavia, who came from Greece with him, obtained leave to visit her brother, she being then great with child, having already borne her husband a second daughter; and as she was on her way, she met Cæsar, with his two friends Agrippa and Mæcenas, and, taking these two aside, with great entreaties and lamentations she told them, that of the most fortunate woman upon earth, she was in danger of becoming the most unhappy; for as yet every one's eyes were fixed upon her as the wife and sister of the two great commanders, but, if rash counsels should prevail, and war ensue, "I shall be miserable," said she, "without redress; for on what side soever victory falls, I shall be sure to be a loser." Cæsar was overcome by these entreaties, and advanced in a peaceable temper to Tarentum, where those that were present beheld a most stately spectacle; a vast army drawn up by the shore, and as great a fleet in the harbor, all without the occurrence of any act of hostility; nothing but the salutations of friends, and other expressions of joy and kindness, passing from one armament to the other. Antony first entertained Cæsar, this also being a concession on Cæsar's part to his sister; and when at length an agreement was made between them, that Cæsar should give Antony two of his legions to serve him in the Parthian war, and that Antony should in return leave with him a hundred armed galleys, Octavia further obtained of her husband, besides this, twenty light ships for her brother, and of her brother, a thousand foot for her husband. So, having parted good friends, Cæsar went immediately to make war with Pompey to conquer Sicily. And Antony, leaving in Cæsar's charge his wife and children, and his children by his former wife Fulvia, set sail for Asia.

But the mischief that thus long had lain still, the passion for Cleopatra, which better thoughts had seemed to have lulled and charmed into oblivion, upon his approach to Syria, gathered strength again, and broke out into a flame. And, in fine, like Plato's restive and rebellious horse of the human soul,[9] flinging off all good and wholesome counsel, and breaking fairly loose, he sends Fonteius Capito to bring Cleopatra into Syria. To whom at her arrival he made no small or trifling present, Phœnicia, Cœle-Syria, Cyprus, great part of Cilicia, that side of Judæa which produces balm, that part of Arabia where the Nabathæans extend to the outer sea; profuse gifts, which much displeased the Romans. For, although he had invested several private persons in great governments and kingdoms, and bereaved many kings of theirs, as Antigonus of Judæa, whose head he caused to be struck off (the first example of that punishment being inflicted on a king), yet nothing stung the Romans like the shame of these honors paid to Cleopatra. Their dissatisfaction was augmented also by his acknowledging as his own the twin children he had by her, giving them the name of Alexander and Cleopatra, and adding, as their surnames, the titles of Sun and Moon. But he, who knew how to put a good color on the most dishonest action, would say, that the greatness of the Roman empire consisted more in giving than in taking kingdoms, and that the way to carry noble blood through the world was by begetting in every place a new line and series of kings; his own ancestor had thus been born of Hercules; Hercules had not limited his hopes of progeny to a single womb, nor feared any law like Solon's, or any audit of procreation, but had freely let nature take her will in the foundation and first commencement of many families.

After Phraates had killed his father Hyrodes, and taken possession of his kingdom, many of the Parthians left their country; among the rest, Monæses, a man of great distinction and authority, sought refuge with Antony, who, looking on his case as similar to that of Themistocles, and likening his own opulence and magnanim-

[9] The soul of man has in it a driver and two horses, the one strong and willing, quick to obey, and eager for applause and for honorable praise; the other unruly and ill-conditioned, greedy and violent, whom only flogging and the goad can control. Do what the driver within us will, our better horse may be seduced at times from his duty, his evil yoke-fellow may obtain the mastery, and bear away all to destruction.

ity to those of the former Persian kings, gave him three cities, Larissa, Arethusa, and Hierapolis, which was formerly called Bambyce. But when the king of Parthia soon recalled him, giving him his word and honor for his safety, Antony was not unwilling to give him leave to return, hoping thereby to surprise Phraates, who would believe that peace would continue; for he only made the demand of him, that he should send back the Roman ensigns which were taken when Crassus was slain, and the prisoners that remained yet alive. This done, he sent Cleopatra into Egypt, and marched through Arabia and Armenia; and, when his forces came together, and were joined by those of his confederate kings (of whom there were very many, and the most considerable, Artavasdes, king of Armenia, who came at the head of six thousand horse and seven thousand foot), he made a general muster. There appeared sixty thousand Roman foot, ten thousand horse, Spaniards and Gauls, who counted as Romans; and, of other nations, horse and foot, thirty thousand. And these great preparations, that put the Indians beyond Bactria into alarm, and made all Asia shake, were all, we are told, rendered useless to him because of Cleopatra. For, in order to pass the winter with her, the war was pushed on before its due time; and all he did was done without perfect consideration, as by a man who had no proper control over his faculties, who, under the effects of some drug or magic, was still looking back elsewhere, and whose object was much more to hasten his return than to conquer his enemies.

For, first of all, when he should have taken up his winter-quarters in Armenia, to refresh his men, who were tired with long marches, having come at least eight thousand furlongs, and then have taken the advantage in the beginning of the spring to invade Media, before the Parthians were out of winter-quarters, he had not patience to expect his time, but marched into the province of Atropatene, leaving Armenia on the left hand, and laid waste all that country. Secondly, his haste was so great, that he left behind the engines absolutely required for any siege, which followed the camp in three hundred wagons, and, among the rest, a ram eighty feet long; none of which was it possible, if lost or damaged, to repair or to make the like, as the provinces of the upper Asia produce no trees long or hard enough for such uses. Nevertheless, he left them all behind, as a mere impediment to his speed, in the charge of a detachment under the command of Statianus, the wagon-officer. He himself laid siege to Phraata, a principal city of the king of Media, wherein were that king's wife and children. And when actual need proved the greatness of his error in leaving the siege train behind him, he had nothing for it but to come up and raise a mound against the walls, with infinite labor and great loss of time. Meantime Phraates, coming down with a large army, and hearing that the wagons were left behind with the battering engines, sent a strong party of horse, by which Statianus was surprised, he himself and ten thousand of his men slain, the engines all broken in pieces, many taken prisoners, and, among the rest, king Polemon.

This great miscarriage in the opening of the campaign much discouraged Antony's army, and Artavasdes, king of Armenia, deciding that the Roman prospects were bad, withdrew with all his forces from the camp, although he had been the chief promoter of the war. The Parthians, encouraged by their success, came up to the Romans at the siege, and gave them many affronts; upon which Antony, fearing that the despondency and alarm of his soldiers would only grow worse if he let them lie idle, taking all the horse, ten legions, and three prætorian cohorts of heavy infantry, resolved to go out and forage, designing by this means to draw the enemy with more advantage to a battle. To effect this, he marched a day's journey from his camp, and, finding the Parthians hovering about, in readiness to attack him while he was in motion, he gave orders for the signal of battle to be hung out in the encampment, but, at the same time, pulled down the tents, as if he meant not to fight, but to lead his men home again; and so he proceeded to lead them past the enemy, who were drawn up in a half-moon, his orders being that the horse should charge as soon as the legions were come up near enough to second them. The Parthians, standing still while the Romans marched by them, were in great admiration of their army, and of the exact discipline it observed, rank after rank passing on at equal distances in perfect order and silence, their pikes all ready in their hands. But when the signal was given, and the horse turned short upon the Parthians, and with loud cries charged them, they bravely received them, though they were at once too near for bowshot; but the legions, coming up with loud shouts and rattling of their arms, so frightened their horses and indeed the men themselves, that they kept their ground no longer. Antony pressed them hard, in great hopes that this victory should put an end to the war; the foot had them in pursuit for fifty furlongs, and the horse for thrice that distance, and yet, the advantage summed up, they had but thirty prisoners, and there were but fourscore slain. So that they were all filled with dejection and discouragement, to consider, that when they were victorious, their advantage was so small, and that when they were beaten, they lost so great a number of men as they had done when the carriages were taken.

The next day, having put the baggage in order, they marched back to the camp before Phraata, in the way meeting with some scattering troops of the enemy, and, as they marched further, with greater parties, at length with the body of the enemy's army, fresh and in good order, who defied them to battle, and charged them on every side, and it was not without great difficulty that they reached the camp. There Antony, finding that his men had in a panic deserted the defence of the mound, upon a sally of the Medes, resolved to proceed against them by decimation, as it is called, which is done by dividing the soldiers into tens, and, out of every ten, putting one to death, as it happens by lot. The rest he gave orders should have, instead of wheat, their rations of corn and barley.

The war was now become grievous to both parties, and the prospect of its continuance yet more fearful to Antony, in respect that he was threatened with famine; for he could no longer forage without wounds and slaughter. And Phraates, on the other side, was full of apprehension that, if the Romans were to persist in carrying on the siege, the autumnal equinox being past and the air already closing in for cold, he should be deserted by his soldiers, who would suffer any thing rather than wintering in open field. To prevent which, he had recourse to the following deceit: he gave orders to those of his men who had made most acquaintance among the Roman soldiers, not to pursue too close when they met them foraging, but to suffer them to carry off some provision; moreover, that they should praise their valor, and declare that it was not without just reason that their king looked upon the Romans as the bravest men in the world. This done, upon further opportunity they rode nearer in, and, drawing up their horses by the men, began to revile Antony for his obstinacy; that whereas Phraates desired nothing more than peace, and an occasion to show how ready he was to save the lives of so many brave soldiers, he, on the contrary, gave no opening to any friendly offers, but sat awaiting the arrival of the two fiercest and worst enemies, winter and famine, from whom it would be hard for them to make their escape, even with all the good-will of the Parthians to help them. Antony, having these reports from many hands, began to indulge the hope; nevertheless, he would not send any message to the Parthian till he had put the question to these friendly talkers, whether what they said was said by orders of their king. Receiving answer that it was, together with new encouragement to believe them, he sent some of his friends to demand once more the standards and prisoners, lest, if he should ask nothing, he might be supposed to be too thankful to have leave to retreat in quiet. The Parthian king made answer, that as for the standards and prisoners, he need not trouble himself; but if he thought fit to retreat, he might do it when he pleased, in peace and safety. Some few days, therefore, being spent in collecting the baggage, he set out upon his march. On which occasion, though there was no man of his time like him for addressing a multitude, or for carrying soldiers with him by the force of words, out of shame and sadness he could not find in his heart to speak himself, but employed Domitius Ænobarbus. And some of the soldiers resented it, as an undervaluing of them; but the greater number saw the true cause, and pitied it, and thought it rather a reason why they on their side should treat their general with more respect and obedience than ordinary.

Antony had resolved to return by the same way he came, which was through a level country clear of all trees; but a certain Mardian came to him (one that was very conversant with the manners of the Parthians, and whose fidelity to the Romans had been tried at the battle where the machines were lost), and advised him to keep the mountains close on his right hand, and not to expose his men, heavily armed, in a broad, open, riding country, to the attacks of a numerous army of light-horse and archers; that Phraates with fair promises had persuaded him from the siege on purpose that he might with more ease cut him off in his retreat; but, if so he pleased, he would conduct him by a nearer route, on which moreover he should find the necessaries for his army in greater abundance. Antony upon this began to consider what was best to be done; he was unwilling to seem to have any mistrust of the Parthians after their treaty; but, holding it to be really best to march his army the shorter and more inhabited way, he demanded of the Mardian some assurance of his faith, who offered himself to be bound until the army came safe into Armenia. Two days he conducted the army bound, and, on the third, when Antony had given up all thought of the enemy, and was marching at his ease in no very good order, the Mardian, perceiving the bank of a river broken down, and the water let out and overflowing the road by which they were to pass, saw at once that this was the handiwork of the Parthians, done out of mischief, and to hinder their march; so he advised Antony to be upon his guard, for that the enemy was nigh at hand. And no sooner had he begun to put his men in order, disposing the slingers and dart-men in convenient intervals for sallying out, but the Parthians came pouring in on all sides, fully expecting to encompass them, and throw the whole army into disorder. They were at once attacked by the light troops, whom they galled a good deal with their arrows; but, being themselves as warmly entertained with the slings and darts, and many wounded, they made their retreat. Soon after, rallying up afresh, they were beat back by a battalion of Gallic horse, and appeared no more that day.

By their manner of attack Antony seeing what to do, not only placed the slings and darts as a rear guard, but also lined both flanks with them, and so marched in a square battle, giving order to the horse to charge and beat off the enemy, but not to follow them far as they retired. So that the Parthians, not doing more mischief for the four ensuing days than they received, began to abate in their zeal, and, complaining that the winter season was much advanced, pressed for returning home.

But, on the fifth day, Flavius Gallus, a brave and active officer, who had a considerable command in the army, came to Antony, desiring of him some light-infantry out of the rear, and some horse out of the front, with which he would undertake to do some considerable service. Which when he had obtained, he beat the enemy back, not withdrawing, as was usual, at the same time, and retreating upon the mass of the heavy infantry, but maintaining his own ground, and engaging boldly. The officers who commanded in the rear, perceiving how far he was getting from the body of the army, sent to warn him back, but he took no notice of them. It is said that Titius the quæstor snatched the standards and turned them round, upbraiding Gallus with thus leading so many brave men to destruction. But when he on the other side reviled him again, and commanded the men that were about him to stand firm, Titius made his retreat, and Gallus, charging the enemies in the front, was encompassed by a party that fell upon his rear, which at length perceiving, he sent a messenger to demand succor. But the commanders of the heavy infantry, Canidius amongst others, a particular favorite of Antony's, seem here to have committed a great oversight. For, instead of facing about with the whole body, they sent small parties, and, when they were defeated, they still sent out small parties, so that by their bad management the rout would have spread through the whole army, if Antony himself had not marched from the van at the head of the third legion, and, passing this through among the fugitives, faced the enemies, and hindered them from any further pursuit.

In this engagement were killed three thousand, five thousand were carried back to the camp wounded, amongst the rest Gallus, shot through the body with four arrows, of which wounds he died. Antony went from tent to tent to visit and comfort the rest of them, and was not able to see his men without tears and a passion of grief. They, however, seized his hand with joyful faces, bidding him go and see to himself and not be concerned about them, calling him their emperor and their general, and saying that if he did well they were safe. For in short, never in all these times can history make mention of a general at the head of a more splendid army; whether you consider strength and youth, or patience and sufferance in labors and fatigues; but as for the obedience and affectionate respect they bore their general, and the unanimous feeling amongst small and great alike, officers and common soldiers, to prefer his good opinion of them to their very lives and being, in this part of military excellence it was not possible that they could have been surpassed by the very Romans of old. For this devotion, as I have said before, there were many reasons, as the nobility of his family, his eloquence, his frank and open manners, his liberal and magnificent habits, his familiarity in talking with everybody, and, at this time particularly, his kindness in assisting and pitying the sick, joining in all their pains, and furnishing them with all things necessary, so that the sick and wounded were even more eager to serve than those that were whole and strong.

Nevertheless, this last victory had so encouraged the enemy, that, instead of their former impatience and weariness, they began soon to feel contempt for the Romans, staying all night near the camp, in expectation of plundering their tents and baggage, which they concluded they must abandon; and in the morning new forces arrived in large masses, so that their number was grown to be not less, it is said, than forty thousand horse; and the king had sent the very guards that attended upon his own person, as to a sure and unquestioned victory. For he himself was never present in any fight. Antony, designing to harangue the soldiers, called for a mourning habit, that he might move them the more, but was dissuaded by his friends; so he came forward in the general's scarlet cloak, and addressed them, praising those that had gained the victory, and reproaching those that had fled, the former answering him with promises of success, and the latter excusing themselves, and telling him they were ready to undergo decimation, or any other punishment he should please to inflict upon them, only entreating that he would forget and not discompose himself with their faults. At which he lifted up his hands to heaven, and prayed the gods, that if to balance the great favors he had received of them any judgment lay in store, they would pour it upon his head alone, and grant his soldiers victory.

The next day they took better order for their march, and the Parthians, who thought they were marching rather to plunder than to fight, were much taken aback, when they came up and were received with a shower of missiles, to find the enemy not disheartened, but fresh and resolute. So that they themselves began to lose courage.

But at the descent of a hill where the Romans were obliged to pass, they got together, and let fly their arrows upon them as they moved slowly down. But the full-armed infantry, facing round, received the light troops within; and those in the first rank knelt on one knee, holding their shields before them, the next rank holding theirs over the first, and so again others over these, much like the tiling of a house, or the rows of seats in a theatre, the whole affording sure defence against arrows, which glance upon them without doing any harm. The Parthians, seeing the Romans down upon their knees, could not imagine but that it must proceed from weariness; so that they laid down their bows, and taking their spears, made a fierce onset, when the Romans, with a great cry, leapt upon their feet, striking hand to hand with their javelins, slew the foremost, and put the rest to flight. After this rate it was every day, and the trouble they gave made the marches short; in addition to which famine began to be felt in the camp, for they could get but little corn, and that which they got they were forced to fight for; and, besides this, they were in want of implements to grind it and make bread. For they had left almost all behind, the baggage horses being dead or otherwise employed in carrying the sick and wounded. Provision was so scarce in the army that an Attic quart of wheat sold for fifty drachmas, and barley loaves for their weight in silver. And when they tried vegetables and roots, they found such as are commonly eaten very scarce, so that they were constrained to venture upon any they could get, and, among others, they chanced upon an herb that was mortal, first taking away all sense, and understanding. He that had eaten of it remembered nothing in the world, and employed himself only in moving great stones from one place to another, which he did with as much earnestness and industry as if it had been a business of the greatest consequence. Through all the camp there was nothing to be seen but men grubbing upon the ground at stones, which they carried from place to place. But in the end they threw up bile and died, as wine, moreover, which was the one antidote, failed. When Antony saw them die so fast, and the Parthian still in pursuit, he was heard to exclaim several times over, "O, the Ten Thousand!" as if in admiration of the retreat of the Greeks with Xenophon, who, when they had a longer journey to make from

Babylonia, and a more powerful enemy to deal with, nevertheless came home safe.

The Parthians, finding that they could not divide the Roman army, nor break the order of their battle, and that withal they had been so often worsted, once more began to treat the foragers with professions of humanity; they came up to them with their bows unbended, telling them that they were going home to their houses; that this was the end of their retaliation, and that only some Median troops would follow for two or three days, not with any design to annoy them, but for the defence of some of the villages further on. And, saying this, they saluted them and embraced them with a great show of friendship. This made the Romans full of confidence again, and Antony, on hearing of it, was more disposed to take the road through the level country, being told that no water was to be hoped for on that through the mountains. But while he was preparing thus to do, Mithridates came into the camp, a cousin to Monæses, of whom we related that he sought refuge with the Romans, and received in gift from Antony the three cities. Upon his arrival, he desired somebody might be brought to him that could speak Syriac or Parthian. One Alexander, of Antioch, a friend of Antony's was brought to him, to whom the stranger, giving his name, and mentioning Monæses as the person who desired to do the kindness, put the question, did he see that high range of hills, pointing at some distance. He told him yes. "It is there," said he, "the whole Parthian army lie in wait for your passage; for the great plains come immediately up to them, and they expect that, confiding in their promises, you will leave the way of the mountains, and take the level route. It is true that in passing over the mountains you will suffer the want of water, and the fatigue to which you have become familiar, but if you pass through the plains, Antony must expect the fortune of Crassus."

This said, he departed. Antony, in alarm, calling his friends in council, sent for the Mardian guide, who was of the same opinion. He told them that, with or without enemies, the want of any certain track in the plain, and the likelihood of their losing their way, were quite objection enough; the other route was rough and without water, but then it was but for a day. Antony, therefore, changing his mind, marched away upon this road that night, commanding that every one should carry water sufficient for his own use; but most of them being unprovided with vessels, they made shift with their helmets, and some with skins. As soon as they started, the news of it was carried to the Parthians, who followed them, contrary to their custom, through the night, and at sunrise attacked the rear, which was tired with marching and want of sleep, and not in condition to make any considerable defence. For they had got through two hundred and forty furlongs that night, and at the end of such a march to find the enemy at their heels, put them out of heart. Besides, having to fight for every step of the way increased their distress from thirst. Those that were in the van came up to a river, the water of which was extremely cool and clear, but brackish and medicinal, and, on being drunk, produced immediate pains in the bowels and a renewed thirst. Of this the Mardian had forewarned them, but they could not forbear, and, beating back those that opposed them, they drank of it. Antony ran from one place to another, begging they would have a little patience, that not far off there was a river of wholesome water, and that the rest of the way was so difficult for the horse, that the enemy could pursue them no further; and, saying this, he ordered to sound a retreat to call those back that were engaged, and commanded the tents should be set up, that the soldiers might at any rate refresh themselves in the shade.

But the tents were scarce well put up, and the Parthians beginning, according to their custom, to withdraw, when Mithridates came again to them, and informed Alexander, with whom he had before spoken, that he would do well to advise Antony to stay where he was no longer than needs he must, that, after having refreshed his troops, he should endeavor with all diligence to gain the next river, that the Parthians would not cross it, but so far they were resolved to follow them. Alexander made his report to Antony, who ordered a quantity of gold plate to be carried to Mithridates, who, taking as much as he could well hide under his clothes, went his way. And, upon this advice, Antony, while it was yet day, broke up his camp, and the whole army marched forward without receiving any molestation from the Parthians, though that night by their own doing was in effect the most wretched and terrible that they passed. For some of the men began to kill and plunder those whom they suspected to have any money, ransacked the baggage, and seized the money there. In the end, they laid hands on Antony's own equipage, and broke all his rich tables and cups, dividing the fragments amongst them. Antony, hearing such a noise and such a stirring to and fro all through the army, the belief prevailing that the enemy had routed and cut off a portion of the troops, called for one of his freedmen, then serving as one of his guards, Rhamnus by name, and made him take an oath that, whenever he should give him orders, he would run his sword through his body and cut off his head, that he might not fall alive into the hands of the Parthians, nor, when dead, be recognized as the general. While he was in this consternation, and all his friends about him in tears, the Mardian came up, and gave them all new life. He convinced them, by the coolness and humidity of the air, which they could feel in breathing it, that the river which he had spoken of was now not far off, and the calculation of the time that had been required to reach it came, he said, to the same result, for the night was almost spent. And, at the same time, others came with information that all the confusion in the camp proceeded only from their own violence and robbery among themselves. To compose this tumult, and bring them again into some order after their distraction, he commanded the signal to be given for a halt.

Day began to break, and quiet and regularity were just reappearing, when the Parthian arrows began to fly among the rear, and the light armed troops were ordered out to battle. And, being seconded by the heavy infantry, who covered one another as before described with their shields, they bravely received the enemy, who did not think convenient to advance any further, while the van of the army, marching forward leisurely in this manner came in sight of the river, and Antony, drawing up the cavalry on the banks to confront the enemy, first passed over the sick and wounded. And, by this time, even those who were engaged with the enemy had opportunity to drink at their ease; for the Parthians, on seeing the river, unbent their bows, and told the Romans they might pass over freely, and made them great compliments in praise of their valor. Having crossed without molestation, they rested themselves awhile, and presently went forward, not giving perfect credit to the fair words of their enemies. Six days after this last battle, they arrived at the river Araxes, which divides Media and Armenia, and seemed, both by its deepness and the violence of the current, to be very dangerous to pass. A report, also, had crept in amongst them, that the enemy was in ambush, ready to set upon them as soon as they should be occupied with their passage. But when they were got over on the other side, and found themselves in Armenia, just as if land was now sighted after a storm at sea, they kissed the ground for joy, shedding tears and embracing each other in their delight. But taking their journey through a land that abounded in all sorts of plenty, they ate, after their long want, with that excess of every thing they met with, that they suffered from dropsies and dysenteries.

Here Antony, making a review of his army, found that he had lost twenty thousand foot and four thousand horse, of which the better half perished, not by the enemy, but by diseases. Their march was of twenty-seven days from Phraata, during which they had beaten the Parthians in eighteen battles, though with little effect or lasting result, because of their being so unable to pursue. By which it is manifest that it was Artavasdes who lost Antony the benefit of the expedition. For had the sixteen thousand horsemen whom he led away out of Media, armed in the same style as the Parthians and accustomed to their manner of fight, been there to follow the pursuit when the Romans put them to flight, it is impossible they could have rallied so often after their defeats, and reappeared again as they did to renew their attacks. For this reason, the whole army was very earnest with Antony to march into Armenia to take revenge. But he, with more reflection, forbore to notice the desertion, and continued all his former courtesies, feeling that the army was wearied out, and in want of all manner of necessaries. Afterwards, however, entering Armenia, with invitations and fair promises he prevailed upon Artavasdes to meet him, when he seized him, bound him, and carried him to Alexandria, and there led him in a triumph; one of the things which most offended the Romans, who felt as if all the honors and solemn observances of their country were, for Cleopatra's sake, handed over to the Egyptians.

This, however, was at an after time. For the present, marching his army in great haste in the depth of winter through continual storms of snow, he lost eight thousand of his men, and came with much diminished numbers to a place called the White Village, between Sidon and Berytus, on the sea-coast, where he waited for the arrival of Cleopatra. And, being impatient of the delay she made, he bethought himself of shortening the time in wine and drunkenness, and yet could not endure the tediousness of a meal, but would start from table and run to see if she were coming. Till at last she came into port, and brought with her clothes and money for the soldiers. Though some say that Antony only received the clothes from her and distributed his own money in her name.

A quarrel presently happened between the king of Media and Phraates of Parthia, beginning, it is said, about the division of the booty that was taken from the Romans, and creating great apprehension in the Median lest he should lose his kingdom. He sent, therefore, ambassadors to Antony, with offers of entering into a confederate war against Phraates. And Antony, full of hopes at being thus asked, as a favor, to accept that one thing, horse and archers, the want of which had hindered his beating the Parthians before, began at once to prepare for a return to Armenia, there to join the Medes on the Araxes, and begin the war afresh. But Octavia, in Rome, being desirous to see Antony, asked Cæsar's leave to go to him; which he gave her, not so much, say most authors, to gratify his sister, as to obtain a fair pretence to begin the war upon her dishonorable reception. She no sooner arrived at Athens, but by letters from Antony she was informed of his new expedition, and his will that she should await him there. And, though she were much displeased, not being ignorant of the real reason of this usage, yet she wrote to him to know to what place he would be pleased she should send the things she had brought with her for his use; for she had brought clothes for his soldiers, baggage, cattle, money, and presents for his friends and officers, and two thousand chosen soldiers sumptuously armed, to form prætorian cohorts. This message was brought from Octavia to Antony by Niger, one of his friends, who added to it the praises she deserved so well. Cleopatra, feeling her rival already, as it were, at hand, was seized with fear, lest if to her noble life and her high alliance, she once could add the charm of daily habit and affectionate intercourse, she should become irresistible, and be his absolute mistress for ever. So she feigned to be dying for love of Antony, bringing her body down by slender diet; when he entered the room, she fixed her eyes upon him in a rapture, and when he left, seemed to languish and half faint away. She took great pains that he should see her in tears, and, as soon as he noticed it, hastily dried them up and turned away, as if it were her wish that he should know nothing of it. All this was acting while he prepared for Media; and Cleopatra's creatures were not slow to forward the design, upbraiding Antony with his unfeeling, hard-hearted temper, thus letting a woman perish whose soul depended upon him and him alone. Octavia, it was true, was his wife, and had been married to him because it was found convenient for the affairs of her brother that it should be so, and she had the honor of the title; but Cleopatra, the sovereign queen of many nations, had been contented with the name of his mistress, nor did she shun or despise the character whilst she might see him, might live with him, and enjoy him; if she were bereaved of this, she would not survive the loss. In fine, they so melted and unmanned him, that, fully believing she would die if he forsook her, he put off the war and returned to Alexandria, deferring his Median expedition until next summer, though news came of the Parthians being all in confusion with intestine disputes. Nevertheless, he did some time after go into that country, and made an alliance with the king of Media, by marriage of a son of his by Cleopatra to the king's daughter, who was yet very young; and so returned, with his thoughts taken up about the civil war.

When Octavia returned from Athens, Cæsar, who considered she had been injuriously treated, commanded her to live in a separate house; but she refused to leave the house of her husband, and entreated him, unless he had already resolved, upon other motives, to make war with Antony, that he would on her account let it alone; it would be intolerable to have it said of the two greatest commanders in the world, that they had involved the Roman people in a civil war, the one out of passion for, the other out of resentment about, a woman. And her behavior proved her words to be sincere. She remained in Antony's house as if he were at home in it, and took the noblest and most generous care, not only of his children by her, but of those by Fulvia also. She received all the friends of Antony that came to Rome to seek office or upon any business, and did her utmost to prefer their requests to Cæsar; yet this her honorable deportment did but, without her meaning it, damage the reputation of Antony; the wrong he did to such a woman made him hated. Nor was the division he made among his sons at Alexandria less unpopular; it seemed a theatrical piece of insolence and contempt of his country. For, assembling the people in the exercise ground, and causing two golden thrones to be placed on a platform of silver, the one for him and the other for Cleopatra, and at their feet lower thrones for their children, he proclaimed Cleopatra queen of Egypt, Cyprus, Libya, and Cœle-Syria, and with her conjointly Cæsarion, the reputed son of the former Cæsar, who left Cleopatra with child. His own sons by Cleopatra were to have the style of kings of kings; to Alexander he gave Armenia and Media, with Parthia, so soon as it should be overcome; to Ptolemy, Phœnicia, Syria, and Cilicia. Alexander was brought out before the people in the Median costume, the tiara and upright peak, and Ptolemy, in boots and mantle and Macedonian cap done about with the diadem; for this was the habit of the successors of Alexander, as the other was of the Medes and Armenians. And, as soon as they had saluted their parents, the one was received by a guard of Macedonians, the other by one of Armenians. Cleopatra was then, as at other times when she appeared in public, dressed in the habit of the goddess Isis, and gave audience to the people under the name of the New Isis.

Cæsar, relating these things in the senate, and often complaining to the people, excited men's minds against Antony. And Antony also sent messages of accusation against Cæsar. The principal of his charges were these: first, that he had not made any division with him of Sicily, which was lately taken from Pompey; secondly, that he had retained the ships he had lent him for the war; thirdly, that after deposing Lepidus, their colleague, he had taken for himself the army, governments, and revenues formerly appropriated to him; and, lastly, that he had parcelled out almost all Italy amongst his own soldiers, and left nothing for his. Cæsar's answer was as follows: that he had put Lepidus out of government because of his own misconduct; that what he had got in war he would divide with Antony, so soon as Antony gave him a share of Armenia; that Antony's soldiers had no claims in Italy, being in possession of Media and Parthia, the acquisitions which their brave actions under their general had added to the Roman empire.

Antony was in Armenia when this answer came to him, and immediately sent Canidius with sixteen legions towards the sea; but he, in the company of Cleopatra, went to Ephesus, whither ships were coming in from all quarters to form the navy, consisting, vessels of burden included, of eight hundred vessels, of which Cleopatra furnished two hundred, together with twenty thousand talents, and provision for the whole army during the war. Antony, on the advice of Domitius and some others, bade Cleopatra return into Egypt, there to expect the event of the war; but she, dreading some new reconciliation by Octavia's means, prevailed with Canidius, by a large sum of money, to speak in her favor with Antony, pointing out to him that it was not just that one that bore so great a part in the charge of the war should be robbed of her share of glory in the carrying it on; nor would it be politic to disoblige the Egyptians, who were so considerable a part of his naval forces; nor did he see how she was inferior in prudence to any one of the kings that were serving with him; she had long governed a great kingdom by herself alone, and long lived with him, and gained experience in public affairs. These arguments (so the fate that destined all to Cæsar would have it), prevailed; and when all their forces had met, they sailed together to Samos, and held high festivities. For, as it was ordered that all kings, princes, and governors, all nations and cities within the limits of Syria, the Mæotid Lake, Armenia, and Illyria, should bring or cause to be brought all munitions necessary for war, so was it also proclaimed that all stage-players should make their appearance at Samos; so that, while pretty nearly the whole world was filled with groans and lamentations, this one island for some days resounded with piping and harping, theatres filling, and choruses playing. Every city sent an ox as its contribution to the sacrifice, and the kings that accompanied Antony competed who should make the most magnificent feasts and the greatest presents; and men began to ask themselves, what would be done to celebrate the victory, when they went to such an expense of festivity at the opening of the war.

This over, he gave Priene to his players for a habitation,[10] and set sail for Athens, where fresh sports and play-acting employed him. Cleopatra, jealous of the honors Octavia had received at Athens (for Octavia was much beloved by the Athenians), courted the favor of the people with all sorts of attentions. The Athenians, in requital, having decreed her public honors, deputed several of the citizens to wait upon her at her house; amongst whom went Antony as one, he being an Athenian citizen, and he it was that made the speech. He sent orders to Rome to have Octavia removed out of his house. She left it, we are told, accompanied by all his children, except the eldest by Fulvia, who was then with his father, weeping and grieving that she must be looked upon as one of the causes of the war. But the Romans pitied, not so much her, as Antony himself, and more particularly those who had seen Cleopatra, whom they could report to have no way the advantage of Octavia either in youth or in beauty.

The speed and extent of Antony's preparations alarmed Cæsar, who feared he might be forced to fight the decisive battle that summer. For he wanted many necessaries, and the people grudged very much to pay the taxes; freemen being called upon to pay a fourth part of their incomes, and freed slaves an eighth of their property, so that there were loud outcries against him, and disturbances throughout all Italy. And this is looked upon as one of the greatest of Antony's oversights, that he did not then press the war. For he allowed time at once for Cæsar to make his preparations, and for the commotions to pass over. For while people were having their money called for, they were mutinous and violent; but, having paid

[10] It seems to have been usual for the guild or company of performers in this part of Asia ("Ionia, as far as the Hellespont"), to have a city of their own, a sort of headquarters, whence they went out, and where once a year they held a festival of their own. Formerly, says Strabo, it had been Teos; intestine troubles drove them thence to Ephesus; king Attalus gave them Myonnesus; and afterwards Lebedus, in Roman times, a half abandoned town, "Gabiis desertior atque Fidenis vicus" was only too glad to receive them. See Strabo, XIV., 29.

it, they held their peace. Titius and Plancus, men of consular dignity and friends to Antony, having been ill used by Cleopatra, whom they had most resisted in her design of being present in the war, came over to Cæsar, and gave information of the contents of Antony's will, with which they were acquainted. It was deposited in the hands of the vestal virgins, who refused to deliver it up, and sent Cæsar word, if he pleased, he should come and seize it himself, which he did. And, reading it over to himself, he noted those places that were most for his purpose, and, having summoned the senate, read them publicly. Many were scandalized at the proceeding, thinking it out of reason and equity to call a man to account for what was not to be until after his death. Cæsar specially pressed what Antony said in his will about his burial; for he had ordered that even if he died in the city of Rome, his body, after being carried in state through the forum, should be sent to Cleopatra at Alexandria. Calvisius, a dependant of Cæsar's, urged other charges in connection with Cleopatra against Antony; that he had given her the library of Pergamus, containing two hundred thousand distinct volumes; that at a great banquet, in the presence of many guests, he had risen up and rubbed her feet, to fulfil some wager or promise; that he had suffered the Ephesians to salute her as their queen; that he had frequently at the public audience of kings and princes received amorous messages written in tablets made of onyx and crystal, and read them openly on the tribunal; that when Furnius, a man of great authority and eloquence among the Romans, was pleading, Cleopatra happening to pass by in her chair, Antony started up and left them in the middle of their cause, to follow at her side and attend her home.

Calvisius, however, was looked upon as the inventor of most of these stories. Antony's friends went up and down the city to gain him credit, and sent one of themselves, Geminius, to him to beg him to take heed, and not allow himself to be deprived by vote of his authority, and proclaimed a public enemy to the Roman state. But Geminius no sooner arrived in Greece but he was looked upon as one of Octavia's spies; at their suppers he was made a continual butt for mockery, and was put to sit in the least honorable places; all which he bore very well, seeking only an occasion of speaking with Antony. So, at supper, being told to say what business he came about, he answered he would keep the rest for a soberer hour, but one thing he had to say, whether full or fasting, that all would go well if Cleopatra would return to Egypt. And on Antony showing his anger at it, "You have done well, Geminius," said Cleopatra, "to tell your secret without being put to the rack." So Geminius, after a few days, took occasion to make his escape and go to Rome. Many more of Antony's friends were driven from him by the insolent usage they had from Cleopatra's flatterers, amongst whom were Marcus Silanus and Dellius the historian. And Dellius says he was afraid of his life, and that Glaucus, the physician, informed him of Cleopatra's design against him. She was angry with him for having said that Antony's friends were served with sour wine, while at Rome Sarmentus, Cæsar's little page (his *delicia,* as the Romans call it), drank Falernian.[11]

As soon as Cæsar had completed his preparations, he had a decree made, declaring war on Cleopatra, and depriving Antony of the authority which he had let a woman exercise in his place. Cæsar added that he had drunk potions that had bereaved him of his senses, and that the generals they would have to fight with would be Mardion the eunuch, Pothinus, Iras, Cleopatra's hair-dressing girl, and Charmion, who were Antony's chief state-councillors.

These prodigies are said to have announced the war. Pisaurum, where Antony had settled a colony, on the Adriatic sea, was swallowed up by an earthquake; sweat ran from one of the marble statues of Antony at Alba for many days together, and, though frequently wiped off, did not stop. When he himself was in the city of Patræ, the temple of Hercules was struck by lightning, and, at Athens, the figure of Bacchus was torn by a violent wind out of the Battle of the Giants, and laid flat upon the theatre;[12] with both which deities Antony claimed connection, professing to be descended from Hercules, and from his imitating Bacchus in his way of living hav-

[11] Suetonius tells us that it was one of the habitual amusements of Augustus to play and talk with children of this kind, who were sought out for him chiefly in Syria and Mauritania. They were specially selected for their smallness; but he had no liking for dwarfs or deformed children, who were often kept by other great people in Rome as their playthings, so called, *delicia* or *deliciæ,* much in the same sense as the pet-bird of Catullus's mistress, "Passer, deliciæ meæ puellæ."

[12] The Battle of the Giants with the Gods was a piece of sculpture in the south wall of the Acropolis, just above the Dionysiac theatre in the side of the rock underneath.

ing received the name of Young Bacchus. The same whirlwind at Athens also brought down, from amongst many others which were not disturbed, the colossal statues of Eumenes and Attalus, which were inscribed with Antony's name. And in Cleopatra's admiral-galley, which was called the Antonias, a most inauspicious omen occurred. Some swallows had built in the stern of the galley, but other swallows came, beat the first away, and destroyed their nests.

When the armaments gathered for the war, Antony had no less than five hundred ships of war, including numerous galleys of eight and ten banks of oars, as richly ornamented as if they were meant for a triumph. He had a hundred thousand foot and twelve thousand horse. He had vassal kings attending, Bocchus of Libya, Tarcondemus of the Upper Cilicia, Archelaus of Cappadocia, Philadelphus of Paphlagonia, Mithridates of Commagene, and Sadalas of Thrace; all these were with him in person. Out of Pontus Polemon sent him considerable forces, as did also Malchus from Arabia, Herod the Jew, and Amyntas, king of Lycaonia and Galatia; also the Median king sent some troops to join him. Cæsar had two hundred and fifty galleys of war, eighty thousand foot, and horse about equal to the enemy. Antony's empire extended from Euphrates and Armenia to the Ionian sea and the Illyrians; Cæsar's from Illyria to the westward ocean, and from the ocean all along the Tuscan and Sicilian sea. Of Africa, Cæsar had all the coast opposite to Italy, Gaul, and Spain, as far as the Pillars of Hercules, and Antony the provinces from Cyrene to Æthiopia.

But so wholly was he now the mere appendage to the person of Cleopatra, that, although he was much superior to the enemy in land-forces, yet, out of complaisance to his mistress, he wished the victory to be gained by sea, and that, too, when he could not but see how, for want of sailors, his captains, all through unhappy Greece, were pressing every description of men, common travellers and ass-drivers, harvest laborers, and boys, and for all this the vessels had not their complements, but remained, most of them, ill-manned and badly rowed. Cæsar, on the other side, had ships that were built not for size or show, but for service, not pompous galleys, but light, swift, and perfectly manned; and from his headquarters at Tarentum and Brundusium he sent messages to Antony not to protract the war, but come out with his forces; he would give him secure roadsteads and ports for his fleet, and, for his land army to disembark and pitch their camp, he would leave him as much ground in Italy, inland from the sea, as a horse could traverse in a single course. Antony, on the other side, with the like bold language, challenged him to a single combat, though he were much the older; and, that being refused, proposed to meet him in the Pharsalian fields, where Cæsar and Pompey had fought before. But whilst Antony lay with his fleet near Actium, where now stands Nicopolis, Cæsar seized his opportunity and crossed the Ionian sea, securing himself at a place in Epirus called the Ladle.[13] And when those about Antony were much disturbed, their land-forces being a good way off, "Indeed," said Cleopatra, in mockery, "we may well be frightened if Cæsar has got hold of the Ladle!"

On the morrow, Antony, seeing the enemy sailing up, and fearing lest his ships might be taken for want of the soldiers to go on board of them, armed all the rowers, and made a show upon the decks of being in readiness to fight; the oars were mounted as if waiting to be put in motion, and the vessels themselves drawn up to face the enemy on either side of the channel of Actium, as though they were properly manned, and ready for an engagement. And Cæsar, deceived by this stratagem, retired. He was also thought to have shown considerable skill in cutting off the water from the enemy by some lines of trenches and forts, water not being plentiful anywhere else, nor very good. And again, his conduct to Domitius was generous, much against the will of Cleopatra. For when he had made his escape in a little boat to Cæsar, having then a fever upon him, although Antony could not but resent it highly, yet he sent after him his whole equipage, with his friends and servants; and Domitius, as if he would give a testimony to the world how repentant he had become on his desertion and treachery being thus manifest, died soon after. Among the kings also, Amyntas and Deiotarus went over to Cæsar. And the fleet was so unfortunate in every thing that was undertaken, and so unready on every occasion, that Antony was driven again to put his confidence in the land-forces. Canidius, too, who commanded the legions, when he saw how things stood,

[13] Toryne is the name which has this meaning.

changed his opinion, and now was of advice that Cleopatra should be sent back, and that, retiring into Thrace or Macedonia, the quarrel should be decided in a land fight. For Dicomes, also, the king of the Getæ, promised to come and join him with a great army, and it would not be any kind of disparagement to him to yield the sea to Cæsar, who, in the Sicilian wars, had had such long practice in ship-fighting; on the contrary, it would be simply ridiculous for Antony, who was by land the most experienced commander living, to make no use of his well-disciplined and numerous infantry, scattering and wasting his forces by parcelling them out in the ships. But for all this, Cleopatra prevailed that a sea-fight should determine all, having already an eye to flight, and ordering all her affairs, not so as to assist in gaining a victory, but to escape with the greatest safety from the first commencement of a defeat.

There were two long walls, extending from the camp to the station of the ships, between which Antony used to pass to and fro without suspecting any danger. But Cæsar, upon the suggestion of a servant that it would not be difficult to surprise him, laid an ambush, which, rising up somewhat too hastily, seized the man that came just before him, he himself escaping narrowly by flight.

When it was resolved to stand to a fight at sea, they set fire to all the Egyptian ships except sixty; and of these the best and largest, from ten banks down to three, he manned with twenty thousand full-armed men, and two thousand archers. Here it is related that a foot captain, one that had fought often under Antony, and had his body all mangled with wounds, exclaimed, "O, my general, what have our wounds and swords done to displease you, that you should give your confidence to rotten timbers? Let Egyptians and Phœnicians contend at sea, give us the land, where we know well how to die upon the spot or gain the victory." To which he answered nothing, but, by his look and motion of his hand seeming to bid him be of good courage, passed forwards, having already, it would seem, no very sure hopes, since when the masters proposed leaving the sails behind them, he commanded they should be put aboard, "For we must not," said he, "let one enemy escape."

That day and the three following the sea was so rough they could not engage. But on the fifth there was a calm, and they fought;

Antony commanding with Publicola the right, and Cœlius the left squadron, Marcus Octavius and Marcus Instelus the centre. Cæsar gave the charge of the left to Agrippa, commanding in person on the right. As for the land-forces, Canidius was general for Antony, Taurus for Cæsar; both armies remaining drawn up in order along the shore. Antony in a small boat went from one ship to another, encouraging his soldiers, and bidding them stand firm, and fight as steadily on their large ships as if they were on land. The masters he ordered that they should receive the enemy lying still as if they were at anchor, and maintain the entrance of the port, which was a narrow and difficult passage. Of Cæsar they relate, that, leaving his tent and going round, while it was yet dark, to visit the ships, he met a man driving an ass, and asked him his name. He answered him that his own name was "Fortunate, and my ass," says he, "is called Conquerer."[14] And afterwards, when he disposed the beaks of the ships in that place in token of his victory, the statue of this man and his ass in bronze were placed amongst them. After examining the rest of his fleet, he went in a boat to the right wing, and looked with much admiration at the enemy lying perfectly still in the straits, in all appearance as if they had been at anchor. For some considerable length of time he actually thought they were so, and kept his own ships at rest, at a distance of about eight furlongs from them. But about noon a breeze sprang up from the sea, and Antony's men, weary of expecting the enemy so long, and trusting to their large tall vessels, as if they had been invincible, began to advance the left squadron. Cæsar was overjoyed to see them move, and ordered his own right squadron to retire, that he might entice them out to sea as far as he could, his design being to sail round and round, and so with his light and well-manned galleys to attack these huge vessels, which their size and their want of men made slow to move and difficult to manage.

When they engaged, there was no charging or striking of one ship by another, because Antony's, by reason of their great bulk, were incapable of the rapidity required to make the stroke effectual, and, on the other side, Cæsar's durst not charge head to head on Antony's, which were all armed with solid masses and spikes of

[14] Eutychus the name of the man, and Nicon that of the ass.

brass; nor did they like even to run in on their sides, which were so strongly built with great squared pieces of timber, fastened together with iron bolts, that their vessels' beaks would easily have been shattered upon them. So that the engagement resembled a land fight, or, to speak yet more properly, the attack and defence of a fortified place; for there were always three or four vessels of Cæsar's about one of Antony's, pressing them with spears, javelins, poles, and several inventions of fire, which they flung among them, Antony's men using catapults also, to pour down missiles from wooden towers. Agrippa drawing out the squadron under his command to outflank the enemy, Publicola was obliged to observe his motions, and gradually to break off from the middle squadron, where some confusion and alarm ensued, while Arruntius[15] engaged them. But the fortune of the day was still undecided, and the battle equal, when on a sudden Cleopatra's sixty ships were seen hoisting sail and making out to sea in full flight, right through the ships that were engaged. For they were placed behind the great ships, which, in breaking through, they put into disorder. The enemy was astonished to see them sailing off with a fair wind towards Peloponnesus. Here it was that Antony showed to all the world that he was no longer actuated by the thoughts and motives of a commander or a man, or indeed by his own judgment at all, and what was once said as a jest, that the soul of a lover lives in some one else's body, he proved to be a serious truth. For, as if he had been born part of her, and must move with her wheresoever she went, as soon as he saw her ship sailing away, he abandoned all that were fighting and spending their lives for him, and put himself aboard a galley of five ranks of oars, taking with him only Alexander of Syria and Scellias, to follow her that had so well begun his ruin and would hereafter accomplish it.

She, perceiving him to follow, gave the signal to come aboard. So, as soon as he came up with them, he was taken into the ship. But without seeing her or letting himself be seen by her, he went forward by himself, and sat alone, without a word, in the ship's prow, covering his face with his two hands. In the meanwhile, some of Cæsar's light Liburnian ships, that were in pursuit, came

[15] Arruntius commanded in Cæsar's centre.

in sight. But on Antony's commanding to face about, they all gave back except Eurycles the Laconian, who pressed on, shaking a lance from the deck, as if he meant to hurl it at him. Antony, standing at the prow, demanded of him, "Who is this that pursues Antony?" "I am," said he, "Eurycles, the son of Lachares, armed with Cæsar's fortune to revenge my father's death." Lachares had been condemned for a robbery, and beheaded by Antony's orders. However, Eurycles did not attack Antony, but ran with his full force upon the other admiral-galley (for there were two of them), and with the blow turned her round, and took both her and another ship, in which was a quantity of rich plate and furniture. So soon as Eurycles was gone, Antony returned to his posture, and sate silent, and thus he remained for three days, either in anger with Cleopatra, or wishing not to upbraid her, at the end of which they touched at Tænarus. Here the women of their company succeeded first in bringing them to speak, and afterwards to eat and sleep together. And, by this time, several of the ships of burden and some of his friends began to come in to him from the rout, bringing news of his fleet's being quite destroyed, but that the land-forces, they thought, still stood firm. So that he sent messengers to Canidius to march the army with all speed through Macedonia into Asia. And, designing himself to go from Tænarus into Africa, he gave one of the merchant ships, laden with a large sum of money, and vessels of silver and gold of great value, belonging to the royal collections, to his friends, desiring them to share it amongst them, and provide for their own safety. They refusing his kindness with tears in their eyes, he comforted them with all the goodness and humanity imaginable, entreating them to leave him, and wrote letters in their behalf to Theophilus, his steward, at Corinth, that he would provide for their security, and keep them concealed till such time as they could make their peace with Cæsar. This Theophilus was the father of Hipparchus, who had such interest with Antony, who was the first of all his freedmen that went over to Cæsar, and who settled afterwards at Corinth. In this posture were affairs with Antony.

But at Actium, his fleet, after a long resistance to Cæsar, and suffering the most damage from a heavy sea that set in right ahead, scarcely, at four in the afternoon, gave up the contest, with the loss of not more than five thousand men killed, but of three hundred ships taken, as Cæsar himself has recorded. Only few had known of Antony's flight; and those who were told of it could not at first give any belief to so incredible a thing, as that a general who had nineteen entire legions and twelve thousand horse upon the seashore, could abandon all and fly away; and he, above all, who had so often experienced both good and evil fortune, and had in a thousand wars and battles been inured to changes. His soldiers, however, would not give up their desires and expectations, still fancying he would appear from some part or other, and showed such a generous fidelity to his service, that, when they were thoroughly assured that he was fled in earnest, they kept themselves in a body seven days, making no account of the messages that Cæsar sent to them. But at last, seeing that Canidius himself, who commanded them, was fled from the camp by night, and that all their officers had quite abandoned them, they gave way, and made their submission to the conqueror. After this, Cæsar set sail for Athens, where he made a settlement with Greece, and distributed what remained of the provision of corn that Antony had made for his army among the cities, which were in a miserable condition, despoiled of their money, their slaves, their horses, and beasts of service. My great-grandfather Nicarchus used to relate, that the whole body of the people of our city were put in requisition to carry each one a certain measure of corn upon their shoulders to the sea-side near Anticyra, men standing by to quicken them with the lash. They had made one journey of the kind, but when they had just measured out the corn and were putting it on their backs for a second, news came of Antony's defeat, and so saved Chæronea, for all Antony's purveyors and soldiers fled upon the news, and left them to divide the corn among themselves.

When Antony came into Africa, he sent on Cleopatra from Parætonium into Egypt, and staid himself in the most entire solitude that he could desire, roaming and wandering about with only two friends, one a Greek, Aristocrates, a rhetorician, and the other a Roman, Lucilius, of whom we have elsewhere spoken, how, at

Philippi, to give Brutus time to escape, he suffered himself to be taken by the pursuers, pretending he was Brutus. Antony gave him his life, and on this account he remained true and faithful to him to the last.

But when also the officer who commanded for him in Africa, to whose care he had committed all his forces there, took them over to Cæsar, he resolved to kill himself, but was hindered by his friends. And coming to Alexandria, he found Cleopatra busied in a most bold and wonderful enterprise. Over the small space of land which divides the Red Sea from the sea near Egypt, which may be considered also the boundary between Asia and Africa, and in the narrowest place is not much above three hundred furlongs across, over this neck of land Cleopatra had formed a project of dragging her fleet, and setting it afloat in the Arabian Gulf, thus with her soldiers and her treasure to secure herself a home on the other side, where she might live in peace, far away from war and slavery. But the first galleys which were carried over being burnt by the Arabians of Petra, and Antony not knowing but that the army before Actium still held together, she desisted from her enterprise, and gave orders for the fortifying all the approaches to Egypt. But Antony, leaving the city and the conversation of his friends, built him a dwelling-place in the water, near Pharos, upon a little mole which he cast up in the sea, and there, secluding himself from the company of mankind, said he desired nothing but to live the life of Timon; as, indeed, his case was the same, and the ingratitude and injuries which he suffered from those he had esteemed his friends, made him hate and mistrust all mankind.

This Timon was a citizen of Athens, and lived much about the Peloponnesian war, as may be seen by the comedies of Aristophanes and Plato, in which he is ridiculed as the hater and enemy of mankind. He avoided and repelled the approaches of every one, but embraced with kisses and the greatest show of affection Alcibiades, then in his hot youth. And when Apemantus was astonished, and demanded the reason, he replied that he knew this young man would one day do infinite mischief to the Athenians. He never admitted any one into his company, except at times this Apemantus, who was of the same sort of temper, and was an imitator of his way of life. At the celebration of the festival of flagons,[16] these two kept the feast together, and Apemantus saying to him, "What a pleasant party, Timon!" "It would be," he answered, "if you were away." One day he got up in a full assembly on the speaker's place, and when there was a dead silence and great wonder at so unusual a sight, he said, "Ye men of Athens, I have a little plot of ground, and in it grows a fig-tree, on which many citizens have been pleased to hang themselves; and now, having resolved to build in that place, I wished to announce it publicly, that any of you who may be desirous may go and hang yourselves before I cut it down." He died and was buried at Halæ, near the sea, where it so happened that, after his burial, a land-slip took place on the point of the shore, and the sea, flowing in, surrounded his tomb, and made it inaccessible to the foot of man. It bore this inscription:—

"Here am I laid, my life of misery done.
Ask not my name, I curse you every one."

And this epitaph was made by himself while yet alive; that which is more generally known is by Callimachus:—

"Timon, the misanthrope, am I below.
Go, and revile me, traveller, only go."

Thus much of Timon, of whom much more might be said. Canidius now came, bringing word in person of the loss of the army before Actium. Then he received news that Herod of Judæa was gone over to Cæsar with some legions and cohorts, and that the other kings and princes were in like manner deserting him, and that, out of Egypt, nothing stood by him. All this, however, seemed not to disturb him, but as if he were glad to put away all hope, that with it he might be rid of care, and leaving his habitation by the sea, which he called the Timoneum, he was received by Cleopatra in the palace, and set the whole city in to a course of feasting, drinking, and presents. The son of Cæsar and Cleopatra was registered among the youths, and Antyllus, his own son by Fulvia, received the gown without the purple border, given to those that are come of

[16] "The Flagons," or *Choës,* was the second day of the Anthesterian feast of Bacchus, and was observed by the Athenians as a special day of conviviality, when they met in parties, and drank together.

age; in honor of which the citizens of Alexandria did nothing but feast and revel for many days. They themselves broke up the Order of the Inimitable Livers, and constituted another in its place, not inferior in splendor, luxury, and sumptuosity, calling it that of the Diers together.[17] For all those that said they would die with Antony and Cleopatra gave in their names, for the present passing their time in all manner of pleasures, and a regular succession of banquets. But Cleopatra was busied in making a collection of all varieties of poisonous drugs, and, in order to see which of them were the least painful in the operation, she had them tried upon prisoners condemned to die. But, finding that the quick poisons always worked with sharp pains, and that the less painful were slow, she next tried venomous animals, and watched with her own eyes whilst they were applied,one creature to the body of another. This was her daily practice, and she pretty well satisfied herself that nothing was comparable to the bite of the asp, which, without convulsion or groaning, brought on a heavy drowsiness and lethargy, with a gentle sweat on the face, the senses being stupefied by degrees; the patient, in appearance, being sensible of no pain, but rather troubled to be disturbed or awakened, like those that are in a profound natural sleep.

At the same time, they sent ambassadors to Cæsar into Asia, Cleopatra asking for the kingdom of Egypt for her children, and Antony, that he might have leave to live as a private man in Egypt, or, if that were thought too much, that he might retire to Athens. In lack of friends, so many having deserted, and others not being trusted, Euphronius, his son's tutor, was sent on this embassy. For Alexas of Laodicea, who, by the recommendation of Timagenes, became acquainted with Antony at Rome, and had been more powerful with him than any Greek, and was, of all the instruments which Cleopatra made use of to persuade Antony, the most violent, and the chief subverted of any good thoughts that, from time to time, might rise in his mind in Octavia's favor, had been sent before to dissuade Herod from desertion; but, betraying his master, stayed with him, and, confiding in Herod's interest, had the boldness to come into Cæsar's presence. Herod, however, was not able to help

[17] It was a name well known on the stage. There were two, if not three, comedies, called the *Synapothneskontes,* and one of them had been translated into Latin by Plautus, as the *Commorientes.*

him, for he was immediately put in chains, and sent into his own country, where, by Cæsar's order, he was put to death. This reward of his treason Alexas received while Antony was yet alive.

Cæsar would not listen to any proposals for Antony, but he made answer to Cleopatra, that there was no reasonable favor which she might not expect, if she put Antony to death, or expelled him from Egypt. He sent back with the ambassadors his own freedman Thyrsus, a man of understanding, and not at all ill-qualified for conveying the messages of a youthful general to a woman so proud of her charms and possessed with the opinion of the power of her beauty. But by the long audiences he received from her, and the special honors which she paid him, Antony's jealousy began to be awakened; he had him seized, whipped, and sent back; writing Cæsar word that the man's busy, impertinent ways had provoked him; in his circumstances he could not be expected to be very patient: "But if it offend you," he added, "you have got my freedman, Hipparchus, with you; hang him up and scourge him to make us even." But Cleopatra, after this, to clear herself, and to allay his jealousies, paid him all the attentions imaginable. When her own birthday came, she kept it as was suitable to their fallen fortunes; but his was observed with the utmost prodigality of splendor and magnificence, so that many of the guests sate down in want, and went home wealthy men. Meantime, continual letters came to Cæsar from Agrippa, telling him his presence was extremely required at Rome.

And so the war was deferred for a season. But, the winter being over, he began his march; he himself by Syria, and his captains through Africa. Pelusium being taken, there went a report as if it had been delivered up to Cæsar by Seleucus, not without the consent of Cleopatra; but she, to justify herself, gave up into Antony's hands the wife and children of Seleucus to be put to death. She had caused to be built, joining to the temple of Isis, several tombs and monuments of wonderful height, and very remarkable for the workmanship; thither she removed her treasure, her gold, silver, emeralds, pearls, ebony, ivory, cinnamon, and, after all, a great quantity of torchwood and tow. Upon which Cæsar began to fear lest she should, in a desperate fit, set all these riches on fire; and, therefore, while he was marching towards the city with his army, he omitted no occasion of giving her new assurances of his good intentions. He took up his position in the Hippodrome, where Antony made a fierce sally upon him, routed his horse, and beat them back into their trenches, and so returned with great satisfaction to the palace, where, meeting Cleopatra, armed as he was, he kissed her, and commended to her favor one of his men, who had most signalized himself in the fight, to whom she made a present of a breastplate and helmet of gold; which he having received, went that very night and deserted to Cæsar.

After this, Antony sent a new challenge to Cæsar, to fight him hand to hand; who made him answer that he might find several other ways to end his life; and he, considering with himself that he could not die more honorably than in battle, resolved to make an effort both by land and sea. At supper, it is said, he bade his servants help him freely, and pour him out wine plentifully, since to-morrow, perhaps, they should not do the same, but be servants to a new master, whilst he should lie on the ground, a dead corpse, and nothing. His friends that were about him wept to hear him talk so; which he perceiving, told them he would not lead them to a battle in which he expected rather an honorable death than either safety or victory. That night, it is related, about the middle of it, when the whole city was in a deep silence and general sadness, expecting the event of the next day, on a sudden was heard the sound of all sorts of instruments, and voices singing in tune, and the cry of a crowd of people shouting and dancing, like a troop of bacchanals on its way. This tumultuous procession seemed to take its course right through the middle of the city to the gate nearest the enemy; here it became loudest, and suddenly passed out. People who reflected considered this to signify that Bacchus, the god whom Antony had always made it his study to copy and imitate, had now forsaken him.

As soon as it was light, he marched his infantry out of the city, and posted them upon a rising ground, from whence he saw his fleet make up to the enemy. There he stood in expectation of the event; but as soon as the fleets came near to one another, his men saluted Cæsar's with their oars; and, on their responding, the whole body of the ships, forming into a single fleet, rowed up direct to the city. Antony had no sooner seen this, but the horse deserted him, and went over to Cæsar; and his foot being defeated, he retired into the city, crying out that Cleopatra had betrayed him to the enemies he had made for her sake. She, being afraid lest in his fury and despair he might do her a mischief, fled to her monument, and letting down the falling doors, which were strong with bars and bolts, she sent messengers who should tell Antony she was dead. He, believing it, cried out, "Now, Antony, why delay longer? Fate has snatched away the only pretext for which you could say you desired yet to live." Going into his chamber, and there loosening and opening his coat of armor, "I am not," said he, "troubled, Cleopatra, to be at present bereaved of you, for I shall soon be with you; but it distresses me that so great a general should be found of a tardier courage than a woman." He had a faithful servant, whose name was Eros; he had engaged him formerly to kill him when he should think it necessary, and now he put him to his promise. Eros drew his sword, as designing to kill him, but, suddenly turning round, he slew himself. And as he fell dead at his feet, "It is well done, Eros," said Antony; "you show your master how to do what you had not the heart to do yourself;" and so he ran himself into the belly, and laid himself upon the couch. The wound, however, was not immediately mortal; and the flow of blood ceasing when he lay down, presently he came to himself, and entreated those that were about him to put him out of his pain; but they all fled out of the chamber, and left him crying out and struggling, until Diomede, Cleopatra's secretary, came to him, having orders from her to bring him into the monument.

When he understood she was alive, he eagerly gave order to the servants to take him up, and in their arms was carried to the door of the building. Cleopatra would not open the door, but, looking from a sort of window, she let down ropes and cords, to which Antony was fastened; and she and her two women, the only persons she had allowed to enter the monument, drew him up. Those that were present say that nothing was ever more sad than this spectacle, to see Antony, covered all over with blood and just expiring, thus drawn up, still holding up his hands to her, and lifting up his body with the little force he had left. As, indeed, it was no easy task for the women; and Cleopatra, with all her force, clinging to the rope, and straining with her head to the ground, with difficulty pulled him up, while those below encouraged her with their cries, and joined in all her effort and anxiety. When she had got him up, she laid him on the bed, tearing all her clothes, which she spread upon him; and beating her breasts with her hands, lacerating herself, and disfiguring her own face with the blood from his wounds, she called him her lord, her husband, her emperor, and seemed to have pretty nearly forgotten all her own evils, she was so intent upon his misfortunes. Antony, stopping her lamentations as well as he could, called for wine to drink, either that he was thirsty, or that he imagined that it might put him the sooner out of pain. When he had drunk, he advised her to bring her own affairs, so far as might be honorably done, to a safe conclusion, and that, among all the friends of Cæsar, she should rely on Proculeius; that she should not pity him in this last turn of fate, but rather rejoice for him in remembrance of his past happiness, who had been of all men the most illustrious and powerful, and, in the end, had fallen not ignobly, a Roman by a Roman overcome.

Just as he breathed his last, Proculeius arrived from Cæsar; for when Antony gave himself his wound, and was carried in to Cleopatra, one of his guards, Dercetæus, took up Antony's sword and hid it; and, when he saw his opportunity, stole away to Cæsar, and brought him the first news of Antony's death, and withal showed him the bloody sword. Cæsar, upon this, retired into the inner part of his tent, and giving some tears to the death of one that had been nearly allied to him in marriage, his colleague in empire, and companion in so many wars and dangers, he came out to his friends, and, bringing with him many letters, he read to them with how much reason and moderation he had always addressed himself to Antony, and in return what overbearing and arrogant answers he received. Then he sent Proculeius to use his utmost endeavors to get Cleopatra alive into his power; for he was afraid of losing a great treasure, and, besides, she would be no small addition to the glory of his triumph. She, however, was careful not to put herself in Proculeius's power; but from within her monument, he standing on the outside of a door, on the level of the ground, which was strongly barred, but so that they might well enough hear one another's voice, she held a conference with him; she demanding that her kingdom might be given to her children, and he bidding her be of good courage, and trust Cæsar for every thing.

Having taken particular notice of the place, he returned to Cæsar, and Gallus was sent to parley with her the second time; who, being come to the door, on purpose prolonged the conference, while Proculeius fixed his scaling-ladders in the window through which the women had pulled up Antony. And so entering, with two men to follow him, he went straight down to the door where Cleopatra was discoursing with Gallus. One of the two women who were shut up in the monument with her cried, out, "Miserable Cleopatra, you are taken prisoner!" Upon which she turned quick, and, looking at Proculeius, drew out her dagger, which she had with her to stab herself. But Proculeius ran up quickly, and, seizing her with both his hands, "For shame," said he, "Cleopatra; you wrong yourself and Cæsar much, who would rob him of so fair an occasion of showing his clemency, and would make the world believe the most gentle of commanders to be a faithless and implacable enemy." And so, taking the dagger out of her hand, he also shook her dress to see if there were any poison hid in it. After this, Cæsar sent Epaphroditus, one of his freedmen, with orders to treat her with all the gentleness and civility possible, but to take the strictest precautions to keep her alive.

In the meanwhile, Cæsar made his entry into Alexandria with Areius the philosopher at his side, holding him by the hand and talking with him; desiring that all his fellow-citizens should see what honor was paid to him, and should look up to him accordingly from the very first moment. Then, entering the exercise-ground, he mounted a platform erected for the purpose, and from thence commanded the citizens (who, in great fear and consternation, fell prostrate at his feet) to stand up, and told them, that he freely acquitted the people of all blame, first, for the sake of Alexander, who built their city; then, for the city's sake itself, which was so large and beautiful; and, thirdly, to gratify his friend Areius.

Such great honor did Areius receive from Cæsar; and by his intercession many lives were saved, amongst the rest that of Philostratus, a man, of all the professors of logic that ever were, the most ready in extempore speaking, but quite destitute of any right to call himself one of the philosophers of the Academy. Cæsar, out of disgust at his character, refused all attention to his entreaties. So, growing a long, white beard, and dressing himself in black, he followed behind Areius, shouting out the verse,

"The wise, if they are wise, will save the wise."

Which Cæsar hearing, gave him his pardon, to prevent rather any odium that might attach to Areius, than any harm that Philostratus might suffer.

Of Antony's children, Antyllus, his son by Fulvia, being betrayed by his tutor, Theodorus, was put to death; and while the soldiers were cutting off his head, his tutor contrived to steal a precious jewel which he wore about his neck, and put it into his pocket, and afterwards denied the fact, but was convicted and crucified. Cleopatra's children, with their attendants, had a guard set on them, and were treated very honorably. Cæsarion, who was reputed to be the son of Cæsar the Dictator, was sent by his mother, with a great sum of money, through Æthiopia, to pass into India; but his tutor, a man named Rhodon, about as honest as Theodorus, persuaded him to turn back, for that Cæsar designed to make him king. Cæsar consulting what was best to be done with him, Areius, we are told said,

"Too many *Cæsars* are not well." [18]

So, afterwards, when Cleopatra was dead, he was killed.

Many kings and great commanders made petition to Cæsar for the body of Antony, to give him his funeral rites; but he would not take away his corpse from Cleopatra, by whose hands he was buried with royal splendor and magnificence, it being granted to her to employ what she pleased on his funeral. In this extremity of grief

[18] A parody on Homer's famous words,

Too many leaders are not well; the way
Is to have one commander to obey,
One king, of Zeus appointed for the sway.

*ouk agathon polu*kaisarie being a slight variation upon *ouk agathon polu*koiranie. *Kaisar* is the Greek form of Cæsar; and *Koiran*, or *Koiranos* is a captain or chief.

and sorrow, and having inflamed and ulcerated her breasts with beating them, she fell into a high fever, and was very glad of the occasion, hoping, under this pretext, to abstain from food, and so to die in quiet without interference. She had her own physician, Olympus, to whom she told the truth, and asked his advice and help to put an end to herself, as Olympus himself has told us, in a narrative which he wrote of these events. But Cæsar, suspecting her purpose, took to menacing language about her children, and excited her fears for them, before which engines her purpose shook and gave way, so that she suffered those about her to give her what meat or medicine they pleased.

Some few days after, Cæsar himself came to make her a visit and comfort her. She lay then upon her pallet-bed in undress, and, on his entering in, sprang up from off her bed, having nothing on but the one garment next her body, and flung herself at his feet, her hair and face looking wild and disfigured, her voice quivering, and her eyes sunk in her head. The marks of the blows she had given herself were visible about her bosom, and altogether her whole person seemed no less afflicted than her soul. But, for all this, her old charm, and the boldness of her youthful beauty had not wholly left her, and, in spite of her present condition, still sparkled from within, and let itself appear in all the movements of her countenance. Cæsar, desiring her to repose herself, sat down by her; and, on this opportunity, she said something to justify her actions, attributing what she had done to the necessity she was under, and to her fear of Antony; and when Cæsar, on each point, made his objections, and she found herself confuted, she broke off at once into language of entreaty and deprecation, as if she desired nothing more than to prolong her life. And at last, having by her a list of her treasure, she gave it into his hands; and when Seleucus, one of her stewards, who was by, pointed out that various articles were omitted, and charged her with secreting them, she flew up and caught him by the hair, and struck him several blows on the face. Cæsar smiling and withholding her, "Is it not very hard, Cæsar," said she, "when you do me the honor to visit me in this condition I am in, that I should be accused by one of my own servants of laying by some women's toys, not meant to adorn, be sure, my unhappy self, but that I might have some little present by me to make your Octavia and your Livia, that by their intercession I might hope to find you in some measure disposed to mercy?" Cæsar was pleased to hear her talk thus, being now assured that she was desirous to live. And, therefore, letting her know that the things she had laid by she might dispose of as she pleased, and his usage of her should be honorable above her expectation, he went away, well satisfied that he had overreached her, but, in fact, was himself deceived.

There was a young man of distinction among Cæsar's companions, named Cornelius Dolabella. He was not without a certain tenderness for Cleopatra, and sent her word privately, as she had besought him to do, that Cæsar was about to return through Syria, and that she and her children were to be sent on within three days. When she understood this, she made her request to Cæsar that he would be pleased to permit her to make oblations to the departed Antony; which being granted, she ordered herself to be carried to the place where he was buried, and there, accompanied by her women, she embraced his tomb with tears in her eyes, and spoke in this manner: "O, dearest Antony," said she, "it is not long since that with these hands I buried you; then they were free, now I am a captive, and pay these last duties to you with a guard upon me, for fear that my just griefs and sorrows should impair my servile body, and make it less fit to appear in their triumph over you. No further offerings or libations expect from me; these are the last honors that Cleopatra can pay your memory, for she is to be hurried away far from you. Nothing could part us whilst we lived, but death seems to threaten to divide us. You, a Roman born, have found a grave in Egypt; I, an Egyptian, am to seek that favor, and none but that, in your country. But if the gods below, with whom you now are, either can or will do any thing (since those above have betrayed us), suffer not your living wife to be abandoned; let me not be led in triumph to your shame, but hide me and bury me here with you, since, amongst all my bitter misfortunes, nothing has afflicted me like this brief time that I have lived away from you."

Having made these lamentations, crowning the tomb with garlands and kissing it, she gave orders to prepare her a bath, and, coming out of the bath, she lay down and made a sumptuous meal. And a country fellow brought her a little basket, which the guards intercepting and asking what it was, the fellow put the leaves which lay uppermost aside, and showed them it was full of figs; and on their admiring the largeness and beauty of the figs, he laughed, and invited them to take some, which they refused, and, suspecting nothing, bade him carry them in. After her repast, Cleopatra sent to Cæsar a letter which she had written and sealed; and, putting everybody out of the monument but her two women, she shut the doors. Cæsar, opening her letter, and finding pathetic prayers and entreaties that she might be buried in the same tomb with Antony, soon guessed what was doing. At first he was going himself in all haste, but, changing his mind, he sent others to see. The thing had been quickly done. The messengers came at full speed, and found the guards apprehensive of nothing; but on opening the doors, they saw her stone-dead, lying upon a bed of gold, set out in all her royal ornaments. Iras, one of her women, lay dying at her feet, and Charmion, just ready to fall, scarce able to hold up her head, was adjusting her mistress's diadem. And when one that came in said angrily, "Was this well done of your lady, Charmion?" "Extremely well," she answered, "and as became the descendant of so many kings"; and as she said this, she fell down dead by the bedside.

Some relate that an asp was brought in amongst those figs and covered with the leaves, and that Cleopatra had arranged that it might settle on her before she knew, but, when she took away some of the figs and saw it, she said, "So here it is," and held out her bare arm to be bitten. Others say that it was kept in a vase, and that she vexed and pricked it with a golden spindle till it seized her arm. But what really took place is known to no one. Since it was also said that she carried poison in a hollow bodkin, about which she wound her hair; yet there was not so much as a spot found, or any symptom of poison upon her body, nor was the asp seen within the monument; only something like the trail of it was said to have been noticed on the sand by the sea, on the part towards which the building faced and where the windows were. Some relate that two faint puncture-marks were found on Cleopatra's arm, and to this account Cæsar seems to have given credit; for in his triumph there was carried a figure of Cleopatra, with an asp clinging to her. Such are the various accounts. But Cæsar, though much disappointed by her death, yet could not but admire the greatness of her spirit, and gave order that her body should be buried by Antony with royal splendor and magnificence. Her women, also, received honorable burial by his directions. Cleopatra had lived nine and thirty years, during twenty-two of which she had reigned as queen, and for fourteen had been Antony's partner in his empire. Antony, according to some authorities, was fifty-three, according to others, fifty-six years old. His statues were all thrown down, but those of Cleopatra were left untouched; for Archibius, one of her friends, gave Cæsar two thousand talents to save them from the fate of Antony's.

Antony left by his three wives seven children, of whom only Antyllus, the eldest, was put to death by Cæsar; Octavia took the rest, and brought them up with her own. Cleopatra, his daughter by Cleopatra, was given in marriage to Juba, the most accomplished of kings; and Antony, his son by Fulvia, attained such high favor, that whereas Agrippa was considered to hold the first place with Cæsar, and the sons of Livia the second, the third, without dispute, was possessed by Antony. Octavia, also, having had by her first husband, Marcellus, two daughters, and one son named Marcellus, this son Cæsar adopted, and gave him his daughter in marriage; as did Octavia one of the daughters to Agrippa. But Marcellus dying almost immediately after his marriage, she, perceiving that her brother was at a loss to find elsewhere any sure friend to be his son-in-law, was the first to recommend that Agrippa should put away her daughter and marry Julia. To this Cæsar first, and then Agrippa himself, gave assent; so Agrippa married Julia, and Octavia, receiving her daughter, married her to the young Antony. Of the two daughters whom Octavia had borne to Antony, the one was married to Domitius Ahenobarbus; and the other, Antonia, famous for her beauty and discretion, was married to Drusus, the son of Livia, and step-son to Cæsar. Of these parents were born Germanicus and Claudius. Claudius reigned later; and of the children of Germanicus, Caius, after a reign of distinction, was killed with his wife and child; Agrippina, after bearing a son, Lucius Domitius, to Ahenobarbus, was married to Claudius Cæsar, who adopted Domitius, giving him the name of Nero Germanicus. He was emperor in our time, and put his mother to death, and with his madness and folly came not far from ruining the Roman empire, being Antony's descendant in the fifth generation.